The Lost Black Scholar

The Lost Black Scholar

RESURRECTING ALLISON DAVIS IN
AMERICAN SOCIAL THOUGHT

David A. Varel

The University of Chicago Press   CHICAGO & LONDON

PUBLICATION OF THIS BOOK HAS BEEN AIDED BY A GRANT FROM THE BEVINGTON FUND.

The University of Chicago Press, Chicago 60637
The University of Chicago Press, Ltd., London

Published 2018
Paperback edition 2020
Printed in the United States of America

29 28 27 26 25 24 23 22 21 20   1 2 3 4 5

ISBN-13: 978-0-226-53488-6 (cloth)
ISBN-13: 978-0-226-75443-7 (paper)
ISBN-13: 978-0-226-53491-6 (e-book)
DOI: https://doi.org/10.7208/chicago/9780226534916.001.0001

Library of Congress Cataloging-in-Publication Data

Names: Varel, David A., author.
Title: The lost black scholar : resurrecting Allison Davis in
American social thought / David A. Varel.
Description: Chicago ; London : The University of Chicago Press, 2018. |
Includes bibliographical references and index.
Identifiers: LCCN 2017041483 | ISBN 9780226534886 (cloth : alk. paper) |
ISBN 9780226534916 (e-book)
Subjects: LCSH: Davis, Allison, 1902–1983. | African American anthropologists—
Biography. | African American college teachers—Biography. | African American educators—
Biography. | African American scholars—Biography. | University of Chicago—Biography.
Classification: LCC GN21.D37 V37 2018 | DDC 301.092 [B] —dc23
LC record available at https://lccn.loc.gov/2017041483

♾ This paper meets the requirements of ANSI/NISO Z39.48-1992
(Permanence of Paper).

CONTENTS

Introduction

Allison Davis was not just a "race" scholar concerned with race issues. . . . He was an American intellectual whose ideas were intended to and did in fact change America.[1]

JOHN AUBREY DAVIS

On a warm summer day in 1970, Allison Davis stepped before a large audience of students and their families to deliver the commencement address at the University of Chicago. As he had considered what to say in the days and weeks before, he'd had a wealth of experiences upon which to draw. His extraordinary sixty-seven-year life had been filled with more than its share of triumphs and travails.

Davis had risen from humble beginnings to become a pioneer in more ways than one. He was one of the first African Americans to secure a truly elite education, earning a BA from Williams College in 1924, an MA from Harvard in 1925, and finally a PhD from the University of Chicago in 1942, after studying once again at Harvard as well as the London School of Economics. In the 1930s he became one of the first black anthropologists in the country, and he soon published two major social-anthropological books, *Deep South* (1941) and *Children of Bondage* (1940). These monographs were theoretically pioneering, exploring the interconnections between culture, social structure, and personality development decades before other social scientists took this approach. His research was also methodologically innovative, combining traditional ethnography with psychological assessments not regularly applied in social science in that era. Furthermore, Davis's publications were socially significant. His most popular books sold tens of thousands of copies between the 1940s and the 1960s.

As if that were not enough, Davis transgressed professional racial boundaries a full generation ahead of most of his peers. When the University of Chicago hired him in 1942, they made him the first full-time black faculty member at a predominantly white university. He did not squander the opportunity. At Chicago he successfully challenged racial segregation in the schools, class inequalities throughout society, and cultural biases within intelligence tests. His efforts prompted Chicago in 1970 to name him the first John Dewey Distinguished Service Professor of Education.

Yet Davis understood that the very exceptionalism of his story testified to the persistent oppression facing African Americans. He knew that his achievements did not open the floodgates for other blacks to follow, for most of them remained constrained by structural inequalities that circumscribed their lives. He would know that, for he spent his career exposing those very inequalities. But Davis also knew that his own story was filled as much with discrimination and hardship as it was with success and achievement, and the scars from those struggles remained.

Sometimes such hardship had taken the form of direct threats of violence. As a sixteen-year-old, he had observed with horror the 1919 race riot in his hometown of Washington, DC. As a graduate student in 1933 he had to flee Berlin as Nazis took control of the city and terrified minorities. As an anthropologist studying the community of Natchez, Mississippi, in the mid-1930s, he had kept a gun nearby to protect against the ever-present threat of lynching. In the middle of the twentieth century, his light-skinned children were targeted by whites and blacks alike on the racially explosive streets of Chicago.

Much of the hardship Davis endured, though, stemmed not from direct threats of violence to him or his family. Rather, Davis, like all African Americans, had to suffer the indignities of racial segregation and exclusion across the country. As a student at Williams College, he was forced to live off campus with the handful of other token blacks at the school. As a faculty member at the University of Chicago, he was barred from the faculty social club until 1948, and he was denied housing in a white neighborhood near the university.

In addition to the psychological effects of such exclusion, Davis had to suffer the restriction of opportunities. In the 1920s and 1930s he was denied teaching positions in the North, and the president of Williams College refused to recommend him for jobs even though he graduated as valedictorian from that institution. In professional social science, his first-rate work was not enough to win him acclaim. For that he relied upon the authority of well-known white professionals who could vouch for him and his work. Even in projects in which he was the lead author and researcher, the greater recognition went to his white collaborators. He also had to muffle his radical views and to constantly control his righteous anger over discrimination to avoid jeopardizing his career. Resisting the larger culture's stamp of inferiority was exhausting and debilitating, though it would have been worse had he not been nurtured by a strong family and a resolute black community.

So as Davis stepped before the microphone to deliver the commencement address at the University of Chicago, he stood poised to deliver his own guiding philosophy of life, which was hard won and battle tested. In the great tradition of the American jeremiad, he recounted the ills plaguing the United States and the world. He captured the sense of anger and frustration boiling over in American society at the end of the 1960s, as the disastrous war in Vietnam pressed on, as Martin Luther King Jr. was assassinated and the civil rights movement lost steam, as armed guards fired upon students at Kent State, and as the threat of nuclear war remained omnipresent. He recognized students' pessimism about the future as they struggled to find worthwhile causes to which they could dedicate themselves.

Then Davis offered up his abiding wisdom. He told the engrossed audience, "Although we seem trapped in the Age of Anger and Despair, the alternatives remain the same as in all other ages. We can scuttle—or we can sail the seas. *Navigare necesse est; non vivere est.* 'One must chart his course and set sail; it is not enough merely to exist.'"[2] As Davis understood it, life was often cruel and full of arbitrary suffering, and it lacked any transcendent purpose. Faced with that absurd plight, people needed to devise their own purposes and dedicate themselves to fallible social projects for the betterment of others. This, he believed, was the only way out of the abyss of despair, and it was the only way to make the most of life.

This book is about the social projects that consumed Allison Davis and the ideas that animated them. In other words, it is an intellectual biography of Davis. Few figures are in greater need of restoration to the historical record, for few people accomplished so much yet remain so little known. Remarkably, Davis's marginalization within the historiography continues despite more than forty years of scholarship focused on recovering the lives of African Americans. We now know a great deal about comparable second-generation black social scientists, such as Charles S. Johnson, E. Franklin Frazier, Ralph Bunche, Abram Harris, Rayford Logan, and Zora Neale Hurston, not to mention less influential figures such as William Fontaine and Oliver Cox. Davis, on the other hand, has had relatively little written about him, and most of it exists in snippets scattered throughout books and articles across the social sciences.[3]

Yet in many ways Davis's accomplishments exceeded those of even his greatest peers. Many of them never received offers of full-time appointments at predominantly white universities, as he had. In the 1930s, when most of his peers were forced to study only the race issue and to follow the research programs set out by white scholars, Davis was leading biracial research teams and developing new theories at the cutting edge of multiple disciplines, many of which extended beyond the purview of race. Indeed, Davis's research emphasized class as paramount, and his fruitful application of class analyses to anthropology, psychology, and education represented a level of theoretical innovation achieved by few others within American social science.

So why do we know so little about Allison Davis? How has he managed to slip through the cracks? What does his marginalization tell us about race and the politics of social science in the twentieth-century United States? And how can understanding his life and career enrich our grasp of other aspects of American and African American intellectual life? In addressing these questions, this book resurrects Allison Davis in American social thought and makes the case that he belongs within the pantheon of eminent twentieth-century American intellectuals.

Davis's striking marginalization has in many ways been the byproduct of his role as a pioneer. This should not really be surprising, for the flip side of being a pioneer is being unconventional and existing within a context often hostile to the change that the pioneer embodies. This was certainly the case for Davis, whose position outside of—even when he was within—the power structure served to trivialize his contributions. Personal characteristics such as Davis's humility and his commitment to nuance also played a role. But the most important reasons for the continued inattention to Davis are threefold: his interdisciplinary involvement, his iconoclasm, and his status as a racial minority in a racist academy. These three qualities can tell us much about Davis—as well as a great deal about the larger society in which he lived.

First and most straightforward, few figures ever moved so fluidly between fields as Davis. His allegiance was at various points to English, anthropology, psychology, and education. This diminished his body of work within each field and made it more difficult for scholars to locate the disciplinary origins of his theories and methodologies. Thus his treatment within the literature remains fragmented, as scholars have examined Davis's work within particular disciplines. Compare this to black scholars such as Charles S. Johnson and E. Franklin Frazier, both of whom remained firmly within sociology and developed a large corpus of work clearly rooted in the tradition of the Chicago School.[4]

Yet precisely because of Davis's interdisciplinary involvement, a study of him over time and across fields reveals connections between areas of inquiry often treated as isolated and distinct. Davis shows how, for instance, the arts and sciences are connected. Quite naturally, he carried his humanistic concerns and literary modes of representation fine-tuned during the New Negro Renaissance to his work in anthropology and education, where he pursued the same ends through different means. His career reminds us that distinctions between disciplines tend to be overemphasized. In our own time, when increasing specialization has erected further barriers between disciplines, Davis's example is instructive.

The second, broader reason for Davis's invisibility was his iconoclasm: he shunned conventional disciplinary traditions and research programs. In the interwar United States, cultural anthropology was the dominant subfield within the part of anthropology that investigated social behavior. But Davis elected instead to pursue social anthropology, a British approach that he and Lloyd Warner brought to the United States in a distinct form. Social anthropology was itself a hybrid field that straddled sociology and anthropology through its focus on social structure rather than values. Partly because anthropologists in the 1930s tended to view Warner as a sociologist, Warner's and Davis's innovative brand of anthropology was marginalized within the discipline.

The two men's anthropology also ran against the grain in its emphasis on social division, power, and conflict within the modern United States. Most anthropologists at that time were committed to studying vanishing "primitive" cultures, and they questioned the applicability of anthropological methods to an advanced civilization. They also strove to document the cohesion of foreign cultures as evident in foreigners' consistent values and practices. Consequently, Davis's and Warner's emphasis on race and class divisions, and their exploration of how people's behaviors often failed to match up with their values—still one of social science's most important insights—kept them far afield from mainstream anthropology.

For the very same reasons, however, Davis's and Warner's anthropology was genuinely new and significant, and it deserves more attention as a vital approach that illuminated social stratification. The two men's "caste-and-class" framework, which explained how race and class intersect to stratify society, was an essential part of this tradition.[5] Furthermore, in *Deep South*, Davis synthesized Marxism and social anthropology in a compelling way, and he and his colleagues provided the most sophisticated portrait of social relations in the Deep South in that generation.

The interdisciplinary field of "culture-and-personality" was another hybrid one outside of mainstream social science, though it became more established as a subfield in both anthropology and psychology. Davis's involvement with culture-and-personality placed him among a small but significant group of social scientists. Culture-and-personality theorists were unique in their willful collaboration across fields and in their theoretical innovation. By scrutinizing processes of socialization, they explored in tangible ways the relation between individual and society, with real influence on public policy.[6] Unfortunately, the difficulties of sustaining research programs that transgress traditional disciplinary boundaries, and of having those programs appreciated within the historical literature, have served to marginalize the contributions of culture-and-personality as a whole.

Yet some parts of culture-and-personality are better remembered than others. The most influential part of the field was centered at Columbia through the work of Ruth Benedict, Margaret Mead, and Ralph Linton. These cultural anthropologists explored socialization within cultures that they perceived to be unified into integrated wholes. They believed that individuals share deeply held values that guide their behaviors and make each culture distinct.

Davis, on the other hand, learned culture-and-personality at Yale, where anthropologist Edward Sapir and especially social psychologist John Dollard developed a novel research tradition. Dollard investigated the importance of early childhood training from a neo-Freudian and social-psychological perspective which emphasized the mutability of behavior. Davis brought his nuanced caste-and-class approach to Yale, where he and Dollard synthesized their theories into a practical research framework. They then applied that form of culture-and-personality to the study of black youths in the Deep South, and the pioneering interdisciplinary result was *Children of Bondage*. The book remains a landmark in theoretical innovation and social insight, but it continues to be marginalized within a culture-and-personality literature focused more on the Columbia tradition.

Applied anthropology is another field that is not well understood or appreciated. When anthropologists move away from traditional forms of research in the field and no longer publish as frequently in anthropological journals, their contributions to other sectors such as education or government are often invisible to the discipline.[7] The partial exception was the application of cultural anthropology to the war effort during World War II, when anthropologists detailed the integrity and cohesion of national cultures at a time of great division. Such studies in "national character," including Margaret Mead's study of America, *And Keep Your Powder Dry* (1942), grew out of a resurgent cultural nationalism that sought to promote unity.[8]

However, Davis's work in the World War II era ran fundamentally counter to that mission. Davis continued to emphasize social divisions, explaining how race and class functioned together as interlocking systems of stratification. He even extended that analysis to the realm of culture, arguing that discrete class cultures characterized the United States. The thrust of his work actually prioritized class over race in compelling ways.

Given that he was a black scholar in a caste society, such a priority calls for explanation. It grew out of two main commitments. For one, he realized that social scientists and others tended to ignore the class divisions within the black community and thereby perpetuated stereotypes that all black people were the same. He wanted to challenge such racism. Equally important, his research in Natchez, Mississippi, during the Great Depression helped him to see the centrality of economic power. He observed how the white upper class pulled the strings of the entire system, while exploiting racial divisions to conceal that fact. As he confided to his friend Horace Mann Bond, "This thing we're in is a class alignment—and how! 'Race' or 'caste' is the wedge, as we knew before, but . . . how cleverly they use it. And right now, for the next 15–20 years, I know they're going to play off colored [folks] against . . . whites for all they're worth."[9] Davis therefore spurned tradition and prioritized class in his intellectual agenda.

Davis's focus on class over race sidelined him in other unexpected ways. Davis violated the racial politics within the academy by becoming—as a black person—a specialist in an area other than race. This worked against him in sometimes subtle ways. For example, in *Commentary* magazine in 1965, Daniel Patrick Moynihan omitted Davis from a literature review of the black scholarship on poverty, even though Davis had contributed more to the subject than almost any other black scholar.[10] When St. Clair Drake criticized Moynihan for that omission, Moynihan responded not that he was unfamiliar with Davis's work but rather that he knew it intimately and simply did not think to include it.[11] The exchange seemed to reveal that Moynihan did not even think of Davis as black and that he had merged Davis's contributions with those of other white scholars at Chicago who could freely pursue research beyond the purview of race. Davis's expertise on class effectively whitewashed him in the minds of some white commentators.

On the one hand, such a predicament was the ultimate compliment for a scholar who wanted to be fully accepted in the mainstream academy based on the quality of his ideas, not the color of his skin. On the other hand, this successful integration marginalized him and his groundbreaking accomplishments as a black scholar.

Davis's disciplinary home in education also contributed to his marginalization. Because education generally lacked the prestige of other social sciences, Davis was less visible there than he would have been in other departments.

Equally important, as a member of Chicago's Department of Education, Davis did not train doctoral students in anthropology or establish a larger research tradition in that field. As a result, Davis's many anthropological contributions to education have been largely ignored. For example, his *Social-Class Influences upon Learning* (1948), which facilitated the abolition of culturally biased intelligence tests and laid the intellectual foundations for antipoverty programs such as Head Start, has been hardly appreciated.

Davis, then, was iconoclastic not only in his affiliation with unconventional research programs but in the specific ideas he held. This was true throughout his career, even before he entered social science. During the New Negro Renaissance, his literary style was steeped in Irving Babbitt's unpopular "New Humanism," which rebuked modernism when modernism was in vogue. Davis also contributed to the Renaissance not from the urban North but from the confines of southern Virginia, where he and his friend Sterling Allen Brown developed a distinct genre of writing I call Negro Stoicism. It humanized ordinary black people through portrayals of their fortitude and resilience amid oppression. Brown remained within the field of English, and he later became well-known for his contributions to the Renaissance. Davis, on the other hand, left the field early on, but not before developing a unique Renaissance voice that reflected his own experiences with race and class in the Upper South and the Northeast. His challenging ideas expand our understanding of the Renaissance, including who was involved, where it was based, and what ideas permeated it.

The two iconoclastic ideas that most defined Davis's career, however, were caste and class. In developing them, Davis used social anthropology to lay bare the intractable structural bases of inequality in the United States. Although his ideas would have resonated particularly during the Great Depression, which was when he developed them, they were not widely read until the outbreak of World War II and the immediate postwar period. In that new context, Davis, like Lloyd Warner and sociologist C. Wright Mills, continued to make the case for structural inequality even amid major social change, understanding the fundamental continuities at work.

Most Americans in the Cold War era, however, found those ideas anachronistic, if not subversive and un-American. African Americans could not be a caste, many reasoned, amid wartime changes in race relations, one of which was symbolized in Davis's own appointment to the University of Chicago. Social class could not be so significant within a society in which the middle class was rapidly expanding and affluence was reaching unprecedented levels. Class as a category, moreover, seemed suspiciously Marxist in the context of the Cold War, in which anticommunism flourished and leftists had to tread carefully or risk unemployment, if not jail or deportation. In such a context, many commentators paid little heed to Davis's empirical investigations into the class biases within major American institutions.

As Davis's conceptual framework became embattled, so too did his methodological ones. He had made a career out of participant observation and community studies. But in the postwar period, those methods were increasingly impugned for yielding subjective and unreliable information. Statistical data and quantitative analysis supplanted them as paths to authoritative, representative knowledge. So by the 1960s, when Americans newly "discovered" poverty, institutional racism, and the flaws within statistics, Davis's prescient ideas and methods had been largely forgotten.

Other ideas of his had been misunderstood from the beginning and were therefore deemed as ill-conceived or irrelevant. Most notably, in works such as *Children of Bondage* Davis wedded cultural with structural explanations of black poverty in ways that humanized African Americans and refrained from stigmatizing them. Yet from the outset, some reviewers misinterpreted the book as primarily documenting the "damage" that poverty and racism exacted upon black people. Damage imagery proved useful in creating moral outrage against racism, but its bitterly stigmatizing portrait of African Americans cemented stereotypes, disempowered poor blacks, and undermined broad movements for social change based upon principles of justice. When notions of cultural pride and power later predominated in the era of identity politics and multiculturalism, commentators looked dismissively, if at all, upon the damage literature, Davis—wrongly—included.

Finally, Davis's status as a racial minority in a racist academy helps to explain his marginalization. Davis's absence from the literature is certainly conspicuous, particularly in several studies in which he was directly relevant.[12] The scholars in most of these studies were simply unaware of Davis and his relevance to their projects, so they unwittingly marginalized his work. But more fundamentally, the division of labor in the mid-twentieth-century academy was explicitly racist to begin with. Though Davis was the lead author of *Deep South* and *Children of Bondage*, the white scholars he collaborated with— especially Lloyd Warner and John Dollard—received more of the credit for the two books' theoretical innovations. Though Davis was also the theoretical leader and chair for *Intelligence and Cultural Differences*, his paramount role was lost within the list of white coauthors.[13] Such was the dilemma of the black scholar of that time, even with a rare appointment at a major white university— perhaps especially then.[14]

The conditions of Davis's appointment make clear that he was kept at arm's length even as a faculty member. He was hired only upon agreement that the Rosenwald Fund would subsidize his salary; he was initially barred from the faculty club where his colleagues ate; and the Department of Education openly debated the appropriateness of his teaching white students. Once Davis entered the University of Chicago and worked in the highly interdisciplinary environment there, his work was subsumed under that of his white colleagues. He came to exemplify the plight of black intellectuals more broadly.

Awareness of these racist divisions of labor has prompted scholars to excavate the past with an eye to the contributions of marginalized actors.[15] Such efforts to "decolonize" historical and social scientific knowledge have highlighted how disciplines have bolstered, or at least perpetuated, racial oppression. In a similar vein, I hope here to show how white social scientists relied upon the labor and experiences of minority peoples to develop their ideas and to advance their careers and burnish their stature. Such a reappraisal should abet a fundamental reorientation of how we understand the politics of knowledge production, the nature of the knowledge itself, and the people involved in constructing it.

As eclipsed as Davis became, so much the more has been his wife, anthropologist Elizabeth Stubbs Davis.[16] She, too, was a pioneer within anthropology, completing graduate work alongside her husband at Harvard and the London School of Economics. She then proved to be an indispensable part of the *Deep South* project, vastly enriching the study through her analyses of black women and miscegenation in Natchez. She further taught anthropology at Dillard University and assisted in the research for *Children of Bondage*. After that, she bore a disproportionate share of domestic responsibilities and took charge of rearing the family's two children, all the while still assisting with Allison's professional endeavors. Elizabeth Davis belongs in the history books in her own right, but also because Allison Davis's career is inseparable from the intellectual guidance, domestic work, and emotional support that she provided him. At the same time, her life exemplifies how race and gender intersected to circumscribe the lives and marginalize the voices of all black women.

Davis's career makes clear how African Americans were central actors in the environmentalist revolution in social thought in which culture unseated biology as king. His example illustrates how African Americans' experiences with racial oppression made them more adept at grasping the social origins of human difference. Given the chance, he and other black intellectuals became leaders in confronting scientific racism. They seized upon the opening of social science within interwar America to further that end.

We should see this intellectual struggle as part of the earlier, more radical phase of the "long" civil rights movement, which prioritized both racial and economic justice. Intellectuals such as Davis understood the centrality of ideas and empirical evidence in galvanizing and sustaining social change. So in addition to promoting class-based alliances and other radical programs, black leaders in interwar America targeted the more rarefied realm of theory and ideas. Their success was extensive, as environmentalist ideas bolstered interracial labor movements in the 1930s, buttressed *Brown v. Board of Education* (1954) and the desegregation movement, and aided antipoverty programs in the 1960s. In this way, the environmentalist crusade was an important, if underappreciated, civil rights struggle that paved the way for the racial change that was to come.

This book traces the life of Davis's ideas over time, while highlighting how those ideas existed not within a vacuum but as a response to concrete social experiences, relationships, and communities of discourse that gave them form and meaning. The fulcrum of the book is the 1930s and 1940s, for this is when the environmentalist revolution in American social thought was in full swing, and this was when Davis contributed his most important work. Yet the full significance of Davis can be appreciated only by taking the long view of his life. This story therefore begins at the dawn of the twentieth century, when Jim Crow was resurgent and fated to transform Davis's world.

CHAPTER 1

Coming of Age during Jim Crow

Dennis learned then, at age 11, exactly what it meant to be a Negro, and he never overcame the trauma, nor trusted white people again.[1]

ALLISON DAVIS

Only a few months after Allison Davis entered the world, W. E. B. Du Bois
published one of the most profound statements on African American life ever
put into print: *The Souls of Black Folk* (1903). For Davis as for so many African
Americans, the book poignantly distilled his own experiences with coming of
age as a black person during the Jim Crow era.[2] Like Du Bois, Davis would
soon learn that despite the lightness of his skin, he was simply a "Negro" like
all other people who had any trace of African blood. He, too, would learn that
to be black was to be a problem; it was to exist as part of a subordinate caste in
a white settler society. Davis would be forced to accept the fact that no matter
how much smarter or more talented he was than the white people around him,
he would be deemed inferior, as well as unclean, uncivilized, and dangerous,
and he would be denied full participation in American life. What is more, he
would have to look on as white Americans and the state disfranchised, exploited, subjugated, harassed, and lynched those like him. These were hard
truths to accept.

For Du Bois, to be African American was to be "shut out from [the white]
world by a vast veil." It was to be denied true self-consciousness and to always
feel one's "two-ness,—an American, a Negro; two souls, two thoughts, two
unreconciled strivings; two warring ideals in one dark body." He famously
wrote, "It is a peculiar situation, this double-consciousness, this sense of always looking at one's self through the eyes of others, of measuring one's soul
by the tape of a world that looks on in amused contempt and pity." Du Bois
used the veil metaphor to evoke the physical and social separation of black
and white people and to illustrate how that separation blinded white people

to the reality of black people's lives. He longed for a pluralist solution to the race problem in which it was "possible for a man to be both a Negro and an American, without being cursed and spit upon by his fellows, without having the doors of Opportunity closed roughly in his face."[3]

Yet Du Bois also emphasized that African Americans were "gifted with second-sight in this American world."[4] Here he meant that African Americans, in having to navigate the white world as well as the black one, gained a better intuitive sense of American social dynamics than the vast majority of white people, who could live comfortably within the white world alone. The soundness of this insight was abundantly evident when those precious few African Americans who gained access to the highest educational institutions in the country harnessed their formal and informal educations to lay bare America's racial system. With *The Philadelphia Negro* (1898) and *The Souls of Black Folk*, Du Bois led the way. Although his work was marginalized within mainstream social science at the time, it exerted a profound influence on the next generation of African Americans, including Allison Davis. Davis's own "second-sight" would later come through powerfully in his anthropology, but it was rooted in the social and intellectual influences of the first third of his life, which took him from Washington to Williams, and from Harvard to Hampton.

BECOMING "NEGRO" IN WASHINGTON

Du Bois's first realization of what it meant to be a "Negro" came when a white girl at school refused to exchange a gift with him. For Allison Davis, that same realization grew out of the horrendous ordeal his father experienced as an employee in the Government Printing Office (GPO) when Woodrow Wilson became president in 1913.

When Davis was born on October 14, 1902, his family was thriving. Over the course of twenty years, his father, John Abraham Davis, had worked his way up from a laborer making barely $500 a year to—by 1906—a counter clerk making $1,400 a year and supervising a crew of ten men, nine of whom were white.[5] Such a coveted managerial position was extremely rare for a black man in those days, even for someone who excelled at school and who graduated as valedictorian from the highly regarded M Street School in Washington.

In part, Davis's position testified to the relative racial progressiveness of the nation's capital at the turn of the twentieth century. However, it was made possible only through Davis's rigorous work ethic, his strong character, and his political prowess. At that time, political patronage carried the day, and Davis was effective at striking up relationships with progressive Republicans,

FIGURE 1.1. John Abraham Davis among the employees he supervised in the Government Printing Office, circa 1904. Davis is seated in the middle of the front row. The only other African American on Davis's team is standing at the far right in the back row. Courtesy of the Davis Family.

including most importantly Iowa senator William Boyd Allison. Senator Allison was instrumental in securing Davis's appointment as a clerk in the GPO in 1899. He also minimized the discrimination Davis continued to face, though Davis was consistently bypassed for raises and promotions.[6] Such help made Davis a faithful Republican who sought to emulate Theodore Roosevelt in dress and appearance. Even more significantly, Davis honored senator Allison by naming his first son William Boyd Allison Davis.

The Davises were also "riding high" during Allison Davis's childhood for other reasons.[7] John and his beautiful wife, Gabrielle Beale Davis, were proud owners of productive property in Virginia and across the District of Columbia. They owned two laundries and several small houses, in addition to one of the largest farms in Prince William County, Virginia. John Davis inherited most of this property from his mother, Caroline Gaskin Davis Chinn, who had bequeathed it to him in 1896.[8] Davis refused to accept any support from his father, a white Washington lawyer named John Mandeville Carlisle, who had had a sexual encounter with Gaskin while she was working as his housekeeper in the 1860s. But Caroline Gaskin was a dynamic woman in her own right, becoming one of the first black women to secure white-collar work in Washington, serving as a clerk in the Treasury Department.[9] At the turn of the century, John Davis and his family were squarely part of the "black bourgeoisie."

Befitting his position, John Davis took up active roles in various fraternal and civic organizations. He served as treasurer of St. Luke's Episcopal Church, founder of Washington's first chapter of the National Association for the Advancement of Colored People (NAACP), historian of the Oldest Inhabitants, and member of various other organizations.[10] His youngest son, John Aubrey Davis, later recalled, "My father used to carry me on his strong shoulders at . . . antilynching demonstrations" in DC.[11] John Abraham and Gabrielle Davis also loved the arts, and they cultivated a rich home environment for their children, reading Shakespeare aloud in the evenings.

Beneath the veneer of affluence, however, lay more precarious circumstances. The properties the Davises held were all mortgaged, and various family members occupied them and prevented them from being profitable. In reality the Davises relied heavily on John's salary at the GPO. For a time

FIGURE 1.2. The Davis family and others on the family farm in Nokesville, Virginia, circa 1908. John Abraham Davis, dressed in a style emulating Theodore Roosevelt, is seated in the chair, with Allison Davis to his right and Gabrielle Davis standing all the way to the right, holding Allison's sister, Dorothy. Courtesy of the Davis Family.

his job seemed relatively secure, as he was clearly a productive worker who, despite opposition, managed to eventually win promotions through tireless work and personal advocacy.

But political circumstances were changing. Senator Allison, Davis's great backer, died in 1908. The following year William Howard Taft became president, and he was no friend of traditional patronage politics.[12] Although it was an imperfect system, patronage was one of the only tools available for African Americans to gain a modicum of power in a system set up to marginalize them.

The election of Woodrow Wilson, the first southern-born Democrat to take the office since Andrew Johnson, sealed the fate of John Davis and many other African Americans in Washington. Wilson never issued clear policy regarding the treatment of black federal workers, but his white southern appointees systematically demoted, fired, segregated, and otherwise humiliated African Americans. Under the Progressive Era guise of efficiency and good government, Wilsonians portrayed black workers as corrupt and inefficient and as obstacles to an orderly government in which ability rather than patronage wins out. The results were stark. Of ninety-seven black civil servants within the Taft administration and the first Wilson administration, "there were 66 promotions and 8 demotions/dismissals under Taft and 23 promotions and 35 demotions/dismissals under Wilson."[13]

John Davis was one of the casualties of the deeply personal, unjust, and devastating nature of Wilsonian racism. After a quarter century of relentless work, Davis had advanced to a supervisory position making $1,400 a year. But his middle-class salary and position of authority over white workers made him a target for racists. In April 1913, Davis was summarily demoted with an almost 15 percent reduction in salary.[14] At first, Wilsonians justified this in the bureaucratic language of a "necessary reduction of force."[15] But months later they continued to persecute him, now claiming that "it is impossible for him to properly perform the duties required (he is too slow)" and requesting that he be "assigned to some other duties in some other division."[16] Davis, in turn, made heartbreaking appeals to his supervisors' "sense of justice and equity" by pointing squarely to the facts of his unblemished employment record, even as he recognized the "almost invariable futility of attempting defence in such cause."[17]

The harassment continued into the following year, when the Wilsonians demoted Davis to the lowly position of laborer with the meager salary of $500. That had been his position and salary when he first joined the GPO back in 1882. His hard-fought gains over thirty years were erased overnight. The stress "affected my nerves, afflicted me with insomnia," and tarnished his reputation, which, he wrote, "I have been able to acquire and maintain at considerable sacrifice of time and effort." His reputation, he continued, "is to me . . . a source of personal pride, a possession of which I am very jealous, and which is possessed of a value, in my estimation, ranking above the loss of salary—though the last to a man having a family of small children to rear, is serious enough." After being forced to return to laborious physical work for the rest of his career, in 1928 he passed away at the age of sixty-six, which his family understood to be directly related to the physical and mental strains placed upon him at work.[18]

Allison Davis was deeply affected by his father's ordeal. He later recounted the essence of the experience in a largely autobiographical novel which he never published:

King saw his father return home early that day. He saw the stricken look on his face. Johnny kept repeating the story as if unable to understand or accept it. "They've kicked me out!" he said in hurt and indignation. "Kicked me out after 21 years. Like a dog without a bone! With nothing! Not even a clerk's job. By God, I've got four children to feed and try to educate! What, in God's name, can be their justification?" His father had tried to relight his pipe, but his hand kept shaking.

"Justification!" his mother said cynically. "What justification? *They* don't need any justification! They'll never care if you slave all your life, or if we go without a crust of bread! If all of us, children and mothers included, starved like dogs, John, I give you my word, white people wouldn't care. They'd think it good riddance!"

King still remembered his mother's sobs and his father's efforts to reassure her. That day, for the first time, he realized his father was too gentle. He'd never get another good job. It was the end of the line for them all!

King never forgot the maiming and crushing of his father. The terrible wounds seared into King's mind and heart forever.

Allison "felt castrated by the maiming of his father." He continued to have nightmares and deep-seated anxieties over the ordeal for the next forty years. He recalled that he "learned then, at age 11, exactly what it meant to be a Negro, and he never overcame the trauma, nor trusted white people again."[19]

John Davis's demotion affected not only the psychological state of the Davises, but also their social and economic circumstances. The family was forced to surrender all their properties except for the home in Washington. The loss of the family farm in Nokesville, Virginia, was particularly difficult to stomach, for it was a source of both family pride and wealth. Out of desperation, Davis sold the eighty-acre land and the accompanying home for only a couple hundred dollars.[20] Additionally, he sold at rock-bottom prices whatever he could of the family's many valuable possessions on the farm, which included "fresh cows and calves, springing cows, horses, Berkshire sows and pigs, sows about to farrow, registered Berkshire boar, vehicles, farming implements and tools, kitchen and household furniture, etc."[21] Along with this loss of property went the Davises' middle-class way of life.

The Davises were "on the skids," as Allison Davis would later call it when investigating downwardly mobile families in the United States. As those later investigations suggest, Davis was profoundly affected by the changing social circumstances of his family.

John Davis, however, did not succumb to despair. He redoubled his efforts to create opportunities for his children, including Allison and his two younger siblings, Dorothy Davis (born 1908) and John Aubrey Davis (born 1912). His experiences with Republican politicians, coworkers, and subordinates at the GPO had led him to believe that northern whites could be allies in the cause of equal opportunity and social advancement.[22] So he began preparing his children to be first-rate students who could secure educations at the best northeastern colleges.

Allison Davis was chastened by his father's experiences, and he was never so optimistic about escaping white racism and advancing socially as a member of a subordinate caste. Still, he pursued excellence in education with a near-singular resolve, hoping that educational achievement would counteract the humiliations he felt.

In reality, Allison Davis's humiliations within America's class and caste systems had begun much earlier, thanks to the ambiguities of American racial divisions, which never reflected the neat black–white distinction that governed social mores. The realities of mixed-raced peoples, interlocking kin networks, the many gradations of skin color, and the practice of passing all undermined popular conceptions of race. At the beginning of the twentieth century, Washington was a laboratory of racial diversity, for it was home to the nation's most elaborate community of mixed-race peoples.

The Davis family embodied many of the complexities. Like many members of the black middle class, the Davises were very fair skinned. As Dorothy Davis later explained it, "The Davises, of mixed racial ancestry, were identified as Negroes by the power structure. Emotionally, socially, and politically they identified as Negroes, though genetically they were predominantly Caucasian."[23]

Indeed, John Davis's father was white, and his mother was less than half black with some Indian ancestry. Gabrielle Beale Davis's father was white, and her mother was of an indeterminate mixed ancestry. Thus Allison Davis's mother, brother, and sister all appeared fully white with fair skin; two of them even had blue eyes. Allison and his father, on the other hand, were identifiably "black" with caramel-colored skin. Allison was easily the darkest member of his family.

This caused difficulties for Allison Davis, who recalled excruciating trips to department stores with his mother. White salesmen would sharply question him about why he was in the store, failing to recognize that he was accompanying his mother, who appeared to them as a white woman and hence not someone who would ever bring a black boy shopping. His mother would lash out at the salesmen and threaten to report them to a manager. She also used her anger in other situations, such as making white insurance agents take off their hats in her home—a demand that violated Jim Crow strictures. For young Allison, the department-store incidents were humiliating and scarring. "His suffering on those Saturday trips with her into the white world," he later wrote, "opened a wound which never closed."[24]

Davis's understanding of the complex social divisions within black communities grew out of the difficult situations he and his family had to navigate during his childhood. As identifiably black, Davis and his father had to ride in the Jim Crow coach of trains while commuting between the family's farm in Virginia and their home in the capital. The rest of the family, though, appeared as fully white, which made commuting together a problem. Davis's mother "was sometimes informed she was in the wrong coach."[25]

In his largely autobiographical novel, Allison Davis described how two of his white-looking aunts shaped his experiences with the color line. Both aunts passed as white to secure jobs otherwise unavailable to them. One aunt, who lived with the Davises, struck Allison as the loneliest person in the world. "Since she 'passed,'" Davis wrote, "she had neither friends nor associates. She neither visited nor was visited; she attended neither church nor theatres." The other aunt "lived in constant fear" of being exposed as black and fired from her job, and of having her white employer exhibit that "flash of recognition—the curling of the lips and narrowing eyes—the snarling 'Nigger!'" As much as these experiences would enrich Davis's social-scientific investigations into African American life, they would also instill in him a deep anxiety about living as a black man in a racist society.[26]

THE DUNBAR YEARS

In 1916, at the age of thirteen, Allison Davis entered Washington's renowned Dunbar High School. Dunbar—formerly the M Street School—was considered the finest high school for African Americans in the country, and it rivaled even the best white schools. Indeed, one of the ironies of segregation was that it could actually benefit leading black educational institutions. As elite blacks were denied career opportunities in other professions, they concentrated a surfeit of talent and knowledge within the walls of schools such as Dunbar. For example, in 1906, twenty of the thirty teachers at M Street had earned degrees from prestigious northern colleges, and five of the others had gained degrees from Howard University, the leading black college.[27] Many of these teachers had also earned advanced degrees in medicine, law, or the liberal arts. When Davis was at the school, faculty members included such luminaries as Mary Church Terrell, Jessie Fauset, Angelina Grimké, and Carter Woodson.

In addition, Dunbar was one of the only black schools accredited on par with top white high schools. This remarkable achievement meant that graduates did not have to spend precious time on remedial schooling before entering universities. Anna Julia Cooper, who served as both a teacher and a principal at M Street for many years, had led the fight for accreditation. Furthermore, realizing the financial obstacles facing many Dunbar students, she instituted scholarships that could support select graduates' educations at Harvard, Brown, Pittsburgh, and Williams College.[28] The advantages of a Dunbar education were not lost on black students in neighboring Maryland and Virginia, who were known to provide false Washington addresses to attend.[29]

Dunbar's faculty members helped to create a school that encouraged black scholastic excellence in the highest traditions of the time. They generally eschewed the vocational route advocated by Booker T. Washington and focused instead on academic training, requiring that students take liberal arts courses in English, foreign languages (Latin, French, Spanish, German), history, and mental and moral philosophy.[30] Davis, for his part, took three years of English, four of Latin, two of French, and one of history, as well as many other subjects.[31]

At the same time, Dunbar was more than half a century ahead of mainstream American high schools in its emphasis on African American history and culture. Carter Woodson's tenure on Dunbar's faculty testifies to the school's unique scholarly prowess early in the twentieth century. Woodson, who had earned a PhD in history from Harvard, was the leading figure in professionalizing the study of black history, forming the Association for the Study of Negro Life and History in 1915, founding and editing the *Journal of Negro History* from 1916 to 1951, and organizing Black History Week (which later segued to Black History Month) in 1926.[32] Woodson's Dunbar taught its black students to take pride in African American history and to approach their education with the utmost seriousness of purpose.

Dunbar produced more than its share of outstanding alumni, among them Charles Drew, Benjamin O. Davis, Charles Hamilton Houston, Rayford Logan, Sterling Brown, Jessie Fauset, Robert C. Weaver, William Hastie, John P. Davis, Will Mercer Langston, W. Montague Cobb, Mercer Cook, and many more. Davis formed close friendships with Sterling Brown and Mercer Cook.[33] Brown became one of the finest poets of the African American experience and served as a professor at Howard for decades. Cook, in addition to being a professor of romance languages, served as the American ambassador to Gambia, Senegal, and Niger. Because the African American intelligentsia in that period was quite small, Davis's education at Dunbar made him familiar with many of the nation's black elite. Some of the relationships he struck up there would persist throughout his life.

Dunbar wasn't all scholastics. Davis took part in many extracurricular activities available there. He eagerly served on the Cadet Corps, appreciating the discipline and black pride it represented. He also played baseball and was captain of the tennis team, which was runner-up in the National Negro Tennis Tournament.[34]

As rich an environment as Dunbar was, however, Davis's experiences were colored by his family's deteriorating social and economic circumstances. When he looked at the affluence of other Dunbar students, many of whom were children of the wealthiest and most powerful African Americans in the country, he came to resent this "black bourgeoisie." He experienced his relative poverty as a humiliation and as a reminder of how far his own family's standing had fallen. Part of him resented having to work all night as an elevator boy to help his family scrape by. As Davis later described it, his

> high-school years were fetid and unsatisfying. He became increasingly conscious of his inferiority to the students whose families were doctors, dentists, and teachers, students who could buy their lunches at the school cafeteria, while he ate from a rumpled brown paper bag, his homemade preserves-on-bread, or possibly a rare and socially fortifying ham-sandwich. When there were dances in the armory and he couldn't dance, when there were track-meets, or football games, for which he didn't have the money, when there were trips across the street at recess to buy ice-cream cones for the girls and he had to slip back into the school, on all these occasions he found excuses to hide the fact—of which he was more ashamed at that time than of anything else in the world—that his family was poverty-stricken; that even nickels and pennies were matters of vital daily concern to them.[35]

FIGURE 1.3. Allison Davis, circa 1918, dressed in his Cadet Corps uniform during his years at Dunbar High School. Courtesy of the Davis Family.

Davis's humiliation translated into deep anger toward more affluent blacks, from whom the Davises grew increasingly isolated. His mother, wrote Davis, "taught her children a fierce and inconsolable pride, to compensate for their poverty; a pride in what she represented to be their intellectual, and especially their moral, superiority." In ways that would influence Allison's own outlook, "she conceived the professional Negroes all to be reprobates, sunken in poker games and cocktail parties, or "debauches," a generic term by which she referred to those who went to anything from a smoker or fraternity dance to a bridge club." Davis's writings in the 1920s would reflect that sentiment.[36]

The belief that the black bourgeoisie was snobbish and condescending was widely held within black Washington around the turn of the twentieth century. That opinion reflected the growing class divisions within the black community. As some affluent blacks began parading around in fur coats and confining themselves to segregated neighborhoods and churches, rebukes from within the black community were pointed. Booker T. Washington declared that "Washington was no place for a Negro who wished to dedicate his life to helping his race; here false standards and selfishness predominated."[37] Langston Hughes later wrote that "never before, anywhere, had I seen persons of influence,—men with some money, women with some beauty, teachers with some education,—quite so audibly sure of their own importance and their high places in the community."[38]

At the root of such critiques was the notion that the black bourgeoisie was violating the sacred African American creed of "lifting as we climb." The Davises were among those intensely critical of the black bourgeoisie for abandoning the black masses in their quest for social mobility. Allison Davis developed his commitment to racial solidarity within this milieu.[39]

Although the Davises had become economically poor, they remained culturally rich, and this facilitated Davis's educational success. John and Gabrielle Davis were highly educated and intelligent people, and they were dedicated to the academic success of their children. By high school, Allison Davis needed little outside encouragement, for he sought to overcome his shame from poverty by "winning indisputable preeminence in the scholarship rankings." In his more vindictive moments, he even sought "to outstrip, and so to subject, to humiliate, this world peopled by those of higher status."[40]

But Davis also partly bought into his father's dream of social mobility through education. He, too, aimed to succeed, and then to help his two younger siblings do the same. So he spent every spare moment studying, from free time on weekends to downtime at work. Years later, as he thought about his own upbringing from a social-scientific viewpoint, it became clear to him just how much social forces informed his own educational motivation and achievement.

Even as Davis spent most of his waking hours studying and competing with his black peers, the larger white world was never far from his mind. At times it intruded into his life with visceral force. In July 1919, the summer before Davis's senior year at Dunbar, a series of race riots erupted throughout Washington and twenty other cities across the nation. Soldiers returning from World War I flooded into cities in search of work, but with demobilization from the war, housing shortages and unemployment were rampant. This was galling to white soldiers in a city such as Washington, where there remained many affluent blacks with good jobs despite Woodrow Wilson's best efforts. The growing assertiveness of African Americans, particularly returning soldiers demanding full citizenship rights after heroically serving their country, also touched a nerve among many white people. Newspapers across town began recklessly inflaming racial tensions by publishing dubious, sensationalistic stories about a "Negro fiend" who was sexually assaulting white women.[41] Then, on the sweltering summer night of July 19, racial tensions finally exploded as white mobs began rampaging through black neighborhoods and viciously assaulting black people.

After a night of violence, the rioting only escalated. In the ensuing madness the next day, Carter Woodson narrowly escaped being attacked by a mob of "hundreds of soldiers, sailors, and marines" who were chasing a black man.[42] Later on he encountered a second mob that "had caught a Negro and deliberately held him as one would a beef for slaughter, and when they had conveniently adjusted him for lynching they shot him. I heard him groaning in his struggle as I hurried away as fast as I could without running, expecting every moment to be lynched myself."[43] That threat was ever present for African Americans in the age of Jim Crow. Twenty-eight were lynched nationwide in the first six months of 1919 alone.[44]

Unlike in other cities, however, African Americans in Washington fought back effectively against the white mobs, presaging the later civil rights struggles. Black Washingtonians had their own grievances. In the previous several years they had watched with resentment as the Wilson administration segregated the capital, pushing black people out of jobs and systematically undermining their precarious social, economic, and political positions. When they realized that the police were not protecting them, they organized. Black citizen groups met and sent out notices telling people to stay home. Other black people bought and distributed guns and responded in force to white violence, initiating deadly clashes that continued for days. Only bad weather and the mobilization of two thousand federal militiamen managed to eventually quell the violence. In all, an estimated 39 people were killed, with another 150 seriously injured.[45]

The riots deeply affected Allison Davis, as they did all black Washingtonians. Davis refused to hide indoors during the terror, though, continuing to commute to work as a bold assertion of his will. This made his mother sick with worry, but luckily he was not harmed. Davis's actions represented not only an assertion of his will and his rights as an American citizen but a refusal to give up his job, which he knew would be jeopardized if he missed a shift. The experience, in fact, taught him to see the economic underpinnings of white racism. By intimidating black people into staying home and missing work, Davis believed, white people were using race to steal black people's jobs. And of course, his father's demotion by white racists, who had filled his former position with a white worker, had already conditioned him to see the connections between race and class.[46]

Amid white racism, black classism, familial difficulties, and the general angst of being an adolescent, Davis fashioned himself as a stoic: strong and resilient in the face of unending toil and hardship. In his youth he had identified more with his gregarious father. But he came to relate more to his sober and taciturn mother, whose wit was sharper and more ironic. Allison had been chastened by the arbitrary nature of his family's and his race's suffering, so he started to believe that "the whole course of the universe was blind, without providence or justice, a matter of chance. Self-pity, therefore, was foolish." Feeling that he had no control over the pain he experienced, he believed that the only path forward was to fight and to endure. As he saw it, "the basic realities of life" were "work, pregnancy, disease, [and] the battle to survive." So "in the end, one faced death as one faced life, by standing up to it."[47]

Even in his adolescence, Davis's experiences with racism and the precariousness of life inclined him toward such existentialist thinking. He would further develop those themes in his literature during the New Negro Renaissance. The stoical strength that many black Washingtonians exhibited in the face of white mob violence also provided seeds for his burgeoning political consciousness. Racial solidarity, he would come to believe, must overcome class divisions. For now, though, such concerns took a backseat to the more pressing goal of achieving unrivaled academic excellence. His stoical view helped him to endure the rigors of his own relentless work ethic. Through herculean efforts, he managed to surpass his outstanding Dunbar peers, graduating as class valedictorian in 1920 and winning a coveted scholarship to Williams College.

WILLIAMS COLLEGE

If Davis had let himself be seduced by his father's optimism about racial egalitarianism in the North, he was quickly disappointed upon his arrival in Williamstown. Tired from a long train ride from Washington to an isolated section of western Massachusetts, Davis followed the scores of other arriving students in attempting to hail a cab from the train station to campus. As he looked around, he already felt like an outcast. Both the color of his skin and the style of his clothing dramatized the vast social gulf between himself and the others. "Every white student had worn a loose-fitting tweed suit, V-neck sweater, a shirt with button-down collar," he wrote, "whereas he wore a pinched ('monkey') back suit, shirt with a large rolled collar and, worst of all, a narrow string tie, all of which stamped him as clearly as if he'd worn a convict's stripes."[48]

Before he even realized it, Davis was standing all alone without a taxi in sight. Refusing to accept the idea that the next four years of his life were going to be filled with further isolation, humiliation, and hardship, he tried desperately "to convince himself he had not been rejected by the cab-drivers for the same reason he'd always been refused by white taxi-drivers in Washington." After waiting a futile half an hour, he picked up his suitcase and began the long walk to campus, hoping against hope "that his skin was not the wrong color in New England" too.[49]

In those days, all-male Williams College functioned as other elite institutions did: as a finishing school for WASP elites. In that world, Davis soon had to accept that the same race and class barriers that circumscribed his life in Washington would limit his life in Williamstown. Capturing that sentiment, he later wrote that African Americans "have no fair country" because "oppression rides with them" wherever they go.[50] While the white boys—with the partial exception of Jews, who had not yet won the privileges of whiteness—took up lodging together in dormitories, Davis was forced to bunk with the few other token black students in a black-owned boarding house off campus.[51]

Furthermore, while the affluent whites at Williams focused on friendship and fun, Davis's precarious economic circumstances demanded that he "find a job in order to eat." He ended up working in a fraternity house, where for "five hours a day" and "seven days a week" he slaved away "serving three meals and washing the dishes," for which he "receive[d] no money, but [was] allowed to eat three meals." Having to serve his classmates was its own special form of punishment. Allison endured the humiliation with characteristic public aplomb, while seething privately.[52]

On one telling occasion, Davis served dinner to the members of the Pipe and Quill, a selective student literary society. After his "duties as a waiter were discharged," he took his place among the Pipe and Quill, of which he was a leading member, and proceeded to present an academic paper.[53] The contrast between black servant and brilliant student was striking, and it left a lasting impression on the president of the college.

Davis's four years at Williams gave him a rich, if demeaning, informal education in the racial dynamics of the North. At times he observed the type of blatant racism he had often encountered in the South. For example, two weeks into his first semester, one white student asserted that his "religion had taught him the races were unequal and blacks must be made to recognize that fact."[54] His position was not without sympathy from others.

More frequently, Davis observed the hollowness of professed racial egalitarianism among liberal white elites. While the president of the college celebrated its token admission of one or two black students per year, he was not much concerned with their happiness while on campus. He oversaw an informal policy of black exclusion from social—but not academic or athletic—affairs, including housing, dances, and any functions in which men and women interacted.[55] In the North, de facto segregation with a smile replaced Southern de jure segregation with a snarl. The practical and psychological effects were largely the same. Davis felt like a leper.

Indeed, when writing about his experiences at Williams years later, he described feeling like an outcast. At a freshman class meeting, Davis took a seat alone near the back of the room, after which "the white students either flowed away from him, or unwittingly sat beside him, but upon looking at him, curved away gracefully. Finally only standing room was left; when that was exhausted, a white boy had to take the seat on [his] right."[56]

His experiences with white women were equally galling. In one case, a woman would talk regularly with him while he was in the college admissions office, but she refused to even acknowledge him in more public places such as Main Street, turning "scarlet with shame, and look[ing] away." Other white women ignored him entirely and "did not regard him as a man." One woman who did take an interest in him made him feel even more invisible than the others. She was a graduate student studying racial problems in the North. But she engaged with him not as an equal person but as a piece of data, and as a clear testament to others that she was more open minded and liberal than they were. She "suffocated him with her condescension and pity," saying "by implication that he was far beneath her, below all the rest of humanity." These experiences help explain why Davis felt he "did not exist" at Williams. "At the end," as he narrated it, "all his memories of college had fused into a picture of cold arrogant white faces."[57]

Among the handful of black students at Williams who shared the same sense of isolation, Davis formed enduring social bonds. He and fellow Dunbar graduate Sterling Brown were particularly close. Brown recalled, "Allison Davis and Ralph Scott and I used to go for long walks, and we decided the race problem, we decided the problem of women, which was a serious thing here." He continued, "So at Williams I made friends with people who have been good friends, good mentors, brothers." Davis's and Brown's shared social experiences informed their common intellectual interests. During the New Negro Renaissance, the two friends were to collaborate to develop a distinct genre of poetry and prose.[58]

Thus Davis's college experiences were complex. He became an active participant in college life, and he won the support and admiration of faculty members and students alike. He himself said that he was "best friends" with "two of the four or five [white] Southern students" there.[59] In addition to taking an active part in the Pipe and Quill and other academic societies, he became a member of Phi Beta Kappa and played on the Commons Club Tennis Team.[60] His fellow students wrote of him in the senior "classbook" that "Dave is a real student, not a grind who plods his way to intellectual petrification. But Davis is more than a student, he is an ardent devotee of basketball, 'touch-football,' and tennis. Moreover, he can entertain you for hours on 'Idealism and Sentimentalism in the English poets.' He has the intense expression of the pre-Raphaelites on his face, and he is the living exponent of constructive satire."[61]

Davis had continued his relentless pursuit of academic excellence, transforming his social humiliations into productive scholastic energy. Before he had aimed to surpass Washington's black bourgeoisie; now he focused on besting white Yankee elites. He and his fellow black classmates were not privileged enough to take college for granted. They understood the need to prove their ability—and hence the ability of black people generally—to succeed there. Davis majored in English, and his coursework included sixteen English courses, four Latin courses, seven French courses, four German courses, two Greek literature courses, two Italian courses, two mathematics courses, two chemistry courses, and two astronomy courses.

Davis's professors testified to his academic and social success. Professor George E. Howes recalled that "Mr. Davis's record at Williams College was almost unique. During his course he received the highest grade in all of his subjects with the exception of two semesters in freshman year—one of Rhetoric and one of Mathematics, in both of which he received the next to the highest grade. . . . At graduation he received highest final honors in English and summa cum laude distinction. He was in the first group elected to Phi Beta Kappa and was valedictorian of his class."[62]

Beyond intellectual brilliance, Davis followed his father in being a model of Victorian character. Howes wrote, "The estimation in which he was held by his classmates is evident from the fact that he was selected by the members of the Phi Beta Kappa group to talk for them at the annual Phi Beta Kappa dinner, at which one member of the graduating class responds to the toast for the Phi Beta Kappa Members of that class. He proved himself, while with us, modest in spite of his excellence in scholarship. He is a young man, I believe, of the highest ideals and absolute integrity of character."[63]

Another professor at Williams, Carroll Lewis Maxcy, reiterated such claims. He considered Davis "one of the best men that have come to my notice during more than thirty years in Williams College. He has a very clear mind, and his work was without exception well and thoroughly done." Noting Davis's personal appeal, he continued, "He won the regard of all who knew him, not only for his intellectual qualities but also for his personal qualities." Perceptively, Maxcy also underscored the difficulties Davis had faced as a black student and his remarkable ability to overcome them. He wrote, "His position was not easy. A colored boy and yet the intellectual superior of his classmates, he might easily have aroused prejudice; but throughout his course, as a student working his way, he conducted himself with dignity and reserve, and won universal respect." Davis's ability to impress but also disarm others would prove essential to his success in mainstream social science.[64]

Davis's almost singular devotion to his studies made him remarkably well versed in modern literature. Great teachers such as George Dutton helped him develop as a writer and thinker. Sterling Brown recalled how "Dutton *taught* me, he *taught* Allison Davis, he *taught* Mortimer Weaver," making them read more than English literature.[65] Dutton's emphasis on critical realism and the modern novel came through in the eclectic readings he assigned, such as Dostoyevsky and Tolstoy, Flaubert and even American authors—widely still seen as inferior to European ones—such as Sinclair Lewis, Edwin Arlington Robinson, and Robert Frost.[66]

These authors taught Davis the ways of critical realism. In Dostoyevsky's writing, Davis observed how a writer could capture the internal psychological conflicts of lowly characters. Reading *Madame Bovary* (1856), Davis took note of how Flaubert developed lifelike characters within a mundane country setting. Through reading Sinclair Lewis, Davis similarly learned to depict authentic American settings while maintaining a critical edge. And like Sterling Brown, Davis "learned from Edwin Arlington Robinson's *Tilbury Town* where he took up the undistinguished, the failures, and showed the extraordinary in ordinary lives."[67]

Robert Frost especially influenced Davis. In his poetry, Frost rendered New Englanders in realistic and stoical ways. Literary scholar Joanne Gabbin nicely describes Frost's "stoicism": "There are no tears in this writer; there are only revelations. The passionless acknowledgement of death's victory over a young sawmill worker . . . the portrait of a tormented husband who silently grieves the loss of his first born . . . the revelation in 'An Old Man's Winter Night' that one

FIGURE 1.4. Allison Davis, circa 1923, in his senior picture at Williams College. Courtesy of the Davis Family.

condition of old age is loneliness—all wed Frost to stoicism."[68] Davis identi-fied with life as a stoical struggle, so he learned from Frost and other Western writers how to capture that sentiment in the written word. His immersion in the Western literary tradition informed his selection of ordinary people as his subjects, and it influenced his portrayal of those subjects in realistic ways.

By the end of his undergraduate career, Davis had developed into a formi-dable student of modern literature and of American social mores more broadly. He secured a fellowship to attend Harvard for a one-year master's program in

English. But his informal education had been even more instructive. At the age of twenty-one, he had already become painfully aware of the race and class inequalities that governed life in varying forms across Virginia, Massachusetts, and Washington, DC. He had the equivalent of many years of participant observation.

Nevertheless, as important as his experiences were in strengthening his later anthropology, he would never have chosen to endure them. Even when his parents came to hear him give the valedictory address at his graduation in 1924, he could not enjoy that moment of triumph. He was convinced that his white classmates would violate tradition and refuse to stand up in recognition of him, thus publicly humiliating him in front of his parents. Fortunately, they did reluctantly stand. But near the end of the visit, his father turned to him and said, "Son, I wish you'd said something about white racism."[69]

HARVARD COLLEGE

In Cambridge, Davis encountered an environment like that of Williams. Boasting the nation's most acclaimed scholars and teachers, Harvard too was still primarily a training ground and finishing school for the nation's white male elite.[70] Although Harvard had historical ties to slavery and the slave trade, it also had a legacy of abolitionism, and Harvard men generally perceived themselves to be racially egalitarian.

Like Williams, Harvard admitted a token number of African Americans, whom it marginalized. By the 1890s it was admitting one or two black students to the college each year, and by the 1920s that number was three or four.[71] A year before Davis matriculated, Harvard had forty-two black students—seventeen undergraduates and twenty-five graduates. Harvard practiced strict equality in the classroom and at formal school events, usually allowing African Americans to play on athletic teams, join political clubs, write for undergraduate publications, and participate on debate teams. Nevertheless, black students encountered the same social isolation and segregation that characterized the North more generally. Just as administrators at Williams were forcing black students to live off campus, President A. Lawrence Lowell of Harvard pushed black students out of the dorms.[72]

During his one year in Cambridge, Davis focused on academic pursuits. He followed in Sterling Brown's footsteps by taking a master's degree in literature, focusing on comparative European literature.[73] Brown and Davis both studied under two famous professors, Bliss Perry and George Lyman Kittredge. Perry was an expert on American literature, and he wrote monographs on Emerson, Whitman, and others. Kittredge was one of the foremost scholars on Shakespeare and English literature.[74] Brown recalled, "At Harvard, I went into careful study of American poetry," including that of Edwin Arlington Robinson and Robert Frost, which George Dutton had already exposed him and Davis to at Williams.[75] When the two young men emerged as Renaissance poets in the years to come, their writings reflected the training they received in the Ivy League.

Davis's greatest intellectual influence at Harvard was Irving Babbitt, leader of a cultural movement he dubbed New Humanism. After Harvard, when Davis started teaching in the South, one of his students, St. Clair Drake, later said he had been "bearing the message of Irving Babbitt's 'New Humanism.'"[76] Indeed, as Davis's writing during the New Negro Renaissance attests, Babbitt's influence was deep. Babbitt's movement remained marginal in its time, though it garnered more mainstream attention in the late 1920s, and it later influenced a range of philosophies ranging from Southern Agrarianism to modern conservatism.[77] Essentially, the New Humanists' perspective developed out of a critique of two major traditions within modern American thought: naturalism and romanticism.

Naturalism registered the impact of science on modern thought. In biology, Darwinian natural selection broke down the dichotomy between humans and animals by seeing all living creatures as subject to the same forces of naturalistic change and evolution. In psychology, behaviorism measured human behavior as a product of socially conditioned stimuli. In philosophy, pragmatism posited truth as relative and dependent upon one's frame of reference. In literature, naturalism portrayed human beings as hapless victims of social circumstances. In all these ways, naturalism was a radically environmental mode of thinking that challenged previous conceptions of human beings as special, unique, and capable of controlling their lives.

Babbitt, along with the three other major New Humanist thinkers—Paul Elmer More, Stuart Pratt Sherman, and Norman Foerster—considered naturalism deeply flawed. Fundamentally, he rejected the conflation of humans and animals, so he reasserted the dualism between humankind and nature. In the first major treatise of the New Humanism, *Literature and the American College* (1908), Babbitt despaired that "Man himself and the products of his spirit, language, and literature, are treated not as having a law of their own but as things."[78] The New Humanists justified their dualistic approach to human beings and nature not on metaphysical grounds but on practical, empirical ones. Specifically, they maintained that human consciousness is an observable reality, as is the ability of human beings to manipulate the environment and to shape their own destinies through self-control and will.[79]

In addition to critiquing the environmental determinism of naturalistic thinking, the New Humanists observed that the underlying cult of science that produced naturalism had other negative consequences. Above all, the emphasis on practical knowledge in the pursuit of technological advancement produced a fixation on a form of "progress" measured in material things. Lost was the higher call to cultivate humanity's spiritual well-being; fading were the traditional forms of knowledge and morality that had nourished that well-being for millennia. And for what? Babbitt was dismayed at Americans for "spending seventy-five million dollars a year on automobiles" while signs of "moral degeneracy" abounded, evident in "the increase in murders, in suicides, in insanity, [and] in divorce."[80] He mocked how Americans could perceive replacing the Bible with the comic strip as a sign of progress.

Romanticism represented the other cultural problem for the New Humanists. In *Rousseau and Romanticism* (1919), Babbitt provided the movement's most sophisticated critique of that intellectual tradition. Babbitt considered a romantic to be "the wrong type of individualist—the individualist who has repudiated outer control without achieving inner control."[81] In other words, he critiqued the cult of individualism that focused on self-expression and the cultivation of each person's unique self. He traced this individualism to Enlightenment thinkers such as Rousseau, who saw civilization as stultifying and who therefore looked with envy upon "primitive" peoples who were freer to develop their individual selves. The rise of modern industrial capitalism and its therapeutic ethos only exacerbated this emphasis on individualistic self-expression as the path to fulfillment. For Babbitt, that strain of individualism was devoid of value, and it fed into the empty materialism of a consumerist society.

By contrast, Babbitt prioritized humankind and the spiritual welfare of the group. He called for individuals to restrict, rather than to cultivate, their temperaments in order to discover their higher selves, which they share in common with all of humanity.[82] The New Humanists took Matthew Arnold's conception of high culture—"the best that has been thought and said"—as humanity's cultural goal, and they castigated modernists' celebration of the debased and the banal.[83] Above all, the New Humanists sought to fortify the spiritual welfare of humankind against what they saw as the individualistic, materialistic, environmental-deterministic excesses of the times.

The twenty-two-year-old Allison Davis found much appealing in Babbitt's philosophy, and likely in the man himself. Babbitt was famous for his energetic, pedantic, no-nonsense approach in the classroom. As one student recalled: "He deluged you with the wisdom of the world; his thoughts were unpacked and poured out so fast you couldn't keep up with them . . . He was at you day after day like a battering ram, knocking down your illusions." Another student felt that "to hear him was to understand the modern world." Babbitt's vast repertoire of facts, carefully chosen cases-in-point from the wisdom and folly of the past, and the force of his personality amazed the students.[84] If nothing else, students had to recognize the depth and breadth of Babbitt's humanist canon, as well as its bearing on contemporary issues.

Davis filtered Babbitt's philosophy through his own experiences with race and class in America. However, Davis, like W. E. B. Du Bois before him, was suspicious of dualistic thinking. He observed with contempt how white thinkers erected dichotomies such as white versus black, or Mongoloid versus Negroid, to posit fundamental biological differences between the "races" of humankind. African Americans saw clearly that such dualism lacked intellectual merit and merely ratified the social subordination of black people. In this way Davis was more attuned to the social construction of knowledge, and he shied away from the New Humanists' attempts to establish a sharp dichotomy between humans and nature.

But other New Humanist ideas resonated with Davis. He identified with the notion that human beings can shape their own destinies through self-discipline and the assertion of will. Although he understood the universe to be indifferent, he had learned through his own herculean scholastic efforts that individuals could at least influence the trajectories of their lives. On a broader level, Davis had learned from his family and teachers that black people, although oppressed for centuries and always susceptible to white racism, did act in all sorts of ways to win social justice and improve their lives, be it the abolition of slavery or the founding of the NAACP. So even as he accepted Darwinian evolution, Davis, like the New Humanists, perceived the environmental determinism within modern thought to be overdone and counterproductive to fomenting change. Striking a balance between environmental and individual forces would become a trademark of Davis's entire thought.

Davis was also drawn to the New Humanists' emphasis on the spiritual welfare of the group over the self-expression of the individual. For many African Americans, religion grounded this sentiment. Yet for Davis, who grew up attending St. Luke's Episcopal Church but who later "had no time for church," spiritualism had a decidedly secular and existentialist bent. As his son recalled, "he never went to church, never said blessing, never. It wasn't a factor, with either [him or his wife], I don't think."[85] Davis's writings reflected these same sentiments, at times strongly rebuking the black church, while generally dismissing Christian theology in favor of an atheistic or agnostic view in which life's only purpose is self-crafted and found in secular projects.

Yet Davis had learned from personal experience that the fates of all black people were linked, despite the class divisions within the black community. As he came to recognize that his people's oppressed ancestors had much wisdom to offer in forging a life of struggle, he developed the New Humanists' insights into a unique literary style during the New Negro Renaissance. He, too, would be critical of modernists' fixation on low culture, but his background taught him to see the "lowly" as also possessing a type of high culture in the Arnoldian sense.

Davis completed his master's degree in one year, graduating in 1925, but he was uncertain what to do next. Even though he graduated "near the top of his class" with an advanced degree—an extreme rarity in those days—from the pinnacle of higher education in the country, he had few job prospects in a university system governed by racial segregation.[86] Though it provided career services to white students, Harvard refused to help Davis find work.

Williams had been no help either. In the previous year its president, Harry Garfield, had refused Davis a teaching assistantship at Williams "on the grounds that," as Davis recalled it, "there were too many Southern students to permit my appointment." A half century later, Davis made clear his continued resentment over the discrimination he faced, saying in an interview, "It was ironic that two of the four or five Southern students were my best friends. Yet the president had to use that excuse!"[87]

Nevertheless, a desperate Davis reached out to Garfield again in 1925, for a letter of recommendation for a position at Hampton Institute. Hampton was a vocationally oriented black school in southeastern Virginia, and it had recently begun offering college courses. He acknowledged in frustration, "I suppose, in view of my race, that it is improbable that I should be considered for appointment in any northern high school or college."[88] In response, Garfield testified yet again to the hollowness of white liberals' racial egalitarianism in the North. He gave lip service to the equality of the races, all the while refusing to support his principles with action, telling Davis, "The difficulty . . . is rather obvious. We all have southern students."[89]

Garfield was, however, more than happy to help Davis secure the Hampton position, which he deemed more appropriate for a black teacher. He wrote with enthusiasm to Hampton's president, James E. Gregg. Although Garfield mentioned Davis's academic successes, he tellingly focused more upon Davis's personal attitudes and behaviors. He called Davis a "fin[e] young man in every respect" who "bore himself modestly" and who had "good traits and pleasant personal ways," which he had learned from his respectable parents. He noted that Davis had been "the head-waiter at the Sigma Phi house," where he "dignified . . . the work of his hands." He also emphasized that Davis had carried out his waiter duties "naturally and apparently without embarrassment." In this way Garfield was signaling to Gregg that Davis, despite his intellectual prowess, would not challenge Jim Crow mores at Hampton nor stir up trouble among Hampton students.[90]

Garfield was wrong.

HAMPTON INSTITUTE

In the fall of 1925, Davis joined Hampton Institute as an instructor of English. Located on the coast of Virginia not far from the border of North Carolina, Hampton was still part of the Upper South, but it was not Washington, DC. And it certainly was not the Northeast. Here Davis encountered more nakedly a resurgent Jim Crow system. He experienced much of his time at Hampton as yet another form of ritualized humiliation. Teaching at an institution that barely qualified as a college and being far from the intellectual mainstream were both hard to stomach. Yet Davis's path mirrored that of most other black academics in the 1920s and 1930s, including Du Bois, Charles S. Johnson, E. Franklin Frazier, Alain Locke, Rayford Logan, William Fontaine, Sterling Brown, Horace Mann Bond, and John Hope Franklin.

This circumscribed path was dictated by financial pressures. Davis could not afford further graduate study, and he needed to help finance the college educations of his two siblings, both of whom were very bright. Dorothy went to Wellesley and later taught English at Dunbar and Howard. John Aubrey Davis followed his brother to Williams and subsequently earned a PhD from Columbia in political science, one of the first black scholars in that field. He also published two books, worked in the Roosevelt administration's Fair Employment Practices Committee, directed the nonlegal research team for the NAACP in *Brown v. Board of Education* (1954), and served as a professor of political science at Lincoln University in Pennsylvania for many years.[91] Amazingly, John Abraham Davis's lofty dreams for his children to secure elite educations and be highly successful were all eventually realized.

Unfortunately, John Abraham Davis did not live long enough to see much of it. He passed away in 1928, after laboring as a messenger in the War Department for the previous eleven years. Allison, on a brief sojourn from Hampton, was at his bedside when he passed. Shocked and shattered, Allison struggled to accept that his father—a source of such stability in a troubled world—could actually be gone.[92] Yet he had little time to dwell on it, as his professional responsibilities quickly called him back to Hampton.

FIGURE 1.5. Allison Davis among colleagues and friends at Hampton Institute, circa 1926. Davis is standing at the far right. Courtesy of the Davis Family.

As infuriating as life in Hampton was for Allison, it placed him in an environment that deepened his understanding of the black masses, of race and class inequalities, and of political protest. The divide between vocationally oriented black institutions such as Hampton and Tuskegee and academically oriented ones such as Fisk, Howard, and Atlanta continued to exist in practice long after the famous Du Bois–Washington debates at the turn of the century. By the 1920s, however, these older debates had begun to take new form. As the slow trickle of black migration northward since the Civil War transformed into a flood during World War I, the social, political, economic, and cultural foundations of black life changed. In 1900 over 90 percent of blacks lived in the South, but between 1915 and 1920 alone, several hundred thousand African Americans migrated northward to industrial centers such as Chicago, Detroit, and New York City.[93] Pushed out of the South by segregation, violence, and a cotton crop devastated by the boll weevil, and pulled north by wartime job opportunities and greater freedom, African Americans initiated a massive demographic transition that would continue for the next several decades and that would result by midcentury in blacks being predominantly urban and northern. Such social changes eventually created new political power, as African Americans began electing black politicians and eventually emerged as an important constituency of the Democratic Party during the 1930s.

Black political protest accompanied World War I and the Great Migration, which was itself a bold form of protest against the prevailing conditions of black life. One important element of this centered on black college campuses in the South.[94] Booker T. Washington's vocational approach dominated most black colleges until his death in 1915, but the wheels of change were in motion. Du Bois captured the new spirit of protest among blacks, declaring, "We are cowards and jackasses if now that that war is over, we do not marshal every ounce of our brain and brawn to fight a sterner, longer, more unbending battle against the forces of hell in our own land. *We return. We return from fighting. We return fighting.*"[95] Having served bravely in combat—and alongside the French and other Europeans who treated them more equally—African Americans became emboldened to fight discrimination at home.[96] More than ever, they realized that this local fight was also a global one, as African Americans partook in the nationalistic spirit of self-determination sweeping the globe and gaining impetus from Woodrow Wilson's postwar rhetoric.[97]

In this fight, African Americans recognized the centrality of higher education and professional training. Both were needed to gain access to skilled middle-class jobs and to cultivate broad-minded race leaders. Yet philanthropy continued to focus on vocational schools, underwriting the continued subordination of African Americans.[98] Black protesters, wrote historian Raymond Wolters, rejected "the condescending belief that whites knew the best methods of Negro education," insisting rather that "black youths must be trained according to principles endorsed by the black community."[99] These tensions exploded into outright protest across black colleges throughout the South.

Such protest is partly explained by the changing profile of the average student at many of these colleges. By the 1920s many of the students were coming from the North. For sufficiently affluent northern families, the schools in the South were often the best option given the dearth of universities that would open their doors to black students in the North. Consequently, these students had high expectations for the type of education they would receive, and they carried with them the sense of protest that had pushed their families northward in the first place. Such students were increasingly unwilling to tolerate white control of black institutions.[100] Because protest in the white South was still far too dangerous, blacks waged their civil rights struggles on the safer terrain of black institutions and colleges.

Hampton Institute was the very exemplar of Booker T. Washington's vocational approach. Founded after the Civil War through the efforts of the Freedmen's Bureau, the American Missionary Association, and other organizations, Hampton initially functioned primarily as a normal school to train teachers who could educate the masses. This was a pressing goal for racial advancement, as slave owners had labored obsessively to deny education and literacy to enslaved people in order to keep them ignorant and tractable. Yet during the school's next phase, from roughly 1893 to 1917, Hampton prioritized vocational training and moral inculcation. Many contemporaries even referred to this approach as the "Hampton Idea," for Washington himself had learned it at Hampton before famously institutionalizing it within Tuskegee Institute in Alabama.[101]

While black discontent with the Washington model was beginning to emerge, Virginia was a hostile place in which to talk about black empowerment at all. In some ways the 1920s were a new low point in race relations there, as the state doubled down on the enforcement of racial segregation. In 1924, Virginians passed the Racial Integrity Law. This repealed the fifteen-sixteenths rule, in which a person could still be considered legally "white" even if he or she had a single great-grandparent who was "non-white." The "one-drop rule" had long governed social affairs, but legal sanction gave discrimination additional force. By outlawing marriages between whites and nonwhites, and by making it a felony to mislead authorities about one's racial heritage, the law empowered the state to enforce the caste system in new and terrifying ways. The Massenberg Bill of 1926 gave still more power to the state by codifying the segregation of places of public assembly.[102] In this time of fear and hate, many white Virginians felt that segregation rooted in custom only was no longer enough to protect the "master race"; white supremacy must be upheld.[103]

In response to such deteriorating circumstances, with segregation becoming all the more entrenched throughout the country and even across the globe, Hampton adapted to the times and did not threaten the status quo.[104] During the 1920s Hampton went so far as to segregate its own residential halls and dining cars, providing separate facilities for white visitors. This amounted to a type of double segregation, as the institution already existed apart from white colleges under the law. One result was that Hampton became "the pet of philanthropy," growing an endowment that far surpassed those of the other leading black colleges.[105] Hampton received, for example, $50,000 per year from the Rockefeller Foundation, $25,000 of which went directly to subsidizing the salaries of teachers such as Davis.[106]

Yet Hampton's concession to racial discrimination came with a cost. Students grew visibly angry with Hampton's paternalism, its redoubling of segregation, and its inadequate educational training. Recognizing this discontent, the institute's white principal, James Gregg, tried to mollify students' concerns. He hired more black faculty members and administrators in what remained a white-dominated institution; he developed programs for black and African studies; and he slowly moved the school toward granting bachelor's degrees instead of offering only vocational training.[107]

Yet Gregg implemented these changes slowly and haphazardly, and he combined them with contradictory steps to appease white philanthropists and segregationists. This included the enactment of rigorous standards of student decorum. In 1919 he issued the bulletin "General Order No. 2, Rules and Regulations," which stated, "Students must be in bed when the lights are out, no talking or whispering is allowed. . . . Every student is expected to bathe at least twice a week. . . . No student is allowed north of the line passing through the center of the Principal's house except when on school business."[108] Furthermore: "Students are forbidden to use tobacco or intoxicating liquors in any form. . . . Rowing, sailing and bicycle riding on Sundays, except on school duty or by special permission, is forbidden.[109] One of Davis's students at Hampton, St. Clair Drake, recalled that "dancing was taboo and semi-military discipline was imposed on the men."[110] The students "marched to lunch every day in military order and to church on Sunday morning. We had regular inspection of our rooms in which one of the officers with a white glove would come on Sunday and make sure that there was no dust."[111]

Unsurprisingly, students responded with indignation to such treatment. They resented what they interpreted as puritanical paternalism. And they were also alienated by symbolic actions such as the trustees' refusal to call Hampton a "college" rather than an "institute" so as not to put off whites who were suspicious of black higher education. When Drake entered Hampton in 1927, "the students were in revolt" and "there was a general mood of protest, impatience with segregation, and willingness to change outdated practices all across the South."[112] In the spring of 1925, for instance, the Hampton choir had walked off a stage in Washington where they were expected to sing black spirituals and submissive plantation melodies to a condescending white audience.[113] Similar episodes of student protest occurred throughout the country. The protest was even more visible in less repressive environments such as Fisk University and Atlanta University.[114] In the pages of the *Crisis*, W. E. B. Du Bois tracked these protests, cataloging for black America their spread from black colleges in the South to schools such as the University of Kansas and Ohio University.[115]

Another Hampton incident was more prolonged, and Davis actively involved himself in it. On Saturday, October 8, 1927, campus administrators refused to turn out the lights during a movie screening in the hopes of discouraging impropriety. The students, interpreting this as yet another affront to their characters, became furious; they launched a protest by skipping class that Monday. At this critical juncture, Davis "conferred with the students informally and helped them 'get it together.'"[116] He likewise resented the paternalism of a black college that, tellingly, had no black full professor or head of a department.[117] Eager to direct students' resentment toward productive ends, Davis helped them form a Student Protest Committee. The students, led by many of the best students on the campus, then presented Principal Gregg with a list of seventeen reasonable grievances.

Gregg responded with fury. He refused to address the grievances or excuse the protesters, and he ended up closing the school for over a month.[118] In addition, he placed hundreds of students on probation and suspended sixty-nine—for the entire year if they were on the Student Protest Committee. Though crushing the strike, Gregg's actions only further alienated the student body and encouraged other forms of resistance. As one alumnus recalled, "Both boys and girls are in the habit of willfully breaking regulations in such ways as going from the grounds without excuse, attending movies without permission, staying away from church, failing to wear regulation uniforms, and neglecting drills."[119] In 1929 Gregg resigned amid such continued opposition.[120]

Davis quickly became "a sort of campus hero" for a small group of the best students. In addition to supporting their protests, students recognized him as having "larger horizons than Hampton."[121] He appealed to those students engaged in the larger black freedom struggle, which they followed in *Crisis* and *Opportunity* magazines, and which they participated in through Hampton's own branch of Carter Woodson's Association for the Study of Negro Life and History.[122] St. Clair Drake recalled, "Davis tried to stimulate young black students to write. He gave magnificent lectures on English literature, and some of us who were majoring in other fields took all of his courses that we could because he was a breath of fresh air at Hampton."[123] Davis exposed his students to the latest critical literary theory, including the New Humanism.[124] Students also formed a small writers club around Davis, and Davis even communicated with Du Bois about their work. For example, in February 1930 he asked Du Bois to publish one of his student's poems, claiming that his student could become a "distinguished poet" and "needs encouragement to stimulate him just now."[125]

St. Clair Drake was the most notable of Davis's students. The two of them eventually became close friends and colleagues within social anthropology.

Drake called Davis "the person who most influenced me [at Hampton]" and who "moved me to want to study, understand, and change the world of Jim Crow."[126] Davis, for his part, recalled that Drake was "both a brilliant student and a very hard worker" whom he found "by far the most able student there, during my six years' teaching."[127] But there were also other significant students, such as Enoch Waters, who later became a well-regarded journalist and editor of the *Chicago Defender*.[128]

This small group of talented students at Hampton sustained Davis while he was there. Still, Drake recalled that Davis "seemed to brood a lot" in those days and that he "didn't interact act much with the student body" apart from his close circle of admiring students.[129] Not surprisingly, Davis struggled with the cultural gap he experienced between his own background and that of Hampton's students, who were predominantly "poor and poorly schooled rural blacks."[130] As he later recalled, he discovered that "teaching in the standard manner made no sense" for them. He desperately "wanted to do something to affect such students," but he grew concerned that he "didn't know anything really to teach them since our backgrounds were so different." For what may have been the first time, he had to seriously consider how his relative affluence and Ivy League education—which made him supremely one of Du Bois's "Talented Tenth"—also put him thoroughly out of touch with the vast majority of American blacks locked in generational poverty and degradation.[131]

After some soul searching, Davis's concerns about being relevant to the black community eventually pushed him toward a career change from the arts to the social sciences. During the 1920s, however, he still strove to contribute to African American life not only through his teaching but also through his poetry and prose. The flourishing of black culture at this time, known as the New Negro Renaissance, afforded him an unprecedented opportunity to make his distinct voice heard.

CHAPTER 2

Harlem from Hampton

It is almost irrelevant to preach race pride and equal rights from the center of New York or on flying trips to Southern cities. It is irrelevant now to *preach* race equality anywhere. The Negro masses want to see the upper class live it in the South.[1]

ALLISON DAVIS

In 1927 Allison Davis published an award-winning essay titled "In Glorious Company," which made clear his literary gifts and artistic sensibility. The essay described the social scene of a train ride north in an almost anthropological way. Davis took stock of numerous black characters including a gambler, porter, college student, one-legged miner, elderly genteel man, prostitute, and older revivalist woman—all cramped together in a segregated boxcar. Despite their vast social differences, Davis captured their sense of racial unity, epitomized in the sense of movement and hopefulness associated with trains. "To them, the mere fact of motion suggests new independence, and incites their trammeled spirits with unbounded enthusiasm."[2] Trains represented the possibility of escape from their torments in the South, and they encapsulated the hope for a better, freer life in the North.

But Davis also conveyed the tragedy and recklessness of these hopes. He knew from his own experiences that life in the North was far from a refuge; discrimination and oppression took familiar forms there. He wrote, "It is pitiable they should not yet have learned they have no fair country, and that oppression rides with them." Yet in the end he portrayed these black figures not as naive and ignorant but as strong and almost heroic:

So it is with them all, escaping the weight of hardship and persecution by some exhilaration of the moment. In an hour now, all will be left at their lonely, country station, while the great engine burns its fiery trail across the black sky, driving on into other lands with happier children. But now they are still in a band and confident.

They have not gone this journey of physical hardship and spiritual cramping without the strength of hope and faith. This faith they will not lose in the newer lands to which they must eventually come, for it is revived daily by the barest victory over disease and poverty, and these will travel with them, to chasten.[3]

"In Glorious Company" conveyed the central themes of Davis's literary style during the New Negro Renaissance. James Weldon Johnson fittingly called Sterling Brown's parallel style "Negro Stoicism."[4] In the face of an unrelenting oppression and tragedy, the black masses in Davis's writing appear as he fashioned himself: resilient, strong, and humble, with a keen sense of irony. Davis thus portrayed ordinary blacks as "stoical" in their ability to endure hardship and oppression, much like the characters he had encountered in the works of writers such as Robert Frost. Davis rendered his characters as finally beautiful and admirable for their quiet persistence against adversity. The central elements of Davis's writing therefore include a focus on ordinary blacks, a critical realist mode of representation, an underlying existentialist philosophy, and the social commitment of engendering sympathy and respect for black folk.

In the same period when he was focusing on literary expression, Davis also wrote articles critiquing black intellectual discourse and black racial leadership. His critiques were often severe in tone, but they signaled the depth of his convictions for achieving racial progress through bold forms of leadership, including sustained intervention in the South. Even though he left the arts for the social sciences early on, his ideas did influence several young black thinkers. His distinctive voice deepens our understanding of the New Negro Renaissance, while also signaling his intellectual maturation.

THE NEW NEGRO RENAISSANCE

While students at Hampton and other black colleges throughout the country were protesting administrative paternalism, the nation's most influential black leaders were launching their own more visible protests—political, cultural, and otherwise. Harlem, the black ghetto in New York City, emerged as the capital of black culture in these years. Marcus Garvey, the Jamaican Pan-Africanist who attempted to orchestrate a Back to Africa movement, powerfully influenced the black masses with his message of racial pride and Black Nationalism. He did this in an era when many African Americans were attempting to integrate into white society by hiding their African heritage, often straightening their hair and dyeing their skin white.

Among many black intellectuals, too, integration rather than separation carried the day during the 1920s.[5] The integrationist program did, however, take new form in the twenties through the arts. Various terms arose to conceptualize this cultural experimentation, especially the "Harlem Renaissance" and the "New Negro Movement." Befitting an era when Americans applied the adjective *new* to all parts of society, "New Negro" captured the sense of novelty characterizing African American life in urban centers such as Harlem.

The Renaissance emerged as an important, if limited, intellectual movement: "a somewhat forced phenomenon, a cultural nationalism of the parlor."[6] The movement was guided by the "Talented Tenth," which comprised approximately ten thousand affluent race leaders among a population numbering over ten million. Race leaders carefully orchestrated the movement through the NAACP's *Crisis* and the National Urban League's *Opportunity* magazines. The idea was that because "the roads to the ballot box, the union hall, the decent neighborhood and the office were blocked," Renaissance leaders looked to the arts and letters to demonstrate black equality.[7] In their fight over the politics of culture, they supplanted racist images of the "Old Negro," who was backward and simplistic, with representations of the "New Negro," who was modern and sophisticated.[8] This often entailed portraying only the more dignified, progressive side of black life as they saw it and suppressing those elements that whites could use to prove black incivility.

Like any movement, the Renaissance evolved over time. Early on, after World War I, white Greenwich Village radicalism—rebelling against Victorianism, entrenched scientific and popular racism, widespread anti-immigrant sentiment, far-reaching antiradicalism, the vigorous suppression of dissent, and white supremacy—encouraged the ideal of a "trans-national" America in which Americans celebrated the nation's racial and ethnic diversity.[9] That notion spread in the twenties, as many intellectuals perceived sterility within WASP culture. Seemingly overnight, white thinkers looked anew upon black people, finding in their oppression and African roots a vibrancy lacking within larger society. If their romanticizing of black culture was unwelcome, their support for black artistic expression was not.[10]

As the Renaissance matured, the NAACP and the NUL brought new black artists to the fore. Leaders such as Du Bois and Charles S. Johnson actively recruited black artists and writers, creating literary rewards and publication forums promoting their work. Yet very quickly the Renaissance came to be "marked by rebellion against the Civil Rights Establishment on the part of many of the artists and writers whom the establishment had assembled and promoted."[11] A younger generation of African Americans, led by artists such as Langston Hughes, rejected the "race chauvinism" of establishment figures who sought to use art only to promote the race's interests.[12] The younger writers wanted to explore the realities of black life among the masses. They wanted their art to capture the wider human experience and to not merely ape white artists' standards.[13]

Allison Davis was one of these artists who was promoted by the black establishment and then turned against it. Charles S. Johnson, the black Chicago School sociologist who headed the NUL at this time, actively recruited Davis—as he did so many other African Americans. One of the main recruitment mechanisms was the annual literary competition held by *Opportunity* magazine, patterned after *Crisis* magazine's similar contest.[14] These competitions held public esteem, partly because highly regarded judges such as Sinclair Lewis, H. G. Wells, Robert Frost, Van Wyck Brooks, and James Weldon Johnson presided over them.[15] The winners gained national attention through publication and recognition at annual awards banquets. In 1927 Davis won one of *Opportunity*'s awards for "In Glorious Company," which Johnson published in the anthology *Ebony and Topaz*. This placed Davis in the company of Langston Hughes, Zora Neale Hurston, Countee Cullen, E. Franklin Frazier, and other Renaissance luminaries.[16]

NEGRO STOICISM

After impressing Du Bois with "In Glorious Company," Davis was invited to publish several literary works in the *Crisis* from 1927 to 1929.[17] Because the *Crisis* was the periodical of record for black America, Davis likely became familiar to a wide audience. His publication in *Opportunity* similarly placed him within the Renaissance mainstream.[18]

Davis's published work elaborated upon themes expressed in "In Glorious Company." In a somber poem called "To Those Dead and Gone," he paid homage to the unsung millions of blacks who suffered and died under slavery and after, insisting that they "still enrich" by bestowing wisdom upon the race through their quiet dignity in the tragic battle against oppression.[19] In another poem, "Gospel for Those Who Must," he highlighted the virtues of two working-class blacks whom he identified as "Fighters": a fisherman and a washerwoman.

> Unbroken
> By the salt spume of the sea.
> Tight-lipped against the whispering fears of age,

He holds her laughing.
In his keen eyes the gleam of one who knows
He must endure all the shifting winds, and hate
Of deep-embittered sons of slaving race,
Must outreach
The hunger of insatiate women,
And broken nets at sea.

Her brave face
Softens with a smile.
And light of youth's long hopes and passion,
Sunk away;—

But she has seasoned in her proper time
And grown to mellow laughter.
Strong.[20]

Davis managed to capture the struggles of his subjects and yet portray them as resilient, dignified, and possessive of "stoical strength."[21] Their hardships never lead to despair or stasis. Life takes its toll, but his characters respond with a heroic willingness to persevere, sustaining one another physically and emotionally. "He holds her laughing" encapsulates that mutual support. The laughter is an acknowledgment of the absurdity of their suffering, but it also represents a dogged desire to carry on.

Others of Davis's writings were more philosophical in nature. Davis's first publication in the *Crisis*, "On Misgivings," was one such essay. Capturing Davis's literary style as a whole, Du Bois remarked that it conveyed "a beautiful philosophy daringly clear, calmly cynical and yet with a final clinging to hope and high ideals.[22] Davis had crafted it during his trying days at Williams College. The article celebrates "misgivings," those rare moments of uncertainty and apprehension when people acknowledge life's ultimate finitude and purposelessness: "He clings to his raft which is actual and palpable, even though he knows it can carry him nowhere. Merely to rest, while one eddies or idly drifts; no bold cutting loose from moorings and plunging into the open sea, where the way is uncertain and perilous—but shoreward! He cannot face the possibility of there being something uncertain, mysterious in life, which would make him ever restless, uneasy, incomplete. To cover such misgivings, he grasps every apparent fact as an anodyne."[23] Davis perceived such shrinking from the realities of human existence to be a type of cowardice, and one that shelters people from the real beauty of life, which can be found only in those "transient and inconstant" moments of misgiving. In this way Davis's philosophy reflected a type of existentialist thought before it ever went by that name, but which grew naturally out of the African American experience with oppression.[24]

Davis's literary style is best understood as a form of critical realism. It represented a Victorian mode of literary expression and an underlying Victorian cultural commitment.[25] In particular, Davis's aesthetic realism—his belief that he could faithfully render his subjects in a way that captured something true about them—was a Victorian method of representation. Modernists, who were at that time coming to dominate the arts, rejected realism as only obscuring authentic portrayals of the human experience. Seeing each piece of art as hopelessly subjective, they sought to embody the flux of human experience before people's minds processed—and hence distorted—it. They also rejected the didacticism of the Victorians, who believed that art could elevate and instruct the masses. Davis's literature was subtly didactic in the sense that it strove to promote racial solidarity through faithful portraits of ordinary black people who were often ignored by other black artists.

Davis's social background and formal education informed his critical realism, but it was the vibrant intellectual discourse of the New Negro Renaissance that gave his literary pursuits form and meaning. Instructors at Williams and Harvard had certainly not assigned black writers, so Davis had to follow the Renaissance on his own time. As he did so, he began to carve out his own position. Among the civil rights establishment he observed a remarkable consensus. Leaders such as Du Bois, Alain Locke, Jessie Fauset, Eric Walrond, and Walter White all tended to see culture in hierarchical terms, with Western standards as the most esteemed. Their chief aim was to develop black art that could demonstrate African Americans' equal capacities to produce high culture according to those standards. Du Bois stated this goal in no uncertain terms, writing that "all art is propaganda for racial advance."[26]

Davis was sympathetic to their cause. Every black person understood the high stakes involved in representing the race. At that very moment, for instance, Columbia historian William A. Dunning and his students were peddling an interpretation of Reconstruction which emphasized the "corruption," ineptitude, and "scandalous misrule of the . . . negroes." Dunning's argument that the return of white supremacy saved the nation from the "mass of barbarous freedmen" dominated the historical profession for half a century. History, culture, and science were all battlefields, and white supremacists had the power to bend the facts to their will.[27]

Black leaders naturally labored to undermine those racist representations by portraying contrary depictions of black equality and civility. Historians call this "race vindication."[28] Du Bois in the *Crisis* and Johnson in *Opportunity* tracked the social successes of African Americans, and they explained any black backwardness as a product of oppression and discrimination rather than racial inheritance. Arthur Schomburg in the Negro Society for Historical Research, and Carter Woodson in the *Journal of Negro History*, cataloged the many achievements of African and African American peoples throughout their rich histories. It followed logically that this older generation of race leaders recognized the Renaissance as an important new opportunity to use art for the same ends.[29]

Yet for a younger generation of black artists, propagandistic Victorian art failed to satisfy. Younger writers shared the broad goal of race vindication, but they criticized their elders when they resorted to "race chauvinism" by offering up inflated portrayals of black achievements. Allison Davis and Sterling Brown grew especially frustrated by race leaders' narrow focus on highlighting only the most successful and lightest-skinned elements of the race.[30] Why not use art to dignify the masses instead? That ultimately became the two young men's central goal.

Davis did not shrink from a realistic depiction of black life in his writing. His inclusion of a prostitute, a gambler, and a "revivalist sister" in "In Glorious Company" was but one example.[31] As David Levering Lewis explains, such subject matter was "in mischievous defiance of the Talented Tenth literary canon" for allegedly providing white racists with fodder for proving black inferiority.[32] But Davis and Brown found this ironic, because they were not even departing from race leaders' vaunted Western tradition when they wrote about the lowly black southerner. As Brown put it, "Major authors everywhere have dealt and are dealing with the lowly," so why should black writers not do the same?[33] In their minds, the failure to represent the lowly was dishonest, cowardly, and contrary to the mission of promoting racial solidarity.[34]

Yet as Davis turned to the work of many of his younger peers, he grew increasingly troubled. He had much to sift through as he developed his ideas. In 1923 Jean Toomer, a fellow graduate of M Street High School, published *Cane*, the first major novel of the Renaissance. Toomer rooted his novel in agrarian Georgia, where he had spent several weeks researching. As a result, the book was realistic in its portrayal of ordinary black life in the South. Zora Neale Hurston accomplished the same thing in her short story "Drenched in Light" (1924), as well as in her one-act play *Color Struck* (1925). Jamaican Claude McKay had helped to initiate the Renaissance with his realistic portrait of Harlem in *Harlem Shadows* (1922). Lewis calls McKay's writing "searingly realistic" in "presenting the world of beach bums, studs, women of easy virtue, and frugal Pullman porters—and no white people or distinguished leaders of the race at all."[35]

Wallace Thurman was another key figure. He led the way in organizing black modernist artists, forming radical but short-lived magazines such as *Fire!!* and *Harlem*. His main goal was to give young black artists the space to experiment with modernism and to revolt against what he called the elders' "editorial astigmatism and their intolerance of new points of view."[36] In "Cordelia the Crude" he broke with establishment decorum and provoked controversy by centering the story on a black prostitute.[37]

Although Davis was impressed with some of the work of younger black artists, he became intensely critical of much of it. On its successes he wrote, "At times the poets achieved something beautiful and significant in spite of their material and creed," citing McKay's "Harlem Shadows" and Hughes's *The Weary Blues* as examples. "There were poems in McKay, Cullen, and Hughes," he argued, "which gave evidence of a higher understanding of Negro life."[38]

Overall, though, Davis believed that these artists' emphases narrowed their vision and corrupted their art. He rebuked their tendency "to capitalize the sensational and sordid in Negro life, notably in Harlem, by making it appear that Negro life is distinctive for its flaming 'color,' its crude and primitive emotion." He noted, "These young writers hit upon two means of injecting primitivistic color in their work; one, the use of the Harlem cabaret and night life, and the other, a return to the African jungles." He denied the authenticity and lamented the stereotypical results of these representations.[39]

Davis did not, however, blame only black artists for their artistic failings. He exposed the wider power dynamics at play by pointing out how "our young writers do not lack white support" for primitivistic art. Indeed, Davis recognized that most black artists depended upon funding from whites to sustain their artistic endeavors, and he knew that this power dynamic allowed white patrons to exert undue control over their work. Because many white Americans in the 1920s looked to African Americans "to bring fresh and primitive forces to a jaded age," it followed logically that much Renaissance art reflected primitivistic tropes. Consequently, when Davis looked at most of the production of the younger writers, he saw art that did not dignify the masses but degraded them. "The total effect of the whole movement was that Negroes are sincerely bestial," he argued.[40]

Davis's critique overlapped those from members of the civil rights establishment, who shared his keen sense of the politics of representation. For instance, one sympathetic reader of the *Crisis* praised Davis's critical essay "Our Ne-gro 'Intellectuals,'" agreeing with him that the modernist artists "have steadily been conveying a most harmful and incorrect impression of the 'New Negro' to many persons who are sincerely desirous of helping us."[41] The positive recep-tion of Davis's criticisms was also evident when that essay won second place in another competition in the *Crisis*.[42]

Yet Davis was nevertheless a modern writer who objected not to the sub-ject matter but to particular representations. He chose to vindicate the race by focusing on those ordinary blacks whom he saw as targets of attacks from both whites and upper-class blacks. He believed strongly that most Renaissance artists hurt the race by eschewing realistic portrayals of African Americans in favor of sensationalized ones. Rather than emphasizing cabarets and jungles, which were so "foreign to the Negro's imagination," Davis chose to represent African Americans' daily struggles. Portraits of these experiences, he believed, would convey the message that "the qualities of fortitude, irony, and a relative absence of self-pity are the most important influences in the lives of Negroes." These qualities, furthermore, "are the secret strength of that part of us which is one with human nature. Our poets and writers of fiction have failed to inter-pret this broader human nature in Negroes."[43]

Davis's literary approach mirrored closely that of his good friend Sterling Brown, now considered one of the finest Renaissance artists. The two men's poetry reflected the same critical realism, the same "Negro stoicism," and the same social aim of fomenting racial solidarity.[44] These similarities are evident throughout their work, including one of Brown's most important critical es-says, "Our Literary Audience."[45] There Brown criticized race leaders' narrow and propagandistic conception of art, referring to them disparagingly as the "NAACP School of Fiction."[46] He argued that "propaganda, however legiti-mate, can speak no louder than the truth. Such a cause as ours needs no dress-ing up. The honest, unvarnished truth, presented as it is, is plea enough for us, in the unbiased courts of mankind. . . . Let the truth speak."[47] With remarkable eloquence, Brown made the case for highlighting the lowly black experience. He reasoned that "rushing away from [the lowly] surely isn't the way to change them." But even more, he insisted, "there is more to lowliness than 'lowness.' If we have eyes to see, and willingness to see," he continued, "we might be able to find in Mamba, an astute heroism, in Hagar a heartbreaking courage, in Porgy, a nobility, and in E. C. L. Adams' Scrip and Tad, a shrewd, philosophical irony. And all of these qualities we need, just now, to see in our group.[48]

Brown's literature was particularly pioneering. Like Davis, Brown es-chewed representations of northern urban blacks, electing instead to portray ordinary southern blacks. He innovatively restored dialect to black poetry in a way that avoided stereotypes and testified to a sophisticated black culture. His book of poetry *Southern Road* (1932) was one of the most stunning achievements of the Renaissance.[49]

The consistency between Davis's and Brown's writing underscores a larger point. The two men's shared experiences and similar generational profiles translated into a specific intellectual style. Like Davis, Brown grew up in an affluent middle-class family in Washington, DC, where he also attended Dunbar High School and won the same valedictory scholarship to Williams College. Brown had also taken an MA in literature from Harvard before teaching at a black college in Virginia.[50] Both men were therefore lighter-skinned middle-class literati who vocally criticized the older generation of black intellectuals, and who did so not from within northern cities where the movement thrived but from the intellectually backward rural South. Such geographical positioning helped them to see how irrelevant the Renaissance was to ordinary black people like their students, and it deepened their resolve to humanize the "low-down folks" around them.

To be sure, Davis's and Brown's exacting criticisms may also have been important in deflecting attacks that they themselves were "race traitors" who abandoned their race through their very privilege and opportunity. More likely, strong rebukes of older race leaders were one way to make their arguments heard and to therefore carve out a position within the black intelligentsia. Their social position and strategy certainly matched those of many of the younger writers. For that reason, their critiques must be seen within the context of a much longer tradition of intergenerational conflict among black intellectuals. By the 1960s many of Davis's generation would in fact become the new targets, as a new group of young radicals criticized them for representing a docile middle class.

THE BLACK BOURGEOISIE

While Davis was highly critical of Renaissance artists for portraying black people in primitivistic ways, he reserved his harshest criticism for the black upper class, or "bourgeoisie," whom he and his mother had come to despise during their family's downward mobility. With "bourgeoisie" Davis referred not to "those producers—scientists, writers, composers, scholars—who are making the Negro's contribution to the civilization of America" but to "the mass of lawyers, doctors, school-teachers, real estate sharpers, business men and society women whose contribution is limited to fur coats, Packards, armchair solutions to the race problem, football classics and fraternity dances."[51]

In a poem in *Crisis* titled "The Second Generation," Davis savaged black physicians and ministers. His treatment of each group had two parts: one rooted in the high ideals of the profession, the other a brutal denunciation of the exploitative behaviors of black professionals. He lambasted physicians, declaring, "You find real pleasure in your work—taking liberties when you examine women, and joking about it later. You prosper by prescribing dope to the slum Negroes for medicine, and taking their money with no serious effort to help them. When you have made your 'pile,' you will move as far away from the Negro section as you can go." Turning to ministers, he wrote, "You make your living by talking through a service about God, and rejoice equally to get a marriage or a funeral. Have you convinced yourself yet that this whole business of a church and confident speaking to God, with you leading, is not a madman's game?" He concluded cynically, "And aren't they fools to be paying you a salary to speak to God for them, when your thoughts are always of a pretty wife and a larger church?" Davis clearly resented black professionals who used their careers as ladders for social mobility while abandoning or exploiting those less advantaged.[52]

Davis expanded his criticisms of the black bourgeoisie in his formal essays. The most important and influential of these was "The Negro Deserts His People."[53] Davis wrote it around 1927 and published it two years later in *Plain Talk*, a Washington-based black magazine. This essay was Davis's most original, passionate, and sustained analysis of black intellectual discourse to date, and it had a significant impact on other young thinkers of his day.[54] Reflecting his experiences with student rebellion and administrative paternalism at Hampton, the article attacked school administrators in the South. He rebuked them for kowtowing to white state officials, running the schools like businesses to maximize profit, and failing to effectively instruct black youths. He lamented the tragedy "of a hopeful and energetic youth in the hands of these 'educators.'" Turning to black lawyers, he argued that their primary aim was to frighten "the common Negro" with "the bugaboo of the law" and force him into "paying out his last cent." The black real estate operator was the worst of all. He conspired with white employers to make "Negroes pay the highest prices for the least desirable property, thereby forcing their living wage still farther down."[55]

For Davis, the black bourgeoisie represented the ultimate failure of leadership. Rather than discovering within the lower classes the great "tradition of sorrow and noble struggle," the bourgeoisie aped white cultural mores and abandoned their black brothers and sisters. Rather than using their social privilege to help the impoverished masses, the bourgeoisie either deserted them

FIGURE 2.1. Allison Davis among colleagues at Hampton Institute, circa 1928. Davis is seated in the middle of the front row. Courtesy of the Davis Family.

or exploited them for social gain. He explained, "Upper-class Negroes . . . close their minds to the tragedy of the common Negro in the South in the past and today. To them it is a nightmare." For the black upper class, he continued,

> black skin is anathema and white, the *summum bonum*. The Negro's faith in the mystic superiority of light skin would be a delightful bit of irony, if it were not so farcically stupid and insane. We are color-mad, duped by a phantasm conjured up by egomaniac whites. Our complete acceptance of the white man's pathological admiration of his skin color entirely unfits us to believe in our own manhood and equality. Black and white, white and black—we are slaves to a myth. Our upper class has set up more social inequalities based upon shades of color than the most ingenious Klansmen could devise.

Having internalized racist color distinctions and the capitalistic model of success, the black bourgeoisie, as Davis saw it, erected insidious barriers between itself and the lower classes.[56]

The reception of Davis's criticisms of the black bourgeoisie was mixed. On the one hand, like-minded young black intellectuals found his criticisms incisive and even inspiring.[57] On the other hand, many older blacks, especially professional men, found Davis's attacks outrageous. W. E. B. Du Bois had to deal with complaints by such men after publishing "The Second Generation." One reader called it an "abhoring [*sic*] . . . condemnation of the twelve million struggling, suffering, abused and defenceless people."[58] Another called it a "damnation," concluding with outrage, "God help the souls under black skins who have so little faith in themselves, and have no faith in their fellows who are likewise covered."[59]

One could not really be neutral about Davis's position. Sterling Brown, naturally supportive of his friend, noted the controversy around "The Negro Deserts His People" and came to Davis's defense, writing, "We resent what doesn't flatter us. One young man, Allison Davis, who spoke courageously and capably his honest observation about our life has been the target of second rate attacks ever since."[60] Du Bois, for his part, attempted to mollify criticism of Davis and to promote an atmosphere of open debate, responding to one critic, "I wonder if you expect every writer in THE CRISIS and in other periodicals to say nothing but that with which you agree?"[61]

The origins of Davis's animus toward the black upper class were diverse. It certainly grew out of the social divisions that he had observed within black Washington, as well as his personal humiliations with poverty. Davis may also have been resentful of having to endure the paternalism and provinciality of Hampton while much of the black bourgeoisie was able to live more comfortably in the North. He simply could not stomach what felt like northern blacks' abandonment of the southern masses while he tried to live a self-respecting life in the South.

Yet Davis's evaluations of the black bourgeoisie were also rooted in larger cultural critiques of America's business culture of the 1920s, such as Irving Babbitt's. The prevailing sentiment among modern writers was a rejection of that culture and its rampant consumerism. Famously, "Lost Generation" authors such as Ernest Hemingway, F. Scott Fitzgerald, and John Dos Passos fled to Europe to live in a more cosmopolitan and less business-oriented atmosphere.[62] While in college, Davis had familiarized himself with the critiques of modern writers. For instance, he read Sinclair Lewis, whose acclaimed novel *Babbitt* (1922) told the story of a businessman who succeeds according to the gospel of materialism but ultimately realizes the emptiness of his life.[63] A wide array of writers in the period took up the word *babbittry* in shared criticism of America's empty materialism.[64]

Davis's philosophical essay "On Misgivings" (1927) positioned him squarely within this larger American critique of consumer culture. The essay makes clear his longing to pierce the surface of reality and to live deeply "in the spirit" that united all human beings, which he understood in secular terms as growing out of humanity's shared fate of certain death and the universe's utter indifference to it.[65] Davis revealed frustration with "practicality" and "all the din and tumult of our iron-vaulted cities," where politicians and scientists spew their "jargon of twentieth-century 'progress.'" In an era obsessed with the "new," Davis reminded readers of all the "departed empires and civilizations, and the long centuries of men, which have appeared and flitted away." Davis therefore saw modern life as full of distractions that only hindered people from realizing the final transience and futility of life, which he believed was a prerequisite for grasping life's real truth and beauty.[66]

To a significant degree, however, Davis developed his critique of the black bourgeoisie in dialogue with younger black intellectuals. He was, after all, speaking *about* the black community *to* the black community. Many of the younger Renaissance artists, especially those from humbler backgrounds, criticized the black upper class along the same lines as Davis. For instance, in the pages of *Opportunity* Langston Hughes indicted the black elite in Washington, DC, for their snobbishness and materialism.[67] Claude McKay delivered a similarly bitter assault on the black bourgeoisie in his novel *Banjo* (1929).

Yet it was the young radicals clustered around Howard University who probably most influenced Davis's views.[68] Among this group, E. Franklin Frazier led the way in lambasting the black bourgeoisie. In 1928 he published a controversial essay titled "La Noire Bourgeoisie." It exposed a stratified black community with conflicting economic interests. For Frazier, many middle-class blacks had fully invested in American bourgeois ideals out of their own narrow self-interest. A cursory glance at black newspapers confirmed for him the bourgeoisie's narcissism. He described the lavish attention devoted to the parties, homes, and jewelry of the elite, alongside regular "What Society Is Wearing" columns. So rather than allying in mutual racial interest by forming cooperatives and labor unions, the bourgeoisie, in Frazier's assessment, aped capitalist mores and lorded it over less affluent blacks for their own social status.[69]

Davis's criticisms of the black bourgeoisie were therefore part of the larger left wing of the New Negro Renaissance. When he wrote that the contributions of black "lawyers, doctors, school-teachers, real estate sharpers, business men and society women" were "limited to fur coats, Packards, armchair solutions to the race problem, football classics and fraternity dances," he reflected the concerns and sentiments of a younger generation of black thinkers who placed class analyses alongside racial ones to devastating effect.[70] Among that group Frazier was the most openly radical, but all of them were socialistic. Even the word *bourgeoisie*, which they employed mockingly, stemmed from Karl Marx's use of it to refer to the capitalists who exploit the working-class masses.

But while Davis shared with other black leftists the worldview that pitted the bourgeoisie against the "masses," he was among the radical few to call for direct action in the South as the prescription for real race leadership.

RACIAL SOLIDARITY

Considering his assessment of the social divisions within the black community and the failures of black leadership, Davis developed his own recommendations for race leadership. These included frank group criticism, substantive cultural and material production, and above all, direct action in the South. Although he emphasized the special role for elites in directing the masses, he called for racial solidarity and close interaction between leaders and the people. He had discovered through his own relationships with students at Hampton that black leaders had much to learn from the wider community.

As a serious thinker, Davis always respected frank and fair critics. Rather than hiding from or inflating certain realities of black life, which he believed the civil rights establishment and "race chauvinists" aimed to do, the real leader must not shrink from those realities. He or she must apply "real and high principles" and "give perspective to the so-called 'men of action.' " "The genuinely qualified critics of Negro life," he continued, "will fix upon the inner strength of Negro character as illustrated in the last three hundred years, and, discounting the trivial and irrelevant, will reinterpret these persistent characteristics for the new Negro to whom he will be as an eye." At a young age, Davis had already laid out a clear conception of the black intellectual's role in society. He would spend his entire career trying to live up to it.[71]

Fairness and judiciousness were, for Davis, essential elements of effective criticism. The ideal critic had "perspective and balance" and was prone to "reflection and contemplation" when assessing others.[72] For this reason he disliked George Schuyler. Commonly known as "the Black Mencken" for imitating the acerbic American satirist Henry Louis Mencken, Schuyler shamelessly satirized black intellectuals. For example, one infamous article titled "The Negro-Art Hokum" ridiculed Renaissance artists for believing that African Americans had anything distinctive to contribute to American art. As Schuyler saw it, "the Aframerican is merely a lampblacked Anglo-Saxon."[73]

In an even more biting article, Schuyler noted derisively that black people's greatest contribution to the United States was to make whites feel better about themselves.[74] Davis interpreted Schuyler as lacking "all standards in his frivolous and universal cynicism" and in "his indiscriminate jeering at all efforts to ameliorate white animosity and injustice."[75] Despite their shared critiques of the black bourgeoisie and of black artists' primitivistic tropes, Davis found Schuyler to lack sound judgment in his unjust and unproductive attacks on black leaders.

In addition to frank, informed, and searching criticism, Davis thought effective black leadership required the production of "creative scholarship, art or business—a contribution of the Negro's best to American civilization."[76] As is evident in his own work, he believed that intellectual production could help to cultivate respect for ordinary blacks as well as demonstrate African Americans' equal abilities to create art. He cited pioneering studies such as W. E. B. Du Bois's *The Philadelphia Negro* (1899) and Charles S. Johnson's *The Negro in Chicago* (1922) to affirm that black social scientists could conduct empirical research that could promote understanding and benefit the race.

Even in owning and operating businesses, which was typically a purview of the black bourgeoisie, Davis found potential for effective black leadership. He rejected conspicuous consumption, but he found black rather than white control over the means of production to be an important step. Chicago in the 1920s was one outstanding example of a place where African Americans had consolidated significant commercial power within the black belt on the city's South Side.[77]

Above all, Davis believed that real black leadership needed to target the needs of the majority of African Americans in the South. He called for "the training and directing of the masses through education, social service, agricultural and industrial guidance, and the encouragement of a positivistic, rather than a religiously fatalistic, attitude toward their situation." Davis echoed Du Bois's top-down conception of social change in his call for black leaders to "act as a leaven throughout the whole mass."[78]

Yet Davis diverged markedly from Du Bois and the civil rights establishment in his call for direct action *"in the South."* He wrote, "It is all very well to grow indignant and eloquent in the relative safety of Washington and New York, but it is a matter of moral and physical courage to live an energetic and self-respecting life in Virginia or Mississippi or Florida or Georgia or anywhere in that area where ten million Negroes *must* live." Here he recognized the central limitation of the Renaissance: it was an attempt "to cure a wound from the top." "The Negro," he argued, "has been bred for centuries to fear the white man's power and hatred. He must now *see in action* Negroes who do not fear the white man and who are successful without sycophancy." Concluding unsparingly, he wrote, "It is almost irrelevant to preach race pride and equal rights from the center of New York or on flying trips to Southern cities. It is irrelevant now to *preach* race equality anywhere. The Negro masses want to see the upper class live it in the South. Otherwise, they know that the upper class is as afraid of the white man as they are." The emphasis on concrete action in the South would later become common wisdom among civil rights activists in the 1930s and beyond.[79]

Davis's model of black leadership refocused attention from whites to blacks. Instead of trying to show white people that blacks were equal to them through art, scholarship, and business, more black leaders needed to worry about gaining the support and directing the energies of the black masses. Despite his socialist proclivities, Davis believed that African Americans had a common racial interest that transcended competing class interests. The black elite, after all, remained only a petit bourgeoisie in relation to white society. If blacks were to recognize their mutual discrimination "by the government and big business," then they would see that allying was in all of their economic interests. The black bourgeoisie could not compete equally with whites, so middle-class blacks relied materially upon the black masses as clients and patrons, not to mention psychologically as allies in the fight against degradation. As Davis put it, "Every man, black, white, purple or green, must exercise his faculties with some degree of fullness if he is to feel any sense of repayment for living. The hard fact is that the upper-class Negro can develop his abilities only in Negro life, because he is cut off from the white world."[80]

Davis's emphasis on race over class solidarity put him at odds with some other black radicals at the time. For instance, black socialist Abram Harris castigated the promotion of racial solidarity by race-based organizations such as the NAACP and the NUL. Harris understood race consciousness as a false identity that was rooted in economic exploitation, and he believed that it undermined interracial class solidarity and labor organizing.[81] E. Franklin Frazier and Ralph Bunche adopted similar positions during the 1930s. Harry Haywood and other black communists likewise placed class over race, although by the late 1920s they subscribed to the "black belt thesis," which held that southern blacks made up an oppressed "nation within a nation" that maintained a unique folk culture.[82]

Davis shared with these radicals an understanding of capitalism as central to racial identity, and he was sympathetic to the idea of interracial labor organizing for social change. However, he believed that African Americans—*all* African

Americans, not just southern peasant blacks, as the communists maintained—possessed a valuable "stoical" tradition that was a source of strength. He also recognized the strength of racism in American society, so he pragmatically recommended racial solidarity to win social gains in that context.

Davis's emphasis on racial solidarity had a practical impact through his younger brother, John, a budding political scientist. After his own graduation from Williams, he had returned home to Washington, DC, where he encountered the dire plight of most African Americans during the Great Depression. Inspired by his brother's ideas, John led the way in forming the intraracial New Negro Alliance (NNA) in 1933. He worked alongside several notable civil rights lawyers, including William Hastie, Belford Lawson, James Nabrit, and George Johnson.[83] The NNA became one of the nation's first "Don't Buy Where You Can't Work" campaigns, and it proved quite successful in leveraging black people's purchasing power to secure employment and fair pay in white-owned businesses in black neighborhoods.[84]

Allison Davis's cultivation of racial solidarity revealed a Black Nationalist component of his thought. His call for racial pride through African Americans' stoical tradition and his emphasis on black mobilization for democratic ends were both parts of this capacious intellectual tradition. However, unlike controversial figures such as Marcus Garvey and Elijah Muhammad, Davis did not advocate separation as a goal.[85] He ultimately desired an egalitarian American society in which racial divisions would break down. Furthermore, he saw the need to ally with and "consult the best spirits among white men" toward that end, even as he remained suspicious of white people.[86] Given the state of race relations, he believed that it was incumbent upon black people to rally together to advance both individually and collectively.

Allison Davis carved out a radical political project during the New Negro Renaissance. He used literature to create sympathy for the masses and to dramatize their oppression as well as their virtues, which he justified as the basis for racial solidarity. Along with his friend Sterling Brown, he crafted a genre of "Negro Stoicism" that worked toward his goals. At the same time, in his literature and his short essays he excoriated black bourgeois leaders for "deserting" their race and futilely attempting to assimilate into white society. He insisted that any hopes for racial uplift relied upon African Americans' supporting one another economically, politically, and spiritually. The most privileged blacks, he believed, needed to serve as true leaders of the race by living among the masses, sharing knowledge and skills, and collaborating with ordinary black folk, who held within them the virtues of the race and the hopes for racial progress.

Although Davis and other young black radicals often failed to live up to these ideals, spending much of their time merely speaking to other intellectuals, they articulated powerful ideas that would resonate through the twentieth century in figures as diverse as Malcolm X and Martin Luther King Jr.[87] That Davis developed his ideas in dialogue with Renaissance discourse and published them in major Renaissance organs, however, makes clear the presence of an important radical part in a movement that is often portrayed as interested only in liberal reformism and artistic independence.[88] Furthermore, the case of Allison Davis shows how ordinary black people—his poor southern students—subtly influenced Renaissance discourse. Such a role suggests a bottom-up element to a movement that is frequently seen as top-down. Finally, Davis's example further reinforces the idea that the Renaissance was a national and international movement that transcended the confines of Harlem.[89] In Davis's case, Hampton proved fertile ground through which to carve out a distinctive and radical Renaissance voice.

By the late 1920s, however, Davis decided to change the terrain on which he would wage his battle against racial injustice. He moved into the arena of mainstream social science, hoping to contribute to debates beyond those within African American intellectual life. Speaking to white America would require him to censor his bold voice, and it would demand that he work alongside white liberals, who all too often could smother black people with condescension, ignorance, and hypocrisy. Yet the rewards could be large. He could have a national impact by pushing empirical research in racially progressive directions.

His decision was not without consequence within the history of social science. His understanding of race and class in the United States, forged through intellectual debate and personal experience, allowed him to portray racial stratification more fully than any of his white peers had done.

CHAPTER 3

The Making of a Social Anthropologist

The social sciences have tended to accept the dogmas of the society as if they were established truths.[1]

ALLISON DAVIS

By the late 1920s, Allison Davis was looking for a way to "become more relevant to Afro-American needs."[2] Like many other black intellectuals of his day, he turned from a career in the arts during the New Negro Renaissance to one in the social sciences during the Great Depression. If the twenties cultural milieu was individualistic, literary, cosmopolitan, and aloof for American intellectuals, the thirties milieu was socialistic, realistic, local, and committed.[3] Although such a distinction is oversimplified, different intellectual styles and goals did accompany the very real changes characterizing life in the Depression. For African Americans, the group always most victimized by economic downturns, the situation was dire. White patronage for artistic expression evaporated, and for some, art suddenly seemed trivial in the face of pervasive suffering.[4] As the Renaissance ended, black intellectuals looked for a new arena in which to fight for racial equality and improve the welfare of the black masses.[5]

The social sciences beckoned as one field of battle. Since the nineteenth century, the devastating power of science to underwrite racism had been all too apparent, but black intellectuals were helpless to counteract it because they were largely barred from higher education. However, some of these barriers began to break down during the interwar period. In the decade after 1926, there were as many black college graduates as there had been in the hundred years previous.[6] At the graduate level, only seventeen blacks had earned doctorates in any field by 1925, but by 1939 that number was at 109, with many more on the horizon.[7] The numbers remained small, but the shift in momentum was large, and even these limited developments would prove crucial in altering scientific knowledge.

Black social scientists undermined scientific racism and demonstrated the importance of the environment over heredity in shaping racial differences. Precisely because of the discrimination they faced, black intellectuals were better able to discern the social inequities that circumscribed their lives. Pioneers such as W. E. B. Du Bois led the way in this fight.

Yet African Americans were not alone in using their experiences as a subordinate group to attack hereditarianism. In much the same way, women combated scientific sexism, and Jews fought scientific racism during the period.[8] African Americans, women, and Jews therefore allied with liberal WASP intellectuals to form an early "American liberal intelligentsia" that fought for equality by exposing the environmental causes of inequality.[9] The nature of social science as an enterprise subject to change and open to new evidence enabled individuals from marginalized groups to transform knowledge. This alluring prospect was one major reason black intellectuals turned to social science in the 1930s.

The transition from literature to social science, though, was not as fundamental as it may at first appear. Indeed, many social scientists of the period understood literary expression as linked closely with scientific research, and in fact many experimented with both.[10] For young black intellectuals like Davis, the vehicle might have changed, but the goal of fighting for racial equality and vindicating the race had not. Even the character of literature and that of social science were sometimes strikingly similar. The realism of Davis, Sterling Brown, and others of the late Renaissance, for example, mirrored closely the empiricism within social science.

Above all, what may usefully be called a "modernist sensibility" united the disparate efforts of Davis and other young black intellectuals in their career change. At the heart of this sensibility was what Dorothy Ross calls "a new understanding of the subjectivity of knowledge," namely, "the recognition that no foundation for knowledge or value exists outside the meanings that human beings construct for their own purposes." Many modernist intellectuals who turned to social science, therefore, did so to "reconstruct the bases of knowledge and value." They worked to demonstrate the centrality of the social environment in shaping human life to create a more just society.[11]

Davis's first two years in social science had a profound influence on the trajectory of his multifarious career. His formal education in anthropology at Harvard and the London School of Economics from 1931 to 1933 included efforts within such fields as African ethnology, social biology, and social anthropology. During this brief span, he forged lasting connections with leading social scientists across the world and with influential foundation officers. In these years he also gained a theoretical orientation and empirical foundation in social anthropology that would ground his later efforts. Here we see the emergence of Davis the pioneering social scientist.

BACK TO HARVARD

When Davis returned to familiar Cambridge in the fall of 1931, he did not travel alone. His new wife, Alice Elizabeth Stubbs Davis, accompanied him. The couple had married on June 21, 1929, in Harper's Ferry, West Virginia. Mordecai Johnson, the first black president of Howard University and a family friend of the Davises, presided.[12] Elizabeth, or Liddie, was a beautiful, brilliant, and outgoing African American woman from Wilmington, Delaware.

Elizabeth came from an affluent family that was firmly part of the black bourgeoisie. Her father, J. B. Stubbs, was a physician who had attended graduate school at the University of Pennsylvania before starting his practice in Wilmington in 1900.[13] Her mother, Blanche Williams Stubbs, was a teacher who teamed up with her husband to take an active role in civic life, including their founding of the Thomas Garrett Settlement House in 1911. Her brother graduated first in his class at Harvard Medical School.

Like the rest of her family, Elizabeth had a first-rate education that rivaled her husband's. However, she had avoided the segregated public schools of Wilmington by attending a preparatory school in Massachusetts. She then earned her BA from Mount Holyoke, which was conspicuous for its rigorous academic and professional training.[14] She was therefore a highly educated, cultured, and proud black woman, and she was Allison's intellectual peer as well as his emotional partner.

By 1929 the Davises were eager to escape the limited horizons of Hampton, Virginia, and to make larger contributions to African American life. Allison's interactions with poor southern blacks had interested him in the study of "the origins of folk-forms among American Negroes."[15] Unlike E. Franklin Frazier and some other black intellectuals of the time, Davis believed that knowledge of Africa is a prerequisite for understanding the culture of American blacks. So in 1929 he began communicating with the world's foremost social and cultural anthropologists in the hopes of studying anthropology in Europe and carrying out fieldwork in Africa. St. Clair Drake explained that Davis's choice of anthropology was logical given that it was "the new field . . . countering the 'intellectual' stream of biological determinism." According to Drake, Davis believed that the black scholar's task was threefold: (1) to make a general theoretical contribution to a discipline, (2) to become an expert in a particular subfield, and (3) "to select a problem that contributed to racial advancement." The Davises found anthropology to be a promising field for their interests and aims.[16]

To be sure, the Davises' decision to enter professional anthropology was an exceedingly rare one for African Americans at that time. Only a handful of blacks studied or practiced anthropology in the interwar period. This was partly because blacks knew the racist past and present of the discipline, which whites consistently used to bolster racial segregation and discrimination. Indeed, the social Darwinism of the founders of anthropology had helped to underwrite *Plessy v. Ferguson* (1896), the Supreme Court decision ratifying segregation on "separate but equal" grounds. For instance, the court looked to the science of Daniel G. Brinton, president of the formidable American Association for the Advancement of Science, to confirm the natural inequality between the races.[17]

Yet even when blacks recognized progressive trends within the discipline, anthropology as a scholarly inquiry still seemed too broad and less immediately relevant than other fields. Sociology, economics, and political science, for example, all dealt more explicitly with contemporary issues of social inequality, and they could be used directly to craft policy.

Perhaps most important, African Americans knew that black anthropologists had few if any prospects for employment in the field. Only the three leading black colleges—Fisk, Howard, and Atlanta—offered any anthropology courses at all, and then only occasionally and through visiting professorships. White universities barred blacks from faculty positions altogether. Recognizing the PhD as a ladder to nowhere, graduate programs sometimes even rejected black applicants on those grounds alone. For these reasons, Allison and Elizabeth Davis were preeminent black pioneers for not only entering into but also succeeding within anthropology.[18]

The Davises targeted European universities for their graduate study. In 1929 Allison Davis began corresponding with Dietrich Westermann of the University of Berlin and Bronislaw Malinowski of the London School of Economics (LSE), both of whom expressed interest in working with him.[19] They helped him see that a year at Harvard could make it easier for him and his wife to secure the funding they needed for study abroad. Consequently, Davis applied for and won a Social Science Research Council grant to subsidize a year at Harvard.[20] He was one of the twenty Southern Fellows selected in 1931 from over two hundred applicants.[21] Yet again, Davis remained squarely within the "Talented Tenth."

Meanwhile, Elizabeth won acceptance to Radcliffe College, which shared many faculty members and facilities with Harvard. Elizabeth was therefore able to study social anthropology along with her husband, despite the formal institutional divide by gender.

Harvard was in the process of developing one of the nation's finest graduate programs in anthropology. Through the support of the Rockefeller Foundation, Harvard had by the 1930s become one of the few institutions with deep enough pockets to support doctoral students in cultural or social anthropology—fields that required subsidizing students' fieldwork across the world.[22] By 1933 Harvard was training thirty-five Harvard students and ten Radcliffe students for PhDs in the discipline.[23] Many of those students specialized in one of the three other branches of anthropology: linguistics, archaeology, and physical anthropology. But cultural or social anthropology was the exciting new field on the rise.

Edwin Embree, vice president of the Rockefeller Foundation and future president of the Julius Rosenwald Fund, signaled the trend. He showed particular interest in supporting the study of isolated non-Western cultures that were "vanishing" across the globe as a result of Western imperialism.[24] The idea was that these traditional and sometimes ancient civilizations would soon cease to exist, so through "salvage ethnography" anthropologists could serve the crucial scientific function of documenting them before they vanished.

Later, as head of the Rosenwald Fund during the 1930s and 1940s, Embree committed that philanthropic institution to improving race relations in the United States. Because the newly reorganized fund was not to exist in perpetuity like other major philanthropies, it had a mandate to harness its resources to maximize impact immediately. Embree took advantage. The fund supported black education at all levels, and it fought for racial integration and equal opportunity, partly through fellowships to outstanding black people. For these reasons, the fund would prove instrumental for Allison Davis and other black scholars of his generation.[25]

The Davises were quick to seize the opportunities at hand. Allison took an intensive year of coursework, completing two semesters of African ethnology with Walter Cline and the famous taxonomist Earnest Hooton, two semesters of physical anthropology, two semesters of European archaeology, one semester of primitive religion, and one semester of American family with Lloyd Warner, in which Davis pursued research on the African American family.[26]

During this intensive year, Davis began to absorb the structural theory that would characterize his mature thought. In one of the African ethnology courses, for example, he wrote a paper on African songs in which he argued for their communal nature.[27] While not dismissing the spontaneity and individual adaptation that characterized the music, he stressed that the songs ran along familiar cultural lines. He summoned his close reading of African American culture in the 1920s to underline the significance of the cultural "whole" in understanding the discrete cultural form.

Similarly, Davis wrote a paper analyzing the functional role that witch doctors played among the Bantu in Africa. The essay explained how the witch doctor was "essentially an organizer of social and religious controls. He stabilized the rule of the chief or king, socially and politically, by giving that figurehead the support of supernatural sanctions. He organized the controls on crime and roguery, around the fear of social condemnation, and of the supernatural."[28] Davis's emphasis on structure and function became a trademark of his thought.

Elizabeth Davis's formal training is less clear, but like her husband she specialized in African anthropology under the tutelage of Earnest Hooton, one of the world's leading racial taxonomists. In a wide range of publications, including such popular books as *Up from the Ape* (1931), Hooton classified the human race according to "the morphological and metrical variations of such bodily characters as hair, skin, nose, eyes, stature, and differences in shape and proportions of the head, the trunk, and the limbs." He used those physical features to divide human beings into four broad categories: "Negroids, Mongoloids, Whites, and Composites," also adding certain white subgroups such as Mediterraneans, Nordics, and Alpines. He generally abstained from making grand claims about the superiority of one race over another, as unabashed white supremacists such as eugenicist Madison Grant did, but Hooton nevertheless saw Negroid groups as having a "generally low state of culture."[29]

One can only imagine the type of awkwardness that Hooton's racism might have engendered with the Davises. Yet Hooton seems to have had no problem working with black Harvard students, and the Davises recognized an opportunity to gain firsthand knowledge of racial taxonomies. How better to understand scientific racism than to study under one of the leading scientific racists?

For a black woman, Elizabeth Davis's graduate education in anthropology is particularly significant. Unfortunately, it can be only dimly viewed from the scant archival record. We know she drafted a paper titled "Rites of Passage among the Ashanti," which made clear her larger investigation into the cultural life of Africans—in this case the Ashanti people, who lived in what is present-day Ghana.[30]

Caroline Bond Day was perhaps the only black woman to precede Elizabeth at Harvard. Day studied intermittently under Hooton for several years, eventually earning an MA in 1930. She studied race-mixing among 346 families, part of which she published as *A Study of Some Negro-White Families in the United States* (1932) through Harvard's Peabody Museum.[31] Gender barriers merged with racial ones to stymie both Day's and Davis's careers, but their examples make clearer the social constraints at the time. They also suggest that individuals transgressed social lines and challenged gender and racial norms from within the academy.

Elizabeth Davis's most important contribution would ultimately come through her relationship with her husband, whose status as a man afforded him more professional opportunities. Indeed, Allison's many accomplishments within anthropology cannot be separated from the intellectual guidance and practical support Elizabeth offered him. The couple became anthropologists together.

The most significant training that Allison Davis received at Harvard was from the young social anthropologist Lloyd Warner. Learning from Warner in the classroom was helpful, but it was nothing compared to studying alongside him in the field. Davis participated in Warner's work and in the process met regularly with him and his large team of researchers, learning Warner's distinct brand of social anthropology.[32]

Warner's innovative anthropology warrants special attention, as it exerted a profound influence on Davis's career within anthropology. The origins of Warner's approach can be traced back his undergraduate days at Berkeley in the 1920s. He had the distinct privilege of learning the discipline from two of Franz Boas's students, Alfred Kroeber and Robert Lowie. Yet Warner hardly took advantage of the opportunity. As an affluent white youth in those days, he rarely took his classes seriously but threw himself into socialist politics instead.

For that reason, A. R. Radcliffe-Brown was Warner's real mentor.[33] Radcliffe-Brown was born in England in 1881 and had studied under W. H. R. Rivers at Cambridge. Radcliffe-Brown conducted extensive fieldwork in the Andaman Islands just west of India from 1906 to 1908, as well as in western Australia from 1910 to 1912. He published some of this research in 1922 in *The Andaman Islanders*, which established him as both a leader in social anthropology and a pioneering theorist of structural-functionalism.

Above all, Radcliffe-Brown was interested in how social structure, including kinship, the economy, politics, and religion, determined human behavior. He theorized that human society is integrated and that every part of it functions together to maintain social stability.[34] Unlike the English cultural evolutionist E. B. Tylor or the German historical diffusionist Franz Boas, Radcliffe-Brown was not interested in the unique or the particular, nor in explaining how cultures developed over time. Rather, he was interested in how patterns of behavior are directed by social structure. He also sought to compare different societies in order to make generalizations, or even laws, about the origins of all human behavior. Émile Durkheim and French sociology loomed especially large in his thinking. Most consequentially, he followed Durkheim in examining social stability even in times of rapid change and in positing a clear dichotomy between "modern" and "primitive" societies, in which class and kinship, respectively, served as the foundational social structures.[35]

Warner's anthropology grew logically out of Radcliffe-Brown's. Before arriving at Harvard in 1929, Warner had spent two years studying the Murngin aborigines in Australia under the tutelage of Radcliffe-Brown. The book he published on that research, *A Black Civilization* (1937), showed his mentor's influence. Yet Warner combined British social anthropology and French sociology in a way that made his brand of anthropology unique within the United States. To be sure, Warner still shared the integrationism and holism dominating American anthropology, evident in his "attempt to correlate specific aspects of Murngin culture with one another" (integrationism) and in his conceptualization of the whole as structuring the parts (holism). But Warner's "sociological philosophy," according to Robert Lowie, made his treatise distinct "in organization and the statement of problems, in fact, in the very nature of the problems themselves."[36] Warner and Radcliffe-Brown, who was a visiting professor at the University of Chicago from 1931 to 1937, helped to bring a sociological approach to American anthropology, which had long been dominated by historical and evolutionary approaches.

Warner's theoretical approach was distinctive, as was his next subject: the investigation of modern, rather than "primitive," societies. The application of anthropological methods to modern society was striking because many cultural and social anthropologists of that era thought participant observation was suitable only for studying cultural "others"; only in such a framework could the anthropologist retain the requisite objectivity.

Warner saw it differently. He insisted on the transferability of his social-anthropological methods. He wrote, "My fundamental purpose in studying primitive man was to get to know modern man better; that some day I proposed to investigate . . . the social life of a modern man with the hope of ultimately placing the researching in a larger framework of comparison which would include the other societies of the world."[37]

Once at Harvard, Warner did exactly that. In 1930 he selected Newburyport, Massachusetts, as the site for his first and most elaborate community study. For Davis, this was to become the laboratory for his initiation into social anthropology. Newburyport was conveniently located not far from Harvard, was of a manageable size, and maintained a largely Anglo-Saxon demographic that appeared relatively stable.[38] As with so many other community studies in that era, including most famously Robert and Helen Lynd's study of Muncie, Indiana, which they called "Middletown," Warner used a pseudonym for the community: "Yankee City." The pseudonym protected the identities of the research subjects, but it also suggested the larger representativeness of the study within New England.

The project was a massive undertaking. Through "participation, observation, and extensive interviews," federally supported researchers, secretaries, and clerks gathered voluminous data about the people and institutions of Newburyport.[39] Warner and his associates spent the next couple of decades organizing and writing up the findings into various monographs.[40] (In addition to his work for Warner, Davis carried out his own research on the very small black community in Newburyport, although his contributions were never acknowledged in later publications.)[41]

Warner organized the voluminous data through a few "leading ideas." One was his functionalist social-anthropological approach that assumed the "interconnectedness" and "mutual dependence" of all parts of the community. Another was Radcliffe-Brown's structural emphasis on the "variety of structure—i.e., the family, the extended kin, the associations and age grading" and its centrality in shaping human behavior and ranking individuals into higher and lower social positions. The final major idea was that societies have "a fundamental structure or structures which integrate and give characteristic form to the rest of the society." Because Newburyport was a modern city, Warner followed Durkheim in seeing the economic system, or class system, as the fundamental social structure.[42]

However, Warner's interests and empirical investigations into Yankee City, along with his attempt to distance himself from communism, prompted him to revise his conception of class.[43] This, too, would have a bearing on Davis's social-science orientation. Warner was interested in what he called "social class," which Davis and other Warner students defined as "the largest group of people whose members have intimate access to one another."[44] They wrote, "A class is composed of families and social cliques. The interrelationships between these families and cliques, in such informal activities as visiting, dances, receptions, teas, and larger informal affairs, constitute the structure of a social class. A person is a member of that social class with which most of his participations, of this intimate kind, occur."[45] Warner argued that a person's social class, or social participation group, was tied to a variety of factors including material ones such as occupation and wealth but also ideational ones such as prestige, family heritage, behavior, and associated symbols. His definition therefore combined the sociological concepts of class and status in a way that would provoke major criticism among sociologists.[46]

In Warner's hands, the economic, or Marxist, dimensions of class were often subsumed under the social aspects. This could result in conceptual confusion and a retreat from economic analysis as paramount. But Warner's aim was partly to revise the economic determinism within Marxism and to reveal how social and cultural forces also play a role in determining a person's class position. Warner divided social class into six imperfect but meaningful groupings: lower-lower, upper-lower, lower-middle, upper-middle, lower-upper, and upper-upper.[47]

Above all, Warner's Yankee City project examined how Newburyport was stratified by social class and how that stratification fundamentally shaped the behaviors, personalities, and patterns of thought of all its residents. Warner, like many of his students, subsequently spent much of his effort tracking residents' movement across class lines to measure the rigidity of social-class distinctions and the possibilities for social mobility.

Because Warner was always interested in comparing different societies in order to formulate general principles of social organization, he quickly moved to initiate other community studies. One idea was for a study of County Clare in Ireland, and the other was for a project in the Deep South. Warner presumed the significance of social class within modern American communities, but he also acknowledged variation across the world's many societies. For example, he saw East Africa as dominated by age grading, India as primarily organized by caste, and Polynesia as principally controlled by status.[48] His interest in a project in the Deep South sprang partly from his belief that the racial division there might have created a novel social system, which would be a useful point of comparison. As of 1932, though, that project was still only an idea in Warner's head.

It was just as well, because Davis had his own concerns. After a year at Harvard, he remained resolved to study African ethnology at the LSE and the University of Berlin, and to then conduct fieldwork in Africa under the auspices of the International Institute of African Languages and Cultures.[49] He planned to use the expertise he acquired to "give courses in African history and contemporary cultures" at Hampton or other black colleges.[50] He found it troubling that no black person was formally qualified to teach that subject, with the result that most black students confined to black colleges could never study a field so relevant to their lives. It is also likely that the Afrocentrism of the Renaissance influenced Davis and inspired him to want to become an authority in a field he saw as too long plagued by either racism or race chauvinism.[51]

Davis also planned to use his African expertise to inform his studies of African Americans. In applying for a Rosenwald Fellowship for study abroad in 1932, he wrote, "After my formal study shall have been completed, I plan to do field work in contemporary Negro folk-life, in certain isolated sections of the lower South . . . with a view toward a more scientific and complete interpretation of its origin and present state, than has yet been made." Indeed, he was "already beginning to trace in the authentic accounts of slavery in America, written in the 17th, 18th, and 19th centuries, the relative influences of African and American forms in the growth of Negro folk-life in this country."[52]

His sense of a rich and sophisticated African American folk life with roots in African society was advanced thinking at the time. Had he pursued this line of research, he could have informed the later debate on African "survivals" that raged between Melville Herskovits, E. Franklin Frazier, and others in the late 1930s. Too often that debate centered on "Africanisms," or isolated cultural forms originating in Africa, rather than on a rich cultural tradition that was sophisticated, diffuse, and adaptable.[53]

Davis put together a remarkably strong application for a Rosenwald Fellowship. He secured laudatory letters of recommendation from faculty members at Williams and Harvard, from Hampton's president Arthur Howe, from Thomas Jesse Jones of the Phelps Stokes Fund, from Will Alexander of the Commission on Interracial Cooperation, and from Malinowski, Westermann, and Alain Locke. Attesting to his success at Harvard, Professor Walter Cline called him "the best student" in his African ethnology course.[54] Earnest A. Hooton credited him as "the most brilliant and able colored student we have ever had," concluding with admiration: "Here at last is a Negro who can make most of his white fellow students 'take his dust.'"[55]

Alain Locke, who was the impresario of the Renaissance as well as a Harvard PhD and professor of philosophy at Howard, rounded out Davis's application by linking his earlier literary accomplishments with his social science objectives. Locke wrote, "The money expended in my judgment will be amply repaid by the equipment of a young man capable for the first time to interpret the Negro point of view in this important field of cultural anthropology; for it requires something of a humanist as well as a scientist to make the proper combination. Mr. Davis's grounding in the humanities at Williams and Harvard make for this unique combination."[56]

Finally, Lloyd Warner also proved instrumental in Davis's success. Warner put Davis in touch with Edwin Embree, whom Warner knew well through his ties to the Rockefeller Foundation and the Rosenwald Fund. Davis then began corresponding with Embree to strengthen his application.[57] This was the beginning of a long and fruitful relationship that was to be essential to Davis's professional success.

Davis won the fellowship. He and his wife left for London later that year.

THE LONDON SCHOOL OF ECONOMICS

The Davises arrived in London in September 1932, and they were both quickly accepted as doctoral candidates in anthropology at the LSE.[58] The LSE had been founded in 1895 by Fabian socialists who believed in a gradual and reformist—as opposed to revolutionary—turn toward government control of private property. In 1900 the LSE joined the University of London, but its leftist orientation persisted.[59]

London itself had long been home to organized radicalism of all sorts, and that inclination became only stronger during the Great Depression. Ralph Bunche, the African American leftist, later diplomat, and good friend of Allison Davis's, studied at the LSE with Malinowski just a few years after the Davises. During his time there, he interacted with a group of radicals including Jomo Kenyatta, C. L. R. James, and Paul Robeson. In fact, Bunche's radical associations almost cost him a chance to do fieldwork in Africa, as the British government was closely monitoring the activities of his friends.[60]

The Davises avoided such controversy, but Allison reported to St. Clair Drake that he "had entered a whole new world." Drake recalled, "He said that he was reading Marx, as well as social anthropology, and that he liked what Lancelot Hogben, a non-dogmatic Marxist, had to say."[61] These were exciting times for the Davises, and their enthusiasm for social anthropology was infectious. Indeed, Allison influenced Drake to begin reading in anthropology as well, and he later enlisted him directly in fieldwork, instigating Drake's long and accomplished career in the field.[62]

Allison Davis's initial hope of completing his PhD at the LSE did not last long. The university had a two-year residency requirement for the degree, so he had to secure an additional year of financial support. Unfortunately, it never materialized, and the Davises had difficulty even making it through the first year. The couple struggled mightily to find an affordable apartment, as landlords typically overcharged students and demanded substantial upfront deposits.[63] Later on, financial constraints also prevented Allison from "spend[ing] the reading period in Paris" to investigate race-mixing.[64]

Even more frustrating, Davis's tutelage under Dietrich Westermann in Berlin in the spring of 1933 was cut short as Adolf Hitler took dictatorial control of Germany, arresting communists, dissolving trade unions, and Nazifying the

FIGURE 3.1. Allison and Elizabeth Davis among friends in Berlin, Germany, in early 1933. The couple is on the far right. Courtesy of the Davis Family.

press and universities.[65] Davis later recalled, "I was a student in Berlin when Hitler came to power. . . . I saw the Nazis burn the books, throw the liberal youth and teachers in jail, and close the University of Berlin to all minority groups. I saw the Brown Shirts attacking the students, the professors, and the anti-Nazis, all in the name of patriotism."[66] Making the matter more personal, Davis observed how one of his good friends in Berlin, a Jew named Rudi, was ordered to sever his relations with his Aryan girlfriend. The two refused and risked their lives by continuing to date in secret.[67] Davis was impressed with their stoical resolve, and he identified with the struggle against an implacable racist foe. After having witnessed the devastating effects of a racism that was clearly global in nature, he and Elizabeth fled back to London as determined as ever to fight racial injustice.[68]

Although their time there was limited, the Davises poured their intellectual energies into their studies at the LSE. As a result, they benefited immensely from the opportunities available there. Among other esteemed faculty members, the LSE employed anthropologists Bronislaw Malinowski and C. G. Seligman, sociologists Edvard Westermarck and Morris Ginsberg, political scientist Harold Laski, and social biologist Lancelot Hogben. At that time, the department of anthropology was focused exclusively on social anthropology, which infused it with an extraordinary energy and focus.[69]

The distinction between social and cultural anthropology was an important one. Cultural anthropology was largely an American field in the 1930s, with Franz Boas as its intellectual leader and Columbia as its institutional home. Boas's students took authoritative roles in the field throughout the country.[70] It was especially through their work that cultural anthropology examined cultures as holistic, integrated entities in which particular values, customs, and symbolic meanings united groups of people.[71] In other words, the Boasian approach was ideational, analyzing the links between values and behavior, and it was "particularistic," conceiving of each culture as distinct, owing to its singular process of historical development.[72]

Social anthropology, on the other hand, was largely a British approach, more scientific than historical. It resembled comparative sociology, and it sometimes went by that name. The field shared the structural emphasis of the Boasians, and it similarly relied upon participant observation as its main avenue to empirical knowledge. However, social anthropology focused on the organization and functioning of social structures within particular communities, rather than on values and meaning. Social anthropologists of this era therefore tended to understand individual behavior as a product of "predetermined sets of behavior" within regulative social structures, whereas cultural anthropologists saw behavior as the manifestation of people's beliefs and values.[73] While cultural anthropology examined each culture as unique, social anthropology was committed to finding commonalities across cultural lines, with the hope of devising general laws of human behavior that could accurately predict how a person would act or think in a particular situation. Davis's interest in Africa had led him to the LSE, and there he reinforced his training in social rather than cultural anthropology.

To be sure, British social anthropology was not unified. It was principally divided between the functionalism of Bronislaw Malinowski, the world's foremost social anthropologist, and the structural-functionalism of A. R. Radcliffe-Brown, described above. Malinowski's approach prevailed at the LSE, but Radcliffe-Brown's approach ultimately had a greater influence on Davis. Malinowski was a Pole who had become the LSE's chair of anthropology in 1925.[74] Between 1914 and 1918 he became a pioneer in his profession by conducting extensive fieldwork in New Guinea and North Melanesia in the South Pacific. That research formed the basis of many important books and his reputation in the field.[75]

Argonauts of the Western Pacific (1922) was his most significant work. The book scrutinized trade, which Malinowski viewed as more than merely an economic transaction. He embedded trade within larger cultural and social institutions. His emphasized the "totality of all social, cultural and psychological aspects of the community, for they are so interwoven that not one can be understood without taking into consideration all the others."[76] The same approach characterized his other works, such as *The Sexual Life of Savages* (1929), in which he looked at sex "in its widest meaning" as "rather a sociological and cultural force than a mere bodily relation between two individuals."[77] As someone interested in better understanding the structure and function of Jim Crow, Davis found Malinowski's functionalism appealing.

Hortense Powdermaker, an American student of Malinowski's in the late 1920s, summed up Malinowski's personality: "He had great vitality and was deeply involved with life—the minutiae and the general, whether in the Trobriand Islands or in London. He was also a man of paradoxes: kind and helpful as well as cruel and sarcastic. Keen perception and sharp wit helped make his barbs effective. Belligerence characterized many arguments with his peers." Powdermaker also remembered that he "delighted in shocking people, particularly those he considered bourgeois and conventional. He boasted about his ability to swear in seven languages and sometimes demonstrated his fluency in inappropriate situations." No evidence suggests that the Davises had a close relationship with Malinowski, but the eminent scholar's theoretical approach to social anthropology—holistic and integrated, seeing all parts of society as unified—did influence them.[78]

Powdermaker reminds us how "strikingly new" this functional approach was within anthropology.[79] Many contemporary practitioners continued to espouse E. B. Tylor's cultural evolutionism, a Victorian approach that depicted culture in hierarchical terms with Western Europe at the top. For cultural evolutionists, "civilization" developed in a clear line straight out of ancient Egypt. Malinowski eschewed this approach and posited cultural relativism, which treated each culture as logical, cohesive, and organized practically to meet people's biological and social needs. In a candid, unproofread letter of recommendation for Davis in 1931, the Polish-born scholar explained his new approach. He taught that "no rigid disdiction [*sic*] is possible as to the methods of studing [*sic*] 'simple' and 'advanced' cultures; the term 'savage' is applied equally to the citizen of London and of Timbuctoo, of Chicago and of any small village in Ashanti or Papua."[80] The Davises perceived the radicalism of relativizing culture, and they found in anthropology a way to attack the all-too-frequent assumption of African Americans' cultural backwardness.

Many critics have contested aspects of Malinowski's thought.[81] Malinowski did explain social institutions as developing not chaotically out of contingent processes of history but rather as logical and organic manifestations of people's natural needs. This emphasis on needs was a primary difference between functionalism and structural-functionalism. Structural-functionalists theorized that social institutions operate according to the dictates of the society as a whole, rather than in relation to the needs of individuals. Malinowski's functional theory could indeed have conservative implications, some of which were rightly criticized. For instance, one might argue, as southern sociologists did, that racial caste developed organically out of individuals' needs and was therefore a natural system.[82]

Nevertheless, functionalism provided serious social insight and had decidedly liberal roots. And as Powdermaker argued, "There is, of course, no reason for a functional point of view to be unhistorical."[83] The fact that the Davises found in functional theory a powerful tool for fomenting racial change testifies to its liberal potential.

The extent of Elizabeth Davis's formal training at the LSE is unclear. But her general anthropological education, at least, was comparable to her husband's. She would never complete her PhD, and after having a child in 1939 and again in 1941, she increasingly focused on rearing them. Once her husband secured a professorship at Chicago, she followed the custom of the time and became more of a socialite. Nevertheless, she continued to underpin her husband's professional success through formal and informal research support and through bearing a disproportionate share of domestic responsibilities. While she served as an instrumental member on several of her husband's research teams, the patriarchal academy marginalized her contributions.

Regrettably, Elizabeth Stubbs Davis continues to be ignored within the history of anthropology despite important attempts to recover examples of early black anthropologists.[84] It speaks volumes of gender dynamics in the academy that even St. Clair Drake, a close associate of Allison Davis and a co-contributor to the Deep South project—in which Elizabeth played a paramount role—failed to include her in his list of the handful of black anthropologists before World War II.[85]

LANCELOT HOGBEN AND SOCIAL BIOLOGY

Malinowski's influence on the Davises was significant, but social biologist Lancelot Hogben (1895–1975) emerged as Allison Davis's most significant mentor at the LSE. Hogben was a public intellectual who used the biological sciences to undermine eugenics by emphasizing the role of the environment over heredity. Hogben consistently put his beliefs into actions, calling his philosophy "scientific humanism." In a 1918 passage about Alfred Russel Wallace, the British biologist who had independently developed the theory of evolution by natural selection, Hogben revealed the nature of his own philosophy: "He was great because his wonderful mentality penetrated the mists of ignorance and battled with superstition; but greater, because he took his part side by side with all good men and women who are engaged in the struggle that will never end, till there is expressed in the structure of society the right of every human being to the good things of life, and a responsible share in the control of his or her own destiny."[86] The requirements of "objectivity" in American social science, especially for African Americans studying race, discouraged Davis from making such public pronouncements. Yet Hogben's scientific humanism mirrored Davis's own philosophy of using science for progressive ends. In his case, this meant combating racial segregation, discrimination, and inequality at a moment when people were using science to support such arrangements.

From early on, Hogben had demonstrated a willingness to put his beliefs into action. As a pacifist who joined the Society of Friends and a socialist who joined the Fabians, Hogben conscientiously objected to World War I and endured imprisonment for it. He elected to sew mailbags in solitary confinement rather than support any aspect of a war that he judged abhorrent and imperialistic.[87] He paid the price for that decision. After five months of imprisonment, in which guards punished inmates with water torture, Hogben was freed in 1917 because his health had deteriorated so severely.[88] He spent the better part of the following year recovering mentally and physically from the ordeal.

Hogben faced other moral challenges while employed at the University of Cape Town in the late 1920s, just as South Africans began instituting the outlines of apartheid. Hogben recalled vividly the introduction of "seven native bills," one of which "made marriage, and even intercourse, between a European and a native a criminal offence. Another tightened up the pass-system which restricted free movement of the natives beyond the reserves, and imposed a period of forced labour on natives found squatting, in effect wandering, on land belonging to our kith and kin, an ex-European farmer." "The most drastic of all provisions of the new legislation," he wrote, "abolished the Cape native franchise and withdrew from the native anywhere in the Union the right of free assembly."[89]

As the racial situation deteriorated, Hogben again faced difficult choices. The local community pressured him to conform to apartheid strictures. Yet Hogben stood by his principles. While the University of Cape Town was beginning to bar black students, Hogben elected to spurn the rules and continue accepting blacks into his class. He also held open houses on Saturday nights and invited various radicals within Cape Town's intelligentsia to participate.[90]

Even more dramatically, Hogben and his wife, Enid, who was also a socialist and a feminist, risked their lives to save two local black leaders from being lynched. They surreptitiously stashed the two men in the trunk of their car and transported them to safety.[91] Hogben's socialist, antiracist, and scientific-humanist philosophy appealed to Davis, as did his activist, morally courageous nature.

In 1930 Hogben fled South Africa and joined the LSE as the chair of social biology, where he used his position to wage an effective battle against scientific racism. The strength of the racialist, eugenicist science in the interwar period was formidable. Indeed, it was not a given that environmentalist positions would displace hereditarian ones. Science could be and was being used to further both racist and antiracist interests. The 1920s represented in many ways the height of scientific racism.

Indeed, racism pervaded the disciplines of psychology, physical anthropology, and biology. Psychologists Edward L. Thorndike of Columbia and Carl Brigham of Princeton, for example, were hugely influential in developing mental tests that scientifically "proved" the superiority of Nordic peoples and the inferiority of other groups.[92] Physical anthropologists continued measuring crania as an empirical guide to human ability.[93] Biologists consistently underemphasized or ignored the importance of the social environment.[94] The scientific racism characterizing these disciplines in turn bolstered the nativism and white supremacy which underlay immigration restriction, eugenics, and lynching in the United States.

Developments on the horizon, including the prolonged economic depression and Hitler's extermination of millions of Jews, were later to fuel an immense shift in social thought toward innate racial equality. In fact, change was already afoot. Cultural anthropologists were leading the way in proving scientifically that the environment has the power to determine a group's potential. Franz Boas and his students, who were the leaders in this fight, also spread the "culture concept" to sociologists in the 1920s, and they had a particularly strong influence on the Chicago School of Sociology.[95]

Social psychologist Otto Klineberg was one of the most important of this new generation of environmentalists. His two books *Negro Intelligence and Selective Migration* (1935) and *Race Differences* (1935) demonstrated that the IQs of individuals within different races varied according to education, region, and socioeconomic background.[96] He found, for instance, that northern blacks had higher IQs than southern whites, which cast profound doubt on the notion that the tests measured hereditary differences.

Nevertheless, throughout the 1930s the environmentalist shift was far from complete, and no antiracist consensus emerged. This was especially the case outside the United States, where cultural anthropology was less influential. Part of the problem was the subdisciplinary division of labor that vested physical anthropologists with authority to speak about matters of race, while cultural anthropologists spoke authoritatively on culture.[97] Most contemporaries did not realize that race is a social construct with no biological basis. The hereditarian biases within biology and physical anthropology therefore continued to underwrite the dominant ideas about racial differences.

This was the scientific context in which Hogben engineered his environmentalist assault on eugenics. Believing that the "rationalisation of race prejudice by appeal to biological principles was then plausible only because human genetics was so immature," Hogben undertook several studies to demonstrate the power of the environment in shaping human beings.[98] Laying the groundwork for Davis's later work, one such study focused on IQ scores. Hogben argued that differences in IQ were much more dependent on the environment than was conventionally assumed, finding the genetic component to be only about 50 percent instead of 80 to 95 percent.[99]

Hogben also argued that biologists continued to overemphasize heredity because they failed to understand how Mendelian genetics had revised Darwin's conception of heredity. Revealing Hogben's influence, Davis later explained: "Darwin and his followers believed that traits were blended, and that they involved 'every structure of the organism in every possible direction.' Mendel discovered that traits are segregated and not blended, and that, as a result, certain combinations of hereditary factors will not appear in all offspring, and some will not appear in any." Consequently, "in view of the intricate operation of such disparate factors in inheritance," he wrote, "we need a much more detailed knowledge of genetic mechanisms before we may be justified in relating any specific behavior to inherited characters."[100]

Hogben also stressed that there is greater variability within races than between them, and he made clear that social inequalities are paramount in explaining differences among groups of people.[101] Through a wide range of articles, speeches, and books, most notably *Nature and Nurture* (1935), Hogben helped to cast doubt on racialist eugenics.[102]

Impressed by the man and energized by his research, Davis began working closely with Hogben, and Hogben directed his studies on race-mixing and blood groups. Davis noted, "He has me come to his home every week for private instruction since he gives no courses. He is the leading English geneticist."[103] Hogben, for his part, wrote that he held "a very high opinion of [Davis's] capability, originality and industry."[104] He no doubt perceived Davis to be a worthy ally in the fight against racism.

The result of their collaboration was Davis's first professional social science article, "The Distribution of Blood Groups and Its Bearing on the Concept of Race," published in the *Sociological Review* in 1935.[105] It was an esoteric and highly specialized article, but its main argument was clear: "Within the human species . . . where there has been widespread interbreeding over a tremendous period of time, genetic segregation of physical or mental characters will not operate so as to distinguish large groups of people in any important biological respects."[106] Davis critiqued various taxonomical approaches, many of which he had learned while studying under Hooton. He took apart their problematic conceptions of "race," using modern genetics to expose the extensive variation in isoagglutination levels within the blood types of each race. His work underlined the role of environmental factors such as ocean barriers, "mountain ranges," and "social prohibitions" in explaining the similarities among groups.[107] In short, Davis took advantage of science's inherent openness to new empirical evidence to launch an environmentalist assault on hereditarianism.

By the end of his two years of graduate school in the social sciences, Allison Davis had gained foundational training in anthropology and social biology. His resolve to fortify environmentalist science and to undermine scientific racism united his disparate pursuits from African ethnology to social anthropology to genetic biology. Diverted from his initial goal of studying at length in Berlin and conducting fieldwork in Africa, Davis nevertheless found an opportunity to work at the cutting edge of social anthropology, while also reaching more quickly his long-term goal of studying black America. The opportunity would take him and his wife into the heart of America's racially explosive Deep South.

CHAPTER 4

Into the Southern "Wilds"

You can't really smash the system if you don't understand how it works.[1]

ALLISON DAVIS

In the early 1930s, people from across the globe became riveted on the Deep South. As St. Clair Drake recalled later, the South "was so much in the news because of Scottsboro, Huey Long, sharecropper rebellions, Klan outrages, and the fact that the Communists spoke of it as the locale of a 'Black Nation' that was justified in struggling for 'self-determination.'"[2]

More than any other event, the Scottsboro Boys case of 1931 fused many issues into one sensational story.[3] The case involved the trial of nine black boys, ranging between thirteen and nineteen years old, who were accused of gang-raping two white women on a train in Alabama. The defendants were immediately found guilty based solely upon the women's dubious claims, which they later retracted. There was little exceptional about this turn of events apart from the sheer number of defendants and the fact that they were so young. But all of that changed when the International Labor Defense of the Communist Party USA (CPUSA) rushed to the boys' defense and won an appeal.[4] Suddenly Americans began to fear the potential radicalism of the masses of southern blacks, and they worried over threats to the capitalist system. It became significantly harder to see the race problem as only a southern issue as leftists linked racism with capitalist exploitation, and as mobs "smashed the windows of the U.S. Embassy in Hamburg, Germany, in protest at the treatment of the Scottsboro Boys."[5]

As these issues transfixed Americans, there emerged a renewed interest in studying the South in a serious way. Drake remembered, "There was a general acknowledgement that little was really known in the North about the Deep South and the potential for other Scottsboro cases."[6] As a result, foundations began lavishing support upon researchers who would study the region, hoping partly to counter the leftists' portrayals of American race relations. For instance, anthropologist Hortense Powdermaker and psychologist John Dollard, both of Yale's Institute of Human Relations, won support to study race in the Deep South.[7] Black educator Horace Mann Bond, through the Rosenwald Fund's Explorer program, also secured funding for his study of southern schools.[8]

Lloyd Warner, for his part, was similarly struck by the racial situation in the South, and he recognized an opportunity to further his comparative research agenda. As the Scottsboro Boys case dramatized for him the black–white divide, he hypothesized that the Deep South was organized by a racial caste system as much as by a class system. So he thought that a comparison between Newburyport and a community in the Deep South would be illuminating as well as socially relevant. He therefore reached out to the Rosenwald Fund and the Laura Spelman Rockefeller Memorial for support, and he too secured funding.

The only major decision that remained for Warner was the selection of the right research team. This was no simple task given the dictates of the Jim Crow system. How would a white researcher gain access to the thoughts and behaviors of black residents who were naturally suspicious of whites? How could a black researcher even associate with whites in a professional capacity when the racial code demanded his or her complete subordination? Moreover, how could any researcher gain access to the lives of both men and women and to the activities of residents within different social classes? Convinced that he needed a diverse team, Warner first enlisted Burleigh Gardner and his wife, Mary Gardner, who were white graduate students in anthropology at Harvard. He then appealed to Allison and Elizabeth Davis to join the project.

With some trepidation, the Davises accepted. They understood the risks and humiliations they would face as highly educated black outsiders studying the South. Yet they were excited to participate in a study that was of historic import, both for its subject matter and for the novelty of its theoretical approach. With heavy hearts, they left the safer confines of London and Massachusetts to live in Natchez as participant observers from 1933 to 1935.

The product of their efforts, *Deep South* (1941), was a landmark study. Most broadly, it was an important part of the larger environmentalist revolution in American social thought, in which social explanations of racial differences supplanted hereditarian ones. The book explained in painstaking detail how the social systems of "caste and class" framed the entire community of Natchez, structuring everything from the day-to-day behaviors of residents to the local beliefs and values that predominated. Allison and Elizabeth's experiences as racial minorities helped to make *Deep South* the richest and most compelling study of southern life in interwar America.

Early in 1933, Lloyd Warner ventured into the Deep South to select a suitable community to study. His contacts at the Rockefeller Foundation put him in touch with John McLaughlin and Howard Odum of the University of North Carolina, who plotted out regional maps for him and helped him find sympathetic people in Mississippi.[9] Warner eventually settled on the town of Natchez, along the Mississippi River in the southwestern corner of the state. The researchers were to study both the urban center of Natchez, which was a trading center for the region and had a population of ten thousand—half of whom were black—and the surrounding rural counties, which were dominated by big plantations and were 80 percent black. The Davises and Gardners later dubbed the former "Old City" and the latter "Old County." Warner found that Natchez residents were more willing than most southerners to tolerate a social investigation, which is not saying very much, but he did find an enthusiastic partner in the town's mayor, a graduate of Yale Law School.[10]

After stopping in Nashville, the Davises stealthily made their way into Mississippi in October. Their entrance into town had to be carefully orchestrated because southerners were extremely leery of outsiders who might "agitate" on the race issue. Shortly before, in 1932, white anthropologist Hortense Powdermaker had met with deep hostility from the residents of nearby Indianola when she attempted to gain the community's cooperation for a study. She recalled, "They were suspicious of a Yankee and did not want their 'niggers' studied by anyone. Their questions, the expressions on their faces, and the tone of their voices indicated both fear and hostility."[11] For an educated black couple like the Davises, the greeting would have been much more hostile. The Rockefeller Foundation therefore put Allison in touch with Will Alexander of the Commission on Interracial Cooperation. Alexander had worked with Powdermaker the year before, and he helped the Davises make the final entry into town.[12] The couple managed to slip "inconspicuously" into Natchez and take up residence with a local doctor in the black part of the city.[13]

The Deep South's rigid racial segregation framed every aspect of the Davises' experiences in Natchez. Socially, they had to conform to strictures that demanded their full subordination and deference to white people. This meant that even with the Gardners, their friends and fellow researchers, they could not interact publicly as equals. Mary Gardner and Elizabeth Davis, for example, were unable to meet either professionally or socially. Decades later, the researchers explained: "Their encounters were limited to an occasional chance meeting at the chain grocery store in the center of town. There they exchanged only a polite, restrained greeting."[14] This type of deference to Jim Crow was exceedingly difficult for the proud and accomplished Davises to perform. Indeed, Davis was "very depressed in those days," and he could not force himself to work on an autobiographical novel he had begun while in Britain.[15] For relief from the ritualized subjugation, "from time to time they left Natchez to spend a few days with friends in the more metropolitan climate of Baton Rouge or New Orleans."[16] Horace Mann Bond and his wife were two such friends with whom they could commiserate.[17]

Although the Davises were familiar with racial subjugation, they experienced the Deep South as a foreign world. They called their travels southward an "expedition into the 'wilds' of the Southern United States."[18] It was truly a nightmare for them, for it was not merely inconvenient and uncomfortable; it was extremely dangerous. Allison even stashed a gun in his car for protection.[19] He knew all too well that a transgression of the racial code, or simply being in the wrong place at the wrong time, could mean his or Elizabeth's life. Such was the naked aggression that undergirded Jim Crow and belied white southerners' claims to peace and harmony among the races.

One of Allison's first conversations with a white man in Natchez revealed this dominant trope of racial harmony. As Davis later recorded it in his journal, the man said, "Oh, yeah, you gonna like Natchez. We don't have no trouble here. I tell you, I don't believe there's a town anywhere below the Mason-Dixon line where Negroes have as good a chance as they do right here in Natchez. We ain't never had no lynching nor matters of that kind here, naw man!"[20]

Reality was another matter entirely. Soon after that conversation, Davis learned of a lynching that had occurred only weeks before in a neighboring county. The story line was a familiar one. A black man had been accused of raping a white woman. He narrowly escaped a mob lynching but was nevertheless tried, convicted, and hanged within a few days in a "legal lynching."[21] Predictably, and as with the Scottsboro Boys, this occurred despite a dearth of evidence and considerable doubt even among white residents that there had been a rape. Such was the danger permeating every experience that the Davises had in the South, where word of each lynching resounded loudly and had a chilling effect.

In subjecting himself and his wife to this danger, Allison may have at least taken solace in the fact that he was living out his prescription for real black leadership. He was embodying moral courage and taking concrete action in the South to foment change.[22] Yet on most occasions that was of little comfort.

Jim Crow was also a constant impediment to the research process. To allay local fears, the researchers concealed the true nature and intentions of their study. They told the community that the Gardners were studying the social history of Natchez and that the Davises were examining the town's black church.[23] This was far less threatening than a study purporting to detail the caste and class inequalities structuring the entire community.

Yet they could not conceal the fact that the two men were working together as colleagues. Burleigh Gardner therefore alerted leading residents of that fact, but "it was explained to them, and generally understood by others, that Allison was working for Burleigh: this was the only acceptable relationship between a white man and a Negro." However, that arrangement strained the research process because Gardner's office was also his personal residence. As the researchers later explained,

> [Because] it was also his home, he could not meet with Allison here for the important exchange of ideas and observations. To do so would be to meet as colleagues, and such a relationship between a white and a Negro was prohibited. It was not enough to *say* that Allison was working for Burleigh; each of them was expected to *behave* strictly according to his caste role. They therefore devised a devious way of meeting. One or the other would telephone to make an appointment. Allison would then wait on a specified street corner in town, Burleigh would drive by to pick him up, and they would ride out into the country, to a back road where they could sit and talk together without attracting attention. In spite of this supposed subterfuge, however, Burleigh learned by chance that both the chief of police and the sheriff were informed of each meeting. Still, no disapproval was expressed, and nothing was done to intervene.[24]

The professional relationship between Gardner and Davis was such a violation of social strictures that the sheriff felt compelled to keep tabs on the two men.

This type of scrutiny created profound anxiety for the researchers. They were painfully aware that the sheriff could seize their notes at any time, exposing the true nature of the larger study and destroying the data they were gathering. To mitigate that risk, "they sent copies of all interviews, observations, etc., to Warner at frequent intervals. Allison, too, sent reports to Warner regularly but less often. Frequent mailings by a Negro, especially an educated Negro, would have aroused suspicion in the middle-aged, middle-class white postal

FIGURE 4.1. Allison Davis in Natchez, Mississippi, in 1934. Courtesy of Fisk University, John Hope and Aurelia E. Franklin Library, Special Collections, J. A. Rogers Collection, 2014.

clerk."[25] As Lloyd Warner described it, "the whole Negro-white research" was "delicate and filled with dynamite."[26]

Yet by keeping their heads low, the Davises and Gardners managed to conduct their research without any major incidents. They relied principally upon participant observation to gather their data. They visited courthouses, churches, social gatherings, fraternal lodges, bars, and other establishments to talk with people and observe the proceedings. They also conducted extensive informal interviews with individuals, which yielded over five thousand pages of research notes. In the foreword to *Deep South*, the researchers explained:

> After about six months of residence, they appeared to be accepted as full-fledged members of their caste and class groups, and dropped their initial roles of researchers. Their observations of group behavior were therefore made in the actual societal context, in situations where they participated as members of the community, within the limits of their caste and class roles. The interviews also were obtained in this normal context, and except where matters of fact, such as factory or plantation management were concerned, few questions were asked. Every effort was made to adapt the principles of "free associative" interviewing to imitate social situations, so that the talk of the individual or group would not be guided by the fieldworkers, but would follow the normal course of talk in that part of the society.[27]

The researchers combined their observations and interviews with newspaper records and statistical data. Allison Davis and Burleigh Gardner labored "to see every Negro-white relationship from both sides of the society, so as to avoid a limited 'white view' or a limited 'Negro view.'"[28]

Like every other American town, Natchez was also stratified along class and gender lines, which created further obstacles to ethnographic work. The research team unfortunately recorded little about the gender dynamics shaping their research, even though the involvement of women researchers was clearly essential to extracting information from Natchez women.

Regarding Elizabeth Davis, the authors did acknowledge that "we are indebted to her in countless ways, but especially for her skillful interviewing of the colored women in Old City and its plantation environment. The data concerning the Negro class system and miscegenation, as well as their interpretation, are in large part her contribution."[29] Yet for reasons that remain unclear, Elizabeth was not credited as an author of the book, though Mary Gardner was. Mary's efforts were essential to gaining information about lower-class white women, but whether she had a larger role in the research and writing process remains difficult to ascertain.[30]

The researchers were more forthcoming about class barriers. From early on, residents associated the Davises and the Gardners with the upper classes in their respective racial groups. This had the unfortunate effect of limiting their chief participation to "the upper and upper-middle classes."[31] That made it difficult to secure reliable information from lower-class residents, who viewed them with suspicion and excluded them from social gatherings.

The research team worked to overcome such limitations in a couple of ways. Mary Gardner volunteered in a social-work capacity to administer federal relief to poor whites.[32] This put her in contact with lower-class residents on a regular basis, although not in the same way as with the upper classes.

More importantly, the researchers enlisted St. Clair Drake to pose as a lower-class black man. He and Davis had remained in touch ever since their days at Hampton Institute. Davis had kept him apprised of his work in anthropology, encouraging Drake to enter the field.[33] Then, in 1935, as the Davises and Gardners wrapped up their fieldwork, Allison offered Drake the opportunity to experience ethnographic work for himself. Drake accepted, and he quickly demonstrated an acuity for participant observation, which he later employed in Chicago while researching *Black Metropolis*, one of the most important social-science books of the period. For the Deep South study, Drake managed to succeed in infiltrating "the bars, juke-houses, shouting churches, and general lower-class areas," compiling rich ethnographic data on the black lower class.[34] He spent the next few years discussing the material with Davis and editing the book manuscript. Given his major contributions, it is surprising that he was not credited as an author. Regardless, despite his important research into the black lower class, the overall study retained a middle- and upper-class bias.[35]

Nevertheless, no research situation could be perfect, and in the end this biracial, dual-sex, seemingly multiclass, five-person research team was exceptionally well equipped to analyze the entire community of Natchez. The novelty of their research design warrants special attention. As Faye Harrison and Ira Harrison explain, "Anthropology's racial division of labor has historically assigned most analysts of color to the study of their own or similar cultures, while whites have been expected to cross racial lines to study dominated peoples, who for the most part are peoples of color." The fact that Allison Davis not only participated in but in many ways actually *led*—he was the first author of the book—this biracial study of the entire community of Natchez made him an anomaly. Indeed, he "went against the grain of research convention" more than any other black pioneer within anthropology. Regrettably, the research design for the Deep South project was not reproduced by other anthropologists, and the importance and novelty of this methodology have been eclipsed.[36]

Theoretically, the researchers followed Warner's holistic, integrationist, structural-functionalist approach to studying modern communities. The difference in Natchez, however, was the stark racial system. As Warner received research reports from his students, he and Allison conceptualized the "caste and class" model that the researchers used to organize the mounds of

FIGURE 4.2. J. G. St. Clair Drake, circa 1935. Courtesy of Fisk University, John Hope and Aurelia E. Franklin Library, Special Collections, J. A. Rogers Collection, 2014.

information they were compiling.[37] In 1936 Warner formally introduced this model to the academic world in a four-page article in the *American Journal of Sociology*.[38] He explained that two fundamental systems organized southern society. One was the social-class system that appeared in Newburyport and elsewhere, but the other was a "caste" system that divided whites and blacks into subordinate and "superordinate" groups. In some ways these systems were "antithetical," for the class system was fluid and provided mechanisms for social mobility whereas the caste system was fixed and allowed for no change in status.[39] Warner nevertheless argued that caste and class had accommodated each other in southern society.

A few years later, Davis and Warner elaborated on the nature of American caste in an important anthology titled *Race Relations and the Race Problem* (1939). They drew from scholarship on the East Indian caste system to explode popular notions that caste implies a completely static social system. By their definition, caste societies—whether in the United States, India, or elsewhere—were ones that "practice endogamy, prevent vertical mobility, and unequally distribute the desirable and undesirable social symbols." Under this definition, caste systems could be found all over the world, and they could be fruitfully compared with one another. Davis and Warner never claimed that American and Indian caste were "exactly the same"; rather, they were "the same kind of social phenomena."[40]

In the South, the authors found ample evidence to meet the basic criteria of a caste system. Endogamy, or the practice of marrying only within one's in-group, was a centerpiece of the racial order. The law, not to mention social norms, prevented interracial marriages and thereby eliminated one means of possible black mobility. That mobility was also restricted by the entire Jim Crow system, which kept the races separate and unequal. The biological markers of skin color and hair form determined where a person fit in the segregation regime. All of this combined with political disfranchisement, an elaborate code of social deference, and other legal and institutional inequities to create a whole "self-perpetuating" system of racial stratification, which Davis and Warner labeled "caste."[41] In this way, the two men laid out a capacious caste theory, applied it productively to the American South, and recommended broader comparative work on caste as a social system.

DEEP SOUTH

Although the fieldworkers had completed the research by 1935, the monograph that emerged from the study was not published for another six years. In the intervening period, the researchers had to sift through their voluminous data and draft a manuscript that was comprehensive and integrated—yet not a thousand pages long. They struggled with this. The publisher, the University of Chicago Press, also insisted upon significant revisions in response to in-depth comments from Charles S. Johnson. Making matters trickier, Chicago had to deal with the threat of potentially libelous lawsuits by angry Natchez residents.[42]

The task of revision was made yet more cumbersome by the Davises' financial and academic concerns. This was the heart of the Great Depression, and the young couple was in desperate need of money. To stay afloat they both ended up taking posts in 1935 at Dillard University in New Orleans, where Allison was saddled with a hefty teaching load of five courses each semester.[43] In addition, he took on several other projects that consumed his time. Luckily, the Rosenwald Fund intervened and paid St. Clair Drake to organize the findings and reduce the monograph by one third. Even so, the delay in publishing the book was to shape its reception.[44]

When it was finally released, it became readily apparent that *Deep South* was the preeminent case study of the "caste and class" school and much more. It remains an invaluable primary source regarding life in the Deep South during the 1930s. Yet the novelty and substance of its argumentation also warrant serious attention.

The authors' chief argument was that caste and class were the primary elements of Natchez's social organization but that caste was "the fundamental division." So they began by describing the caste system. Here they partly reiterated arguments from Davis and Warner's article. They made clear that caste was dynamic and variable across social class, age, occupational, sex, skin color, and geographical lines. Their point was that caste theory helped to explain the social *controls* individuals faced, as well as the adjustments that individuals made in response to those controls. While underlining the importance of endogamy to the system in familiar ways, they also exposed innovatively the dynamics of interracial sex within Natchez. That was a taboo subject rarely explored in social science at the time. Furthermore, the authors tackled the general ideology of black inferiority with its component beliefs about black people as "unsocialized" and "childlike." In their view, this ideology grew out of and sustained the caste system. Finally, the authors described rituals of behavior such as deference, spatial separation, extralegal punishment of blacks, and other caste realities in the same structural-functionalist way. They did all of this while juxtaposing their explanations to long quotes from residents, which breathed life into their interpretations.[45]

After establishing caste as central, the authors explained how the class system overlay the caste one. Burleigh Gardner was the principal author of this section of the book, and he followed Warner in describing social classes as essentially "participation groups."[46] The researchers were all deeply interested in social interaction, or who associated with whom, in this racially divided town. They believed that a person's social group, or "clique," was a microcosm of the larger social class system, which they divided into Warner's six parts: upper-upper, lower-upper, upper-middle, lower-middle, upper-lower, and lower-lower.

In the first part of the book, the researchers explicitly distinguished their conception of "social class" from the Marxian, sociological definition of "class" centered on economic groups. To be sure, they found much parity between the two. They acknowledged that economic groups shared similar "incomes, economic possessions, and economic functions," as well as comparable "attitudes and dogmas with regard to property and money." Yet because such groups "seldom participate with one another in group action," they did not adequately account for class disparities. Essentially, the authors combined sociological categories of class, status, and association into one broad definition of class that they believed could be used to more accurately describe people's class positions. The class system they delineated in Natchez was a highly stratified one.[47]

Regarding African Americans, the authors argued that the caste system truncated the black class system. Because caste denied African Americans white-collar work, adequate education, and political office, a full 75 percent of the black caste was confined to the lower class, whereas only about 50 percent of the white caste shared that position. Yet the authors insisted that "to the Negro community the distinctions of social class determine thought and action to a high degree."[48]

Here Allison and Elizabeth's knowledge of the black community became a real asset. They took the lead in explaining the link between skin color (black, brown, olive, yellow, white) and class status, with lighter skin color correlating positively with higher class status. The "blue-vein" group of African Americans—whose skin was light enough that you could make out their blue veins—proved the point. The blue-veins in this area were six mixed-race upper-class families who guarded their relative social privilege by marrying among themselves and keeping apart from other black people.[49]

Echoing Davis's earlier criticisms of the black bourgeoisie, *Deep South* also explained how middle- and upper-class blacks sometimes perpetuated the caste system for their own gain. More affluent blacks, for example, had occasionally cooperated with white leaders to keep lower-class blacks from emigrating North during World War I because it threatened their control over a cheap labor supply.[50] The larger achievement of the authors' analysis here was that it portrayed a complex system of tradeoffs in which social groups interacted across caste and class lines to further their own interests. Contrary to previous studies that examined "race relations" in the South, the authors captured complicated interactions among many different social groups, framing them as outgrowths of the caste and class system.

Deep South issued a remarkably conservative assessment of the black church and black associations. Allison Davis authored this section, which he later expanded into a book-length research memo to Gunnar Myrdal, a Swedish economist appointed by the Carnegie Corporation to head up a monumental study of American race relations. Myrdal incorporated Davis's work into his final product, *An American Dilemma* (1944), arguably the most important social-science book in the United States of its time.[51] It was through this influential study that Davis's ideas were to reach a wide audience.

Yet in many ways Davis's analysis of the black church and black associations was the least compelling part of his research.[52] Essentially, he focused on the "function of Negro churches and associations in maintaining both the caste and class structures in the deep South."[53] Here Davis's structural-functionalist orientation at times appeared more stilted than revelatory. Still, he was unsparing in arguing that associations reflected and reinforced class stratification within the black community. Reminiscent of his attacks on the "black bourgeoisie" in the 1920s, he detailed, for instance, the exploitation by lodge leaders—such as embezzlement of lodge monies—and the popular hostility toward some lodges as a result.[54] In Davis's hands, black associations sometimes appeared as little more than pathetic, exploitative organizations.

His analysis of the black church was more useful, but it did portray the church as a particularly conservative institution. Rather than focusing on how the black masses used the church for their own ends to help them endure oppression, Davis examined how the church's leaders, dogmas, and rituals actually buttressed the caste-and-class systems. Specifically, he explained how the church suppressed race and class conflict by encouraging passive acceptance of one's inferior social station. He also emphasized the status that black ministers derived from their position of power. Just as he did during the New Negro Renaissance, he rebuked them for preaching that "antagonism was futile" and that "a good church member should be an obedient tenant and a faithful worker for his (white) landlord." To be sure, he did acknowledge that the Christian dogma of "the brotherhood of man" helped to nurture "a resentment to [blacks'] lower-caste position." But he nevertheless argued that the Christian ideology tended, above all, to give "supernatural sanction to the humble and deferential role demanded of Negroes by the caste system." When he found that church symbols tended to equate whiteness with holiness and virtue, it only confirmed for him that the black church all too often supported "the superordination of whites to Negroes."[55]

In the end, Davis understood well the importance of the church for the black community, but his leftist perspective and his structural-functionalist orientation led him to issue an excessively critical assessment of the black church in the social life of African Americans. When civil rights activists in the postwar period effectively used the church as a base for a mass movement against Jim Crow, the flaws within this thinking became evident.

Within *Deep South*, though, Davis's analysis of black social institutions is peripheral. The book's primary focus is on detailing the larger caste-and-class system that cemented social inequality. The most important section of the book is part 2, of which Davis was the principal author.[56] This part examines the ways in which caste and class were integrated into Natchez's larger political and economic system. Anthropologist Faye Harrison notes that this section "illuminated the economic underpinnings of Southern race relations in a way no other work published around that time did."[57] Indeed, even though *Deep South* never received as much attention as John Dollard's *Caste and Class in a Southern Town* (1937) or Hortense Powdermaker's *After Freedom* (1939), the authors of *Deep South* were pioneering in arguing that the caste system grew out of and maintained the economic advantages of the white upper class. In this view, caste was a byproduct of the class system, even if it had taken on self-sustaining features.

The authors go to great lengths to establish the economic underpinnings of the caste system. In particular, they argue that caste divisions ensured a steady supply of cheap, docile workers after slavery's demise and obstructed interracial organizing among lower-class workers. In the rural, cotton-oriented society of Old County, the researchers observed how caste combined with tenantry to ensure the power of the upper class. For example, because caste restrictions prevented blacks from defending their interests in the courts or through the political process, planters were free to violate contracts and trap black tenants within a system of debt peonage.[58] Indeed, planters preferred black tenants over white ones precisely because they had more control over them. The cotton economy of the rural South represented caste divisions at their most severe, so the authors spend seven chapters describing that environment.

The second part of the book thus reveals the authors' strong understanding of economic power. Here they emphasize the economic rather than social dimensions of class. In many ways, that interpretation guides the entire book. St. Clair Drake later recalled, "Davis and Gardner had gone originally to study the social-class aspects of the system, but as they began to look at it, they were struck by its economic features." He continued, "Although they might have started without Marxian concepts, they were nonetheless driven to examine the system from what was essentially a Marxian angle." In recounting the ensuing interactions, Drake helped to explain why this was the case.

> Mississippi had a Prohibition Law which was always defended on the grounds that black laborers would not work well if liquor was available, and that they would probably rape white women when drunk. But that wasn't the real story. In the county where we were doing our research, a law officer owned the stills and his black assistant made the liquor. No liquor was sold until Friday night

and then it was sold all over the place. On midnight Saturday, the police started arresting people for disorderly conduct. One dollar per head was budgeted for feeding the prisoners, but they were fed for twenty cents. On Monday mornings, the judge starting giving out sentences—one month in jail or ten dollars fine. All the planters then would come to ransom "their Negroes," because they needed their labor. That money went into the political machine. Thus, there was the profit from selling the liquor, a "rake-off" from feeding the prisoners, plus the money the political machine got from the fines. That was the system.

In the face of such blatant examples of profiteering, in which individuals selectively transgressed racial mores when it was in their interest to do so, Davis and the other fieldworkers saw clearly the economic basis of life in Natchez. Their real accomplishment lies in what Drake refers to as "interfac[ing] the Marxian analysis with Warner's sociology." That is, they make clear how the economic and social aspects of the community related to one another, functioning together as a powerful system that directed the behavior of Natchez residents.[59]

Despite such accomplishments, *Deep South* is at times inconsistent in its presentation. Although its final interpretation is at root economic, the authors downplay that fact, and in the first part they discuss social classes along lines that closely follow Warner's framework in Newburyport. The reasons for the book's inconsistency are threefold. First, the authors, like Warner, did legitimately wish to extend class beyond the economic sphere. The recognized that class divisions had social components that were not always aligned with a person's wealth and economic power.

Second, the book was drafted by different authors with somewhat different interpretations. The evidence suggests that the Davises and Drake, like other black intellectuals of the time, held more Marxian ideas than did mainstream white social scientists such as the Gardners and Warner. The structural racism experienced by the black researchers allowed them to better grasp America's structural inequalities along both race and class lines. Their contributions therefore pushed the book in more Marxian directions. Burleigh Gardner, on the other hand, as his later work in business consulting suggests, was less radical and more inclined to see business as capable of functioning to mitigate social inequality.[60]

Finally, the deeply antiradical environment within the United States played a role. Great Depression or not, most Americans saw communism as dangerous and extreme, so even sympathetic intellectuals distanced themselves from Marxism to avoid being discredited or fired.[61] The importance of this hit home when, in 1935, the Illinois Senate investigated the University of Chicago for any "subversive communistic teachings and ideas" on campus.[62] Such a violation required nothing more than a complaint by one man: Charles R. Walgreen of the Walgreen Drug Store family. He requested the investigation after his niece, a student there before he withdrew her, reported having to read Karl Marx in one of her classes. Although the investigation proved fruitless, the limits on academic freedom were clear to all. The inconsistencies in *Deep South*, therefore, grew partly out of the authors' aims to defend themselves against attacks of communist bias on the one hand and yet to convey their fundamentally economic interpretation of social stratification on the other.

As for Allison Davis, he may be best understood as a pragmatic and free-thinking left-liberal whose ideas were never neatly in line with Marxism or any other philosophy. His worldview was secular and generally leftist, but he frequently revised or expanded upon Marxian ideas. Most notably, he critiqued the narrowly economic interpretation of racism, which held that racism was merely a byproduct of economic inequality that would disappear along with economic disparities. He recognized the social as well as economic dimensions of race, and he knew that race or caste had become a somewhat independent social system. His approach was always pragmatic and realistic, so he avoided making ideological pronouncements. Instead, he aimed to maximize his potential influence by calibrating his language to the audience at hand, which in the American setting meant differentiating himself from Marxists. American antiradicalism and the requirements of "objectivity" in social science always informed Davis's public statements. Perhaps Drake said it best: "Davis, I'm sure, didn't consider himself a Marxist," but he did at times employ "a Marxian approach."[63]

A final contribution of the second part of the book was its portrayal of the ultimate mutability of caste. Throughout this section the authors detail the circumstances in which caste strictures were modified or loosened. For example, they describe the social changes wrought by the Great Depression, urbanization, and the penetration of outside corporations and the federal government into life in Natchez. Just as their depiction of the southern environment is not static, neither is their interpretation of the caste system, which allowed for the loosening of caste strictures through a complex system of tradeoffs.

The authors argue that it was in the economic sphere that caste underwent the most modifications. Whereas "in the familial, class, associational, church, legal, and political structures all colored persons are subordinated to all white persons," the same was not true in the economic sphere, where some blacks were more powerful than some whites. From the authors' vantage point, such realities constituted "only a modification, and by no means an abrogation, of caste as it applies to economic relationships."[64]

Underpinning this structural-functionalist analysis was the notion that significant social change could and would occur if power dynamics changed. After the research for *Deep South* was complete, Drake and Davis actually felt optimistic that "profound change in American race relations was possible."[65] *Deep South* makes the case that people's social positions, as opposed to their psychological states, direct their behaviors and ideologies. People thus behave according to the caste- and class-ways of the system, rather than immutable cultural mores or deep-seated personal prejudices. While most contemporaries emphasized the latter, the researchers for *Deep South* found those approaches flawed. The degree to which Natchez residents modified their behavior in different contexts delegitimized most cultural and psychological interpretations.

The authors therefore explore the social, economic, and political factors that maintained the caste-and-class system, and they make clear that changes to the system will result in changes to people's behavior. "The theory was that once political power was in the hands of Blacks," Drake recalled, "whites would modify their behavior to achieve new economic, political, and social gains."[66] In this way, *Deep South* laid bare the South's social system, but it also showed that significant change was possible—if blacks could be empowered.

DEBATING CASTE AND CLASS

Deep South was published on the eve of the United States' entry into World War II. But even the turmoil of the war did not prevent the book from finding an audience larger than that of most academic books. Davis reported to Edwin Embree that *Deep South* sold "over 1,000 copies in just over four months."[67] People continued to buy several hundred copies each year for the next three decades, totaling almost ten thousand copies by 1965.[68] The book became "basic reading in sociology" as universities such as Harvard, Yale, Chicago, California, Syracuse, Ohio State, Colorado, Iowa, and Atlanta University used it regularly.[69]

The success of *Deep South* did not stop there. In 1965, at the height of the civil rights movement, the University of Chicago Press issued an abridged edition of the book, which continued to sell well through the 1970s. As one journalist remarked, "We must study the racial situation in the South of a generation ago to begin to understand the conflict today."[70]

St. Clair Drake was the boldest in stating the book's importance. He wrote, "I feel that the real significance of Davis' work was its effect on all students of Southern life. Stokely Carmichael, Rap Brown, James Forman, as well as Martin Luther King, were exposed to it in college." He continued, "For the Supreme Court desegregation case in 1954, Kenneth Clark used data from *Deep South* in the social part of the brief. So the study by Davis, which dealt with the problem of rigidity and flexibility in the Southern social order, fed into the process of social change when the Freedom Movement decided to smash the caste system."[71]

By 1972, Davis proudly reported that *Deep South* was "still the most widely used study of Southern life."[72] Although he may have overstated it, the book was quite successful, not least because of its wide adoption in sociology courses.

Yet the book also managed to find an audience outside the academy. Major Christian periodicals were one group that translated *Deep South*'s findings to a popular audience. For instance, the *Christian Century*, the flagship journal of mainline Protestantism which had a circulation of around forty thousand at midcentury, praised the book. It even called for fiction writers to ground their stories in the empirical realities of the South as documented in the study.[73] A reviewer in a similar periodical, the *Protestant*, used the book to dispel eight pervasive stereotypes about African Americans, such as their alleged laziness, dishonesty, and thievishness.[74] The reviewer exposed not only how inaccurate those stereotypes were but also—following Davis—how they originated from powerful whites who used them to shore up their own social power.

Other northern and national periodicals similarly praised the book. The *New York Age* synthesized the book's findings for lay readers, while the *Nation* called it a "penetrating study" that "every student of the South can consult . . . with great profit."[75] Daniel Bell, editor of the *New Leader* and later a renowned sociologist, called it "important for its detailed descriptions of the class systems within the Negro caste, and the class and clique system, over on the white side of the tracks, as well as the barrier between."[76] A reviewer in the national magazine of the Republican Party praised it on several fronts, commending the book for exposing the contradiction between America's democratic values and the existence of a caste system. He or she also made troubling comparisons with racism abroad, writing, "The thoughtful reader . . . cannot fail to compare the facts presented in this book with certain recent trends in thinking concerning the underlying causes of the present world conflict. The strictness of the Southern Colored caste system is strongly suggestive of Nazi racial doctrines."[77]

More surprising were the sympathetic reviews from southern newspapers, notably in the Upper South.[78] These papers often justified their reviews by invoking the book's objectivity. The *Morning Tennessean*, for instance, called it a valuable study of race relations that was conducted "objectively and scientifically" and "without bias."[79] The reviewer's rhetoric in the *Virginia Teachers Bulletin* was even stronger, stating that "the microscopic eyes of Davis and Gardner" told "the story . . . without bias or emotion."[80] This helped these reviewers promote work that southerners might otherwise immediately dismiss as anti-southern.

There was even at least one sympathetic review from a newspaper in the Deep South, the *Clarion-Ledger* of Jackson, Mississippi. Moreau Chambers, an employee of the Mississippi Department of Archives and History, wrote, "This work is valuable in that it supplies an unvarnished picture of the real life in a small Southern city of the white in his relationship to the Negro."[81] In what must have infuriated the few locals who knew the nature of the book, he extolled the book's "accuracy and care" and "soundness."[82] Edwin Embree reported happily to Davis, "The comment in the Jackson paper seems to me so significant that I have sent a note of congratulations to the editor."[83]

Others understood the book differently. One review in the *Wichita Daily Times* praised *Deep South* for its objectivity and its abstention from issuing calls for reform. Misreading the book as merely a "factual and statistical book," this reviewer understood objectivity to mean not explicitly condemning race and class inequality in the South. In this way the reviewer used *Deep South* to condemn other work as less "objective." Playing up a sense of southern regionalism, the reviewer concluded, "When and if the prescription is written, it will not be by anthropologists or by non-Southerners."[84]

Although most southerners surely shared that sentiment, most southern commentators simply ignored the book. The same was true for Gunnar Myrdal's *An American Dilemma* and Rayford Logan's anthology *What the Negro Wants* (1944), both of which called for an immediate end to segregation.

Social scientists offered more substantive reviews of *Deep South*. Many recognized the novelty of the research design, which grounded anthropological methods in the study of a modern rather than primitive community. Participant observation and informal interviewing over a long period of actually living in a Western community added something that sociological research did not.[85]

Many influential figures praised the rich, detailed findings on Natchez social life that such a method yielded. John Dollard proclaimed, "There is no other single book which does such an excellent job of portraying the social and economic systems of a community."[86] W. E. B. Du Bois commended the book's analysis of social cliques and the larger economic system.[87] Margaret Mead noted that this "inside story of an American community" allowed readers to see "life from one highly constricted category, defined by caste, sex and class." Unlike many other reviewers, she argued that the book "falls short of the standards of complete objectivity." However, she found this to be a good thing, because the authors remained responsible and made clear "the extent to which the ideals of social, political and economic democracy to which Americans do lip service is contravened." Giving voice to Davis's own hopes, Mead concluded by suggesting that *Deep South* "should prove an effective background for the kind of thinking which leads to social change."[88]

The book also received several criticisms. Some were minor, such as the authors' occasionally "labor[ing] the obvious," or the book's being somewhat outmoded by the time of publication because caste theory had been written about elsewhere.[89] Others were more substantial, including complaints about the book's faulty organization and lack of integration. Although the authors had worked to streamline the book's organization during the revision process, the difficulties in balancing the perspectives of five researchers, and in navigating the complex caste-and-class theoretical framework, militated against a completely clear presentation. One reviewer commented that some parts of the book were "too technical" and not related to the main theme.[90] Lewis C. Copeland, in the *American Journal of Sociology*, criticized the disjuncture between the first and second parts of the book, suggesting that "two complete books might have been preferable." He also complained that the authors overemphasized caste and class, which he thought were insufficient to explain the complexities of the community.[91]

Another reviewer took the opposite approach, critiquing the book's overly complex portrait of society. He wrote, "There seem to be too many social groups for the size of the entire population. Under such a thorough and minute system of stratification, there is a tendency to make society too complex to be understood by anyone other than a specialist in community organization." This was a problem, in his view, because "the maintenance of these class or caste lines" within the community depended upon residents' consciousness of those social divisions.[92]

Another substantive criticism centered on the book's methodology. As social science began to move away from the era of the community studies and toward the era of statistical sampling, reviewers became critical of the lack of quantification in *Deep South*.[93] One reviewer criticized the researchers' reliance on interviewing, which produced data that were subjective and hard to generalize.[94] Although John Dollard attributed the lack of quantification to the "exploratory design of this kind of research," he wished there had been "more quantitative support to [the authors'] findings."[95]

The harshest review came from Robert Schmid in the *American Sociological Review*. Clearly defensive of sociology's turf, he argued that social-anthropological methods were insufficient for studying a modern community. He assailed the authors for their lack of quantification and the ultimate dubiousness of their findings as a result. Schmid maintained that "the project bit off more than it could chew," concluding mockingly that " 'Old City,' Mississippi, is not just another collection of native huts on the banks of the river; it is a tremendously complex segment of a culture so vast that one wonders at the audacity of the four men and women who seek to comprehend it and indeed to generalize about it after mingling with the inhabitants and taking copious field notes for two years."[96]

Perhaps unexpectedly, black writers had only mixed reviews for the book, especially the caste theory undergirding it.[97] They were sensitive to the implications of representing black people as part of a profoundly subordinate caste. In *Opportunity* magazine, Alain Locke issued a typical critique, arguing that "numerous anomalies and exceptions" essentially invalidated caste theory. Blaming the authors for taking residents' "stock rationalizations" as literal truths about community life, he ultimately criticized *Deep South* for being a static "retrospective" study that failed to account for the significant social changes taking place. He wrote, "Scant attention has been paid . . . to the insecure economic structure of the entire society or to the increasing conflict of economic interests with the traditional stock values both among the whites and Negroes."[98]

Locke shared with other black intellectuals, especially the Chicago School sociologists Charles S. Johnson, E. Franklin Frazier, and Oliver C. Cox, the fear that whites would use caste theory for nefarious ends.[99] Such fears were not groundless. Howard Odum, the leading white southern sociologist, argued that the book "shows conclusively that racial divisions in the southern regions of the United States are culturally organic and are products of long, evolutionary development." Accordingly, he promoted inaction: "It is unreasonable, therefore, to expect that through mere process of legislation or coercion or propaganda a situation so organically and culturally conditioned over so long a period of time can be changed overnight."[100]

To combat such conservatism, Locke and the black sociologists emphasized the racial change that was already taking place and that would likely continue. In the process, they undermined Davis's and Warner's "caste-and-class" school of race relations, which portrayed a hardened system of stratification. As an alternative, they and most of the social science community came to embrace Donald Young's minority theory, which treated African Americans as only one among many racial minority groups in the United States and hence downplayed the special condition of black people because of their history of chattel slavery.[101] As these scholars criticized caste theory, they followed white sociologists' reductive definitions of caste as a permanent, unchanging system, therefore sidestepping the Davises' and Gardners' more sophisticated definition of caste as a complex, evolving system. Ironically, such critiques effectively minimized the significance of a study and a research tradition that had powerfully laid bare the structural racism that black intellectuals were working to subvert.

Allison Davis's conservative assessments of black institutions also had an intellectual impact. Davis briefly summarized this material in *Deep South*, but it was in the book-length research memorandum to Gunnar Myrdal that he developed his interpretations and eventually transmitted them to a larger audience. In particular, Myrdal drew heavily from Davis in his treatment of the black church, arguing in *An American Dilemma* that it was "inefficient and uninfluential" as "an instrument of concerted action." He maintained, furthermore, that the church kept blacks "from going against the caste system" and that it "conformed to the power situation of the time and locality" and "favored a passive acceptance of one's worldly condition." His indictment of the black church's "political fatalism" and "timidity and disinterest" reflected the influence of black radicals such as Davis, Ralph Bunche, and St. Clair Drake, all of whom wanted the church to lead the fight against caste-and-class inequality rather than to passively accommodate it. Myrdal predicted that if the church failed to reform, it would "decline . . . as an active influence in the Negro community."[102]

Though their critiques were valid and influential, Myrdal, Davis, and the others underestimated the church as a source of political leadership and cultural sustenance for the black community. Black clergy later heeded such criticisms and actively reformed their practices to stay relevant to black people's needs. The bold leadership practiced by the next generation of preachers, which Martin Luther King Jr. exemplified, measured the distance that the black clergy had come.

Myrdal's treatment of black associations also drew from Davis and likewise reflected a harsh judgment of their roles within the black community. However, Myrdal went even further than Davis in calling black associations "pathological." He argued that "Negro clubs and lodges" embodied cultural lag, following "a pattern a generation behind the general American pattern." Whereas white America had begun abandoning the lodges and their "secret rites and elaborate ritual" thirty years earlier, the institutions remained popular within black communities. Myrdal viewed black associations as pathological because they "accomplish so little in comparison to what their members set out to achieve by means of them." Myrdal's critiques were not without basis, but once again his almost exclusive emphasis on politics and power hindered him from taking seriously the social and cultural importance of black organizations.[103]

Through the commercial and institutional success of *An American Dilemma*, Davis's ideas on the black church and black associations reached a wide audience. This became problematic, though, because of the rapidly shifting contexts in which those ideas took hold. Davis, along with E. Franklin Frazier and Ralph Bunche, issued those leftist critiques of black institutions during the depths of the Great Depression in the hope of galvanizing a widespread struggle against race and class inequality. Unfortunately, as historian Walter Jackson explained, "Myrdal's version of their critique led not to a process of socialist transformation but rather to a white perception of blacks as a people afflicted with social pathologies calling for the cure of social engineering and adjustment to the norms of white, middle-class society." Myrdal's view of black social life as primarily an outgrowth of oppression rather than a potential wellspring of strength played into that process. On such a rapidly shifting discursive terrain, Davis did adapt, and he began pointing out the virtues within black culture, which most white writers failed to recognize.[104]

Finally, *Deep South*'s portrayal of Natchez's class system evoked strong reactions. Sociologists generally found Warnerian social class to be confusing and problematic because it conflated class (economic) with status (social).[105] A reviewer criticized Davis's work along these same lines, writing that "clique, friendship, kinship and caste relations are in certain respects different from class positions *in so far as* these latter are oriented to a competitive order in the occupational structure. In particular . . . they are oriented to *who you are* rather than to *what you have* or *what you do*, or can do."[106] Others simply found such categories as "upper-upper" and "lower-lower" to be "forced and meaningless," if still correlated with actual divergent experiences within the community.[107] Another reviewer agreed, criticizing the "somewhat sweeping generalizations concerning status, attitudes, and behavior of members of these [social] classes."[108]

Yet other reviewers found much of value in the book's class orientation. Leftists Arthur Brown and Herbert Aptheker recognized the implicit Marxian analysis framing *Deep South*, and they naturally praised the book for it.[109] However, they were both annoyed by the book's inconsistent discussions of social class and by the authors' attempt "to disassociate themselves from Marxism." Brown remarked that "the primary importance of the economic organization is unwittingly revealed."[110]

Meanwhile, the esteemed sociologist Edward A. Ross found the book's class framework to be rich. He ranked *Deep South* among the "best five studies in American society," and he credited the book's anthropological approach with providing the "soundest and most exhaustive analysis of class hierarchy and description of class characteristics I have ever met." Indeed, he confided to Lloyd Warner that "DEEP SOUTH is the first presentation of the class structure of contemporary Americans that I am quite unable to see any fault in."[111]

Margaret Mead was similarly enthused by the book's caste-and-class framework. She called it a "working descriptive formula" that makes it "easier to think." Albeit with exaggeration, she predicted that the class "categories which are used will prove so useful and so stimulating that within a few months the reading world will be tossing about the classifications of 'upper upper,' 'lower middle' or 'upper lower,' applying them to the behavior of their friends, to the latest novel, or the latest political ideology."[112]

None of these commentators, however, represented the majority of American opinion. Liberal and leftist intellectuals who insisted upon the centrality of class divisions within American society became marginalized during and after World War II. The war stoked a powerful and insular form of cultural nationalism. As Americans faced an external military threat, and as they witnessed the fall of democratic governments at the hands of fascistic regimes, many intellectuals closed ranks and sought to locate and nurture a distinctive "American Way of Life" that could defeat the forces of aggression abroad.[113] Emphases on class divisions did not fare well in such an environment.

Mead exemplifies the shift. She had written her laudatory review of *Deep South* and its class framework on the very eve of the Japanese attack on Pearl Harbor. By 1942 she had already backed away from her position. In her study of American national character, *And Keep Your Powder Dry* (1942), she directly challenged Warner and Davis's class conceptualization, arguing that "the American system is really a classification based on a ladder, up which people are expected to move, rather than upon orderly stratification or classification of society, within the pigeon-holes [in] which people are born."[114] Amid global conflagration, Mead applied cultural anthropology's holistic approach to American society, hoping partly to stoke unity and promote the virtues of America's democratic culture. In such an environment, Davis's focus on conflict, division, and social stratification became increasingly anathema.

The Cold War only exacerbated these trends. Although the Soviets had been their wartime allies, Americans soon perceived themselves to be locked in life-and-death struggle with the Soviet Union. That struggle fueled a deep suspicion of the class concept, because it suddenly seemed suspiciously Marxist and hence communist and "un-American." Various anticommunists exploited this context to orchestrate a second Red Scare.[115] Politicians smeared their foes and launched dubious investigations of communist infiltration into the federal government, Hollywood, and elsewhere. All of this heightened Americans' fears that a powerful communist menace was indeed threatening the country. The anticommunism that then swept the nation, assuming its most virulent form during the McCarthy era from 1946 to 1954, had a chilling effect on social discourse. It became unpopular, if not risky, to speak of class stratification at a time when democratic capitalism was supposed to be the righteous alternative to Soviet communism.

Postwar American intellectual life was dominated by notions of mobility and opportunity, not stratification. In a 1946 article Maxwell Brooks exemplified this trend, arguing that class did not exist within the United States because of the remarkable social mobility offered to all Americans. He preferred to refer to a "*status system*, in which individuals of different origins compete for the SAME statuses," instead of a more hardened class system.[116] Brooks therefore mobilized conceptual critiques of Warnerian social class to reject altogether the existence of a class system within the United States. In the context of this type of conservatism, *Deep South* and Warnerian social anthropology became important ongoing testaments to the existence of class stratification, even as such analyses were marginalized.

Above all, *Deep South* should be seen as a deeply environmentalist project. The book emphasized the power of the caste-and-class systems to shape southern society, including the distribution of power, status, and wealth, as well as the character of both individual and collective behaviors, attitudes, ideologies, and symbols. By focusing on the larger social structures that molded the fate of all individuals, the researchers attacked reductive individualistic explanations of social inequalities. For the eugenicist who pointed to biology to explain racial differences, *Deep South* exposed the social origins of those differences. For white southern apologists such as the Southern Agrarians, who extolled the greatness of southern society and its plantation tradition, *Deep South* depicted a savagely cruel, unfair, and even deadly society that arbitrarily ranked individuals and circumscribed their lives. For the liberal who perceived racism to be a problem of individual prejudice, *Deep South* revealed a prejudice that was systematic in nature and rooted within an exploitative economic system. And for the optimist who believed that gradual social change would end racial inequities, *Deep South* portrayed a system defended by powerful vested interests which could be overcome only by concerted action and revolt against the *entire* system. Systematic problems, after all, demanded systematic solutions.

For Allison Davis, *Deep South* represented the culmination of his early career within social science. He had left his life in English for one in social science with two major goals in mind: to better understand structural racism and to contribute to a new science of society. That science was environmentalist, antiracist, and geared toward social engineering. With *Deep South* he left a lasting testament to the social systems that delimited the lives of African Americans, not to mention poor whites. He translated his modernist sensibility into an environmentalist project that restored humanity to an entire group of people. His work in social science, then, like that in literature before it, was part of his concerted aim to fight for equality and fairness across the color line. After 1935 he found new ways to build upon his earlier research and to become a leader within interdisciplinary social science.

CHAPTER 5

Caste, Class, and Personality

It may be we shall eventually have to go the whole way and state that there is a single social science and that what now seem like discrete fields or sciences are really shadings and points of emphasis in a unified field of scientific observation.[1]

JOHN DOLLARD

In the early 1930s Allison Davis was at the cutting edge of social anthropology. He continued to interpret his findings and refine *Deep South* over the next several years. Yet well before the book ever reached print, he was already exploring bold new approaches within social science. With remarkable speed, he learned new interdisciplinary methods, carried out new interdisciplinary research, and published an important book on this material, *Children of Bondage*, in 1940, one year before the University of Chicago Press released *Deep South*.

Such achievements were especially significant for a black anthropologist. Most black scholars were systematically denied opportunities to develop new social theories and methods, and they were typically forced to study only black life or the "race problem" in support of white scholars. Indeed, as St. Clair Drake explained, Davis was "the only one of the first group of Afro-Americans" with training in anthropology who "contributed to the debates about concepts and methods that went on during the thirties."[2] The years from 1935 to 1940 were therefore important ones not only in the evolution of Davis's thought but also in the broader history of social science.

In this period Davis collaborated with social scientist John Dollard, who "interested [him] seriously in the *processes of human socialization.*"[3] The emphasis on socialization was not serendipitous. Rather, it was the central research priority of a small but growing cohort of social scientists involved with the culture-and-personality movement. Culture-and-personality theorists aimed to integrate anthropological, sociological, psychological, and psychiatric theories into a broader framework for understanding human behavior. The focus on socialization, or the process through which individuals learn social norms, logically became the locus for this interdisciplinary investigation.

From early on, Davis recognized the liberal ends to which he could put such theorizing. Above all, it allowed him to humanize the individuals who were being scrutinized. So Davis eagerly shifted his focus from explaining the structure of the caste-and-class systems to investigating the points at which individuals encountered them. The product of his labors, *Children of Bondage*, is an underappreciated landmark within culture-and-personality, and one that shaped Davis's career and reputation, though not always in ways he would have hoped.

DILLARD UNIVERSITY

Having completed his nearly two years of fieldwork in Natchez in early 1935, Davis was eager to write up his findings. But he was even more desperate to earn some income to support himself and his wife. He therefore accepted a professorship in anthropology at the newly established Dillard University in New Orleans, where Elizabeth Davis also took up teaching and research responsibilities. He also headed up the Division of the Social Sciences. The young couple spent the next few years at Dillard, with Allison laboring under a heavy teaching and service load while still pursuing ambitious transnational research projects.

Dillard was the product of collaboration among the Rosenwald Fund, the General Education Board, the American Missionary Association, and the Methodist Episcopal Church to develop another first-rate black university in the Deep South. Edwin Embree of the Rosenwald Fund envisioned Dillard as rivaling the three other major black research institutions—Howard, Atlanta, and Fisk. He spearheaded the development of Dillard, which merged two struggling institutions, New Orleans University and Straight College.[4] Through support from the foundations and from local white philanthropists, Dillard managed to weather the Depression.[5] It was even able to attract impressive faculty such as educationalist Horace Mann Bond and historians Lawrence D. Reddick and Benjamin Quarles.

In the vibrant metropolis of New Orleans, Dillard offered a unique social laboratory. As Davis had discovered during occasional flights from fieldwork in Natchez, New Orleans was a more liberal and permissive place than the surrounding areas.[6] The whole state of Louisiana, in fact, remained in the throes of "Longism" even after charismatic governor and US senator Huey Long was assassinated in September 1935. In the Depression, Long was able to dominate

Louisiana politics and to mobilize populist resentment against income inequality, business, and the banks. His impractical but seductive "Share Our Wealth" campaign, which called for massive wealth redistribution through taxes, continued to capture Americans'—and especially Louisianans'—imaginations in these years.[7]

New Orleans also had a racial demography unlike any other. Its Creole community was of mixed European and African ancestry, but that European background was more frequently Spanish or French (Cajun) than English.[8] This led New Orleans to have one of the only US communities of black Roman Catholics, as well as the only black Catholic university, St. Xavier.[9] So beyond providing a more tolerant atmosphere for conducting social research, the city offered Davis the opportunity to compare different cultures.

During his years at Dillard from 1935 to 1938, Davis tried to do just that. He aimed to advance the field of comparative social anthropology in new directions. This included building the nation's first department of social anthropology, as well as developing a Caribbean studies program.[10]

He drafted a research proposal that laid out his research agenda. Titled "Comparative Study of Negro Societies in New Orleans and the Caribbean Islands," the proposal made clear Davis's ongoing interest in the type of transnational diasporic study of African peoples that he had originally planned to undertake in Africa. Davis proposed to investigate "four Negroid communities," including both a "colored Creole community" and a "Negro community" in New Orleans.[11] He then sought to compare those communities with analogous ones in the Caribbean and the British West Indies.

Such a study had an important goal. Davis believed that knowledge about race "can make little further progress until scientific studies of the range and variation of Negro societies outside of the United States have been completed."[12] Implicit here was the recognition that an accounting of the great diversity among African Diasporic peoples across the world could be used as ammunition to fight racism at home. White Americans frequently relied upon the experiences of African Americans—who all shared the burdens of the particular caste system in the United States—to make bogus generalizations about all African-descended peoples. Even a cursory knowledge of the diversity among black people, Davis thought, would explode such generalizations. His strategy here followed that of cultural anthropologists such as Ruth Benedict and Margaret Mead, who studied the broad variation in "patterns of culture" across the world in order to critique social arrangements at home.[13]

Unfortunately, Davis's project never came to fruition. He lacked the time and funding to support it. That predicament was the norm at the time for black scholars, almost all of whom were forced to work at underfunded and under-staffed black colleges. At Dillard, Davis was required to teach five courses each semester, which severely handicapped his ability to conduct further research and to write up his Natchez material.[14] The foundations, for their part, offered far less research support for black colleges than for white ones, and during the interwar period they were tepid about funding transnational research projects on the race issue.

Davis's comparative race project would have been well ahead of the type of African Diasporic studies that began in the postwar era, when African de-colonization movements reshaped research priorities. Nevertheless, his men-tee St. Clair Drake would eventually make a career out of precisely that type of study.[15] Building upon Davis's original research agenda, Drake became a prolific pioneer in the field.[16]

Although Davis faced many frustrations at Dillard, he was able to use his professorship there to get involved with numerous organizations supporting black people's practical needs. Davis believed that "the ultimate aim of science should be social action," so he enjoyed working for organizations that had tangible effects on the lives of African Americans.[17] One appointment was as "State Director of the Survey of the Training and Employment of White Collar and Skilled Negro Workers in Louisiana," for which the state empowered him to coordinate the study and appoint supervisors in such cities as New Orleans, Shreveport, Monroe, and Baton Rouge.[18] The National Urban League also asked Davis to serve on a committee to determine whether a local chapter was needed in New Orleans.[19] Most important, Davis served on the Committee on Co-ordination and Prevention, which focused on meeting the needs of youth in New Orleans amid the devastating impact of the Depression.[20] He spelled out for the government the crises facing southern youth—especially black youth—in procuring food, shelter, clothing, education, and recreation. That work directly informed his study of black personality.

All these undertakings proved useful for Davis. On the one hand, they further grounded him in the social circumstances of that region of the Deep South. On the other hand, they developed his practical administrative skills and put him in contact with various levels of government. Davis's relation-ship with members of President Roosevelt's "black cabinet," such as his friend Robert C. Weaver, helped him to effectively navigate various government bureaucracies.[21]

Davis's most important project during the Dillard years was his study of "Negro personality," which grew out of pressing national concerns. The New Orleans Committee on Co-ordination and Prevention observed that "throughout the United States at the present time, there has developed a grow-ing recognition that one major result of the depression has been the unsettling and thwarting of the normal opportunities for youth. Educational opportu-nities have been reduced and employment avenues closed. Many millions of youth have graduated from school with no opportunity and very little hope of any."[22] In response, the Roosevelt administration formed the National Youth Administration, which in turn established the American Youth Commission (AYC) in 1935 to investigate the nature and extent of the crises facing the na-tion's youth.[23]

The crisis among African American youth garnered special attention in the 1930s. At least since the trial of the Scottsboro Boys in 1931, Americans had feared the potential for radicalism among African Americans enduring economic, political, and social oppression. Such fears of the "Negro prob-lem" only deepened as the Depression lingered on, and as black people began organizing to confront fascism at home. As Robert L. Sutherland, the orga-nizer of the AYC studies, explained, "At a time when the world conditions are challenging the stability of our nation's democratic institutions, the peaceful solution of our own minority problem takes on a special urgency." He further noted, "Negro youth are becoming increasingly conscious of political discrim-inations which deny or make meaningless their participation in government, and are becoming increasingly impatient with the vocational and social bar-riers that limit their individual advance and place a stamp of inferiority upon their group." In response, foundations began sponsoring studies of African Americans, and the federal government began appointing more African Ameri-cans to government positions. These were timid yet important steps toward improving the condition of the black masses.[24]

At the AYC, Sutherland and Edwin Embree worked to ensure that Davis was appointed the director of the Southern Urban Division. Davis and Suther-land then formally proposed a project to the General Education Board that would address the question "What effects does their minority racial status have upon the personality development of Negro youth?" The study would analyze the social environment in diverse locales to address that question. It would use case studies compiled through in-depth interviewing, attitude tests, and personality inventories. Davis and Sutherland argued that the findings would be "invaluable to institutions responsible for [a black youth's] education, to private and public agencies concerned with his economic welfare, to religious and humanitarian groups that have regard for his social status, and to the larger public."[25] They therefore recommended wide distribution of the find-ings through monographs, brochures, poster presentations, conferences, and journal publications. Convinced, the General Education Board approved the research plan and awarded the researchers the staggering sum of $110,000.[26]

The AYC project ultimately took the form of four primary research studies. E. Franklin Frazier studied black youths in two urban areas of the Upper South: Washington, DC, and Louisville, Kentucky. Charles S. Johnson focused on eight rural counties across the South, including ones in Alabama, Mississippi, Georgia, North Carolina, and Tennessee. Lloyd Warner looked at the urban North, specifically Chicago. And Davis and John Dollard studied black youths in the urban Deep South, including Natchez and New Orleans. Each project drew support from other researchers, including such notable scholars as Kenneth Clark, Horace Cayton, St. Clair Drake, Harry Stack Sullivan, and Hortense Powdermaker. The monographs that emerged from these studies—*Negro Youth at the Crossways*, *Growing Up in the Black Belt*, *Color and Human Nature*, and *Children of Bondage*, respectively—were all important contributions to the nation's understanding of the plight of black youths. However, only *Children of Bondage* was theoretically pioneering, with its unique culture-and-personality orientation.[27]

Davis and Dollard's theoretical innovation grew out of sustained collaboration between the two differently trained men. Davis's social-anthropological caste-and-class approach offered Dollard a sophisticated way to understand black youths' social environment. Dollard's expertise in social psychology and psychoanalytic theory allowed Davis to understand how individuals learn to behave and think under such larger social systems. As with any collaboration, its success depended upon the two parties' eagerness to learn from one another. Luckily, Davis and Dollard could scarcely have been more enthused in that regard.

The final product of their labors made explanations for human behavior rooted solely within a single discipline suddenly seem strikingly incomplete. Yet the nature of their achievement lay partly in the distinct brand of culture-and-personality theory that Dollard had worked out.

SAPIR, DOLLARD, AND CULTURE-AND-PERSONALITY

John Dollard was an energetic and iconoclastic thinker who, like Lloyd Warner, had pioneered his own variety of social theory. Born in Menasha, Wisconsin, in 1900, Dollard studied English and commerce at the University of Wisconsin, earning his BA in 1922.[28] Shortly thereafter, he enrolled in the University of Chicago's renowned Department of Sociology, taking his PhD in 1931 under the supervision of William Fielding Ogburn. But Dollard had a penchant for disciplinary eclecticism, so when anthropologist Edward Sapir offered him an assistant professorship in social psychology at Yale, Dollard jumped at the opportunity.[29] At Yale he served as a research associate in the university's exciting new Institute of Human Relations (IHR). The IHR had been founded only recently, in 1929, but it quickly became a major center for advanced interdisciplinary social science.

Much of the IHR's early innovation can be credited to Sapir. Anthropologist Regna Darnell argues convincingly that Sapir was the single most important theorist and early advocate for culture-and-personality research, which combined analyses of culture and society (from anthropology and sociology) with analyses of the individual (from psychology and psychiatry). In 1909, Sapir had earned his PhD from Columbia under the supervision of the world's leading cultural anthropologist, Franz Boas, who served as an early guide into the field.[30]

Boas's interests in psychological anthropology especially appealed to Sapir. In *The Mind of Primitive Man* (1911), Boas had already emphasized the importance of early childhood socialization, and he speculated about the unconscious processes at work in acquiring culture and language.[31] However, he questioned the cross-cultural validity of psychoanalysis, and he believed that much more historical-diffusionist work—which reconstructed the development of cultures over time and space—needed to precede studies of cultural acquisition. Boas therefore left the field of psychological anthropology wide open for Sapir and his other students.

During the 1930s, after establishing himself as North America's leading linguist, Sapir focused on cultivating the culture-and-personality movement. By that time, Columbia had become the leading center for such research, with Ruth Benedict, Margaret Mead, and Ralph Linton leading the way. Yale's contributions to the field have been overshadowed by Columbia's, though Sapir had shaped the orientation of both Mead and Benedict before a personal falling out with them in the 1920s.[32] The field's first major theorist, Sapir published two important articles that laid out the agenda of the burgeoning science.[33] He called for social scientists to "bring every cultural pattern back to the living context from which it has been abstracted in the first place and, in parallel fashion, to bring every fact of personality formation back to its social matrix."[34]

In this period, cultural anthropology reached its apex in one phase of culture theory. Anthropologists conceptualized each culture as inherently unique (owing to its singular path of historical development), as fully integrated into a coherent whole, and as remarkably powerful in determining the behaviors and values of individuals within that culture. The terminology for these ideas was cultural particularism, holism, and determinism, respectively. Benedict's influential *Patterns of Culture* (1934) marked the culmination of this approach.

As culture theory evolved, however, anthropologists caught up with Sapir in seeing how the holistic portrait of culture failed to explain how cultures change and are transmitted to individuals. Sapir led the way in criticizing anthropology for erecting a mechanical model of culture in which individuality was nonexistent and individuals were used merely to "prove" the existence of the generalized culture.[35]

At the same time, Sapir criticized psychiatry and psychology for seeing individual development as the unfolding of a universal biological process in which culture played no role. Along with the "neo-Freudians," Sapir pointed to the power of culture to direct people's psychological development. His mastery of language dynamics enabled him to see how concepts such as "the individual" and "culture" were merely "cultural construct[s]" that people used to make sense of the world. For Sapir, no such distinctions were plausible within human life, because all people are deeply enmeshed with one another. So Sapir set out to study that enmeshment. "The true locus of culture," he argued, "is in the interactions of specific individuals." Accordingly, social scientists in their respective disciplines needed to study the dynamic interrelation between the individual and the culture.[36]

In order to investigate the links between self and society, Sapir prescribed a focus on child development and the processes of socialization. He refused to see culture as "a neatly packed-up assemblage of forms of behavior handed over piece-meal . . . to the passively inquiring child." Rather, he believed that social scientists needed to approach the acquisition of culture, or acculturation, as a problem to be investigated. How exactly does an individual learn a particular way of life? How is a person added to the group? Sapir contended, "As soon as we set ourselves at the vantage point of the culture-acquiring child . . . everything changes," because individual personalities "are destined from the very beginning to interpret, evaluate and modify every culture pattern, sub-pattern, or assemblage of patterns that it [*sic*] will ever be influenced by." Sapir always saw the individual as an active agent in making culture rather than as a passive recipient of it. Consequently, he recommended scrutinizing the child "from birth until, say, the age of ten" to see how "cultural patterns . . . appear in his psychic world." The emphasis on learning, socialization, and children would all become givens within the culture-and-personality school.[37]

One culture-and-personality approach that Sapir promoted, and which his mentee John Dollard adopted, was the life-history method. Dollard's *Criteria for a Life History* (1935) revealed Sapir's influence throughout, particularly in its passionate call for culture-and-personality studies via intensive analysis of individuals over time. Dollard defined the life history as "a deliberate attempt to define the growth of a person in a cultural milieu." Like Sapir, he argued that a close understanding of individuals could help explain how cultures were transmitted to people—"the group *plus* a person"—and, in turn, how those cultures reproduced themselves and changed over time.[38]

Dollard likewise believed that focusing on individuals would provide new answers to old questions. On the one hand, he saw clearly the limits of generalized explanations of human behavior provided by sociologists and anthropologists. For example, although the Chicago School of Sociology was adept at explaining the social origins of criminality, it failed to make clear why individuals within those groups could have very different experiences. Why did one gang member rise in rank while another did not? On the other hand, Dollard argued that psychologists and psychoanalysts missed how culture "forms a continuous and connected wrap for the organic life," making the individual "a microcosm of the group features of his culture." In calling for a synthesis between anthropology and psychology through analysis of individuals over time and in relation to culture, Dollard was operating very much in the realm of Sapirian culture-and-personality thought.[39]

Yet Dollard's brand of culture-and-personality also departed significantly from Sapir's. This came mainly through his emphasis on psychoanalytic and social-psychological theory. In 1931 Dollard studied psychoanalysis in Germany under Hanns Sachs, whom Dollard later referred to as his "portal to . . . Freud."[40] According to Regna Darnell, Dollard returned "committed to fairly orthodox Freudianism," which quickly produced tension with Sapir, whose aims were more anthropological than psychiatric.[41] Led by director Mark A. May, Yale's IHR moved culture-and-personality studies in increasingly psychological directions. In 1935 psychologist Clark Hull introduced behavioristic psychology as a potential integrating device that could "reconcile learning theory with Freudian psychology." Dollard, Hull, and the psychoanalyst Earl Zinn began to test whether the "basic generalizations in psychoanalysis could be deduced logically from principles of behavior and learning theory."[42] All of this would come to shape Allison Davis's thinking.

In 1935 Dollard, Hull, and Zinn held a seminar that examined aggression as a response to frustration, which they eventually published as *Frustration and Aggression* in 1939. In this book, the authors acknowledged Freud as their most important intellectual influence. They followed his insight that "the tendency to seek pleasure and avoid pain" was "the basic mechanism of all mental functioning" and that "frustration occurred whenever pleasure-seeking or pain-avoiding behavior was blocked," thus producing aggression as "the 'primordial reaction' to this state of affairs." In a chapter titled "Socialization in America," the authors again followed Freud in emphasizing the centrality of early childhood socialization and the attendant frustrations that accompany social learning. Anticipating material in *Children of Bondage*, the book examined feeding, cleanliness training, and early sex training as inherently frustrating experiences that shape personality.[43]

Dollard and the other IHR theorists were nevertheless "neo-Freudian" in that they modified Freud's ideas in several ways.[44] First, Dollard and the others did not focus exclusively on early childhood socialization as Freud did, for they understood socialization as an ongoing process throughout life. Second, although they emphasized the repression and frustration involved with socialization, they acknowledged that there are also rewards and satisfactions in it. Finally, they understood that socialization is not a universal biological process but varies significantly across cultural lines.[45]

Dollard and Neal E. Miller laid out the IHR's social-psychological approach in *Social Learning and Imitation* (1941). Here the two theorists took Clark Hull's principles of learning, which he originally developed through animal experiments, and applied them to human beings' social learning.[46] In his life-history study of personality in Indianola, Mississippi, *Caste and Class in a Southern Town* (1937), Dollard had already made the empirical case that individuals had to be understood in relation to the social structures framing their lives.[47] Dollard and Miller now explained how behavioristic theories of learning, including concepts such as drives, cues, responses, and rewards, could be fruitfully integrated into sociological and anthropological theory. Specifically, to learn a behavior, a person must "want something, notice something, do something, and get something."[48] But the nature of what a person wants, sees, does, and receives, they claimed, is entirely dependent upon that person's cultural lens and social position. Allison Davis's caste-and-class model went a long way toward providing that social information for one region of the United States.

Edward Sapir found such behavioristic learning theory to be simplistic and problematic, but Dollard had managed to integrate psychology, psychoanalysis, sociology, and anthropology into a compelling practical framework for conducting culture-and-personality research.[49] Indeed, one scholar noted that "few social scientists worked as hard to bind theoretical, empirical, and social interests as Yale's John Dollard."[50] At a time when most culture-and-personality theorists were emphasizing the links between holistic, value-based cultures and individual personality, Dollard worked with Davis to insert social-anthropological analyses of stratification into the mix. The result of their efforts, *Children of Bondage*, was a sophisticated analysis that incorporated a valuable material component into culture-and-personality discourse. For a group of theorists who sometimes lapsed into hopeless abstraction, that was no small accomplishment.

CHILDREN OF BONDAGE

As two bright young social scientists interested in studying the South, Allison Davis and John Dollard seemed fated to meet. Lloyd Warner made it happen. He learned of Dollard's proposed community study of Indianola sometime around 1934, so he advised Dollard to meet up with his students. When Dollard "went to Natchez to visit Burleigh and Jackie Gardner and Allison Davis," he "first got the idea of caste and class."[51] He immediately recognized the value of those concepts and incorporated them into his study.

Like the men themselves, Davis's and Dollard's community studies were different yet complementary. This was not lost on them. Dollard admitted that his study was weaker in its explication of caste and class, but he believed that it was superior to *Deep South* in its "strong basis in Freudian analysis." He argued, "Without the Freudian analysis, the study was structured without content. To get a complete sense of the southerner, I had to show him loving and hating, laughing and breathing. In this way, Freud is unparalleled in describing human life." In many ways Davis came to agree, finding Dollard's psychological approach compelling. So a few years after they met in Mississippi, Davis asked Dollard to work with him on the AYC project on black youth, initiating a fruitful collaboration.[52]

Between 1937 and 1938, Davis and Dollard carried out their research using the caste-and-caste model as the structural framework of their life-history study. In all, they gathered thirty-five life histories of adolescents in either Natchez or New Orleans, situated throughout the caste and class hierarchies. Davis oversaw the research and appointed various educators and social researchers to conduct in-depth weekly interviews of the adolescents over the course of four to seven months, along with briefer interviews of the adolescents' parents, teachers, and friends.[53]

The staff administered an array of standardized tests, measuring students' personal attitudes, values, occupational aspirations, views of color differences among people, and intelligence.[54] Elizabeth Davis once again served as a valuable member of the research team. She helped her husband and Dollard train the others, many of whom struggled to overcome the social "gulf between the interviewer and the person being interviewed," particularly "when that person [was] a lower class [or caste] person."[55]

FIGURE 5.1. Allison and Elizabeth Davis in New Haven, Connecticut, in 1939. Courtesy of the Davis Family.

During the summer of 1938 and especially during the first half of 1939, Allison Davis and Dollard collaborated intensively while analyzing the data and writing. At the beginning of 1939, Davis was appointed as a guest research associate at Yale's IHR, so he and his wife spent the next several months in New Haven with Dollard and other IHR scholars.[56] While Davis offered Dollard "actual practice in perceiving American social class relationships," Dollard, Davis said, gave "his time and energy to instruct me in those elementary principles of Freudian and of stimulus-response psychology which I was able to absorb."[57]

By July 1939 the two men had completed a manuscript, which they tentatively titled "Not Black in Their Hearts." Apparently the publishers insisted upon "Children of Bondage" as the title of the book. Davis was not pleased with the stigmatizing imagery, complaining to Edwin Embree that it was a title "which I did *not* choose!"[58]

The book was organized to appeal to a large audience, evident in how it centered on eight compelling case studies. Davis and Dollard sought to reach "teachers, social workers, and guidance people" as well as "the great body of general white readers." With the Great Depression still wreaking havoc on African Americans, the authors' larger aim was to mobilize public support to help desperate black youths across the country. Therefore, much like elements of Davis's earlier work, the book provided "a vivid and intimate presentation of the humanity of Negro Children." Despite resistance from AYC officers, Davis eventually convinced them to publish the book in a format that foregrounded the black youths' lives and personalities.[59]

Children of Bondage deserves serious attention for both its theoretical innovation and its humanistic qualities. Like *Deep South*, *Children of Bondage* would become a landmark study, one of the two most important ones carried out by Davis. Davis and Dollard divided the book into two main parts. One part, placed mainly at the end of the book, explains the theoretical approach. The other part, constituting the bulk of the book, provides detailed case studies of eight black youths, representing each of the different social classes. The authors hoped that readers would use each case study to "vicariously experience life in each of the class positions" and to understand and sympathize with black youths from different social strata.[60]

The book's central argument is straightforward: caste and class intersect to fundamentally shape the lives and personalities of black adolescents in the Deep South, but class is the more influential—a conclusion the other AYC studies did not come to.[61] The authors portray caste as an additional deprivation for black people, but they insist that its central importance lies in simply exacerbating class inequalities. They attribute the disproportionate power of class over caste to the fact that "social class governs a much wider area of the child's training than do the Negro-white controls." In other words, because caste so separated the races, a person's racial status was not paramount in his or her daily socialization, apart from the broad outlines of social, economic, and political deprivation that it guaranteed. By Davis and Dollard's accounting, not only were the vast majority of blacks lower class, but in proportional terms there were three times as many blacks as whites in the lower class.[62]

The life-history method undergirded Davis and Dollard's interpretations. The authors examine caste and class not as holistic structures abstractly shaping individuals but as concrete realities to which individuals actively adapt over the course of their lives. They ask, What forms do caste-and-class structures take in the lives of the maturing child? How do caste and class present tangible social controls on an individual's life experiences? They draw from behaviorist psychology to explain the socialization process. In particular, they argue that individuals experience the social structure as a series of rewards and punishments beginning at birth.

Davis and Dollard maintained that "the goals and sanctions of both the family and the intimate social clique are determined principally by the class-ways, that is, by the criteria of status in *their part of the society*." They consistently used concepts such as "class-ways," class "mores," class "modes of living," and, evoking William Graham Sumner, class "folkways." In effect, they were contending that social class functioned as a type of culture, such that fundamental differences in social experiences, behaviors, and attitudes existed between the middle and lower classes. Stated succinctly, the classes socialized children differently.[63]

The book especially emphasizes the differences between the lower and middle classes. While finding the cultures of the upper and middle classes to be quite similar, Davis and Dollard observe that the "social experiences and available goal responses of lower-class and lower-middle-class people are separated by a virtual chasm."[64] The middle classes enjoyed higher levels of education, greater social status, and far better jobs that paid more and were relatively secure. The lower classes, on the other hand, were poorly educated, economically insecure, and forced to live in environments defined by violence and aggression.

The cultural patterns of the classes were similarly distinct. The middle classes labored to delay gratification, to work hard and save, and to invest in long-term goals for educational and career success. This type of ethic was geared toward preserving class privilege. The lower classes faced different social and economic realities, so they necessarily focused more on immediate gratification and meeting short-term goals, while condoning more aggressive and sexualized behavior. The lower-class ethic was calibrated to survival in a harsh and insecure environment.

Davis and Dollard then explain how these different class environments translated into disparate patterns of socialization. Drawing from Freudian theory, the authors perceive early childhood socialization as foundational. They maintain that the ways in which parents deal with their children's early feeding habits, cleanliness training, and sex training all have far-reaching effects on the children's personalities. Essentially, children encounter the restraints on how and when they can eat, defecate, urinate, and explore their bodies as punishments to their organic drives. Depending on the severity of this early training, children can develop lifelong anxieties that will shape their personalities. Interestingly enough, Davis and Dollard found no real caste and class differences among these forms of early childhood socialization, so this theorizing did little to support their thesis that caste and class are fundamental.[65]

Aside from early childhood training, however, Davis and Dollard perceived middle- and lower-class socialization as worlds apart. Through the process of punishing unwanted behaviors and rewarding desired ones, parents, social cliques, teachers, and other socializing agents taught distinct behaviors to children in distinct classes. Middle-class parents allied with teachers to "exert a powerful and continual pressure upon their children to study, to repress aggression at school, to inhibit sexual impulses, to avoid lower-class playmates, to attend Sunday school regularly, and to avoid cabarets, night clubs, pool parlors, and gambling houses. They set before their children the goals of a high school education, a skilled or white-collar occupation, and a 'good' marriage."[66] Through constant supervision, middle-class parents worked to control the environments of their children and to shelter them from adult life. They had the economic and social resources to carry out these efforts.

The lower-class boy, on the other hand, "is a man sociologically at a much earlier age." Because lower-class parents had very different life experiences and conceptions of parenthood, and because economic realities forced them to work more and spend less time with their children, lower-class children tended to grow up in the streets and face very different environments. The lower-class child

> is surrounded by people of quite different habits who make other demands and set other goals before him. His parents are very likely to separate several times during his life. Extramarital partnerships are common for both husband and wife. Fighting with fists and knives occurs within most families and is common in their cliques and their neighborhoods. Gambling and magic are accepted class-ways. . . . The parents have attended only a few grades in school and the educational goal they set for their children is not much higher than their own. . . . Illegitimate birth runs from one-fourth to one-third of all lower-class births; delinquency is far higher than in the lower-middle class and school retardation is almost universal.

As a result, Davis and Dollard argued, lower-class and middle-class children grew up to be very different people.[67]

One of the authors' most remarkable achievements is their nuanced portrayal of how class cultures shape specific individuals. This comes through most clearly in their explanation of the competing patterns of class acculturation that shaped the black youths. For example, they argue that one adolescent, Julia Wilson, experienced middle-class training from her mother but lower-class training from her father.[68] When Julia ultimately adopted more of the lower-class behaviors, the authors interpret it as a way for her to release the frustrations she had developed during early childhood socialization. So rather than striving for upward social mobility by adopting the middle-class ways of her mother and her teachers, which other adolescents they studied did, Wilson made no effort to change her class status. As Davis and Dollard saw it, these were fateful decisions because class acculturation is central to actual social mobility.

The authors' interpretations had radical implications. Davis and Dollard made the case that all people are equally socialized, even though "it is common practice, even of sociologists, to speak of the lower class as 'unsocialized,' from their middle-class point of view." The authors thus exposed the middle-class bias of many commentators that prevented them from seeing the very real, but different, code of behavior governing lower-class life. For instance, the lower class was indeed more tolerant of sexual promiscuity and violence, but it generally condemned prostitutes, drug addicts, criminals, and homosexuals. The lower class did have sets of standards and ethics, permissive as they might have seemed to the middle class.[69]

The same biases also shaped perceptions of intelligence. Davis and Dollard observed that psychologists often failed to recognize the intelligence of lower-class youths if it did not manifest itself on intelligence tests, even if teachers and family members had different assessments of the youths' mental abilities. The groundwork for Davis's later empirical investigations into the cultural biases of intelligence tests was being laid during this research.

Davis and Dollard proceeded one step further by arguing that the behaviors of lower-class people were actually realistic, logical, and adaptive to difficult environments.[70] Without romanticizing members of the lower class, the authors point to their virtues and resiliency. For example, they show how one lower-class child, Mary Hopkins, learned to use violence as a necessary tool of defense in her life. At the same time, they explain why it was a rational, proactive decision for another lower-class child, Edward Dodge, to become a gang leader in order to gain social status and power otherwise unavailable to him.

Furthermore, the authors maintain that the ability to enjoy immediate gratification and to avoid certain anxieties that accompanied middle-class training were potential "gains" for lower-class people.[71]

To be sure, Davis and Dollard were clear that lower-class life was above all hard, unfair, and debilitating. Lower-class people adapted as best they could, but their behaviors were adjustments to oppressive circumstances. The root problem was that lower-class life offered few educational, economic, and social opportunities, and it was therefore "crippled by the scarcity of available rewards" that could modify destructive behavior. "The long-range goals do not seem to be 'there' in [the lower-class person's] world," the authors conclude.[72]

Although it is less central to their argument, Davis and Dollard also explain how black youths learned their place within the caste system, again through a series of rewards and punishments: "Caste controls appear as sanctions defining the conditions under which [a black person] may reach the basic biological and social goals. They are experienced as privileges and punishments which facilitate or block the road to certain basic goals," including the freedom to move about, to acquire and spend money, to have sex, to avoid physical punishment, to access education, and to participate in politics. The lower caste therefore experienced the deprivations of caste as a succession of punishments, which taught black people to learn caste behavior in order to avoid future punishment. The authors portray the black youth as frustrated by caste deprivations, which then translated into resentment and aggression toward whites. However, caste strictures ensured that this aggression was channeled away from violence and into verbal remarks and internal resentment. Above all, the authors explain caste behavior as a rational and adaptive response to an oppressive environment defined by punishments.[73]

Davis and Dollard's approach of seeing caste as a system of controls humanized individuals by explaining behaviors not as reflections of maladaptive, idiosyncratic characteristics but as reasonable responses to discriminatory systems. It explained how behavior stemmed from the power dynamics within immediate social situations, not simply from the stable "values" a person acquired from the larger culture. Yet this portrait of caste was not monolithic but variable. As in *Deep South*, caste controls did not govern economic matters as much as they dictated social and political ones, nor were they as powerful in urban communities as in rural ones.[74]

Davis and Dollard's interpretation was also remarkable for emphasizing individual agency and resistance. They explain that "within the bounds of [the black youth's] caste position he may adopt substitute modes of aggression toward whites," such as "sabotage of his work (slowness, lack of punctuality, clumsiness), and the use of flattery, humor, secretiveness, 'ignorance,' and other behavior for outwitting white people," which are all "learned at an early age."[75] Here Davis's own experiences with racial oppression and his knowledge of African American culture put him a generation ahead of mainstream social science in understanding black life. Only by the 1960s and 1970s, when the new social history took root, did mainstream scholars begin to follow Davis's lead.[76]

The bulk of *Children of Bondage* analyzes the life histories of eight black youths. The authors' use of psychoanalysis is uneven and not especially revealing, but their culture-and-personality orientation is compelling. Davis and Dollard examine the nature and origin of their personalities. They are particularly successfully in humanizing Julia Wilson, an angry and abusive girl. Rather than condemn her, the authors unpack the deep traumas and difficulties at the root of her behavior: she experienced severe illness as a child, intense sibling rivalries, limited affection from her mother, a sweeping flood that destroyed her home, and devastating losses of family and friends to violence. Wilson had learned from early on to expect only pain from the world and to exploit others to secure her basic needs.[77]

Davis and Dollard then deftly tie such traumas—which could easily appear to lay readers as unique to Wilson—to the larger social forces of caste and class, which systematically reproduced similar traumas for youths from the same social station. For instance, lower-class people had inadequate health care and therefore more disease; they had more broken families owing to economic insecurity; they faced municipal neglect because of their lack of political capital; and they encountered a police force indifferent to black-on-black crime under the segregation regime.[78] Wilson's behaviors suddenly appear to be systematically conditioned rather than idiosyncratic.

Yet despite the book's structural emphasis, the authors also convey that the youths' behaviors could change abruptly depending on the immediate social situation. They show, for example, that Wilson's behavior shifted dramatically in response to her audience: a middle-class interviewer, a lower-class interviewer, or a friend on the street. In this way Davis and Dollard make a quieter but innovative social-psychological argument about the ephemerality and adaptability of human behavior. This was a vital revision to cultural interpretations that explained behavior as consistent and as patterned according to deep-seeded cultural mores. It was also a crucial corrective to psychological explanations that posited behavior as principally a reflection of stable personality traits. Stanley Milgram's infamous studies of obedience to authority in the 1960s and 1970s—which revealed that the vast majority of people would torture someone if an authority figure told them to—would underline for a larger audience just how fundamentally the immediate social situation shapes human behavior.[79] A generation earlier, Davis and Dollard were already making that point in a subtler manner. In the end, *Children of Bondage* was a compelling environmentalist and humanist portrait of life in the face of terribly unjust social conditions.

READING AND MISREADING *CHILDREN OF BONDAGE*

By 1948 *Children of Bondage* had sold over thirteen thousand copies.[80] That number only scratched the surface of the book's influence. As part of the AYC project, the American Council on Education did much to promote the resulting case studies (through a series of brochures and other forms of advertising, for example) and to distribute them to universities, teachers, social workers, government agencies, and the general public.[81] In 1942 Robert L. Sutherland, the director of the AYC project, published *Color, Class, and Personality,* "a summary volume coordinating the results and recommendations of the four main area reports." Accordingly, it helped to disseminate Davis and Dollard's ideas. Moreover, even though the chief purpose of the black youth project was "research, not implementation," Sutherland and others spelled out recommendations for practical efforts to implement their ideas.[82]

Davis himself did much to publicize *Children of Bondage* and its interpretations. He gave several presentations at key venues, including the IHR, the Progressive Education Association, the American Sociological Society, and the National Conference on Family Relations.[83] Once he was at the University of Chicago, he presented his research before the Child Development Study group organized by Professor Daniel Prescott there. He recalled that this group was "very receptive to the method and theoretical framework" and that "Professor Prescott feels that the approach should be presented to the people dealing with the practical problems of education."[84] Davis also led special summer courses at Atlanta University in 1940, even briefly heading up its department of education and serving as an editor of *Phylon,* the journal of black history and culture. The courses he offered dealt with the region's "social and economic problems . . . and their implications for teacher education."[85] Finally, from 1940 to 1942 Davis served as a staff member of the Division on Child Development and Teacher Personnel of the American Council on Education. There he shared his ideas with notable educationalists such as Margaret Mead and Kurt Lewin.

In addition, Davis began publishing his ideas in various journals. In 1939 he contributed to a special volume of the *Journal of Negro Education*, which focused on tracking the status of African Americans amid the Great Depression.[86] He presented his findings alongside leading black social scientists such as W. E. B. Du Bois, E. Franklin Frazier, Ralph Bunche, and Charles Johnson. Davis also published his work in the *American Sociological Review* and *Scientific Monthly*.[87] At the same time, the Society for Research in Child Development selected Davis as a contributor to a sourcebook on child development.[88] Davis's essay, "Child Training and Social Class," grew directly out of a chapter in *Children of Bondage*.

In general, *Children of Bondage* itself was well received. Notable figures such as Margaret Mead, Clyde Kluckhohn, and several professors of education at Ivy League schools were "quite enthusiastic."[89] In 1941 the book was "used as a text or required reading at about thirty institutions, including Yale, Harvard, Columbia, Stanford, California, Cornell, Illinois, Chicago, Mt. Holyoke, and a large number of teachers' colleges."[90] Robert Havighurst said it had "sparkle" beyond that of the other AYC monographs and other social science books in general.[91] Edwin Embree gave it a glowing review in the *Survey* and remarked to Davis, "I am the more impressed because in general these psychoanalytic and behaviorist approaches are confused in thought and written in a hopeless jargon," but "you have outlined most difficult vistas in a way that makes them understandable to the layman."[92] Indeed, Embree was convinced that Davis was "likely to become one of the really important social students of the next twenty years, especially in that realm which attacks social problems from the psychological viewpoint."[93]

Reviews in academic journals were more critical, though still generally positive. One criticism centered on Davis and Dollard's social-class schema, which most reviewers agreed had not yet been empirically established and was therefore problematic as a basis for analyzing the lives of black youths.[94] Little could be done to avoid this critique. The empirical bases for Warnerian social class had already been established among these researchers, but they had not yet been published. Davis and Dollard left it up to the forthcoming volumes of *Deep South* and the Yankee City series to legitimate their approach.

Relatedly, critics took issue with the limited methods the authors employed: essentially only interviews and a few personality inventories and intelligence tests. In the *Journal of Negro Education*, the reviewer argued that such a heavy reliance on interviewing allowed the analysts to select the material that suited their interpretation and ignore what did not.[95]

Other critics thought that the authors failed to synthesize eclectic theories into a comprehensive, convincing scientific approach. In the *American Journal of Psychology*, for instance, Wayne Dennis complained that the book employed a sociological framework only "touched . . . up with Freudianism and some terminology from conditioned response theory" that ultimately "failed to improve the product."[96] Davis and Dollard understood that their interdisciplinary efforts were not perfect and would encounter resistance, yet they saw these as vital.[97]

The authors' use of Freudian and behaviorist psychology became a point of contention in itself. Psychoanalysis remained marginal within social science because of its unempirical, even unscientific, nature. Reviews in *Phylon* and the *American Journal of Sociology* questioned the ability of psychoanalysis to elucidate social behavior. The *AJS* review also rightly pointed out the "disjunctive" use of Freudian theory, some of which seemed "almost dragged in by the heels."[98] Furthermore, echoing Edward Sapir's earlier critiques, several reviewers argued that Davis and Dollard's social psychology was overly simplistic. As another critic wrote, "To explain learning in a complex social situation by the simple principles of conditioning, under reward and punishment, appears over simplified."[99] In the *American Sociological Review*, Donald Marsh similarly noted, "Sociologists may take some issue with Davis' and Dollard's fundamental thesis of frustration-aggression as an oversimplification of a more complex social situation."[100]

Equally galling to some observers was the book's emphasis on class over race. One reviewer complained, "The book is somewhat disappointing if one expects it to shed much light on the impact of race upon a minority group."[101] While Davis and Dollard stood by their interpretation, the ideological context of interwar America also played a role. During Davis's fieldwork in Natchez, he had come to see how effectively the white upper classes played up racial differences to divide lower-class workers of all races; he called race "the wedge" in what was effectively "a class alignment."[102] This helps to explain why Davis focused this book and much of the rest of his career on class rather than race stratification.

Finally, some reviewers criticized Davis and Dollard for overemphasizing the role of the social environment. As the reviewer in *Phylon* put it, "The setting is considered so completely, that, at times, the personality itself seems either neglected or of secondary importance."[103] This emphasis was a conscious revision of the racialist and hereditarian dogmas of the day, but many commentators thought the book went too far in the environmental direction.

Reviewers nevertheless had much praise for *Children of Bondage*. What some critics saw as weak points others saw as strengths. For instance, one review in the *American Journal of Sociology* praised the environmentalism of the book, calling it "one of the best things we have in American sociological literature" for showing how one's "position in the social system is a powerful determiner of personality."[104] Indeed, this comment underscored one of the major achievements of Davis and Dollard: the addition of sociological analyses of social stratification into culture-and-personality, which had been far more focused on holistic, unified cultures and the individuals within them. Davis and Dollard inserted a vital material edge into culture-and-personality.

In a 1948 anthology, anthropologist Clyde Kluckhohn and psychologist Henry Murray drew directly from this work to map out one of the four types of culture-and-personality studies. In addition to "constitutional determinants," "role determinants," and "situational determinants," Kluckhohn and Murray conceptualized "group determinants" in the development of personality.[105] Here they referred not merely to national and ethnic cultures as analyzed by cultural anthropologists but also to a person's position within the social structure as articulated by social anthropologists such as Davis. Such a position was outside the mainstream of culture-and-personalities studies, but Davis's theorizing had an impact all the same.[106]

Many reviewers also recognized *Children of Bondage* as an important early contribution to interdisciplinary scholarship. Donald Marsh wrote, "The fundamental importance of the study lies in its attempt to add something to the knowledge of factors involved in the socializing process no matter what racial or nativity group is considered."[107] Wayne Dennis praised the authors' clear explication of the diverse theories, while another reviewer applauded Davis and Dollard's "significant illustration of the contribution which sociology has to make to education."[108] Another scholar noted similarly that the book "indicates that some fruitful cross-fertilization is underway" and that "the products will be increasingly important as time goes on."[109]

Almost universally, reviewers praised the book's readability and its compelling case studies. Leonard Cottrell, in the *American Journal of Sociology*, said it best. Whereas the case studies of other AYC books were "stilted and depersonalized," Davis and Dollard's reflected "flesh-and-blood personalities."[110] The popular press echoed that sentiment. For instance, the *Washington Star* called *Children of Bondage* "an intensely human book" that "achieves color unrivaled by fiction," while the *Washington News* wrote of it, "The authors . . . have combined sociology and psychology to produce in this volume a stirring human document as well as a study of scientific and social importance."[111] Recognizing the significance of this humanizing portrait, Cottrell stated, "One very important result of this method of presentation is that the reader, almost in spite of himself, identifies with the person in their experiences and develops a real appreciation for the way the subjects view their world of caste and class."[112]

Black journals largely echoed the reviews of the white-dominated mainstream journals. Three exceptions are notable. One was an excessively negative review in *Opportunity*. The reviewer there considered the book a total failure, even calling for the omission of all the case studies—two thirds of the book.[113] Surmising that some personal dislike must have informed the review, Davis wrote to Embree: "I don't know whether the reviewer dislikes me or Dollard or the book worst—all three, I imagine!"[114]

Black journals were particularly attuned to certain contributions of the book. Black scholars understood well the politics of racial representation in the United States. The reviewer in the *Journal of Negro History* therefore praised the book for "blast[ing] the absurdity of the 'convenient ideology that all colored people are identical.'" Indeed, a determination to explode stereotypes and to convey the complexity of the black experience had guided Davis's choice to analyze class divisions within the black community. Notably, that same reviewer also praised the authors for their finely etched portrait of black life.[115]

The final exception is even more revealing. W. M. Brewer's review in the *Journal of Negro History* rightly focused on the book's implications for black people and for black social life. However, Brewer, one of Carter Woodson's protégés and a principal of black schools in Washington, DC, said nothing at all about its emphasis on class, focusing instead on the debilitating effects of caste on the personalities of black youth. Brewer wrote about the "cancerous effects of caste" and how "caste barriers preclude . . . normal personality development," producing "dwarfed characters and personalities."[116] Thus he used the book as confirmation that the caste system crippled black people.

That reading of the book would stick, and it would have lasting consequences. The rhetoric of "damage" became prevalent in the postwar era as a means of creating white opposition to racial prejudice and discrimination.[117] Despite its title, *Children of Bondage* did not fit in well with that discourse, but that did not stop later commentators and historians from lumping it in with classic delineations of damage, such as Abram Kardiner and Lionel Ovesey's *The Mark of Oppression* (1951).[118] Later, during the age of identity politics and multiculturalism, when expositions of damage became anathema, other scholars were not inclined to look seriously, or at all, at the damage literature. Consequently, *Children of Bondage* has never garnered the attention it deserves.

Ironically, *Children of Bondage* never belonged within the damage literature. The book emphasized black youths as struggling under the weight of caste-and-class oppression, but not as permanently damaged by it. The heart of Davis and Dollard's analysis highlighted the contingent nature of black social behavior. The authors implied that changing the environment, or the reward-and-punishment regime, would change individual behavior. Later, summing up this underlying philosophy, Davis wrote, "We must always remember that man is a learner. No matter how deprived he may have been, he still possesses the highest of human capacities, the ability to improve himself by learning. Given the opportunity, he will learn his way up and out."[119] The behaviorist learning framework within *Children of Bondage* actually lent itself to a portrait of black youth who were resilient and adaptable to varying conditions.

To be sure, the book's psychoanalytic emphasis on early childhood socialization at times ran counter to this portrait by pointing to the enduring consequences of that socialization.[120] Such a contradiction was inherent in the application of both Freudian and behaviorist theories, which were in many ways incompatible. In any case, the authors in the end applied psychoanalysis unevenly, and sometimes barely at all, as several reviewers acknowledged. The behaviorist orientation was the stronger message of the book, and it pointed to black youths' adaptability and potential for change. *Children of Bondage* was no narration of damage.

Allison Davis's involvement with the AYC project marked a fundamental turning point in his career. By seeking out and collaborating with John Dollard, Davis became part of the culture-and-personality school that scrutinized processes of socialization in order to better understand the relationship between the social structure and the individual. By combining Davis's social anthropology with Dollard's social psychology, the two scholars developed a pioneering brand of culture-and-personality thought, which they articulated most clearly in *Children of Bondage*. Their emphasis on social stratification and conflict was anathema to much of culture-and personality, but it added a vital material dimension to a movement focused more narrowly on cultural cohesion and shared values. In the 1950s, when a group of social scientists did a follow-up study to *Children of Bondage*, published as *The Eighth Generation* (1960), they testified to Davis and Dollard's achievements, calling their work "a classic of modern social science."[121]

And yet the book that emerged from the Davis-and-Dollard collaboration is much more than a pioneering theoretical work. It is a compelling, intimate text that humanized black youths whom most white Americans typically feared or despised. This was even more impressive in the context of the burgeoning damage literature, which too often reduced black people to pathetic objects of pity. In the end, even if the book was frequently misunderstood and underappreciated, it continued to deepen Americans' knowledge of race relations for the next three decades.

CHAPTER 6

Bending the Academic Color Line

In the present proposal we have an unusual chance to make possible a demonstration of friendly and effective cooperation between white professors and a brilliant and able Negro scholar and thus conspicuously to raise the ceiling of Negro opportunity.[1]

EDWIN EMBREE

In the fall of 1939, fresh off his fellowship at Yale's Institute of Human Relations, Allison Davis enrolled in the University of Chicago's doctoral program in anthropology, supported by a Rosenwald Fellowship. For an established scholar like Davis, gaining the PhD was less about learning a field than about ensuring professional legitimacy. That was always a struggle for black scholars in the white-controlled academy. Yet earning the capstone credential proved even more important for Davis because of a quirk at Harvard. At that time the college refused to award a second master's degree to students, meaning that Davis's earlier MA in English disqualified him from earning an MA in anthropology, despite having completed all requirements for the degree.[2] The lack of an advanced degree in his field would have seriously limited his career prospects, regardless of the quality of his work.

On the other side of the color line, things were different. Harvard had had no problem hiring Lloyd Warner as a tenure-track professor despite his lack of any advanced degree whatsoever. The academy was rife with such racist double standards.

Davis also pursued doctoral work for other reasons. He wanted to build further connections with world-renowned scholars at Chicago, which along with Columbia, New York University, and Ohio State was then one of the few northern universities hospitable to black graduate students.[3] Chicago was the most logical choice because his mentor Lloyd Warner had moved there in 1935. On a more practical level, Davis's decision to return to graduate school was also informed by his heavy teaching and service load at Dillard. Taking

FIGURE 6.1. Elizabeth Davis with her two sons, Allison S. Davis, Jr. and Gordon J. Davis, in Chicago in December 1942. Courtesy of the Davis Family.

three classes at Chicago afforded him more time to focus on his publications than did teaching five classes at Dillard.

Since he was already a professor with a mature research agenda and two forthcoming books, Davis's graduate education at Chicago was not especially notable for its intellectual impact. Far more important was how his time there helped to transform him into an ideal candidate to desegregate Chicago's faculty. As his professors recognized his first-rate mind and his pioneering research program, they began looking to recruit him.

This all happened relatively quickly, against the backdrop of a world made new. Just as Davis entered his PhD program, Hitler invaded Poland and inaugurated World War II. And as Davis was completing his degree, the Japanese attacked Pearl Harbor, dragging the United States into a conflict in which fascistic forces stood poised to conquer the world. Davis was too old for the military draft, so he looked elsewhere to make his contribution. In particular, he recognized that the global conflagration opened new possibilities for racial progress at home. Through his own scholarly success, he found himself uniquely positioned to strike a blow against racial segregation and to help win a "double victory" against fascism at home as well as abroad.

The personal stakes of these struggles soon became even greater for Davis. During these years, he and Elizabeth welcomed their two children into the world: Allison Stubbs Davis in 1939, and two years later Gordon Jamison Davis. These were exhilarating times, but the two children added significant financial strain for a young family barely subsisting on fellowships and a paltry salary from Dillard. In 1941 the Davises' future seemed as precarious as ever.

Yet in 1942, Allison Davis, a newly minted PhD, secured a three-year contract as an assistant professor of education at the University of Chicago. He was, by one authoritative account, "the first African American scholar of record to serve with full status in a predominantly-white university in America."[4] This accomplishment was a civil rights landmark in an era when similar ones were still on the horizon—such as desegregation in the defense industries, in professional baseball, in education, in the courts, and in other arenas. For that reason Davis's appointment was immensely important, both for the Davis family and for American history as a whole.

A CHANGING RACIAL CLIMATE

In 1941, when Edwin Embree and Chicago professor of education Ralph Tyler moved to challenge the academic color line and appoint Allison Davis, they saw American society as in flux and newly ripe for racial change. During the 1930s, environmentalist interpretations of racial difference, including Davis's *Deep South* and *Children of Bondage*, had displaced hereditarian ones in social science.[5] In American culture more broadly, the leveling effects of the Great Depression impressed upon many Americans the power of the environment to shape their destinies. The ideological justifications for racial inequality began to slowly break down.

Political movements aided this process, as leftists made racism a public issue as never before. Beginning in the 1920s, but erupting with the Scottsboro

Boys case in 1931 and the Angelo Herndon case in 1932, the Communist Party USA linked racism to capitalist exploitation in a way that indicted America's entire economic and political system.[6] Communists exposed how capitalists exploited racial divisions to divide workers and weaken labor. They also publicized the fact that black people were an oppressed "nation-within-a-nation," as white southerners denied African Americans social justice. In this period, communists united with socialists and liberals in a broad-based "popular front" that fought for workers' rights and economic equality.[7] Alliances across the color line were crucial to empowering all workers, so many began to support interracial unionizing. That such a union—the Southern Tenant Farmers' Union—materialized in 1934 in the heart of the Deep South demonstrated the extent to which economic inequalities could challenge racial divisions.[8] All of these efforts eventually pushed the federal government to pass the National Labor Relations Act (1935), which empowered the drive to unionize workers into interracial industrial unions. The rapid growth of the Congress of Industrial Organizations, a federation of industrial labor unions, further testified to the bold changes.

International events served to further weaken the power of America's color line. The rise of fascism abroad, especially in the form of Nazism, exposed the horrifying consequences of a racialist ideology taken to its logical conclusion. The black press was particularly successful in linking domestic racism and lynch law with the activities of Hitler, Mussolini, and Franco.[9] At the time, Americans sought to differentiate their nation and to locate a native culture that could resist fascism's expansion both at home and overseas.[10] Many began extolling the virtues of America's democratic culture, to which de jure racial subordination became increasingly anathema. In that context, headlines in black newspapers such as "Seven Days in Open Lifeboat Hell, but Seaman Finds U.S. Jim Crow Worse" became newly unsettling.[11]

The 1936 Olympic Games in Berlin provided Americans with a model for the type of racial egalitarianism that their country could embody. Many Americans cheered African American sprinter Jesse Owens against "Aryan" runners. In doing so, they were able to celebrate their own society for being more racially tolerant than Nazi Germany.[12]

As the global crisis escalated, World War II further altered the racial situation at home. Wartime mobilization continued the Great Migration of African Americans from the rural South to urban centers across the country—a process begun during World War I and accelerated during the Great Depression. The Great Migration made "the Negro problem" a consciously national rather than southern issue. It also provided a sufficiently powerful base for blacks to force political and economic concessions from the government, labor unions, and other institutions.[13]

The most significant concession grew out of the March on Washington Movement led by labor activist A. Philip Randolph. As African Americans became increasingly organized, and as the federal government sought to tout its democratic values and downplay the country's subjugation of black people, the movement pressured President Franklin D. Roosevelt into desegregating the defense industries in July 1941.[14] The victory was monumental. It opened up hundreds of thousands of good jobs for African Americans, and it encouraged the growing resolve among blacks to secure racial justice through mass protest and other means.

Meanwhile, the NAACP had won a major victory in its decades-long approach of using the courts to effect social change. In *Gaines v. Missouri* (1938) the Supreme Court broke with decades of inaction and ordered the admission of a black man into the University of Missouri's law school. Other practical realities combined with such progressive changes to make education an especially suitable field for desegregation efforts. Above all, there was a teacher shortage in higher education. Total college enrollment swelled 529 percent from 1900 to 1940, while the population as a whole increased by only 73 percent.[15] The postwar boom and the GI Bill only exacerbated the teacher shortage, creating an urgent need to recruit scholars to fill positions within the rapidly expanding universities.

Auspiciously, African Americans had recently gained graduate educations at unprecedented levels. "By the mid-1940s," according to James Anderson, "there were approximately 3,000 African Americans holding master's degrees and more than 550 with Ph.D.s," many of which were from the most elite American universities.[16] These scholars stood poised to challenge America's academic color line as never before.

SELECTING A TEST CASE

Embree was ever mindful of the larger changes characterizing American education and race relations, which he had played an important role in fostering. After becoming president of the newly reorganized Julius Rosenwald Fund in 1928, Embree focused its monies on improving race relations and providing new opportunities for African Americans. He expanded the fund's program beyond building schoolhouses in the South to include "aid to colleges for teacher training and Negro leadership, fellowships for promising Negroes and whites, research on Negro health and medical services, book subsidies for county and school libraries, appropriations for specific social studies, and contributions to agencies and individuals working in the field of race relations."[17]

The fellowship program for outstanding black individuals was particularly important to Embree. He believed in a "Talented Tenth" model of top-down change in which exceptional leaders could demonstrate the equal capabilities of African Americans and thereby foment far-reaching racial change.[18] The list of recipients of Rosenwald fellowships amounted to a virtual who's who of the black intelligentsia. W. E. B. Du Bois, James Weldon Johnson, Charles S. Johnson, Charles Drew, and Kenneth and Mamie Clark were but a few of the notable recipients. The fellowships were instrumental in allowing talented but poor blacks to reach their goals. Charles Drew's pioneering work on blood plasma, which saved thousands of lives, was but one of the significant consequences of investing in black human capital in this way.[19] Perhaps the most enduring testament to the significance of these fellowships was the sheer number of fellows who played major roles in the NAACP's landmark desegregation case, *Brown v. Board of Education.*[20]

Allison Davis quickly emerged as one of Embree's favorite Rosenwald fellows. After Lloyd Warner introduced the two men and helped Davis win his first Rosenwald Fellowship for study abroad in London, Davis and Embree maintained a close professional relationship.[21] Embree supported Davis's work at Dillard University, and he helped Davis win another Rosenwald Fellowship to subsidize his doctoral work at the University of Chicago. Embree and the fund also approved a grant to St. Clair Drake to help revise the *Deep South* manuscript, as well as to John Aubrey Davis for doctoral work in political science at Columbia.[22] Once Allison Davis arrived at the University of Chicago in 1939, Embree's relationship with him grew even closer as the two men interacted personally in Chicago. Embree observed with interest how well Davis fit in at Chicago.

Davis's primary fields of doctoral study were "ethnology, sociology, and recent anthropological literature," and his primary advisers were Lloyd Warner and Robert Redfield.[23] His dissertation committee also included eminent sociologist Everett C. Hughes and anthropologists Fay-Cooper Cole and Fred Eggan. Davis was at home in a department still pervaded by structural-functionalism, which A. R. Radcliffe-Brown had inspired there as a visiting professor from 1931 to 1937.

Davis refined social anthropology with insights from American cultural anthropology, especially as practiced by Robert Redfield. Redfield examined "primitive" societies, and he followed the Boasians in seeing culture as holistic, ideational, and unifying. Davis's emphasis on class divisions within modern culture was generally anathema to cultural anthropologists like Redfield, but Davis nevertheless won his mentor's admiration.[24] Redfield wrote, "No other Negro student who has ever worked with me has to so great a degree aroused my respect or created confidence in his ability."[25] Davis revealed Redfield's influence when he began more explicitly employing the concept of culture in his work, specifically in relation to "class cultures."[26]

Davis also sharpened his understanding of linguistics, closely studying the works of Edward Sapir. He was especially drawn to Sapir's notion that "primitive" cultures had languages that were just as sophisticated as those within advanced industrialized nations.[27] He built upon such insights to critique intelligence tests in *Social-Class Influences upon Learning*: "Sapir denied explicitly that our so-called 'advanced' European languages really showed any greater complexity, or intellectual ability, than the languages of many primitive peoples. His scientific judgment is a necessary antidote to the almost universal academic views that facility with standard English is a mark of superior intelligence. Many American Indian languages are equally complex!"[28] Davis innovatively extended that idea to the languages of marginalized groups in modern societies, which he saw as equally sophisticated and well suited to their social environments.

In education, Davis was most influenced by Daniel Prescott and Ralph Tyler, the new head of the department, but it was clear from the beginning that Davis had as much to offer them as they did him. Lloyd Warner wrote of Davis's involvement: "I hear very high reports of his contributions. . . . I believe he is doing a great deal of good on synthesizing the Chicago educationalist group to realizing the necessity of understanding the culture in which a school has to operate."[29] Chicago's faculty on the interdisciplinary Committee on Human Development prized Davis's ability to offer an anthropological analysis of the socialization process. Tyler had been looking for a faculty member who could conduct research into the problems of the rural and urban poor from that very perspective.[30] In 1940 Davis was also appointed as a lecturer in the Department of Education, making him one of the first black teachers at Chicago.[31] In that role he demonstrated his ability to be an effective teacher of white and black students alike.[32] Meanwhile, he developed national contacts while serving on the American Council on Education's Commission on Teacher Education.[33] It quickly became clear to many of those involved that Davis would make a great addition to the faculty at Chicago.

This was not lost on Embree, who understood clearly that Davis's success was a powerful illustration of the virtues of the fund's fellowship program. Having found key figures at a major white university who were eager to appoint

Davis, Embree felt confident that Davis's list of accomplishments would make his appointment to Chicago beyond reproach. Indeed, by 1941 that list was quite long. Davis had published two major social-science books and had developed an impeccable record at first-rate white institutions. The fact that he had proved himself to be an affable colleague and inspiring teacher further cemented his position as an ideal candidate for desegregating academia.

The question of how and where exactly the Rosenwald Fund could challenge the academic color line seemed finally to have an answer. Chicago itself was an ideal institution, given that it was prestigious, had close ties to the Rosenwald Fund, and was private and hence less subject to political considerations than public schools. Yet even as Embree, Tyler, and others began consulting about the prospects of appointing Davis, they knew it would be no simple matter. The strong faculty support from some quarters was counteracted by resistance elsewhere, including that of Georgia-born sociologist William Fielding Ogburn.[34] Nevertheless, Tyler and Embree joined together in the recognition of, as Embree put it, "an unusual chance to make possible a demonstration of friendly and effective cooperation between white professors and a brilliant and able Negro scholar and thus conspicuously to raise the ceiling of Negro opportunity."[35]

THE FIGHT FOR THE APPOINTMENT

When the Japanese bombed Pearl Harbor on December 7, 1941, the US racial context changed abruptly. President Roosevelt moved immediately to quell racial conflicts at home in order to shore up the war effort and present an image of the United States as the "arsenal of democracy." Key figures at the Rosenwald Fund and the University of Chicago exploited the moment by trying to appoint Davis as a faculty member. After behind-the-scenes maneuvering by Tyler and Embree, Lessing Rosenwald, a trustee of the Rosenwald Fund and a son of department-store magnate Julius Rosenwald, wrote to University of Chicago president Robert Hutchins regarding "the propriety of a grant by the Fund to the University for Allison Davis." Lessing Rosenwald made clear to Hutchins his desire for the university to appoint Davis. The fact that it was a beneficiary of the fund's philanthropy was not lost on Hutchins, especially given the fund's substantial gift to Chicago for its recent Fiftieth Anniversary Campaign. In addition, Hutchins was a longtime friend of Embree's and a trustee of the foundation. He told Lessing Rosenwald that Davis's appointment was "an object that I admit is a good one." He decided to back the appointment and present it to the university's board of trustees.[36]

Hutchins knew he had to tread carefully. Because of the controversy involved in appointing a black faculty member, he believed that the board of trustees might use wartime financial constraints on the university as an excuse to reject the proposition. He therefore proposed that the fund subsidize the appointment to allow him "to present the matter squarely to the trustees on its merits, without the possibility of any discussion as to financing or other matters which might be used to avoid the issue."[37] With Embree and Lessing Rosenwald promising financial support, Hutchins presented the appointment to the board, and the board approved it without issue—so long as the Rosenwald Fund agreed to underwrite the costs.

Then a controversy embroiled the Rosenwald Fund and nearly torpedoed the appointment. One of the members of the fund's board of trustees, a white southern liberal named Edgar B. Stern, took Embree and the others by surprise when he voiced strong opposition to the subsidy and then proceeded to obstruct the process.[38] Stern was a wealthy businessman and philanthropist in New Orleans who had married one of Julius Rosenwald's daughters. He became active in African American issues in the 1920s. He served on the board of trustees of the Tuskegee Institute and was a member of the Committee on Interracial Cooperation. His most significant philanthropic activities centered on Dillard University, where he served as president of the board of directors. As a white southern liberal, he supported black uplift, but only within the framework of segregation. So even though he gave generously of his time and money to support Dillard University for over thirty years, he was unwilling to support Davis's appointment to Chicago because of the challenge it posed to segregation. The loss of one of Dillard's best scholars may have also weighed on his mind.[39]

Stern's arguments were typical of many Americans' views of desegregation. He made the case that desegregation was "a new and radical departure in racial relations" that had to come about "naturally" rather than through fund intervention. Because he thought that segregation was natural, he portrayed those who were attempting to undermine it as dangerous agitators. He also suggested that Davis was not qualified for the job and that he was being selected only because he was black. He wrote, "The purpose of this move is to have Davis join the Chicago Faculty, not in spite of the fact that he is a Negro but because he is a Negro." Ignoring the realities of racial discrimination which prevented even qualified blacks from gaining access to mainstream institutions, Stern evoked a sense of reverse discrimination in Davis's selection, while dismissing Davis's clear qualifications for the job.[40]

Finally, Stern argued that the practical effects of Davis's appointment would be counterproductive—deleterious to race relations. Instead of demonstrating

African Americans' ability to serve as valuable scholars in white universities, he contended that the fund's subsidy would only demonstrate that Chicago was beholden to foundations. The fallout from the move, he said, would undermine public support for the fund and jeopardize its ability to carry out other programs such as school building in the South. Rationalizing his segregationist stance, he concluded that Davis and other black scholars would do more good for their race by holding positions at black colleges.

Stern's dissent halted any decision making about the subsidy until the next board meeting, scheduled for April 1942.[41] He also succeeded in rallying other opposition, including that of Adele Levy, one of Julius Rosenwald's five children, who was "inclined to agree with Mr. Stern against the appointment of Mr. Davis to the University of Chicago Faculty."[42]

Nevertheless, Stern and Levy remained squarely in the minority, and their opposition only spurred Embree and others to action. Embree immediately began challenging Stern's objection, calling it "grievously wrong."[43] In a letter to Stern, Embree took issue with Stern's central proposition that the appointment would be good only if it occurred naturally from within the university and not with fund support. Embree explained that the idea of the appointment did in fact originate organically within the University of Chicago, where faculty members from the anthropology, sociology, and education departments supported it. He argued that the only obstacle was financial, given the wartime context. This was not entirely correct, but he knew that Stern would read any opposition to the appointment not as racism to be confronted but as proof that intervention was imprudent.

Embree then argued on principle that it is the distinct and important role of foundations to foment positive social change: "The whole purpose of foundations is to bring about higher standards and wiser practices than would occur in the normal course of events. In some cases foundations start movements that might not otherwise get started at all. In all cases they hasten these movements."[44] He thus carried Stern's argument to its logical conclusion. If the fund should not intervene in this case, then it should not intervene in any case, including building schools in the South, because those activities were likewise not occurring "naturally."

In the end, Embree did not have to convince most of the board of trustees, which included such notable racial progressives as Eleanor Roosevelt and Charles Johnson. Most of them enthusiastically supported the appointment without qualms. Even the influential white southern sociologist Howard Odum expressed his approval, and in doing so he revealed as much about the state of race relations in the United States as Stern had in his objection. Like

Stern, Odum was a gradualist on the race question, and he generally supported increased economic and educational opportunities for African Americans only within the framework of segregation.[45] With the onset of World War II, however, he had begun to change his position. He explained his evolving mindset in a letter to Embree:

> More and more it must be clear that this great field of race relations and what we call the problem of the Negro in American life is no longer merely a southern problem. It is a national problem; it is more specifically what we call a regional-national problem, which means that not only the South, but other regions, working through our broader principles and practices of American democracy, must cooperate, not merely in fine statements, but in making practical ways and means available to implement the thing we are talking about. It will mean a great deal to the Negro and to the nation at large to have a major university say to the world that it is putting into practice and into administrative channels procedures whereby this opportunity for participation in American professional life may become real. For the new generation of southerners who are working toward an increasingly larger participation of the Negro in cultural and economic life, such a move would clear up a situation which results in the common assertion: "Why should we expect southern universities to do more when universities in other regions do less?"[46]

Odum saw that the war had made race relations a clearly national issue. He also observed the growing political power of African Americans, who began mounting a "Double V" campaign—victory against fascism at home and abroad. In this context, he recognized the importance of offering black people avenues to participate in mainstream American life, and of therefore slowly allowing for racial integration. Amid a growing and more radical black civil rights movement, the appointment of an esteemed black professor at a white university no longer seemed so challenging. In fact, as Odum saw it, the appointment could serve to defuse black militancy and head off more radical changes.

With men such as Odum now supporting the appointment, the Rosenwald Fund's board of trustees agreed in April 1942 to subsidize two thirds of Davis's salary for his three-year contract as an assistant professor of education at Chicago.[47] Chicago officially appointed Davis that same month—and thus a significant racial barrier in the United States was transgressed.

The fact that Chicago appointed Davis to the Department of Education rather than to the Department of Anthropology, the field of his PhD, warrants further discussion. Scholars have not fully understood this disciplinary shift. Michael Hillis, for example, portrays Davis's move to education as more ambiguous and serendipitous than it was.[48] Bruce Kuklick attributes the change to an entrenched disciplinary racism within social science.[49] Such racism, he argues, barred Davis from joining Chicago's Department of Anthropology, which was a more prestigious discipline and hence less willing to break with social norms. Kuklick thus implies that Davis's disciplinary shift stemmed mainly from his desire to gain employment at Chicago in whatever way possible.

Although Kuklick may be right that there was more entrenched racism within anthropology, both interpretations miss the fact that Davis's turn to education, especially to Chicago's highly interdisciplinary Department of Education, was a logical outgrowth of his intellectual development. Davis's initial graduate studies and fieldwork were in social anthropology, but by 1935 he was already involved in the culture-and-personality school, which combined anthropology, psychology, and psychiatry. His focus on the processes of socialization—or learning—led him logically into the field of education. As he completed graduate work at Chicago, many of his chief affiliations were actually with the Department of Education. He also served as a staff member of the Division of Child Development of the American Council on Education.[50] His appointment as a professor of education at Chicago was therefore logical, predictable, and more than a product of disciplinary racism.[51]

BEING TESTED AT CHICAGO

Securing Davis's appointment was only the beginning of the integration process. The success of this "demonstration" project depended above all on Davis's ability to succeed at Chicago. If he failed, his example could become fodder for segregationists. But success was not easy given the increased pressure, disproportionate expectations, and outright racism he encountered. The latter was best symbolized by the fact that he was barred from the faculty Quadrangle Club—where most of the faculty regularly ate lunch—for his first six years.[52] It took a resignation threat from President Hutchins to finally integrate the club. African Americans were similarly denied access to the university nursery, Laboratory School, and hospitals throughout much of the 1940s.[53]

The Davises were also subject to racism within the larger community. Real estate agents denied them housing in the Kenwood neighborhood where many Chicago professors resided.[54] Not until 1956, eight years after the Supreme Court ruled in *Shelley v. Kraemer* that racially restricted covenants were unconstitutional, did the Davises finally move into Kenwood.[55] Like the other

350,000 African Americans packed into Chicago's black belt, Davis and his family also faced local discrimination and de facto segregation in employment, housing, medical services, financing, entertainment, and education.[56] His sons, owing to their light skin color and racially ambiguous status, faced threats of assault by whites and blacks alike.[57]

At the same time, racism affected Davis's ability to carry out his research projects. For example, white administrators across the Southwest refused to help him in his study of the acculturation of minority peoples in that region. As one of them explained to Davis, "It would be like playing with dynamite if a Negro were to undertake such a study in New Mexico as you suggest," because "minority groups are extremely sensitive."[58] Davis experienced such segregation as a form of ritualized humiliation, and his experiences only fanned the flames of his deep resentment of racial caste. He nevertheless continued to effectively channel his anger into his scholarship, avoiding unproductive conflicts by eating off campus and keeping his hair closely cropped.[59]

On the plus side, the city of Chicago did have its thrills for African Americans. Davis's son Gordon later recalled his father's love of black culture and music, for which Chicago was a mecca. He remembered that "his father once decreed that Louis Armstrong playing 'West End Blues' 'may be the greatest thing American civilization has ever produced.'"[60]

Still, Davis's early years at the University of Chicago were very difficult. The blatant racial exclusion took its toll, although perhaps not as much as the more pervasive, pedestrian racism. He had to deal with university personnel and local residents who thought he did not belong there and who suspected that he was getting special treatment, as Edgar Stern had assumed. Davis confided to Ralph Tyler, "In my kind of a situation, it is not easy to feel even moderately secure, and especially is this tension present when the minority-group member seeks to 'compete.' . . . I am absolutely certain that had it not been for your encouragement, I would have had an unhappy, instead of a very satisfying life here."[61]

Sympathetic colleagues such as Tyler, Redfield, and Warner helped Davis to cope, but he still had to deal with a university that was ambivalent about his presence. Shortly before his appointment he received a letter from the university, generated by Robert Redfield, stating that it "cannot assume responsibility for Mr. Davis's personal happiness and his social treatment. It is quite probable that some members of the Quadrangle Club would object to his being invited to membership, and that other types of embarrassing personal-social incidents will occur. The University can assume only responsibility for his professional treatment."[62]

Racism further affected Davis's career by warping the very standards of success used to measure his achievements. A white scholar at Chicago with Davis's extensive publication record, his successful teaching and service efforts, and his involvement in innovative research projects sponsored by major foundations would have been considered a huge success and would have had no difficulty earning tenure. This was not the case for Davis. He had to fight to get reappointed after the three-year Rosenwald Fund subsidy expired, with the university citing financial duress caused by World War II. Once more Ralph Tyler, Davis himself, and others intervened to push the fund to further support Davis financially, now by playing up his many accomplishments.[63]

MAKING THE APPOINTMENT A SUCCESS

Luckily, playing up Davis's achievements was not difficult, because he had been exceptionally productive in his early years at Chicago. Between 1942 and 1945 he published or had accepted for publication eight scholarly articles; he taught courses that were well attended by students of all racial groups; he collaborated on and led interdisciplinary research projects that won foundation support from the General Education Board and the Rosenwald Fund; and he consulted with local schools and teachers on how to practically implement his ideas regarding socialization and the school.[64] To underline those achievements, Davis sent around a list of his accomplishments to President Hutchins and other members of the university community.[65] It met with success. Chicago agreed to hire him for another three-year appointment so long as the fund contributed one third of the monies for Davis's salary and work.[66] Under this arrangement, he was able to continue his impressive research, teaching, and consulting.

By 1947, when Davis was up for tenure, the national civil rights scene looked very different. A series of lynchings of African Americans in the South in 1946 garnered national attention and sparked organized protest.[67] President Harry Truman responded by forming the President's Commission on Civil Rights, which presented its report, *To Secure These Rights*, in 1947. The report made clear how liberals had, in only a few short years, come to adopt an ambitious civil rights program. The report's recommmendations included antilynching legislation, an end to poll taxes, desegregation of the armed forces, a permanent Fair Employment Practice Act, the abolition of restrictive covenants in housing, the general "elimination of segregation, based on race, color, creed, or national origins, from American life," and many other significant reforms.[68] Recognizing the increasing political clout of African Americans and the prevailing civil rights sentiment among liberals, Truman endorsed the report's recommendations in his successful bid for the presidency in 1948. Congress effectively stymied most civil rights reforms during Truman's next term, but the endorsement nevertheless set an important precedent in national politics.

In this new context, Chicago was more than willing to promote Davis and keep him as a permanent faculty member. Without qualms, he was granted tenure in 1947. Even more remarkably, only one year later Davis was promoted to full professor. All these accomplishments were racial landmarks.

Because Davis became part of a wealthy, esteemed, and well-connected institution, his appointment had far-reaching consequences. He knew well that his position "made it possible for me to do things which I could not have done at a small black college."[69] The larger foundation support, the lighter teaching load, and the greater authority of scholarship produced at Chicago all combined to extend the reach of Davis's progressive ideas on social stratification, socialization, and schools.

Davis's appointment also had other significant effects. His very presence demonstrated to white colleagues, white students, and the nation as a whole that an African American was capable of being a first-rate scholar who could collaborate effectively with whites. For a man who had forged friendships with white southerners at Williams College and elsewhere, it was not necessarily surprising that he was also an effective teacher of white southern students.[70] But the impact of having a major research university endow a black person with such a prominent position was considerable. White students had an example of a brilliant, articulate, caring black teacher to belie the pervasive racism and stereotypical thinking of the day. The facts that white faculty could have a black colleague they liked and respected and that white students could have a black teacher and mentor they admired were both important, if difficult to quantify, forces for progressive social change.[71] When three of Davis's students came to head education departments across the country, they testified to his influence as a teacher and a mentor.[72]

The effect of Davis's appointment on the black community was at least as significant. His prestigious post symbolized the racial change that was occurring across the United States, opening new possibilities for black people. Surprisingly, the black press did not make much of the initial appointment. The *Chicago Defender* and the *Afro-American* buried their brief announcements on their seventh and ninth pages, respectively, and they said nothing of the racial barrier that Davis had broken through.[73] Nevertheless, African Americans across the country heard of Davis's position and saw it as a sign of hope and inspiration. The black press, including the *Chicago Defender*, the *Chicago*

Bee, the *Afro American*, and other organs, ensured that visibility by publicizing Davis's scholarly achievements to the black public.[74]

Black readers wrote to Davis conveying their pride in his accomplishments. For instance, a black teacher in South Carolina named Jesse E. Weston sent him a letter stating, "I learned that you are the only colored Professor at Chicago University which I am very proud of the fact. I am contacting you because I am colored. I have been reading about you in the *Afro American*, and I feel that if you can help me that you will."[75] Weston went on to ask whether Davis would help him get into graduate school at Chicago. Such a request shows that African Americans understood Davis's position as not only a symbolic achievement but also a tangible one that could be leveraged to open doors long closed to their people. In these ways, Davis's appointment reflected the significance of academia as both a physical and an intellectual terrain of the larger black freedom struggle.

THE LIMITS OF RACIAL CHANGE

Despite the practical and symbolic significance of Davis's appointment, his story demonstrates continuity in race relations as much as change. To be sure, his appointment did establish an important precedent that some progressive universities soon followed. Fred G. Wale, director of education at the Rosenwald Fund, sought to build upon the success of Davis's appointment to push more northern universities to hire black academics.[76] From 1945 to 1947 he corresponded with six hundred university presidents, providing them with a list of several hundred exceptionally talented black scholars which included the likes of Robert Weaver, E. Franklin Frazier, Charles Johnson, W. E. B. Du Bois, Horace Cayton, W. Montague Cobb, Ralph Bunche, Abram Harris, Rayford Logan, John Hope Franklin, and many more. Between 1945 and 1946, twenty-three African Americans on the list secured full-time employment at northern white universities, while twenty-seven more gained temporary appointments.[77] Roosevelt University in Chicago led the way, hiring four full-time black scholars, including St. Clair Drake.

Yet the real legacy of Wale's campaign was to highlight the institutional racism that largely defeated efforts to appoint black scholars. Of the six hundred university presidents that Wale contacted, four hundred of them refused to even reply. Of the two hundred who did reply, most professed principles of meritocracy but declined to honor them in practice. Because the academic achievements of the black scholars on Wale's list were beyond dispute, these presidents justified their exclusion based on criteria such as " 'institutional needs,' 'geography,' 'population,' and 'local community attitudes.'"[78] Almost all of them ignored Wale's request to hire black scholars, even though many of them boasted of their institutions' record of hiring black people in non-academic roles, such as library assistants or even janitors. Many university presidents thus legitimated the traditional exclusion of black people from the academy while professing otherwise.

A generation later, Allison Davis and John Hope Franklin exposed how little had changed within higher education. They observed that those few blacks who had managed to attain faculty positions at white universities were kept part time or without tenure.[79] As with desegregation in other arenas, the process occurred slowly and intermittently, and it sparked organized opposition. In the field of K–12 education, for instance, the Supreme Court ruled in *Brown v. Board of Education* that de jure segregation was unconstitutional, yet desegregation did not proceed until the social protest of the civil rights movement forced integration. Even then, the decision could not touch educational segregation by residence and income, nor could it prevent white flight to private schools, which became the new vehicles for race and class segregation.[80] Within higher education, it was not until the 1970s that the Black Power movement forced academia to substantively change by hiring more black professors and by offering courses in black studies and African American history.[81] Even fifty years after Davis's initial appointment, the *Journal of Blacks in Higher Education* found that the University of Chicago had only nine black professors with tenure out of a total of 719 tenured faculty.[82] Such underrepresentation remained the national norm.

Those African Americans who managed to secure full-time faculty positions in higher education, furthermore, remained constrained by the larger institutional racism that set limits on the type of scholarship they could undertake. The fact that foundations and universities froze out black radicals such as W. E. B. Du Bois and Oliver Cox, who in spite of their brilliance struggled to gain an audience for their work or to even maintain employment at black colleges, shows the limits placed on all black scholars.[83] The people like Davis who managed to enter the mainstream had to muffle their radicalism, play up their objectivity, construct close alliances with authoritative white faculty and foundation officers, and choose research projects that foundations deemed permissible.[84]

Throughout his career, Davis managed to negotiate these constraints well, and his progressive ideas on education and social stratification reached a wide audience. Yet his contributions were often subsumed under those of the white scholars with whom he typically coauthored his major books and articles.

Despite being the senior author on many of these works, including *Deep South*, *Children of Bondage*, and *Father of the Man*, Davis was often denied the credit he deserved. This is an example of the double bind that Davis and other African American scholars faced: blacks needed the approval of powerful white scholars for their work to gain authority, but the process of collaboration resulted in their contributions being slighted. Davis ended up choosing collaboration in order to reach a wider audience and to effect change—if in less conspicuous ways—at powerful institutions. The result, unfortunately, was relative obscurity. That sad fate prompted St. Clair Drake to remark, "I am led to wonder if co-authorship with white scholars may not work to the disadvantage of their Negro colleagues."[85]

Although Davis's appointment was an important barometer and progenitor of social change, it did little to overcome institutional racism within the academy or the wider society. Persistent race and class discrepancies combined to ensure that "most blacks in Chicago could aspire to do nothing higher than a job working as a Pullman porter or a civil servant in the post office," according to the *Journal of Blacks in Higher Education*.[86] Class barriers prevented African Americans from gaining access to higher education even when racial barriers began to erode.

Davis's appointment to Chicago offers a revealing case study of desegregation and the anatomy of social change. Liberal individuals with access to social power seized opportunities to challenge the color line within higher education in hopes of galvanizing larger changes.[87] In the process, they made clear that academia could be a multifaceted terrain for racial change, including both scholarly production and physical racial integration. Yet the degree to which they had to methodically plan their maneuvers, the extent of the resistance they faced, the discrimination Davis had to deal with, and the glacial pace with which other full-time black appointments occurred all reveal the power of entrenched interests and the limits on racial change. Davis was exceptional, and was therefore an exception that proved the general rule of racial inequality. A close look at his appointment reveals less the relentless forward march of racial justice and more that individual achievement is a poor measure of group success. Davis spent his career elucidating the systems of racial and class oppression that circumscribed the lives of people of color and the poor. He, more than others, would have wanted people to see his story as a reminder of the tenacity of racial inequities even amid progressive racial change.

CHAPTER 7

Critiquing Middle-Class Culture

The behavior which we regard as "delinquent" or "shiftless" or "unmotivated" in slum groups is usually a perfectly realistic, adaptive, and—in slum life—respectable response to reality.[1]

ALLISON DAVIS

Allison Davis's affiliation with the University of Chicago transformed his career. Chicago was renowned for its interdisciplinary social science, which was a perfect fit for a man who made a career out of transgressing disciplinary boundaries. Through groups such as the Committee on Human Development, Davis joined an impressive group of scholars that included Lloyd Warner, Ralph Tyler, Robert Redfield, Robert Havighurst, and many others. These men worked together to carry out pioneering research on human development and education that emphasized the social conditions under which socialization takes place.

Davis's contributions to this work were part of the burgeoning field of applied anthropology. In the 1940s Davis brought his culture-and-personality framework to bear on a wide variety of issues within human development, such as those relating to the family, the workplace, the ethnic group, and the school. As in *Children of Bondage*, he explored how racial caste and above all class shape the socialization patterns of Americans. In this period he began to refer to distinct "class cultures" as characterizing the lower and middle classes. He worked with his colleagues to apply this framework to an array of institutions with an eye to providing practical guidance for reform. In particular, he recommended ways for parents to rear children, employers to treat their workers, and teachers to instruct their students. The primary audience for this work was middle class, but his aims were quite radical at the time. He wanted middle-class Americans to understand that a rigid class system divided their country and created profound cultural barriers between people. Even more, he wanted Americans to question their own class biases and to recognize the inherent dignity and resiliency within the lower class—which African Americans inhabited at disproportionate levels.

Davis had his work cut out for him. Most Americans in the 1940s began to see the class framework as irrelevant, if not subversive. The type of applied anthropology that garnered more attention, and that was more in line with the cultural nationalism and anticommunism of the period, was Margaret Mead's studies in "national character." As Mead "returned from the natives" to apply her anthropological insights to American foreign policy during the Second World War and the Cold War, she made the case that modern nations were largely unified into distinctive national cultures and that anthropological knowledge about those cultures would be useful in international relations. Her effort was part of a broader campaign sponsored by institutions such as the Council of Intercultural Relations, which lavished funding on "a series of systematic understandings of the great contemporary cultures so that the special values of each may be orchestrated in a world built anew."[2] In this ideological context, Ruth Benedict's famous portrayal of culture as "a more or less consistent pattern of thought and action," which she presented in *Patterns of Culture* (1934), carried the day.[3]

Meanwhile, Davis and his colleagues continued to emphasize social division and conflict. They investigated class divisions not only as economic realities in the United States but also as cultural realities that had profound implications for social policy. The iconoclastic nature of their work made it particularly innovative, but it also marginalized these scholars' voices within mainstream debates.

INTERDISCIPLINARY RESEARCH AT CHICAGO

The University of Chicago's Department of Education had a long tradition of drawing from the other social sciences. When Charles H. Judd became head of the department in 1909, he worked to "dismantle [John] Dewey's edifice."[4] He moved the department's focus away from teacher training and the laboratory schools, and he made education more "scientific" by establishing a graduate department that focused on research and drew faculty from the social sciences. When Ralph Tyler took over as head in 1938, he continued that mission. He reorganized the Committee on Child Development, enlarging it to the Committee on Human Development (CHD) and making it more interdisciplinary.[5] The CHD drew personnel from anthropology, sociology, psychology, economics, education, and other fields, ensuring that educational research at Chicago would be grounded in the larger social order.[6] Allison Davis fit perfectly within such an environment.

Ralph Tyler had a long record of leading progressive efforts within education. In the 1930s he was a major figure in the Progressive Education Association, through which he highlighted innovative research coming out of the Iowa Child Welfare Research Station. For instance, he propagated Kurt Lewin's and George Stoddard's research showing that the environment played a central role in shaping educational success and IQ scores. Tyler also challenged traditional assumptions about educational purpose, pushing teachers to formulate teaching objectives and to assess their own teaching effectiveness rather than merely the knowledge and ability of students.[7]

When Tyler took over at Chicago, he began assembling a first-rate group of theorists to continue his efforts. He brought in the like-minded Robert J. Havighurst of the General Education Board, and he collaborated closely with Lloyd Warner. After helping to secure Davis's appointment to the Department of Education in 1942, Tyler had, in Havighurst's judgment, assembled a "critical mass" of social scientists to continue progressive trends within education.[8]

The Department of Education's most important work during this era grew out of its involvement with the CHD, which focused on two central questions: "(1) How does development of human beings take place? (2) What is a good environment for the favorable development of human beings?"[9] Its research program examined individuals over long periods of time. It evaluated the physical, mental, and social elements of human development, but it privileged social factors above all else.[10] For empirical evidence of environmental influences, the CHD drew from comparative social-anthropological research on communities throughout the country, including Warner's "Yankee City" studies; Davis's "Deep South" study; and Buford Junker's "Hometown, USA" study of Dowagiac, Michigan. The CHD eventually settled upon the small town of Morris, Illinois, to intensively study human development. Its efforts resulted in a wide range of publications.[11] Then, in 1945, the CHD launched another research program in the larger city of Rockford, Illinois, to supplement work conducted in Chicago. Here again, faculty and graduate students conducted diverse studies—including work on intelligence testing as described in the next chapter.

Warner's social-class framework guided all of the CHD's efforts.[12] In the early 1940s, faculty members and students began to clamor for a course focusing on how the CHD's community research could inform the study of education. Warner and Havighurst began offering a seminar called Social Status and Learning. They eventually developed this material into an important book, *Who Shall Be Educated?* (1944), in which they rooted the school in the social order and analyzed its social function. They argued that schools are ineffective instruments of social mobility, functioning chiefly to reflect and reinforce existing class inequalities.[13] The book issued a passionate call for a more democratic and egalitarian educational system.

Building from Warner's social-class schema, the authors contended that schools were thoroughly middle-class institutions that discriminated against lower-class pupils. They developed their argument in a number of ways. For one, they explained how curricula reinforced class differences by tracking middle- and upper-class students into academic and commercial courses while placing lower-class students in vocational ones.[14] Such tracking, they believed, stemmed from that fact that teachers and school administrators were overwhelmingly middle class themselves (over 95 percent). School personnel therefore failed to understand the abilities and behaviors of lower-class students.

According to the authors, the actual subject matter of courses was also alien to the experiences of lower-class youth. Middle-class students were better prepared for the school's focus on language, reading, and arithmetic because their parents had taught them these skills early on and consistently used more sophisticated language at home. Lower-class children started at an immediate disadvantage in gaining such skills. Schools' reliance on intelligence tests, which in the authors' view measured class training more than native ability, only legitimated the consignment of lower-class students to vocational courses.[15]

Finally, *Who Shall Be Educated?* noted that the behavior patterns of lower-class children were anathema to middle-class standards. Teachers spent little time trying to understand the cultural environments of lower-class pupils, which promoted more aggressive behavior. As a result, teachers interpreted lower-class behavior as reflective not of environmental factors but of innately deviant dispositions that were poorly suited for classroom learning.

Davis's own research supported and extended these lines of argument. He proved to be a major force within Chicago's intellectual community.

THE FAMILY

While the bulk of Davis's research came to focus on the school, he began his critiques of middle-class culture by examining the family, which he recognized as the most important socializing agent. For the young child, the family is, according to Davis, a "microcosm of society." It "teaches the basic human behaviors and feelings" and "humanizes (or socializes) man by teaching him the cultural solutions to the basic problems of group living: how to survive as an individual, how to help perpetuate the group, how to win the group's approval by learning its culture." Unfortunately, social scientists knew little about the childrearing practices of American parents because they occurred within the privacy of the home. Davis and Havighurst sought to remedy that by exploring scientifically this "unknown country of human development."[16]

In the early 1940s Davis and Havighurst organized a study of the socialization patterns of Chicago families. They analyzed middle- and lower-class families within both black and white communities. They interviewed 100 middle-class mothers, including 50 whites and 50 blacks, and 102 lower-class mothers, again split equally between the races. The interviewers asked the mothers a set of two hundred questions over the course of a few hours. They then combined those interviews with an "intensive study of children in their families": "these children were observed and studied in their homes" for between nine months and two years.[17] The project was a clear extension of Davis's approach in *Children of Bondage*, only this time the researchers investigated both black and white families, and they did so in a northern setting.

The research, published principally in *Father of the Man* (1947), produced some significant findings. Above all, it uncovered vast social, economic, and especially cultural differences between the lower and middle classes. Explaining the broader implications of their findings in the *American Sociological Review*, the authors wrote, "A detailed understanding of American social-class cultures and motivational patterns is now a *sine qua non*" in studying the child's socialization. Social class "determines not only the neighborhood in which he lives and the play-groups he will have, but also the basic cultural acts and goals toward which he will be trained." Social class therefore "defines and systematizes different learning environments for children of different classes." Pushing back strongly against the retreat from class analyses taking place in the postwar period, Davis and Havighurst placed class inequalities at the very heart of American life.[18]

Davis's research into the family also lent further empirical support to many of his earlier arguments. For one, *Father of the Man* stressed class over race in directing children's socialization. As Ralph Tyler summarized it for Edwin Embree, "This study shows that the methods of child rearing are more alike between whites and Negroes of the same class than they are between lower class and middle class families of the same race."[19] To be sure, the authors did find some differences along racial lines, such as the black tendency to be "much more permissive than whites in the feeding and weaning of their children."[20] But they attributed little significance to that finding.

Davis and Havighurst also confirmed that the racial caste system existed not only in the Deep South but also in the North. They pointed to Chicago's "highly organized residential segregation of Negroes" and its "highly segregated system of so-called 'public' schools" as evidence of the caste system.[21] Similar to *Children of Bondage*, *Father of the Man* presented the argument that caste is most important in its social-class effects—specifically in relegating most blacks to the lower class.

Father of the Man is notable for having targeted a popular audience. This reflected Davis's attempt to be a public intellectual who was relevant to debates beyond the academy. He and Havighurst provided practical childrearing advice to parents at the end of each chapter. They consistently recommended that middle-class parents socialize their children far less rigorously than was typical. Instead of perpetually managing their children's behaviors and instilling anxiety in them at every turn, the authors advised parents to simply model the behaviors they wanted their children to learn.[22] The book offered a clear rundown of Davis's ideas for a wider audience, even if it had little new to contribute theoretically and was probably still too academic for the average parent.

Father of the Man received mixed reviews among the relatively few publications that did review it. Various newspapers reported its general findings to a wider audience, and *Parents' Magazine* gave it an honorable mention for its annual "best book on child guidance" award.[23] But the substantive reviews were similar to those of *Children of Bondage*. One reviewer, for instance, praised the book's popular style and "skillful integration of the anthropological, psychological, and psychoanalytic points of view."[24]

Harvard anthropologist John Whiting was one of the few people to recognize the larger contribution of the book: it exposed the class divisions within American society at a time when most social scientists were reflexively equating national culture with middle-class culture, which led them to mistakenly perceive cultural cohesion while ignoring many segments of society.[25]

Yet while Whiting and others found value in the book's approach, many commentators did not. Chicago School sociologist Ellsworth Faris, whose research findings were directly challenged by Davis and Havighurst's, spoke for the critics when he issued a harsh review in the *American Journal of Sociology*. He charged that the authors overemphasized early childhood socialization and drew unconvincing conclusions from their simplistic behaviorist orientation. Even more telling, however, was Faris's rejection of the authors' claim that slum society had a "culture" at all—let alone one that was not wholly inferior to middle-class culture. He was not alone when he wrote that "much of what is here called 'culture' is termed disorganization in the vocabulary of the sociologist."[26] Faris rebuffed Davis and Havighurst for portraying lower-class life as an integrated culture that had its own virtues. Davis's ideas were radical and challenging.

THE WORKPLACE

Davis soon extended his class critiques from the family to the workplace, taking aim at industrialists and business managers. This work grew out of his membership in Chicago's Committee on Human Relations in Industry (CHRI), the brainchild of his old friend Burleigh Gardner. After finishing the research for *Deep South*, Gardner had completed his PhD at Harvard and worked with a private firm before becoming a professor of business at the University of Chicago in the early 1940s, alongside Davis. In 1943 he helped found the CHRI, which initially focused on "studying and resolving the racial problems which they anticipated when blacks from the South entered wartime industry in the Chicago area." However, the primary focus of the CHRI soon became the practical application of Warner's class framework to industrial relations. The committee—Davis, Gardner, Warner, Havighurst, William Foote Whyte, Everett C. Hughes, and others—secured numerous corporate sponsors, and for each sponsor it "planned a special study which addressed some problem of interest to the company." One notable result of these efforts was the book *Human Relations in the Restaurant Industry* (1948).[27]

In the mid-1940s the CHRI also planned a series of lectures that were eventually published in the book *Industry and Society* (1946).[28] Committee members and nonmembers alike, including business executive Chester Barnard and labor educationalist Mark Starr, presented on topics related to social class and industry. Hundreds of audience members—mainly business people—attended each lecture. The lectures shared a

> well-integrated point of view and methodology. We see the society and any of its segments, whether a neighborhood, a factory, or a work group, as having a social structure comprised of the relations among individuals. While there are obviously those individual differences which we call "personality," much of the behavior whether in acts or talk or thinking is an expression of the place of the individual in the social system rather than an expression of his own unique personality pattern. The primary interest in this research is directed to the understanding of the social structure and the way in which it controls and molds the individual. In order to study this we rely almost completely on interviews

and observation, which means that the research people must actually go out into factories and homes. Thus the analysis and understanding grow out of an intimate knowledge of the way the people actually act, think, and feel.[29]

Industry and Society brought Warner's social-anthropological framework to bear on industrial relations, both in its theoretical emphasis on social class and in its methodological focus on participant observation and interviewing.

Allison Davis's contribution to the anthology was an essay titled "The Motivations of the Underprivileged Worker," in which he presented challenging ideas about lower-class workers. Based upon his and his colleagues' research, which examined six hundred families in all, including four hundred lower-class ones, Davis argued that lower-class behaviors—which managers typically understood as reflecting " 'innate' perversity," such as " 'shiftlessness,' 'irresponsibility,' absenteeism, and . . . quitting the job"—were in fact "*normal responses* that the worker [had] learned from his physical and social environment." He insisted, furthermore, that "these habits constitute a system of behavior and attitudes which are realistic and rational in *that environment*." His lecture proceeded from this decidedly progressive position.[30]

Davis began by underlining the deprivation that pervaded the lives of lower-class people.[31] He emphasized the "miserable housing," the "recurrent homelessness," the malnutrition, and the much higher rate of disease, especially tuberculosis. Without adequate sleep or basic health, workers could not work consistently. Nor could they invest in long-term middle-class goals such as formal education and homeownership. Lacking even a "minimum of *physical security*," such goals made little sense. Instead the lower-class worker had to focus on mere survival and to constantly "narrow, limit, and shorten his goals with regard to the care, nutrition, education, and careers of his children." Reacting rationally, workers pursued the satisfactions that were within reach, which often centered on "visceral, genital, and emotional gratification."[32]

Davis also explained that lower-class patterns of behavior were not simply dysfunctional products of poverty. Rather, many of these patterns were impressive adaptations to oppression. For example, he took the fact that poor people had large families as evidence not of irresponsibility or stupidity but of the creation of a "*protective* circle" that shielded the lower class from chronic economic insecurity. This was especially true for poor black families, who had an average of 4.9 children, compared to 3.3 on average in the white lower class and 2.2 in the white middle class. As Davis highlighted, the larger network of family and friends, which included both kin and non-kin groups, helped to ensure that lower-class people could find a place to stay even when they were unemployed and displaced. So rather than being "disorganized" as Chicago School sociologists maintained, the large family, for Davis, was actually a resource. These communal groups practiced an "organized, cooperative system of sharing" of "food, money, clothes," beds, and work.[33]

Davis did not shrink from discussing plainly those lower-class behaviors most stigmatized by the middle class. He acknowledged, for instance, that lower-class workers would sometimes spend their entire paycheck within the first couple of days on drinking and carousing. They would then be forced to rely on loans from friends for basic necessities until the next paycheck came. Most middle-class people could not understand behavior that so violated their ethic of working hard, saving, and delaying gratification. Yet Davis emphasized that middle-class people had *learned* that ethic in their privileged upbringing. In the lower-class environment, workers learned different behaviors. Namely, they learned to survive, and to see education and delayed gratification as unrealistic avenues for social mobility. So they took advantage of the physical pleasures and social gains that were actually available to them. Davis explained this behavior as "part of a practical cultural system" in which each worker shared his or her paycheck with a couple of friends, who would later support him or her when their paychecks came. In this way the workers "actually had developed a system of getting money every Friday or Saturday, instead of only every second week, on payday."[34] Lower-class people were thus not merely rational but creative in adjusting to their conditions, and were capable of adaptation should their circumstances change.

To make workers more consistent and efficient, Davis recommended a few practical solutions. Above all, he underscored the necessity of offering robust economic opportunities for the lower class. He wrote, "We must offer the underprivileged worker real rewards," including a "permanent, decent home" and a "steady job and good wages." Only then would it be possible to raise a worker's "ceiling of aspiration for education, for respectability, for skills, and for better training." As in his earlier work, Davis therefore put the onus for change on the wider social environment. Although this essay was his only publication that examined industrial relations, it revealed the potential progressive application of Davis's class-as-a-culture ideas to the workplace.[35]

Businesspeople had their own interests in Davis and Warner's research. Many of them may have been sympathetic to social reform for humanitarian reasons, but they were in the end driven far more by maximizing profit and solidifying their position in the marketplace. Consequently, they ignored the scholars' more radical recommendations for change, which included granting workers more control over the workplace and redistributing wealth to alleviate social inequality. Instead they exploited sociological knowledge for their own gain.

Businesspeople looked to Warner's social-class framework to more effectively market their products. Warner's emphasis on social status and participation, rather than on inherent conflicts over the means of production, suited their interests. They marshaled his six-part class system, with its descriptive details about each class's interests and goals, to better market to each segment of the marketplace. That is, they treated his analysis as market research. When the *Journal of Marketing* "heralded Warner's 1948 book *Social Class in America* as 'the most important step forward to market research in many years,'" it made clear that businesspeople were exploiting Warner's research for their own ends.[36]

Warner at times aided industry's appropriation of his research. For instance, he informally instructed Pierre Martineau, director of research in the *Chicago Tribune*'s marketing division in the 1950s, about social class in America.[37] Martineau then published articles such as "Social Classes and Spending Behavior" in the *Journal of Marketing*, and books such as *Motivation in Advertising*, which taught marketers how to exploit class divisions to maximize sales.[38] Burleigh Gardner went even further, in 1946 resigning from the University of Chicago to consult full time through the organization he founded, Social Class, Incorporated.[39]

Unfortunately, the net effect of Warner's and Gardner's consulting efforts was to shore up corporate profits. In an ironic twist, their work did promote class consciousness, but only among businesspeople. Business owners shielded that consciousness from consumers and instead peddled the idea of a classless society that was newly possible through mass consumption. In this context, it is not too surprising that Davis's more radical ideas about class fell largely upon deaf ears.

EDUCATION FOR DEMOCRACY

As part of the Department of Education at Chicago, Davis naturally focused most of his energy on schools, which he perceived as rife with middle-class bias. More than in other areas of his research at the time, his approach was shaped by larger intellectual trends. The most significant one was the rise of a widespread and lavishly funded "intercultural education" movement. Davis participated while also trying to steer the movement in a progressive direction.

Intercultural education was a response to the widespread racial, ethnic, and religious conflicts of interwar America. The movement had grown especially out of the turmoil of the 1920s. Liberals were bothered by the vitriolic anti-immigrant, anti-Catholic, and antiblack sentiment pervading the country, so many of them responded by promoting tolerance. After World War II, Americans became increasingly critical of the subjugation of ethnic, racial, and religious minorities.

The intercultural education movement took numerous forms, and the number of organizations combating ethnic hostility soared in the late 1940s.[40] Local activists in the movement followed the lead of organizations such as the Commission on Intercultural Education, which the Progressive Education Association formed in 1937. One of the commission's programs was called Education for Democracy, and it celebrated the contributions of immigrants to American society. Growing numbers of Americans, including religious leaders within the Federal Council of Churches, openly condemned racial prejudice and discrimination.

Intercultural educators took a variety of steps. They "developed public school programs, teacher education courses, adult education forums, pamphlets, religious programs, discussion groups for businesses and unions, films," and other means to wage the battle against intolerance.[41] Anthropologist Hortense Powdermaker was one educator who used her expertise on race relations, developing a text for high school students called *Probing Our Prejudices* (1944). Davis was directly involved in this type of work, and he read and commented on Powdermaker's book.[42] More important, Davis helped to institutionalize the intercultural education movement at Chicago by forming the Center for Intergroup Education in 1948 alongside Tyler, Havighurst, Louis Wirth, and Hilda Taba.[43]

William Vickery and Stewart Coles's *Intercultural Education in American Schools* (1943) laid out the intercultural approach, arguing that ethnic, religious, racial, and socioeconomic conflicts need to be addressed through the educational process. As educationalist William Kilpatrick wrote in the foreword, "The problem *is* essentially an educational problem, since all the prejudices involved in it have been acquired by each individual during his lifetime." Schools, therefore, must "mitigate some of the present evils by teaching the young to see the unjust pain which certain of their present thoughtless practices and prejudices inflict on their fellows."[44] Vickery and Cole recommended that classrooms be student centered and discussion based, that social studies teachers take the lead in the schools, and that the cultivation of critical thinking be prioritized—all with the goal of strengthening democracy.[45] Davis became a major advocate for all of these ideas.

Yet as much as Davis shared the pedagogical aims of intercultural educators, he found their exclusive focus on prejudice and the role of education to be problematic. As St. Clair Drake later recalled, he and Davis had emerged from their research for *Deep South* believing that the idea of prejudice was essentially "meaningless."[46] The concept typically portrayed racism as some fixed, acquired trait that existed within the minds of individuals. That interpretation missed the structural nature of racism, its ties to specific social realities and power dynamics. Furthermore, Davis and Drake understood that people's behaviors often fail to match up to their ideas. In Natchez they had observed that residents frequently ignored caste strictures when it was in their interest to do so. This discrepancy suggested that ideas are less important in determining human behavior than the particular circumstances in which people act. Davis therefore wanted to change the environment in which Americans interacted with one another, rather than to simply teach people not to be prejudiced.

Resisting the emphasis on prejudice would be difficult. The belief that prejudice was a problem in white people's minds, and that it could be educated away for intergroup harmony, was prevalent. Gunnar Myrdal's *An American Dilemma* had helped to solidify that priority, and in subsequent years foundations proved unwilling to support studies that focused on black people or structural inequality; instead they lavished funds on studies of white prejudice.[47]

Consequently, the stature of psychological and psychoanalytic studies of prejudice rose.[48] Books such as Robin M. Williams's *The Reduction of Intergroup Tensions* (1947), Theodor Adorno et al.'s *The Authoritarian Personality* (1950), Abram Kardiner and Lionel Ovesey's *The Mark of Oppression* (1951), and Gordon Allport's *The Nature of Prejudice* (1954) dominated the intellectual landscape. Although these works were sophisticated and innovative, they largely ignored the social-structural nature of racism. To be sure, many of these studies emphasized the intractability of prejudice, locating it within early patterns of socialization that cannot easily be undone. Still, the focus on prejudice among white people reinforced the idea among more optimistic thinkers that education can indeed promote profound change. As intercultural educator Robin M. Williams Jr. stated it, "What is needed here is not something the government can do for us—no new political credo nor even, for the most part, new laws—but a new social code, one that shall animate our continuous behavior, a social code worthy of a civilized people that believes in its own democracy."[49]

Although Davis saw the widespread emphasis on prejudice as misguided, he seized upon the liberal moment to strike against social injustice. Davis, Warner, and other Chicago faculty members pushed the intercultural educators to see that class stratification is significant and that it, too, translates into cultural differences that provoke prejudice and discrimination.[50] They believed that class prejudice is as important to address as racial, ethnic, or religious prejudice and that it can in fact masquerade in those forms. Here, Davis sought to ground psychological thinking on cultural prejudice within the larger social context.

Davis entered the fray of intercultural education through his abortive project on school acculturation. The project was a logical extension of his previous work. He followed Redfield, Edward Sapir, Ralph Linton, and Melville Herskovits in defining acculturation as "the learning of a culture different from that of one's birth group." It was therefore a subset of socialization, which Davis defined generally as "the life-long process through which the human organism learns a culture, or possibly several cultures."[51] But while the pioneering theorists of acculturation focused on ethnic and national cultures, Davis investigated class cultures. Like intercultural educators, he evaluated how schools could acculturate students to new behaviors and values, especially those of the middle class. His larger hope was to find practical ways to equalize education for the "underprivileged" masses.[52]

In early 1943 Davis wrote up a proposal for a comparative school acculturation project. He made plans to study schools in "the Southwest, Hawaii, Jamaica, and Guatemala" in order to "gain a firsthand view of the practical measures involved in the education of colored peoples who possess many different types of subordinate culture and status in relationship to various white groups." He contended that such a study would "furnish a concrete frame of reference for expanding the intercultural understanding of teachers" and that it would "provide rich resources of practical educational measures for improving the understanding and tolerance of all groups."[53]

In this way Davis once again attempted to use his comparative social-anthropological training to extend current debates over race and class beyond the confines of the United States. His hope was to allow Americans to see local conditions within a global context. Yet unlike the similar project he failed to launch at Dillard, Davis now narrowed his investigation to the study of one process (the acculturation of people of color) in one institution (the school) across a few different countries.

This time around, foundations were supportive—in part because World War II had made Americans more globally conscious and in part because Davis was now part of a prestigious predominantly white university. The General Education Board (GEB) quickly granted him $4,000 for the project.[54]

Yet securing funding proved to be the least of Davis's problems. He immediately encountered trouble making travel arrangements to Hawaii while the war was still raging. Davis therefore tried to begin his investigation in the American Southwest. His prospects at first proved little better there. His Rockefeller and Rosenwald contacts in Texas ignored him completely, while those in New Mexico advised him to stay away.[55] Throughout the entire project, Davis had to curtail his research plans after hitting obstacles.

However, his persistence was eventually rewarded. Edwin Embree's contacts in California proved more helpful. Davis studied schools in Los Angeles, San Diego, Oakland, and San Francisco from January 9 to March 10, 1944. He visited thirty-three public schools and observed 116 classes, where he "had the opportunity to observe . . . pupil activities, to interview administrators, teachers, and pupils, and to collect records in 16 elementary schools, 9 junior-high schools, and 8 senior-high schools."[56] In the summer of 1944, he wrote up a 175-page research report on this material and submitted it to the GEB.

Davis's report, "The School's Most Costly Weakness: The Public Schools and the Cultural Assimilation of Americans of Negro, Mexican, and Chinese Background," laid out his interpretation of the school's role in acculturating underprivileged students. In most ways, his ideas paralleled those within the broader intercultural education movement. He likewise recognized three major types of culture within the United States: (1) "the general American cultural behaviors, such as the monogamous family, or American food habits"; (2) "the social-class cultural behaviors, such as the lower-class approval of overt aggression, or characteristic lower-class food habits"; and (3) "the ethnic or nationality-group cultural behaviors, such as the speaking of Polish or Spanish, or the habitual use of Italian, or Negro, songs and dances."[57]

Of those cultures, however, Davis argued that the second one was the most important. He never discounted the importance of ethnic cultural differences, but his strategy was to explain how ethnic differences translate into a particular social status within the American class system—which is where he believed the bulk of social power resides. For example, the Chinese veneration of scholarship and learning mirrors the middle-class American value on education. So even though Mexican culture is more closely related to American culture because of its partly European roots, Chinese students actually fare better within American education.[58]

Regarding African Americans, Davis was even blunter. He argued that blacks are "overwhelmingly American in their culture." As he saw it, "The cultural stigmas, which American whites react to in most Negroes, are not foreign in any sense. They are stigmas of lowerclass people, of their habits, symbols, and values." Lower-class culture "has become equated with 'Negro behavior' in the popular thinking," Davis argued, because "the color barriers in occupations, education, and politics keep the great majority of Negro Americans in lower-class positions."[59]

While aware of the influence of Africa on the culture of African Americans, Davis continued to argue that the American class system is the most significant factor shaping black culture and life. Davis had not abandoned his earlier conviction that African Americans retain cultural ties with Africa. He admired the work of Melville Herskovits and Lorenzo Dow Turner on that subject. Yet as E. Franklin Frazier and Herskovits debated the existence of "Africanisms" among American blacks, Davis elected to more quietly pursue research centered on class inequalities.[60]

Davis's career paralleled Frazier's in many revealing ways. Frazier was one of the most significant black social scientists in the United States by midcentury. He became the first black president of the American Sociological Society in 1948, and he published some of the most important books on the African American experience, including *The Negro Family in the United States* (1939) and *The Negro in the United States* (1949).[61] Like Davis, he was a radical who had long critiqued class stratification within the black community as well as within the larger society, and he worked for a more socialistic system. But also like Davis, Frazier maintained an objective stance in his professional career, and he was empirical in his approach. Both men retained their leftist sympathies in the postwar period, but they adapted their work to the ideological context of the times. Frazier "emerged as a major exponent of integration and assimilation" after World War II, emphasizing the damage that racism had exacted upon American blacks and working toward racial integration.[62] Although Davis eschewed expositions of damage, he, too, used his professional stature to aid the process of racial integration in the postwar period. His leadership in intercultural education was part of this effort.

So Davis was not alone when he described African American life as primarily a product of social stratification. As he explained it, because caste and class have relegated the majority of blacks to the lower class, "the problem of acculturation for American Negroes" is "to learn habits and values more similar to the middleclass way of life." He continued, "This form of acculturation involves not only the changing of habits of language, housing, and manners, but requires also the more difficult learning of new methods of child-rearing, and of basically different controls upon aggression, sexual response, and other gratifications. It also involves the final difficulty of learning new values or social goals." To gain status and power within the United States, one needs to learn middle-class culture.[63]

Davis recognized schools as crucial agents of middle-class acculturation. Because American public education is universal, and because schools are staffed predominantly by middle-class people, schools offer a unique pathway for assimilating underprivileged groups to the culture of "native, middleclass, white Americans."[64] Davis was critical of aspects of that culture, but he pragmatically argued that it should nevertheless be available to underprivileged groups. In his own words, public schools provide students with "daily opportunities to imitate and to identify with each other."[65] Accordingly, schools afford underprivileged children "sufficiently prolonged and close-range association with middleclass teachers and pupils," which could "motivate their learning of certain aspects of middleclass culture."[66] The importance of social participation and interaction—trademarks of Warner's anthropology—continued to loom large in Davis's thinking.

Yet Davis also found that schools were ultimately failing in middle-class acculturation. One reason for this was that school personnel did not understand their own class biases. For Davis, teachers and administrators—much like the middle-class families and businesspeople he was also studying—failed to see how their ideas were informed by middle-class cultural training. That ignorance prompted them to interpret the behavior of lower-class students as evidence of individual deficiencies or innate racial inferiority, instead of as logical adaptations to lower-class life.[67] This did not bode well for student learning. Davis found that teachers consistently failed underprivileged pupils and treated them as behavior problems. In contrast, teachers identified with middle-class students, who had been trained to value education and to exhibit behaviors that appealed to teachers' middle-class sensibilities.[68]

Opening up another line of attack, Davis explained that schools failed to acculturate underprivileged youth because of the endemic racial segregation characterizing American schools. He found that de facto racial segregation in the North and West, enforced by restrictive covenants as well as by violence and intimidation, led to a level of segregation that was comparable to that of the South. "Group isolation," he wrote, "is the most powerful obstacle to acculturation."[69] "If people of different cultures cannot associate intimately," he continued, "they cannot learn one another's special forms of language, manners, morals, and social goals."[70] He soon expanded his critique of segregation to practices *within* schools, such as ability grouping, which perpetuate race and class segregation.

Speaking more broadly, Davis also criticized segregation for undermining America's democratic culture. He recognized that segregation, by its very existence, trains children to perceive one another differentially, thereby sowing division rather than solidarity. Similar to John Dewey in *Freedom and Culture* (1939), Davis understood democratic culture to be learned and not inherited.[71] So he and his CHD colleagues made the case that the schools need to be bulwarks for democracy by educating all students together and teaching them to value fairness, cooperation, reasoned debate, and community activism.[72] He maintained that greater social equality and extensive intercultural interaction are important preconditions for the successful inculcation of democratic values.

Davis recognized social studies teachers as paramount in promoting democracy. He considered them "the most essential people in the schools." As he saw it, "they were helping the children of the masses learn . . . the meaning of justice and of injustice in America. They were teaching a devotion to democratic ideals of fairness, and a group disapproval of injustice and oppression." In all these ways, Davis claimed, schools should function not merely to promote social mobility but to bolster democracy.[73]

As the 1940s wore on, Davis kept trying make progress on the larger comparative acculturation project that he had initially proposed. However, wartime developments and other professional responsibilities obstructed his progress. He first decided to abandon his proposed study of Jamaica and Guatemala and focus instead on Brazil.[74] He then had to push that research back until the fall of 1945, at which point he visited Brazil for only a brief period. Unfortunately, the trip proved fruitless. The war had disorganized the schools, and he struggled mightily to secure the requisite travel permits, housing, and means of transportation.[75] At that point Davis finally gave up on the Latin American aspect of the project altogether and focused instead on examining acculturation in Hawaiian schools.

Because Hawaii was home to the nation's most racially integrated school system, it was a major research priority.[76] After more delays and difficulties, in the spring of 1947 he and his family finally spent a few months in the territory while he conducted his research. The report he produced, "The Public Schools and America's Most Successful Racial Democracy: Hawaii," did provide some significant ethnographic accounts of Hawaiian society and its unique school system.[77] If anything, the research only further convinced him that schools need to racially integrate, promote democratic culture, and counteract class inequalities. In the end, however, a few months proved insufficient for such a complex setting, and little new on acculturation emerged from the project.

Although the acculturation project struggled to get off the ground, Davis did convey his conclusions to a variety of audiences. For example,

FIGURE 7.1. Allison Davis in Hawaii in 1947. Courtesy of the Davis Family.

he presented a paper titled "The Role of the Public Schools: Acculturation of Mexican Americans in California" before the Institute for Social Research in August 1944.[78] More informally, he discussed his findings on the segregation of Mexican American students in California—still de jure until 1947—with Carey McWilliams, a prolific journalist and advocate for minorities who incorporated Davis's ideas into his influential work.[79] Davis also spoke before Chicago schools and PTA meetings on topics such as "our schools' contribution to democracy."[80]

Davis continued such work into the 1950s. In 1951 he presented his research at the annual meeting of the American Home Economics Association. Newspapers covered that talk closely, and they helped to propagate Davis's ideas. A journalist for the *New York Times* quoted Davis at length: "The only institution in our society in which the lower-class children have sufficient contact with middle-class people to be able to learn their habits of nutrition, health care, language, saving, budgeting and economic skills is in the public schools. . . . It is precisely for that reason that the public school in America is the ladder of the people."[81] Davis's arguments also came through in publications, such as *Social-Class Influences upon Learning*, as well as major presentations, such as one at the White House Conference on Children and Youth.

Davis also used the CHD as a platform for the dissemination of his ideas. In his own classes and in the CHD workshops he held, he underscored the public school system's central role as "the essential training ground for a democratic society." According to Davis, schools should both "decrease the antagonisms between the social strata in American society" and "give the children of the various social levels and races a chance to interact with one another and to learn to accept certain common loyalties and standards of justice." This was education for democratic ends.[82]

Davis also laid out concrete measures for school personnel to more effectively instruct their students. In the *Journal of Educational Sociology* he advised teachers to conduct "socialized interviews" with all of their students in order to better understand their cultural backgrounds. The point was to "discover where the pupil is situated in the learning process" in order to surmount the "cultural obstacles which the pupil faces in learning."[83] He also recommended extensive in-service teacher training and suggested that teachers become familiar not only with social class in America but with the particular communities of their students.[84]

Relatedly, Davis insisted that school curricula needed to be more realistic and interesting to students. In his view, too much of American education emphasized reading and the memorization of formal English. More productive would be the cultivation of problem-solving skills, rooted in material closely connected to the lives of the students. He elaborated on those ideas in an article in *Progressive Education* in which he criticized classrooms as merely laboratories for the inculcation of formulaic middle-class culture.[85]

Several of Davis's other recommendations remain relevant today. For instance, Davis promoted the use of discussion and active student participation. Through discussion, teachers could locate where their students stood in the learning process. Even more important, discussion would make students active participants in that process. The results of this approach could be particularly striking in a diverse classroom setting, where students could learn to understand the different class, race, and ethnic cultures of their peers through extensive interaction. Within an atmosphere of intercultural learning and tolerance, teachers could help students adopt long-term middle-class goals pertaining to educational and career success.[86] Davis presented these ideas widely, including in journals such as *Educational Leadership*.

Davis's strategy of using the schools to acculturate underprivileged students to the dominant middle-class culture was not narrowly assimilationist. He never naturalized middle-class culture or prescribed it uncritically, even though that objective loomed large in the ideological universe in which he operated. In fact, much of his work on the family, industry, and the schools amounted to a critique of middle-class culture. His work in all those fields pushed middle-class people to discover their own cultural biases in order to transcend them, and then to judge lower-class people on their own terms. He portrayed lower-class behavior as fundamentally reasonable, logical, and adaptive with the larger environment of oppression, and he pressed parents, businessmen, and teachers to discern the fortitude within the underprivileged.

However, as much as Davis wanted to transform aspects of middle-class culture and to challenge its values, he understood the importance of first creating opportunities for the underprivileged to succeed in a society dominated by that culture. Like other civil rights leaders, he recognized the value of breaking down social barriers and allowing equal access to social, economic, and political opportunities. As Gunnar Myrdal summarized it, "American culture is 'highest' in the pragmatic sense that adherence to it is practical for any individual or group which is not strong enough to change it."[87]

To be sure, the postwar emphasis on "intercultural education" and "access" was conservative in many respects. It did not address institutional forms of racism, and it emphasized social change through acculturation rather than political mobilization, social solidarity, and cultural pride among disadvantaged groups. All of this would invite criticism in the coming years.[88] Nevertheless, intercultural education and access did offer practical opportunities for mitigating social injustice. According to St. Clair Drake, "The enduring contribution made by this type of research was the incorporation of its ideas into textbooks, thus sensitizing a wide circle of educators to the need for understanding disadvantaged children, irrespective of their race."[89] Drake directly linked intercultural education with the successes of the civil rights movement, which he knew depended upon white Americans' viewing racial discrimination and prejudice as a problem.[90]

Davis took advantage of the new impetus for racial integration and cultural assimilation to foment social change. Yet he also subtly challenged that agenda by questioning the very tenets of the dominant culture that many Americans had naturalized as superior.

Allison Davis's class-as-a-culture framework proved effective for generating progressive research on the family, the workplace, and the school. That framework emphasized the different experiences and behaviors of people within the different social classes. In the context of the 1940s and 1950s, this emphasis was especially valuable because so many Americans continued to perceive their country as a "classless" one. Davis understood that middle-class audiences needed to recognize social class as real before they could understand—let alone appreciate—the different lives and behaviors of people within the lower class.

In a different context, sharpening the distinctions between people within different classes was less useful. For example, later in the twentieth century, when white Americans came to see urban ghettos as fundamentally alien spaces, it became important for social scientists such as sociologist Sudhir Venkatesh to make clear that the urban poor, despite living in very different environments, shared many of the same values as other Americans, including the desire to build a community.[91] Moreover, Venkatesh emphasized that governmental, philanthropic, and commercial institutions linked all people together.

In Davis's time, however, he found it necessary to sharpen the distinctions between the classes. This allowed him, first, to document the existence of a stratified class system and, second, to humanize the people at the bottom of that system. In all of his work, he found willing and able colleagues at the University of Chicago to further his research goals. At every turn, he benefited from Chicago's power and prestige to carry out that research. His work on the family, the workplace, and the school in this period represented one important way in which intellectuals applied culture-and-personality theorizing for practical ends.[92]

Yet it was in the arena of intelligence testing that Davis and his colleagues had their greatest influence. In other arenas Davis struggled at times to carry out his research or to reach a large audience. Not so with intelligence testing. His work in that sphere led to practical reforms and initiated a far-reaching debate on issues of class bias, fairness, and ability. In many ways, that work marked the culmination of his career.

CHAPTER 8

Rethinking Intelligence

How shall one measure by standardized tests the skills of a boy who has learned to acquire the fruits of stealing and at the same time to escape being put into jail?[1]

ALLISON DAVIS

The reforms that Allison Davis galvanized within intelligence testing were the most lasting achievements of his career. Davis led the first quantitative empirical studies of cultural biases within intelligence tests. He and his colleagues found extensive biases along class lines, and they reported those biases to an American public immersed in standardized tests. Although intelligence testing had first emerged only around World War I, it quickly proliferated and became a staple within American society by World War II. For that reason, Davis's research assumed remarkable importance in helping to revise testing practices. His work ultimately opened up opportunities for poor and minority people, who were the ones most victimized by the tests.

Yet despite the strength of his ideas, the impact of Davis's research was not always immediate. As throughout his career, Davis once again swam against the tide of public opinion in establishing his position on intelligence tests. He continued to emphasize stark class divisions at a time when Americans were more focused on abundance and affluence. He also faced fierce opposition from psychologists, publishers, and other parties invested in the proliferation of the tests. In the 1940s and 1950s, such vested interests muffled many of Davis's and his colleagues' criticisms of the tests and conspired to prevent systematic changes to testing practices. Nevertheless, Davis's ideas found a receptive audience among many educators, African Americans, and other test critics. And during the 1960s and 1970s, when prodemocratic, antipoverty, and civil rights activists mounted powerful movements for social change, his ideas found new life. Various parties took up his research to bolster their calls for social change. Many others never knew of his contributions, but they nonetheless built upon his pioneering work to help reform American testing practices.

INTELLIGENCE TESTING AND THE SCHOOLS

By the 1940s, intelligence testing was deeply entrenched within American society, especially within the schools. In the previous half century, the nation's dramatic urbanization, industrialization, and immigration had left schools with swelling enrollments, bewildering student diversity, and massive budget shortfalls. From 1890 to 1915 alone, total public-school enrollment increased 55 percent, from 12.7 million to 19.7 million. The most dramatic increases occurred at the high school level, where enrollments mushroomed 554 percent, from 203,000 to 1.3 million. The trends continued in the interwar period, as total enrollments rose 22 percent and high school enrollments doubled between 1920 and 1930 alone.[2]

The profundity of the challenges spurred educators at all levels to adjust, often creatively. During the Progressive Era, when there was a real effort to order the chaos, educators tried sorting students into different tracks—a practice commentators referred to variously as "tracking," "ability grouping," and "homogeneous grouping"—based upon their perceived abilities. Had intelligence tests never been invented, schools would still have functioned as sorting mechanisms.

Intelligence testing, however, played an important role in exacerbating the sorting trends within education. Professional psychologists, as both developers and chief proponents of the tests, played a key role in the tests' proliferation. The process began during the late nineteenth century when psychologists tried to distance themselves from metaphysical speculation and labored to sever their ties with philosophy, religion, and spiritualism. This involved professionalizing the discipline and placing it within the more authoritative natural sciences.[3] They did this by establishing an experimental quantitative psychology.

A number of figures led the way here. German philosopher Wilhelm Wundt designed the first experimental lab in Leipzig in 1879. British scientist Sir Francis Galton placed psychology on scientific rather than metaphysical grounds through his use of the quantitative method. He also laid the groundwork for an applied psychology through his emphasis on eugenics. One of his students, Charles Spearman, used correlative methods to theorize the existence of a single intelligence factor, which he referred to as g.[4] In the United States, G.

Stanley Hall followed his mentor, Wundt, and established the first psychology laboratory in the United States in 1883. James McKeen Cattell, Wundt's first American graduate student, brought Wundt's and Galton's ideas to the United States, and he worked with Hall and William James to lay the basis for a psychology that measured intelligence.[5]

Yet it was Frenchman Alfred Binet who was the most significant person in the burgeoning field of mental testing. Commissioned in 1904 by his government to devise ways for diagnosing "feeblemindedness" among schoolchildren, Binet was the first to develop a practical test to measure intelligence. In 1905, along with his assistant Theodore Simon, he developed the first scale of intelligence—the Binet-Simon—which identified the "mental age" of the test taker. Underscoring the significance of Binet's innovation and its long shadow on mental testing, Allison Davis later pointed out that "in the thirty-five years since Binet's last work, virtually no new types of problems have been included in either the individual or group intelligence tests."[6]

Indeed, the second generation of American measurement specialists abandoned Binet's own reservations and seized upon his creation to introduce intelligence testing on a mass scale. Henry Herbert Goddard was the first to translate Binet's scale into English in 1908, and shortly thereafter he allied with Lewis Madison Terman, Edward Lee Thorndike, and Robert Mearns Yerkes to institutionalize the tests within the United States.[7] World War I was a major boon to their cause, providing the funding and research sample (1.7 million soldiers) necessary to bolster their science; it enhanced professional networks among psychologists and politicians; and not least of all, it supplied a compelling example of the potential value of classifying large numbers of individuals.[8]

The new cohort of psychological testers quickly moved to exploit their successes and spread intelligence testing throughout society. For them, it was a patriotic cause. Like most progressives of the time, they believed that urban industrial society needed to be ordered and rationalized, not reconstructed. They also understood heredity as the paramount factor in determining a person's ability. Accordingly, they sought to measure innate mental capacity in order to streamline the sorting of Americans into different jobs, classes, and social roles, all of which would increase social efficiency. Despite their generally good intentions, they mistook social disparities for biological ones and therefore enshrined, rather than mitigated, social inequality. And it was precisely such aspects of their thinking that made it so amenable to Americans during the 1920s, when deep-seated racism, sexism, classism, and xenophobia predominated. Amid cultural conflict, measurement specialists found many opportunities to peddle tests which seemed to provide scientific justification for the social disparities people observed.[9]

After World War I, education emerged as the central terrain for the proliferation of intelligence testing. To be sure, corporations, asylums, courts, and the military all began institutionalizing the tests as well, but it was in education where the tests reached the most people and were administered the most widely.[10]

Lewis Terman became the central spokesman for this effort. Exploiting psychology's new authority, he helped to embed intelligence tests within the schools by convincing administrators and teachers that they were effective tools for scientifically sorting students. He also led efforts to disseminate the tests. His success is registered by that fact that by the 1920s, schools, publishing houses, and the discipline of psychology had all established deep institutional and financial investments in intelligence testing.

As Allison Davis surveyed the scene a couple decades later, he observed that those investments had only grown stronger. With the end of World War II and the passage of the GI Bill, the nation stood poised to accelerate the application of intelligence tests within the schools at an unprecedented rate.[11]

Because the proliferation of the tests had occurred so rapidly, critiques were often muted, and major debates over the tests' validity and utility took place only after the fact. In their haste to reform society and to professionalize their discipline, psychologists largely ignored the significant criticism that was present from the beginning, even among the test developers themselves. Even Alfred Binet had been concerned with the class and cultural biases inherent in his creation, and he was critical of American psychologists' commitment to the large-scale quantification of test data.[12] In the 1910s, other psychologists built upon Binet's critiques, consistently questioning the ability of the tests to measure something as complex as human intelligence.[13] These critiques, however, continued to be marginalized within the field.

It was not until the 1920s—after the tests were already deeply institutionalized—that real public debate, or at least acrimony, erupted. Educator William C. Bagley began the charge. In *School and Society*, a progressive education journal, he questioned the psychologists' definition of intelligence and lambasted the "educational determinism" inherent in the tests' application.[14] Meanwhile, black intellectuals voiced their own dissent. In the pages of *Opportunity* and *Crisis*, for instance, Davis's friend Horace Mann Bond criticized the tests as racially biased.[15]

The most public controversy occurred in the *New Republic*, as journalist Walter Lippmann roundly criticized the tests over the course of several articles.[16] His attack was multifaceted. He questioned the notion that the tests measured hereditary ability more than environmental influences; he contended that psychologists' definitions of intelligence were unclear and unscientific; and he argued that the tests were far too susceptible to misuse and abuse in ways that subverted democracy.

In most of these debates, Lewis Terman was the opponent. In crusading fashion, Terman responded that intelligence was a hereditary trait, that the tests did measure it accurately, and that the tests should be used in all parts of society to classify people into different spheres. With characteristic zeal, he proclaimed, "If this, or even half of it, should be found true ... eugenics would deserve to become a religion."[17]

In the end, the controversies did not lead to practical reforms within intelligence testing. The tests had become too institutionalized, and the racist and xenophobic atmosphere of the time was not conducive to launching a social movement against them. Moreover, most public critics did agree that testing could be beneficial if implemented correctly, and most relied upon democratic theory as a basis of critique. The imposing language of science and engineering, and the sheer amassing of empirical data, lent more authority to the psychologists than to democratically minded critics to shape testing practices in the 1920s. It was not until the 1940s, when Allison Davis launched his empirical investigations into the cultural biases of intelligence tests, that critics would begin to confront mental testing on its own terms.[18]

TOWARD A NEW STUDY OF INTELLIGENCE TESTING

Davis's plan to challenge intelligence-testing practices had been brewing for some time. As a black intellectual looking to vindicate his race, Davis saw early on how intelligence tests were yet another tool to oppress African Americans. They did so by erroneously "proving" black people's mental inferiority and thus justifying racial disparities as natural. His friendship with Horace Mann Bond, who had examined the tests, only deepened his understanding of the tests' flaws.

Davis also looked to the burgeoning environmentalist research of the 1930s, which Columbia social psychologist Otto Klineberg epitomized.[19] Klineberg conducted a series of pathbreaking studies which exposed the power of the environment to shape a person's score on intelligence tests.[20] His work, in Davis's words, "has shown ... that the I.Q.'s of Negro children born in the South improve steadily with length of residence in New York or Philadelphia."[21] Recognizing the significance of that finding, Davis concluded that it "indicates the great power of better schools to raise the level of achievement by Negro pupils."[22]

Social biologist Lancelot Hogben was another prominent interwar voice whose environmentalist critiques of intelligence testing influenced Davis long after their time working together.[23] Davis later explained the importance of Hogben's work in human genetics as it pertained to his own project on intelligence:

> No geneticist, of any national or international standing, furthermore, will venture even the opinion that lower-class groups are genetically inferior. The leading men in the field of human genetics, like J. B. S. Haldane, Lancelot Hogben, and H. S. Jennings, have advanced both theoretical (mathematical) and specific evidence against the probability of the genetic inferiority of the lower social strata. Hogben, probably the most distinguished social biologist in the world, has said, in his *Nature and Nurture*, with specific reference to intelligence: "In the light of the new evidence derived from the study of twins, no conclusions about *inborn* differences based on comparisons of different occupational and racial groups, have any scientific validity."[24]

Thus Davis drew from the latest biological science to inform his developing critique of intelligence testing.

Yet another intellectual influence was the research emanating from the Iowa Child Welfare Research Station in the 1930s. The University of Iowa emerged as a major center for early environmentalist critiques of intelligence testing. Under the leadership of George Stoddard and Kurt Lewin, the Iowa Station demonstrated how IQ scores varied considerably depending on one's early childhood experiences within nursery schools, foster homes, and other learning environments.[25] Ralph Tyler, Davis's colleague and mentor at the University of Chicago, had been involved with propagating the Iowa School's findings through the Progressive Education Association. Davis was exposed to this work through Tyler, as well as the American Council on Education.[26]

Davis's own administration of intelligence tests also informed his critique. For his study of black adolescent personality, the American Youth Commission mandated that he and John Dollard use an array of intelligence tests.[27] The researchers found clear discrepancies between their own assessments of the youths' intelligence and the scores yielded by the tests. In *Children of Bondage* they highlighted the problem: "Mrs. Martin says that Edward has always been a smart boy. The psychologists disagree; they grant him an I.Q. of 71. The Doc, however, tended to agree with the mother. How shall one measure by standardized tests the skills of a boy who has learned to acquire the fruits of stealing and at the same time to escape being put into jail?"[28] For Davis it became clear that the formulaic nature of the tests rewarded middle-class training and punished students from lower-class backgrounds.

Davis's later studies of school acculturation only further proved to him that the intelligence tests were both deeply flawed and socially damaging. In 1944 he emerged from his two-month investigation of California schools convinced that the most pressing goal within education was the reform of these tests. As he saw it, they penalized lower-class children and stigmatized "the Negro and Mexican-American, and other low-status groups" as intellectually inferior. He lamented how teachers "use this 'scientific' judgment, as symbolized in the I.Q., to justify the schools' discrimination against colored pupils, and their own inefficient teaching." He recognized the urgency of the problem, for educators throughout the nation were routinely using these tests for such discriminatory ends.[29]

Notably, Davis's solution was not simply to eradicate the tests but to reform them and make them more objective. Like many of his contemporaries, he sought to use the power of social science to inform decisions and to engineer social practices. In his mind, the development of unbiased, or "culturally fair," tests was "the most practical inexpensive aid to the education of underprivileged white and colored groups in this country."[30] It was to this task that Davis now turned.

In 1945, as part of the Committee on Human Development (CHD), Davis began by spearheading an extensive study of the relationship between social-class background and performance on intelligence tests. As mentioned previously, this study was based in Rockford, Illinois.[31] Writing to the General Education Board, he proposed a three-year program through which researchers would uncover the class biases of traditional intelligence tests and then develop new, culturally fair ones.[32] The GEB approved a $25,940 grant to the University of Chicago in January 1945.[33]

Although Davis took the lead in conceptualizing the project, others ultimately carried out most of the fieldwork. A sociology graduate student named Charles Warriner and his wife completed much of the research in 1946, after which Kenneth Eells performed the statistical work.[34] Ernest A. Haggard, Robert J. Havighurst, Virgil E. Herrick, Edith Lind, and Ralph W. Tyler all participated in this project too.[35]

The team effort resulted in a wide-ranging study. In all, the investigators tested over forty-eight hundred Rockford children aged nine, ten, thirteen, and fourteen. They then correlated the results with Warner's and Eells's Index of

Status Characteristics, which sorted the children by social class.[36] By 1951 the team published the full research report, titled *Intelligence and Cultural Differences*.[37] The essential propositions of that book included—at times verbatim—the arguments that Davis and his colleagues had made in previous years.

SOCIAL-CLASS INFLUENCES UPON LEARNING

The most important statement of the study's intellectual orientation and contribution was in Davis's *Social-Class Influences upon Learning* (1948). This book was a published version of Davis's 1948 Inglis Lecture at Harvard University. In November 1947, Harvard's Graduate School of Education honored Davis for his work on social class and education by inviting him to give its prestigious annual lecture on American secondary education.[38] Previous Inglis lecturers included such notable figures as John Dewey and Edward Thorndike. For this presentation, Davis was forced to step back from the details of his research and convey his ideas to a wide audience. The one-hundred-page product was much more than a critique of traditional intelligence tests. It was a synthesis of Davis's almost two decades of social science research. By deeply contextualizing the problems of intelligence testing within the larger social-class system, Davis ultimately made a compelling argument against traditional intelligence tests.

Davis organized *Social-Class Influences upon Learning* into five parts, each of which marked a stage in his own intellectual evolution. In the first part he draws from his social-anthropological research to explain that social classes, ethnic groups, and color castes determined American social status. Each system dispensed rewards and punishments unequally depending upon one's social position.[39] Different social classes amounted to different social worlds. The second part explains the impact of social-class differences on patterns of early childhood socialization, drawing from Davis's culture-and-personality research. He argues that lower-class parents were generally more lenient, while middle-class parents tended to socialize their children more rigorously.[40]

The third part of the book discusses the different cultures, or learning environments, of the lower and middle classes. This section is Davis's fullest published examination of lower-class culture, in which he explains the logic of lower-class behaviors. He makes clear that lower-class people have their own standards of decency and morality, though these differ from those of the middle class.[41] This is only natural because the lower class developed its standards in a very different social, economic, and political environment.

The fourth part of the book examines the links between social class and intelligence scores. Here Davis finally discusses his latest research on intelligence testing. Davis and his colleagues found that "a large proportion of the items in each of these tests 'discriminated between' children from the highest and lowest socio-economic levels." The researchers discovered that certain tests and test items were more discriminatory than others, often because of the language used in them. For example, in test items using the word *sonata*, which lower-class children were almost never exposed to, only 28 percent of lower-class children scored it correctly, compared to 78 percent of children in the high socioeconomic group. But when intelligence tests used items with language that was easily understood across class lines, such as *cutting tool*, the class differentials nearly disappeared.[42]

Davis then launches into a general critique of intelligence-testing practices. He argues that psychologists, in their haste to devise practical tests of intelligence, failed to grasp the incredible complexity of a concept such as "intelligence." Drawing from A. R. Radcliffe-Brown's structural-functionalism, Davis explains that mental behavior is "a system in the sense that all 'mental' acts are interdependent and interconnected."[43] He understands intelligence not as an "essence" but as something that is phenomenal, organic, and inextricable from the larger human organism. He takes issue with psychometricians such as Charles Spearman who conceptualize intelligence as "one essential human ability," which they call "the general factor, or g."[44] Such psychometricians, Davis contends, fail to understand the difficulty in measuring something as intricate as intelligence, which is a complex "system of acts," none of which can be meaningfully isolated and then assessed independently.[45]

Still, Davis maintains that the tests' most significant problems could be resolved by accounting for cultural differences. He argues that "culture 'teaches' the individual not only to recognize certain phenomena, but also certain symbols of phenomena, and the logical relationships among them." Culture, furthermore, "sets the goals of human problems, and teaches the inferences (logic) which people in a particular culture regard as justifiable." Because individuals within particular social classes share similar social experiences, sanctions, patterns of behavior, and cultural logic, he believes it makes sense to conceptually isolate "class cultures" for the purpose of studying them. Using this reasoning, he makes the case that intelligence tests need to eliminate class biases if they are to assess general intelligence in any meaningful way. The point is always to measure individual ability rather than cultural training.[46]

Davis therefore spells out criteria for the creation of "culturally fair" tests; such tests must (1) refer to experiences equally common in the life of all socio-economic groups, (2) "be expressed in symbols, in words or pictures" equally common to all classes, and (3) "be such as to arouse approximately equal interest, attention, and desire to achieve their solution" among all socioeconomic groups. Notably, he does not seek "culture-free" tests, because he understands culture as inextricable and omnipresent.[47]

For Davis, culturally fair tests would control for social-class variables and draw from a "common American culture." It was here that Davis and his colleagues ran into their most intractable problem, for what precisely could count as "common culture" in a nation so racially, ethnically, and linguistically diverse? In the nationalistic postwar environment of "consensus," even Davis and other American intellectuals could genuinely believe in the possibility of a clear "American culture" or "American way of life."[48] Yet the hollowness of Davis's statements about this American culture belie the legitimacy of such a concept. For example, Davis refers vaguely to "American food habits" and cultural behaviors such as monogamy.[49] Rarely does he examine American culture more concretely. Creating test problems drawn from this notional common culture would prove difficult.

Consequently, Davis and his colleagues spent more energy purging social-class biases from intelligence tests, which they found to be legion. Davis discovered that two types of test questions predominated: those based upon "(1) verbal relationship and complex academic phrasing (such as verbal 'analogies' and 'opposites,' and 'syllogisms'); and (2) rare words (used in vocabulary tests and 'definitions')." Even though the more self-aware test creators recognized the cultural biases of tests so reliant upon language, they nevertheless held that the traditional tests were effective prognosticators of students' scholastic success. The problem was that such success really registered only the cumulative effects of social privilege. Moreover, Davis explains, "test-makers and academic people persist in the belief that verbal facility is the highest expression of mental capacity. Their own careers and training have emphasized linguistic skill above all other forms of learning." As a result, "since they make and administer the tests, they build into the tests, as most important, that particular element or factor which is most important in their own academic culture." Like middle-class families, industrialists, and school personnel, test makers are people who enshrined their class biases within testing.[50]

Davis draws from linguistic theory to critique the widespread notion that fluency in language equates with higher intelligence. He explains, "Any language is a highly formalized system of cultural behavior" that "must be learned by long experience in that cultural group which possesses the language." Stated differently, facility with language represents cultural training more than native ability. Furthermore, he declares, "the lower socio-economic groups have a different language-culture than the higher groups." Davis cites the work of Edward Sapir and Morris Swadesh in showing that the language of any particular group—"primitive" or "civilized"—is well suited for the needs of that group.[51] Davis extrapolates those ideas to lower-class groups, contending that their nonstandard dialects are as complex and functional as academic English. Intelligence tests therefore need to control for language differences if they are to measure innate ability.[52]

Davis concludes by discussing the preliminary findings of his and his colleagues' experimental tests of intelligence. After reducing class biases and better equalizing motivation for completing the tests successfully, Davis found that they had drastically reduced social-class differences with the intelligence tests.[53] From here he extends these insights into American education as a whole. Although purging the class biases of the tests is paramount, Davis argues that all aspects of education required transformation in light of his findings of class bias.

This is especially true for the curriculum, which is defined by members of the middle class. Thus schools overemphasize verbal fluency and comprehension. Davis finds the emphasis on reading to be problematic because reading "consists chiefly of learning to recognize written symbols, to pronounce them, and to paraphrase them." Learning to decode the language of others, Davis argues, is far less important than teaching a child "how to think, to develop his reason, his insight, his invention, his imagination." Education's main objective, then, should be to teach students how to solve problems and be effective workers and citizens in a democracy.[54]

Davis sees American schools as falling far short of this objective. He observes that schools tend to perpetuate, rather than mitigate, social inequality, and not only through intelligence tests. While the most important of these practices is racial segregation, Davis here criticizes the widespread practice of homogenous ability grouping. Very early in a student's career, teachers combine intelligence tests, reading scores, and their own assessments—all of which are culturally biased in favor of the middle class—to segregate students into different ability groups. In effect, ability grouping leads to segregation along class lines. This segregation stigmatizes lower-class children as intellectually inferior, and it further alienates them from an educational system that already seems unrealistic and largely irrelevant to them. Thus ability grouping sets up "different social and cultural groups within the school" and establishes "different learning environments." The net result is harm for all students. Rather than learning the diverse skills and experiences of children from different backgrounds, segregated students are denied opportunities for cultural exchange and engagement.[55]

In the end, *Social-Class Influences upon Learning* offers a concise and compelling examination of social-class stratification within American education. Each part synthesizes years of research into an accessible framework that made all of Davis's social science work comprehensible to a wide audience. The book was most influential, however, for its indictment of intelligence-testing practices.

FINDING AN AUDIENCE

Social-Class Influences upon Learning met with immediate commercial success. By 1950 the book was in its third printing and had sold over forty-five hundred copies, more than any other Inglis Lecture in the previous twenty years. In addition, "many of the largest universities" used it as a text and would continue to do so for the next three decades.[56] Davis also gave talks at major universities all over the country, including Berkeley and Minnesota.[57]

One of the most important professional forums for his ideas, however, was the esteemed journal *Scientific Monthly*. In April 1948 he and Robert Havighurst published an article that conveyed their research findings on class biases within intelligence testing.[58] Tellingly, *Scientific Monthly* had recently published a racist article by Henry E. Garrett, chair of Columbia's Department of Psychology and former president of the American Psychological Association. He was a eugenicist and an ardent proponent of racial segregation who vocally condemned *Brown v. Board of Education* (1954). In his article, he argued that it was "extremely unlikely . . . that environmental opportunities can possibly explain *all* the differences found" between the test scores of whites and blacks, and thus revealed the extent to which racist thinking endured within mainstream social science.[59]

Yet those who believed in innate racial differences in intelligence were only one group of Davis's critics. The psychologists who developed the tests and the industries that profited from their proliferation were the two biggest groups. Arthur S. Otis, one of the leading intelligence-test makers and a onetime director of Test Services for World Book Company, soon gave voice to such critiques in a long rejoinder to Davis and Havighurst's article. Otis argued that the authors were biased in assuming, but not proving, the equal intelligence of people from different socioeconomic groups. In social-Darwinian fashion, he contended that "logical reasoning" makes clear that higher socioeconomic groups would be more intelligent. As he understood it, "in the long run the less favored individuals—those with less hereditary ability to solve life's problems and adjust themselves, especially in these days of insecurity—must necessarily tend to gravitate into the lower socioeconomic groups."[60] Henry Chauncey, director of the Educational Testing Service, a private nonprofit testing company founded in 1947 that fundamentally transformed testing practices in the United States, was another prominent person who expressed the same thinking.[61]

Davis and Havighurst quickly refuted Otis's arguments. They explained, first, that they had not simply assumed that all socioeconomic groups are equal in intelligence. Rather, they drew that idea from the latest genetic science. Citing the work of J. B. S. Haldane, Julian Huxley, and Lancelot Hogben, the authors showed that genetics refuted Otis's "logical reasoning" at every turn. Above all, they argued that genetic adaptations among humans occur very slowly over long periods, meaning that socioeconomic differences over the course of a few generations would not affect innate intelligence.[62]

They then pivoted to a practical argument. They reasoned that even if some innate differences do exist, there would still be far more lower-class individuals endowed with greater innate intelligence than in the upper classes, simply because there are so many more lower-class people. Finally, they critiqued the oft-proclaimed defense of intelligence tests as useful and harmless prognosticators of individuals' scholastic success. Davis and Havighurst explained that the tests do not merely predict success but are active in determining it, favoring affluent people and penalizing those worse off.[63]

That such arguments took place within the pages of *Scientific Monthly* illustrates the wide interest that Davis's ideas were garnering. Indeed, readers began writing to Davis to profess support for his position and to request further information. One was Orval Hobart Mowrer, who became the president of the American Psychological Association in 1954. In correspondence with Davis, Mowrer said that Davis's arguments were more compelling than Otis's.[64] Davis reported his satisfaction to the General Education Board that "Havighurst's and my rejoinder to [Otis] brought a good response from psychologists."[65]

Intelligence and Cultural Differences was another important instrument for the diffusion of Davis's ideas. In addition to regular sales, the authors distributed two hundred copies of the book to "leaders and influential persons in the field of mental testing and measurement."[66] In the book Davis reprinted largely verbatim his work from *Scientific Monthly* and the Inglis Lecture. However, because *Intelligence and Cultural Differences* was reviewed widely, it better exposes how the social science community greeted his ideas.

Scholars at home and abroad reviewed the book quite positively in venues including *Elementary School Journal* and *U.S. Quarterly Book Review*.[67] A reviewer in the *Teachers College Record* reported that the book was "so important and so challenging" that it occasioned a symposium "organized around the

'Implications of the Chicago Studies of Intelligence and Cultural Differences' at the annual meeting of the American Psychological Association'" in 1952.[68]

Criticisms of the book centered on a few areas. First, some reviewers disliked the presentation of the book. Anthropologist Charles F. Harding called it "overly long and detailed" given the "essential simplicity of the conclusions reached."[69] Second, some reviewers sought greater theoretical clarification, with one arguing that the results would be clearer if the authors had made "distinctions between three types of intelligence: genetic, developmental, and test."[70] A third and more telling criticism revolved around the authors' recommendation to abolish the traditional tests. Sociologist William H. Sewell, along with many others, wanted to salvage the current tests, arguing that abolition was unnecessary, unrealistic, and problematic. Sewell maintained that there were "many legitimate uses for existing intelligence tests," particularly predicting scholastic success.[71] Like Arthur Otis, Sewell sidestepped the problem that the tests did not merely predict success but actually helped to determine it.

The richest review by far was that of psychologist S. Stansfeld Sargent in the *American Journal of Sociology*. Sargent contextualized the study in the history of social scientific investigations into intelligence testing. He praised the book for exposing the social-class biases within intelligence tests, and he admired its interdisciplinarity. Yet he also perceived the fundamental weakness of the research project: the "common-culture" approach required "limiting the test to such a narrow range of experiences that it could not possibly be representative of the most important kinds of problem-solving ability in either high-status or low-status culture." He exposed the hollowness of the concept of a "common culture." Social class, in the end, informs every aspect of people's behavior, values, and motivations. Eliminating class bias is therefore not only impossible but also fatal to the potential value of any intelligence test. The authors recognized the predicament, and this helps to explain why Davis and his colleagues ultimately failed to develop commercially viable alternative tests.[72]

The real importance of Davis's work was in rethinking intelligence more broadly, in light of the cultural biases throughout the educational system. For that reason, professional educators paid close attention to his ideas, especially when he published them in various educational organs.[73] In response to one article in *Educational Leadership*, the National Education Association journal, which reached over four hundred thousand readers, Davis received "more than 350 letters."[74]

Davis used other forums to broadcast his ideas as well. He gave presentations at Harvard, Columbia, Northwestern, Iowa, the American Psychological

FIGURE 8.1. Allison and Elizabeth Davis in Washington, DC, on December 6, 1950. Courtesy of the Davis Family.

Association, the American Educational Research Association, and the International Society for the Study of Exceptional Children, to name a few. Most important, Davis presented at the 1950 White House Conference on Children and Youth.[75] Remarkably, he was "the only speaker on the program with President Truman on the morning of December 5, 1951."[76] The conference, held every ten years since 1919, this time focused on personality development and adjustment.[77] Many of the nation's foremost scholars in the field, including

Benjamin Spock, Margaret Mead, Bruno Bettelheim, Erik Erikson, and Franz Alexander, convened to present their research.[78] Black psychologist Kenneth Clark also presented a paper on the effects of prejudice and discrimination on children's personalities. He cited his famous "doll test," in which black children's preference for a white doll over a black one seemed to suggest their internalized belief in their own racial inferiority.[79]

Davis calibrated his conference talk, "Socio-economic Influence upon Children's Learning," to appeal to Americans in the context of the Cold War.[80] Rather than make moralistic arguments about helping the underprivileged, he made practical, nationalistic arguments. Davis revealed that the United States wasted nearly 60 percent of its human resources by failing to develop and take advantage of the abilities of lower-class Americans. The reasons for this failure were "(a) the failure of intelligence tests to measure the real mental ability of the children from the lower socio-economic groups, and (b) the failure of the schools to recognize and train this ability."[81] The crisis was clear:

> This country cannot survive as the leading world power, unless we learn how to discover, recruit, and train more of the brains in the lower-income groups. If we cannot find more people with quick minds and native-ability in the great reservoir of the lower-income groups in the United States . . . we shall not be able to compete with the vast populations of western Europe or Asia. . . . If our society is to increase its strength, we need to recruit ability of all kinds from the lower socio-economic groups. When any nation stops recruiting or slows it down through the failure to discover the able but poor children, and to develop their abilities, that nation starts to decline and die. There have been no exceptions to this rule in the history of modern nations.[82]

This jarring language resonated with many Americans in the context of chronic insecurity and anxiety surrounding the Cold War and the Red Scare. Davis's provocative talk was circulated to a national audience by various news organizations.[83]

The late 1940s and early 1950s marked the height of Cold War fears about nuclear holocaust and another global conflagration. In rapid succession, a series of foreign and domestic developments created an atmosphere of insecurity. Joseph Stalin denied free elections in Poland, took control of Czechoslovakia, and hardened the Soviets' position in Eastern Germany. In 1949 the Soviets developed an atomic bomb and China had a communist revolution. All of this pushed the United States to enter a war in Korea in June 1950 to prevent what policy makers perceived as communist aggression.

Speaking shortly after Davis at the White House Conference on Children and Youth, President Truman sought to garner support for his aggressive foreign policy. He alerted Americans that "the effort of the evil forces of Communism to reach out and dominate the world confronts our nation and our civilization with the greatest challenge in our history." He insisted that only massive rearmament and permanent military readiness "can insure our survival as a nation."[84] In this context, Davis's call to mobilize all the country's human resources for national strength was compelling.[85]

Yet of all of them, it was probably his presentations before the American Association of School Administrators (AASA)—what Ralph Tyler called "the most powerful education association in the country"—that proved the most important in disseminating Davis's ideas.[86] The high-level administrators in this organization had broad authority in setting school policy.[87] In 1949 Davis presented his research on intelligence testing at the AASA's regional meetings in San Francisco, St. Louis, and Philadelphia. The San Francisco conference alone included "four thousand superintendants, educators, college professors and other administrators," while the Philadelphia meeting drew five thousand.[88] In part because Davis had already made personal and institutional connections with educators in California through his earlier study there, his presentation in San Francisco proved the most influential. Indeed, Davis's ideas soon prompted Lewis Terman to defend intelligence tests at the International Council for Exceptional Children.[89] The president of Science Research Associates later confided to Davis, "your lectures created a sensation on the West Coast."[90]

Davis was already aware of the sensation because of the deluge of letters he received from conference participants. One field representative for the California Teachers Association thanked him for his "powerful address."[91] Another told him that papers like his "embody a kind of leadership that America badly needs."[92] Almost everyone who wrote Davis asked him for more information, or even for copies of his presentation to share with others.[93] The director of secondary instruction of San Diego City Schools summed up many educators' sentiments when he wrote, "I believe that it will cause more discussion by educators the country over than any talk that has been given before such groups in recent years."[94] Soon members of the black community also wrote letters to him. One teacher in the public schools gave voice to the common sentiment that the tests had "not been used wisely," then thanked Davis for being so "far-seeing."[95]

The *New York Times* spread the sensation by publishing two articles that discussed the nature and impact of Davis's presentation in San Francisco.

Reporter Benjamin Fine spent one third of his main article, intended to cover the entire conference, on Davis's "extremely provocative and challenging paper." After summarizing Davis's main arguments about intelligence testing, Fine reported, "Educators were quick to see the far-reaching implications of this report." The conference attendees "realized that if the Chicago study holds up under further analysis, many of the accepted dogmas and principles of our school program would have to be seriously revised." Because "the I.Q. tests are used to separate children into various groupings either in or out of the classroom," Fine declared that "the entire concept of the 'intellectually gifted classes' and the 'superior' groupings in school rooms throughout the country would have to be reconsidered.[96] Another article two days later reiterated the same points.[97]

The *Times* articles prompted personnel at institutions as diverse as Boston University, the Detroit Board of Education, and the Pine Mountain Settlement School in Kentucky to write Davis to voice their support and ask for more information.[98] Davis had tapped into a widely held concern among educators that their assessments of students' abilities failed to match up with IQ scores. A professor of education at West Virginia University, for instance, explained to Davis that his skepticism about "so-called intelligence examinations . . . was greatly increased during my period in the United States Indian Service when I discovered that Indian children appeared always to rate so much lower by these tests than white children, whose intellectual capacity I would have rated no higher."[99] Another educator in Kentucky reached the same skeptical position after working with children "who are supposed to be 'inferior' on more than one count, being not merely Southern and rural but 'mountain.'"[100] Here experience taught educators to recognize bias.

African Americans were already keenly aware of the cultural bias of traditional intelligence tests. They understood that Davis's work was as much about race as it was about class, since blacks were disproportionately lower class and hence disproportionate victims of the tests. Black newspapers praised Davis's work, with an editorial in the *Chicago Defender* referring to Davis's project as of the "utmost importance to Negro America," while also recognizing that African Americans had in fact been waging "the battle on the I.Q. front" for many years.[101] The editors knew both intuitively and empirically that the "failure of intelligence tests is that essentially they measure the literacy and culture of a person rather than their native intelligence."[102] The color-caste system, black critics maintained, ensured that black people's access to literacy and culture was always impeded. Most educators, however, according to the editors of the *Chicago Bee*, missed this environmental explanation for racial differences. The devastating consequences were profound: "the public schools used the present unsound tests as the basis for saddling Negro pupils with inferior equipment, curricula, and standards of education."[103] Other black columnists feared even more dire consequences from such racist views of intelligence. Reporter Jacqueline Lopez, for instance, explained that they "periodically lead to violence." Indeed, Lopez continued, "most notorious of these misconceptions—that some human beings are innately inferior to others—gave rise to the Nazi 'superman' philosophy, and is used by Americans to justify the persecution of the Negro."[104]

The impact of Davis's work was significant, though it is impossible to know how many school districts discontinued their use of intelligence tests around this time. The outpouring of positive responses to Davis's ideas among superintendents, teachers, and professors of education suggests large numbers. Yet Davis was probably more effective in pushing educators to use tests more critically and alongside other diagnostics. Perhaps even more important, many of the tests themselves became less culturally biased as the testing industry worked to fend off Davis's critiques by revamping them.[105]

REFORM DEFERRED

Despite their many achievements, Davis and his colleagues could not successfully orchestrate more systematic changes to intelligence testing in the 1940s and 1950s. The timing was simply not right. To be sure, Davis had tapped into a deep populist resentment against intelligence testing. But such latent hostility ran up against practical concerns, not to mention the entrenched interests of several groups. Challenging the interests of publishing companies, schools, corporations, and psychologists required more than sound critiques. It demanded a social movement.

Postwar America was not conducive to such a movement. With wartime demobilization and the beginnings of the "baby boom," the need to sort Americans into segments seemed only to increase. Applied psychology proliferated as psychologists devised practical ways to "adjust" Americans to various social institutions.[106] The Great Depression had nurtured radicalism and prompted Americans to mobilize against social inequality, but in the postwar period Americans focused more on expanding opportunity than on confronting the power structure.

It might have helped if Davis and his colleagues had been more successful in developing alternative, "culturally fair" tests that could have supplanted the traditional tests. This proved more difficult than Davis and his colleagues had imagined. By 1948, when the GEB's three-year grant ended, the CHD had made very little progress on that front, and it failed to win an additional grant to help with "developing and standardizing the new tests."[107] Thus the task of developing new tests increasingly fell to Davis alone. In August 1950 he reported, "I have taken off four quarters from teaching, without salary, in order to construct my tests. That is, I gave up salary for that period. I have therefore put the equivalent of about $11,000 into the tests, in addition to $750 which I have paid of my own money for the drawing of items."[108]

By 1951 Davis and Kenneth Eells finally succeeded. They developed a "common-culture" test, which became known as the Davis-Eells Test.[109] Davis marketed the test not only to schools but also to industry and the military.[110] He argued that all these institutions needed to better identify and recruit lower-class ability. The Davis-Eells Test was a valiant effort to measure mental ability in unbiased ways. It consisted of a series of cartoons in which test takers would interpret images of ordinary people in easily recognizable situations. For example, one test item showed the examinee a particular image while an examiner (who had established rapport with the examinees) read aloud the following:

> This picture shows a woman; it shows a man with a bump on his head; and it shows a broken window. A boy is outside the window. Look at the picture and find out the thing that is true. (1) The man fell down and hit his head. (2) The ball came through the window and hit the man's head. (3) The picture does not show how the man got the bump on his head. Nobody can tell because the picture doesn't show how the man got the bump.[111]

The test required no reading, and it had no time limit—both of which were factors favoring middle-class test takers.[112] The Davis-Eells Test aimed to measure general reasoning ability and practical problem-solving skills in unbiased ways. To assess older and brighter students, the items demanded that test takers draw increasingly complex inferences and judgments from the cartoons.

Davis, Eells, Robert Hess, and others at the University of Chicago ultimately found the tests to be successful in reducing class bias.[113] Equally important, they found that the tests remained effective in measuring individual differences while also predicting scholastic success. Not surprisingly, most psychologists disagreed. An array of independent studies reported that the Davis-Eells Test produced a similar level of discrimination along social-class, ethnic, and rural–urban lines.[114] One study concluded that "the Davis-Eells Games do not tend to reveal a 'hidden intellectual potential'—by virtue of their elimination of culturally unfair items—not tapped by other intelligence tests presumed to be culturally biased."[115] Professional symposia also featured attacks on the test, illustrating yet again how challenging Davis's ideas were at the time.[116]

The Davis-Eells Test may not have been a great alternative to traditional tests. It was cumbersome to administer and arguably not very effective in predicting scholastic success. Furthermore, the idea of a "common culture" was hopelessly vague, and the cartoon format made it difficult to assess more sophisticated types of thinking. Nevertheless, the seriousness of Davis's critique did not rise and fall on the tenability of any particular alternative test. His challenge was not merely to traditional tests but to traditional methods of schooling and customary ways of thinking about intelligence. Test specialists emphasized the weaknesses of the Davis-Eells Test to cleverly divert attention from the irrefutable charges of cultural bias. In the 1940s and 1950s they were largely successful in muffling Davis's critiques and overseeing a continued proliferation of the traditional tests.

Despite the success of vested interests in the 1950s, the situation looked very different two decades later. In 1972 Davis surveyed his own influence and reported satisfactorily: "This was one time I got what I wanted: a direct effect on society from social science research."[117] Indeed, Davis's work was rediscovered and redeployed during the 1960s and 1970s in movements for social change. Even though his contributions were not always acknowledged and appreciated, his efforts in overseeing the first quantitative, empirical studies of cultural bias in intelligence testing underpinned progressive changes in testing in the next generation.

The process began in the 1960s, when an atmosphere of protest over inequality and suspicion of expert authority prevailed. Young Americans questioned Jim Crow, poverty, sexism, Cold War foreign policy, and antidemocratic practices everywhere. The civil rights movement fueled the protest and empowered African Americans and others to demand social justice in many arenas. In this environment, Davis's critiques of the biases within intelligence testing influenced a variety of activists. Davis continued to speak on these issues in the 1960s, and he found an increasingly interested public. For instance, he gave a talk on the social factors shaping IQ scores before the American Home Economics Association in 1965, which the *Chicago Tribune* and the *Washington Post* broadcast to a larger audience.[118] A year earlier Ralph McGill, an opponent of segregation and a Pulitzer Prize–winning journalist, drew directly from Davis's research in objecting to the tests, which he said were "based on a super middle and upper class culture."[119] Commentators found Davis's earlier studies to lend validity to their own social critiques and thus to bolster their movements for social change.

As African Americans fought for the end of Jim Crow, for fair housing and employment practices, and against institutional racism of all sorts, many of them also harnessed the power of their movement to critique intelligence testing. The Association of Black Psychologists (ABP) led the way here. Black activists formed the organization in 1968 after the assassination of Martin Luther King Jr. Recognizing the institutional racism within white-dominated organizations such as the American Psychological Association, ABP members exemplified Black Nationalist trends across the country by developing their own black-controlled institution dedicated to black liberation from poverty and racism.

One of the founders of the ABP was Robert L. Williams. When Williams was in high school, he had scored 82 on an IQ test. Had he scored only three points lower, he would have been placed on a special-education track. His counselor told him that he was clearly not equipped for college and that bricklaying suited him well. Williams ignored his advice and eventually went on to earn a PhD and become a professor of psychology at Washington University in St. Louis.[120] His own experience had made him painfully aware of the tests' biases, which he gradually came to see as racial in nature and systematic in effect.

Williams therefore took the lead in ABP efforts to challenge intelligence-testing practices from within the discipline. He built explicitly from Davis's research to carry out further research showing that intelligence tests were biased in favor of the white middle class.[121] Reflecting the more confrontational attitudes of the time, Williams also developed two tests—provocatively called the B.I.T.C.H. (Black Intelligence Test of Cultural Homogeneity) and the S.O.B. (Son of the Original Bitch test)—that measured white people's knowledge, or lack thereof, of the black experience.[122] The idea was to reveal in humiliating fashion just how ignorant whites were of black culture, and just how racially biased all the intelligence tests were, because of the vastly different cultural experiences of white and black people. In an earlier context, Davis had sought to exploit opportunities for racial integration by deemphasizing cultural differences between the races and attacking intelligence tests on class grounds. But in the era of Black Power, black critics rejected the idea of assimilation into white culture, and they celebrated what they perceived to be a unique and vibrant black culture. Consequently, Williams emphasized the racial as well as the class biases of the tests.

At the ABP's 1969 annual meeting, Williams and other members called for an immediate moratorium on the testing of African Americans' IQs. The members charged that the tests

1. Label black children as uneducable;
2. Place black children in special classes;
3. Potentiate inferior education;
4. Assign black children to lower education tracks than whites;
5. Deny black children higher educational opportunities;
6. Destroy positive intellectual growth and development of black children.[123]

By drawing upon Davis's empirical studies of the biases of intelligence tests, the ABP's arguments gained further credibility and validity.

With a larger social movement behind the protests, major changes began to take place. Members of marginalized groups took to the courts to challenge the discrimination in intelligence tests, and the courts began to rule in their favor. In *Hobsen v. Hansen* (1967), Circuit Judge J. Skelly Wright outlawed the tracking system in Washington, DC, on the grounds that it was used to perpetuate racial inequality and to resist the mandated racial desegregation of the schools.[124] Criticizing the tests along the same lines as Davis, Wright wrote, "The skills measured by scholastic aptitude tests are verbal. More precisely, an aptitude test is essentially a test of the student's command of standard English and grammar."[125] He continued,

> Whether a test is verbal or nonverbal, the skills being measured are not innate or inherited traits. They are learned, acquired through experience. It used to be the prevailing theory that aptitude tests—or "intelligence" tests as they are often called, although the term is obviously misleading—do measure some stable, predetermined intellectual process that can be isolated and called intelligence. Today, modern experts in educational testing and psychology have rejected this concept as false.[126]

Wright may not have been familiar with Davis's work in particular, but the modern expertise to which he referred was built upon Davis's empirical investigations two decades earlier.

Other rulings across the country used analogous reasoning, including *Diana et al. v. California Board of Education* (1970) and *Larry P. et al. v. Wilson Riles, Superintendent of Public Instruction for the State of California* (1979). The latter case outlawed the use of IQ tests for all black children in California schools.[127]

By the 1970s, critics of intelligence testing had largely won the public debate. This was striking, given that serious public interest in the issue had surfaced only a few years before, notably with the publication of Banesh Hoffman's *The Tyranny of Testing* in 1962. The fierce criticism that greeted psychologists Arthur Jensen and Richard Herrnstein when they reiterated the role of heredity within group intelligence testified to the new hostility toward the tests, which many now saw as antidemocratic and racist.[128] In 1972 the National Education Association (NEA) captured the spirit of the times by making its annual conference theme "Tests and Use of Tests—Violations of Human and Civil Rights." The NEA's objective was "to create greater national awareness of an immediate need for concerted action to prohibit the use of IQ and other test scores as indicators of growth potential; especially for the culturally different learner."[129] Davis's position, once marginal and muted, had finally become mainstream.

Throughout the ensuing years, further devastating critiques of mental testing arose, even as the tests ironically remained a staple within American society.[130] Registering the distance Americans had come on the issue, when Richard Herrnstein allied with political scientist Charles Murray in 1994 to publish yet another hereditarian tract on human intelligence, *The Bell Curve*, the critical response was once again overwhelmingly negative.[131]

In all these struggles, Allison Davis's shadow loomed large. He built from the long tradition of environmentalist thought to develop the first quantitative, empirical critiques of cultural bias within intelligence tests. He also underlined the significance of his findings by emphasizing the devastating social— and more subtly, moral—effects of wasting human potential. He argued that intelligence-testing practices, by arbitrarily circumscribing individual development and ratifying social inequality, actively subverted democracy and the principles of fairness and equality that underpinned it. At midcentury, he and his colleagues at the University of Chicago labored in an environment often hostile to their work. But their research nevertheless paved the way for future critiques, and it informed the social activism of the next generation, which was better positioned to foment major social change.

CHAPTER 9

From *Brown v. Board* to Head Start

What is now required is not equality of *access* to education. What is needed to solve our current as well as future crises in education is a system of compensatory education which can prevent or overcome earlier deficiencies in the development of each individual.[1]

ALLISON DAVIS

Following his efforts on intelligence testing, Allison Davis entered a less productive stage of his career. He had finally gained a modicum of financial stability after earning tenure at Chicago in 1947, but the decades of vigorous work and the string of racial humiliations he had to endure all took their toll. Surely the challenges of being an iconoclast also wore him down. His pioneering work on racial caste was misunderstood and often seen as irrelevant in postwar America. So, too, was his work on social class. And in intelligence testing, mainstream psychologists and others were rebuffing his alternative tests and squelching efforts for serious reform. So by the 1950s, some of the very traits that made Davis such an important figure deepened his own frustration as people failed to appreciate his work and to act upon his ideas.

Davis's personal life at times contributed to a gloomy mental state. In the 1950s his wife Elizabeth struggled with health problems. By the mid-1960s she was dying of cancer, to which she succumbed in January 1966. Around that time Allison had written a retrospective essay for a new abridged version of *Deep South*. He gave a copy to his son Gordon inscribed: "I wrote my Retrospect, 1965 when my wife was ill. I thought I couldn't write then. Upon reading it in print I regret only that I have spent so little of my last 20 years in writing. It is a solid reward. And I am proud of what I wrote here."[2] In a moment darkened by the loss of his emotional and intellectual partner of almost forty years, he confided to his other son, Allison, that his life had always been "miserable." The remark registered the psychological toll of living as a black person in a caste society and of a lifetime spent in near-singular pursuit of academic excellence. Davis's declining productivity by the 1950s was partly the product of

FIGURE 9.1. The Davis family after the graduation of Gordon Davis from Williams College in 1963. Left to right: John Aubrey Davis, Elizabeth Davis, Allison Davis, and Gordon Davis. Courtesy of the Davis Family.

burnout and despair, but also a new resolve to enjoy life and to make it about more than work.

After his grief subsided, Davis took pleasure in the opportunities still ahead of him. In the late 1960s he began courting Lois S. Mason, a close friend since his years at Dillard University. The two married on January 7, 1969, and Mason's exuberant nature boosted his and his children's spirits.

Davis's two sons also provided him with a deep sense of pride and hope for the future. Allison S. and Gordon J. Davis had become significant figures in their own right, following the example of race leadership which their father had embodied. Both sons chose the legal profession as a practical way to fight racial discrimination and inequality. Allison S. Davis worked for racial integration as a senior partner in housing development firms in Chicago, one of which employed Barack Obama in the 1990s. In the 1970s Gordon Davis served as the first African American commissioner of New York City's Department of Parks and Recreation, and he later worked as a partner in various firms supporting progressive causes relating to real estate, land use, and the environment.[3]

FIGURE 9.2. Allison Davis, circa 1960. Courtesy of the Davis Family.

Even while W. Allison Davis struggled with despair, he continued to be a quintessential professional. He threw more energy into teaching, and he developed meaningful relationships with students such as Leon Forrest, who became a notable African American novelist and professor of English at Northwestern. Reed Ueta, a historian at Tufts University, recalled Davis's teaching style of the early 1970s: "Davis used a type of Socratic method to explore students' thoughts about human development in childhood, adolescence, and adulthood. However, unlike other professors who used it in a confrontational way to produce a preconceived conclusion for students to accept, Professor Davis used it in an encouraging way to create an open discussion in which students expressed their insights and interpretations." Capturing Davis's appeal to generations of students, Ueta noted further that Davis "created an atmosphere in class that was intellectually uncompromising, while remaining respectful of differing views and unpoliticized. He interacted with a modest, caring and understanding attitude. He responded to students who approached him with an inviting sensitivity and amicability, touched with a sense of good humor."[4]

Davis did continue various lines of research. One project analyzed the psychology behind middle-class socialization patterns, work he had begun with *Children of Bondage*. In 1960 the University of Pittsburgh invited him to give its Horace Mann Lecture, which he published as *Psychology of the Child of the Middle Class* (1960).[5] In a familiar fashion, he argued that middle-class patterns of socialization which encouraged delayed gratification and sublimation were psychologically costly, resulting in heightened levels of anxiety among middle-class youth. This approach was useful in highlighting problems within dominant patterns of socialization that many people accepted unthinkingly. Elsewhere, Davis further explored the role of anxiety, aggression, and identity in facilitating social mobility.[6]

Another project was a longitudinal study of young people which he conducted with Robert Hess in the 1950s and 1960s. In *Achievement in Adolescence and Young Adulthood* (1963), he and Hess argued that, contrary to received wisdom, adolescents do not resolve their identity crises nor complete their ego development during adolescence.[7] The authors found that people do not fully develop psychologically until early adulthood, which implied that adolescents should not yet be treated as full adults and that adolescents need to be better supported throughout the development process. Davis fine-tuned these ideas while serving as a fellow in the Center for Advanced Study in the Behavioral Sciences in Palo Alto, California, from 1959 to 1960.

Even though the depth and breadth of Davis's research waned after 1950, that did not stop him from being involved in some of the most historic developments in American society in the postwar years. The Supreme Court's ruling in *Brown v. Board of Education* and the launching of the federal Head Start program were two such watershed moments. His involvement was both direct and indirect, but it was above all the rigor of his earlier scholarship which underpinned his contributions.

Nevertheless, as before, some of Davis's relevant ideas did not become part of these larger efforts for social justice because they challenged dominant assumptions. In *Brown*, Davis's refusal to emphasize the psychological damage that segregation exacted upon black people minimized his direct intellectual contribution. In Head Start, which the Johnson administration inaugurated speedily and haphazardly, Davis provided empirical support for the program, but he also went further by stressing the need for greater educational support throughout childhood and adolescence. Finally, in the fierce debates over poverty in the wake of Head Start, in which misguided conceptions of a "culture of poverty" prevailed, Davis's own scholarship had much to offer. Unlike most white liberals discussing poverty, Davis emphasized the complex interplay between economic and cultural forces, and he documented the resiliency of the poor while not stigmatizing them.

That Davis was not more widely consulted revealed how much institutional racism and his own iconoclasm had marginalized him. But as he bore witness to this history, his example makes clearer the power dynamics, ideological contexts, and missed opportunities characterizing these heady years.

BROWN V. BOARD OF EDUCATION

Davis helped to lay the intellectual foundations for *Brown v. Board*. Three areas of his research made particularly strong cases against segregation.[8] For one, Davis's social-anthropological analyses of racial caste amounted to a devastating indictment of segregation and racial stratification. His environmentalist critiques confirmed that segregation was arbitrary, unfair, and debilitating for African Americans. Furthermore, by linking caste to the class system, this work showed that caste exacerbates class inequities that hurt most white people as well.

Davis's culture-and-personality research was also influential. It explained that racial caste unjustly circumscribes the lives of black youths across the country. Although Davis humanized the youths and explained their behaviors as rational adaptations to difficult environments, he also showed that caste controls create frustration and aggression among them and therefore hinder their healthy social development.

Davis's third critique of segregation was even more directly relevant. It dealt explicitly with the effects of racial segregation in the schools. In his research on school acculturation, he showed that segregation prevents lower-class and minority children from learning the dominant middle-class culture, and thus served to maintain rather than offset social divisions. Davis argued that school segregation hurts more privileged Americans, too, by preventing them from learning the skills and cultures of people in other social strata. All of this underpinned the contention that school segregation undermined American democracy as a whole, which was an abiding concern of the Supreme Court.

Indeed, if a successful democracy depends upon not only opportunity for all but also rigorous engagement between citizens, then school segregation was a pressing national concern.

Yet despite its relevance, Davis's research played a surprisingly minor role within the *Brown* proceedings. The reasons soon became clear. The chief NAACP attorney, Thurgood Marshall, made the discourse of "damage" central to the plaintiff's arguments. As he later explained it, "We had to try this case just like any other one in which you would try to prove damages to your client. If your car ran over my client, you'd have to pay up, and my function as an attorney would be to put experts on the stand to testify to how much damage was done."[9]

Marshall and other NAACP attorneys turned to recent social-psychological research on racial prejudice to bolster their arguments. They had much to draw from. Postwar social science deemphasized analyses of racial stratification, prioritizing instead studies of racism as a psychological problem in the minds of individual white people. The standing of books such as Theodor Adorno et al.'s *The Authoritarian Personality* (1950), Abram Kardiner and Lionel Ovesey's *The Mark of Oppression* (1951), Gordon Allport's *The Nature of Prejudice* (1954), and Kenneth Clark's *Prejudice and Your Child* (1955) testifies to the dominance of this type of social science, which emphasized how racial prejudice damages black personalities. The NAACP's Legal Defense and Education Fund (LDEF) fittingly chose Clark to head up its social science team. His research strengthened the claim that segregation caused psychological damage to black children.[10]

In December 1952, Clark and other social scientists submitted an amicus brief that laid out the damage themes. The brief, which the *Minnesota Law Review* published for a wider audience in May 1953, argued that segregation "damaged children of the minority groups." He continued, "As minority group children learn the inferior status to which they are assigned—as they observe the fact that they are almost always segregated and kept apart from others who are treated with more respect by the society as a whole—they often react with feelings of inferiority and a sense of personal humiliation." Most disturbingly, he claimed, segregation leads a black person "to self-hatred and rejection of his own group." In addition to citing an abundance of social science research, Clark and the NAACP-LDEF also solicited signatures from leading social scientists. Thirty-two of them—including Allison Davis—signed Clark's brief and enhanced the document's authority.[11]

On May 17, 1954, Chief Justice Earl Warren explicitly cited the social scientists' work when he wrote the court's unanimous opinion that segregation violates the Fourteenth Amendment. He used that research to lend credence to the court's decision that de jure school segregation deprived the plaintiffs of equal protection under the law.[12] Furthermore, Warren's argument that "separate educational facilities are inherently unequal" depended upon the idea that segregation causes psychological damage to black children. In public, the justices downplayed the influence of social science in their ruling because most jurists saw it as irrelevant to the constitutional issues at hand. But the ruling was nevertheless rooted in and justified by the damage imagery.[13]

Although Davis signed the amicus brief, his research was not very helpful in delineating segregation's damage. Indeed, the bulk of Davis's work eschewed expositions of damage. Davis always put the onus for dysfunction on the social system itself, and he generally elected to emphasize the resiliency and rationality of individual black people as they navigated environments of inequality and discrimination. In *Scientific Monthly*, he stated directly that black children's "racial status had a somewhat minor influence on their personalities."[14] The difference here between Davis and his peers was profound. A later generation of scholars schooled in the civil rights movement would come to reject expositions of damage as inaccurate and insulting, but in Davis's time, his position made him a marginal countervailing voice among a chorus of proponents of damage imagery.

Nevertheless, Clark and the attorneys in *Brown* still mobilized parts of Davis's work in the case. In the amicus brief, Clark explicitly cited Davis's 1939 article in the *Journal of Negro Education* to support the claim that segregation causes maladaptive frustration and aggression in some black youths.[15] Clark also cited Myrdal, and in this way Davis's analyses of black churches and associations as pathological influenced the brief. Finally, Clark relied upon research showing that no racial differences in intelligence existed, which Davis had a major hand in developing.

The *Brown* litigants did not, however, marshal the majority of Davis's work for the case, including his most potent criticisms of school segregation and racial caste. In many ways this was a logical outcome of the liberal consensus among social scientists to close ranks and achieve desegregation by whatever means necessary. This involved tabling the stronger argument that segregation was unconstitutional because it maintained white supremacy—not because it hurt black people's feelings. The Supreme Court was not yet ready to accept that reasoning in the 1950s, only; it did not change course until *Loving v. Virginia* (1967), which struck down antimiscegenation laws. Davis's signature on Clark's brief demonstrates that he, too, took part in the broader cause, even though his own research contradicted many claims about damage. In that historical moment, social scientists like Davis cared less about how damaging school segregation in particular was for black youth and more about how debilitating the *entire system* of racial caste is for African Americans. Davis and his peers realized that *Brown* represented an opportunity to strike a major blow to de jure segregation as a whole, so they creatively interpreted parts of their own research to achieve that end.[16]

In many ways, this was an entirely defensible position. In their minds educational segregation could not be fairly isolated from segregation as a whole, but the proceedings of the law in this case demanded that it be. So without guilty consciences, Davis and his colleagues testified against the system of segregation itself, if in narrower terms than they would have liked.[17]

The pragmatic emphasis on damage to black personalities was nevertheless a fateful one that would later be used to subvert racial justice. In addition to weakening the larger constitutional argument, it stigmatized black people and focused attention on their psychological problems rather than the equal rights and protections that they deserved as citizens. Later on, conservatives co-opted the damage imagery for their own ends, including attacks on government programs benefiting black people.

Davis contributed to the landmark case in still other ways, in part through his relationship with his younger brother John Aubrey Davis. John Davis served as the director of nonlegal research for the NAACP in *Brown*. After hearing the oral arguments of the case in December 1952, the Supreme Court justices called for a reargument of the issues in June 1953.[18] The justices asked the plaintiffs and the defendants to make new arguments in response to five nonlegal questions. The first three questions had to do with the historical circumstances surrounding the passage, ratification, and implementation of the Fourteenth Amendment. The last two questions related to how school desegregation should be carried out in light of a potential ruling that segregation was unconstitutional. As the director, John Davis appointed a group of historians, including Horace Mann Bond, John Hope Franklin, and C. Vann Woodward, to address the first three questions, and he appointed Kenneth Clark to direct the research into the latter two questions.[19]

John Davis then involved his brother. In September 1953, shortly before the nonlegal team submitted its brief, the NAACP-LDEF held a three-day conference in New York. There Allison Davis was one of the forty-two attendees who critiqued the team's work. Yet that formal collaboration was surely less important than the more informal collaboration Davis had with many of those involved. He had intimate ties to his brother and Horace Mann Bond, and he had close relationships with numerous others among this tightly knit group of black scholars, many of whom had also been Rosenwald Fellows. The gathering included colleagues and friends such as Rayford Logan and Charles H. Thompson. Davis was very much part of the community that helped to win *Brown*.[20]

Davis also contributed in subtler ways to the earlier litigation that led up to the case. His mentor and eventual colleague at the University of Chicago, anthropologist Robert Redfield, served as an expert witness on race and desegregation in a number of cases, including *Sweatt v. Painter* (1947) and *Sipuel v. Oklahoma State Regents* (1948). For his testimony, Redfield drew from his personal experiences with Davis's desegregation of the faculty at the University of Chicago. While arguing that segregation undermined "public security and general welfare," he was able to contrast that reality with the successful appointment of Davis, who had proved to be an esteemed colleague, a productive researcher, and an inspiring teacher to students of all races.[21]

After *Brown*, Davis played a part by taking to the press to clarify the significance of the ruling. The *New York Times* interviewed several influential social scientists of race relations including Davis, Charles S. Johnson, and Harvard psychologist Gordon Allport. The reporter discussed Davis's response first and in greatest detail. Davis said that the decision "makes it clear that our democratic government is vital, because it is adaptive, able to respond vigorously to the processes of cultural and economic change." He also emphasized the international significance of this democratic victory, saying that it "makes it clear to the colored peoples of Japan, Africa, India and Indonesia, as well as to the European colonial powers . . . that the United States is not defending a color hierarchy in the world but is defending a democratic political system which is proving itself efficient." Davis also argued for hastening the implementation of the ruling by underlining its significance for national strength: "When this decision is implemented, it will result in a tremendous increase in the fund of ability and skill available to our country. Outnumbered as we are, the survival of the United States seems to depend upon its developing the ability of millions of our citizens whose capacities have been crippled by segregation."[22]

In the next few years, Davis persisted in trying to spur on the desegregation process and shape the national debate over desegregation. Disappointingly, it was not until May 31, 1955, that the court remanded the cases to the federal district courts within each state and passively directed them to desegregate the schools "with all deliberate speed."[23] The court's ruling in *Brown II* only emboldened states to delay desegregation, and in those areas where integration efforts had begun, there was often a strong counterreaction.

Examples of southern intransigence abound. In Louisville, Kentucky, locals found that "Negro pupils were about two years below the level of achievement of their white classmates."[24] Hearings in Washington, DC, soon reported that the same discrepancy existed nationwide. Such findings galvanized resistance among white parents who did not want their children's education to be jeopardized by an influx into the classroom of students who needed to catch up. Yet even more troubling for southerners was the clear challenge that desegregation posed to white supremacy and the caste system. Floyd Fleming, a member of the Citizen's Council in Washington, DC, argued that "intermarriage . . . is what integration in the schools leads to and as that comes to pass, the white race becomes a mongrelized race and history records that the breeding is downward instead of upward."[25]

Southern congressmen followed the lead of their constituents and fueled the flames of resistance. In March 1956 Georgia senator Richard Russell responded by drafting a "Southern Manifesto," which declared that "outside agitators are threatening immediate and revolutionary changes in our public school systems. If done, this is certain to destroy the system of public education in some of the States."[26] Most southern congressmen signed it.

In such an environment, figures emerged spouting racist epithets about inherent black inferiority. For instance, Frank C. J. McGurk, a psychology professor at Villanova University, argued that "as far as psychological-test performance is a measure of capacity for education, Negroes as a group do not possess as much of it as whites as a group." According to journalist Eve Edstrom, such "alleged intellectual inferiority of Negroes" was also "inferred during the congressional investigation of the District's integrated schools." In these ways southerners attempted to deploy intelligence testing to further the segregationist cause.[27]

On October 15, 1956, Davis and seventeen other renowned social scientists responded with a joint statement condemning the false, racist statements about black intelligence. Davis, Otto Klineberg, Gardner Murphy, Kenneth Clark, Theodore Newcomb, and others confirmed the scientific consensus that no "innate racial difference in intelligence" exists.[28] They explained that this scientific conclusion had in fact already been established decades earlier and that "no new research" had emerged to challenge it.[29] Although these social scientists agreed that the average level of black educational achievement was behind that of the average white student, they attributed that fact to systematic racism and discrimination. To substantiate their claims, they cited studies such as Klineberg's, which demonstrated that African Americans' scores on intelligence tests improved drastically—even exceeding those of whites—upon migration to the urban North, where schools were better and more racially integrated.[30] To redress the problem, Davis and the others called for immediate desegregation.

Even if the average segregationist cared little about their statements, their arguments were nevertheless an important public refutation of the segregationist position. As always, it would depend upon the mass mobilization of grassroots activists to force the issue. For his part, Allison Davis played the role in the black freedom struggle that he was best positioned to play: social science expert, social commentator, and educator.

HEAD START

In the early 1960s, poverty became a national issue in a way that it had not been since the Great Depression. In the 1940s and 1950s, despite the work of social scientists such as Davis, Lloyd Warner, and C. Wright Mills who continued to delineate class stratification, most American commentators had focused on the country's affluence and rising standard of living.[31] And not without reason. Americans experienced a 19.2 percent increase in per capita income over the 1950s.[32] On the back of unionization, progressive taxation, and government support of education, social welfare, suburbanization, and infrastructural development, the United States built a large and thriving middle class in the postwar years.[33]

Underneath this growing middle class, however, was an entrenched lower class that did not benefit. In fact, the bottom quarter of the population was in some ways harmed by the macroeconomic growth. The skills gap deepened in these years, and suburbanization eroded tax bases from the cities and created isolated pockets of poverty.

In response, Michael Harrington, a Catholic socialist, investigated the problem and reported it to a national audience.[34] His influential exposé of American poverty, *The Other America* (1962), helped to frame the issue for sixties liberals. It revealed that 25 percent of Americans were trapped within a "vicious circle" of poverty from which they could not escape. Focusing on structural factors, the book described how unemployment and underemployment combined with inadequate education, housing, healthcare, and nutrition, as well as with age and race discrimination, to systematically produce an "underclass" even amid a booming economy. Harrington also explained how the effects of poverty extended to the realm of culture. He drew from anthropologist Oscar Lewis to argue that "poverty in the United States is a culture, an institution, a way of life." Controversially, he portrayed the poor as hapless victims whose "will and spirit" were warped and who lacked "the social energy and political strength to turn [their] misery into a cause."[35]

The Other America had a major impact on the Kennedy and Johnson administrations. John F. Kennedy was already primed to do something about the Appalachian poverty he had observed while campaigning in West Virginia in 1960.[36] After reading social critic Dwight Macdonald's laudatory review of *The Other America* in the *New Yorker*, Kennedy took concrete steps to initiate a "war on poverty."[37] After he was assassinated, the task fell to Lyndon Johnson.

Surprising many within his new administration, President Johnson acted swiftly. In his first State of the Union address on January 11, 1964, he proclaimed boldly, "This administration today here and now declares unconditional war on poverty in America." He aimed to eradicate the web of poverty which he understood as growing out of "our failure to give our fellow citizens a fair chance to develop their own capacities—in a lack of education and training, in a lack of medical care and housing, in a lack of decent communities in which to live and bring up their children."[38]

Head Start became the most enduring and popular program within the War on Poverty. It was, however, implemented hastily in 1964 without consultation from many experts such as Davis. Sargent Shriver, director of the Office of Economic Opportunity, backed a comprehensive program for childhood intervention that included medical care, nutrition, social skills, and basic education. Dubbed Head Start, the program began in the summer of 1965, and by the end of that summer it had already served over a half million children. The program quickly became a permanent and popular year-long program.[39]

The work of Allison Davis was not closely connected with the creation of Head Start, but his work nevertheless played a significant role in Head Start's success. This came partly through his relationship with Benjamin S. Bloom, a longtime fellow professor of education at the University of Chicago who is generally credited as one of the main intellectual architects of Head Start.[40] Notably, Bloom testified before Congress in support of the Economic Opportunity Act.[41] There he reported the findings from his influential book *Stability and Change in Human Characteristics* (1964), which drew directly from Davis's environmentalist work, particularly *Intelligence and Cultural Differences*. Davis's extensive investigations into early childhood socialization clearly informed Bloom's research. Bloom's novel contribution in *Stability and Change* stemmed not from his observation that early childhood education is vital but from the data he collected proving that learning actually occurs more quickly during that period of life before slowing down and stabilizing. The implications were clear: early childhood intervention programs were essential.[42]

Once the War on Poverty was under way, Davis collaborated directly with Bloom. In June 1964 they organized a four-day Research Conference on Education and Cultural Deprivation, which led to the publication of a timely book coauthored by Bloom, Davis, and Robert Hess, titled *Compensatory Education for Cultural Deprivation* (1965). The authors sought to capitalize on the sudden interest in early childhood poverty in order to steer public policy in more progressive directions. They argued that "what is now required is not equality of *access* to education. What is needed to solve our current as well as future crises in education is a system of *compensatory education* which can prevent or overcome earlier deficiencies in the development of each individual." "Essentially," they continued, "what this involves is the writing and filling of educational prescriptions for groups of children which will enable them to *realize their fullest development.*"[43]

Davis, Bloom, and Hess recommended practical measures to counteract the social, economic, and cultural disadvantages of poor students. Reinforcing the emerging Head Start program at every turn, the authors proposed a guaranteed breakfast and midday meal each day, a physical exam and regular health services, and clothing. They understood that students needed to secure basic needs before learning could be addressed. They also endorsed a nursery and kindergarten system that could help poor children develop educational skills that they did not learn at home. Recognizing the racial disparities of poverty, furthermore, the authors drew from Davis's work to advocate the racial integration of schools. Finally, the authors went further than Head Start by recommending guidance programs that would mentor students and track their struggles throughout adolescence.[44]

Even before the inauguration of Head Start, Davis was sharing his progressive ideas on child poverty. For instance, in December 1962 he spoke before 150 people at the City Club of Chicago's annual civic assembly, where he stridently criticized the Aid to Dependent Children welfare program for failing to understand and address poverty. Three years before the advent of Head Start, he laid out practical solutions such as "day care centers and nursery schools . . . to help children 3 to 5 years old to learn language, basic cultural habits, and academic skills that enable them to do better work in elementary school."[45] At the same time, he proposed regular biweekly interviews with all ADC children in grades one through ten, and he recommended the development of "residential vocational centers, summer camps, and youth corps projects . . . for ADC youths 14 to 16 years old."[46] He continued to speak widely on these issues in the coming years, helping to create the context in which programs such as Head Start could be successful.[47]

Realizing that his goals required more than the presentation of his ideas to different audiences, Davis also took briefly to politics in the 1960s. He aligned with the National Urban League, the NAACP, and many other civil rights organizations to demand reforms to the school-board nomination procedure in Chicago. One major objective was "to give more representation to Negroes and labor groups, among others." On March 12, 1964, he told the Chicago branch of the National Council of Jewish Women that the Chicago school system was failing to provide quality education for its students, especially African Americans, because of the "gerrymandering of school attendance boundaries." He joined twenty-four civil rights groups in calling for a radical reconstruction of the Chicago school board, beginning with the dismissal of School Superintendent Benjamin Willis, who continued to resist racial integration of the public schools.[48]

Davis's efforts won him some acclaim. Several local groups recognized him as an effective leader in the fight, so they nominated him for the mayor's advisory committee on school board nominations.[49] On the national level, Davis's work earned him membership in President Johnson's Commission on Civil Rights (1966–67), in the Department of Labor's Commission on Manpower Retraining as vice chair (1968–72), in the Conference to Insure Civil Rights, and in the White House Task Force on the Gifted.[50]

Ironically, even though Davis was important in laying the intellectual foundations for Head Start, his and his colleagues' work also led some contemporaries to question the value of the program. This is evident in the reception of James S. Coleman's similar research. Coleman was a colleague of Davis's at the University of Chicago from 1956 to 1959, and he worked alongside Robert E. Cooke at Johns Hopkins University, the lead expert on whom Sargent Shriver relied in setting up Head Start. In 1966 Coleman published *Equality of Educational Opportunity*, commonly known as the Coleman Report.[51] The report paralleled Davis's work in arguing that students' family background and socioeconomic status matter far more than school resources in shaping educational outcomes.[52] Also like Davis, Coleman recommended bold educational and social interventions, such as racial integration, compensatory educational programs, rigorous teacher training, and strong antipoverty programs.[53]

To the great frustration of Davis and Coleman, some contemporaries interpreted the Coleman Report as proving the futility of interventions such as Head Start amid an entrenched class system. Some research at the time— above all, an extensive study by the Westinghouse Learning Corporation— found that the gains from Head Start dissipated within the first few years after children left the program.[54] Critics used such findings to discredit Head Start as ineffective and wasteful. Davis, of course, pleaded that such findings only underscored the need for increased and prolonged interventions, not the abandonment of them.

In one form or another, Davis's ideas were never far from the heated debates over education and poverty in the 1960s.

THE CULTURE OF POVERTY

No debate was more heated than the one over the "culture of poverty." On one level, there was nothing new about discussing the cultural dimensions of poverty. Indeed, Davis had done so for many years. But in the hands of white liberals eager to stoke white middle-class outrage in order to galvanize reform, the notion became controversial and deeply problematic. This was readily apparent in Michael Harrington's *The Other America*, which portrayed the poor as hapless victims of a debilitating environment of despair and dependency.

It was Daniel Patrick Moynihan, the assistant secretary of labor under President Johnson, who sparked a national uproar. In 1965, hoping to spur policy to combat black poverty, he circulated a memo to White House staff framing the issue. He argued, "Three centuries of injustice have brought about deep-seated structural distortions in the life of the Negro American," creating a "tangle of pathology" within African American society. Drawing from E. Franklin Frazier, he located the fundamental pathology within the black "family structure," whose single-parent matriarchal practices he observed as deeply pathological. Perhaps most controversially, Moynihan viewed such pathology as "capable of perpetuating itself without assistance from the white world."[55] Thus he placed undue emphasis on the nature of the black family itself, rather than on the structural forces that gave it form. The memo made painfully clear just how problematic many liberals' conceptions of poverty were at the time. When the memo became public in August 1965, critics rightly attacked Moynihan's bitterly stigmatizing portrait.[56]

Well-meaning white reformers could have benefited from the sophisticated, eclectic approaches in Davis's extensive body of work on black poverty. His structural-cultural orientation, which maintained a clear focus on the structural realities of poverty while also exploring its cultural dimensions, would have been helpful. His social-psychological approach, which explained behavior as conditioned by the power dynamics within the immediate environment, could have exposed the limits of portraying behavior as the response to a stable, inherited set of cultural values. Finally, his cultural relativism and humanism allowed him to see agency and virtue in lower-class peoples at a time when most middle-class commentators could see only pathology. All of these approaches anticipated the mounting critiques of the culture of poverty in the 1960s and 1970s.[57]

Although Davis was rarely consulted in national discussions of poverty, he did attempt to enter the fray during debates about the welfare program Aid to Dependent Children (ADC). As always, he emphasized the structural factors shaping the effectiveness of the program, while also explaining the behavior of recipients as logical given their circumstances. In familiar fashion, he charged that ADC was crippled by the middle-class biases of its architects, which prevented them from developing a program that could change the conditions in which the poor lived. Specifically, because ADC offered no means to develop social goals, "no method for improving the skills of the poor, and no services which would raise the hope and occupational level of the children whom it is supposed to serve," it degenerated into a dole.[58] For Davis, the lack of a constructive program encouraged the poor to simply incorporate the funds "into their already established survival patterns."[59]

Davis's analysis implied that poor people were not only rational but also sophisticated. They had adopted patterns of behavior that enabled them to survive under circumstances of extreme deprivation. Because the poor recognized that the system was stacked against them, they knew that hopes for social mobility were often unrealistic and even dangerous to entertain.[60] In the context of a system that blocked their advance and reinforced their subordination, a pittance of welfare money did nothing to inspire them to change. For that reason, Davis argued that only a bold program offering real avenues to success could begin to address the problem.[61]

Given his many insights and clear expertise on the subject, why was Davis not consulted in debates about the culture of poverty? One answer is that reformers were not looking for nuance but rather for shocking details that could prod white middle-class people into action. But the full answer is more complicated than that. The degree of marginalization of Davis's work was striking for a man who continued to present at conferences alongside people such as Oscar Lewis, the original architect of the culture-of-poverty concept.[62]

Institutional racism within the academy played a significant role. The contributions of black intellectuals such as Davis often failed to reach mainstream social science, and if they did, they were often whitewashed, or subsumed under the contributions of white scholars. Writing in 1967, after the Watts uprising had fueled national hysteria about the state of black America, sociologist Lee Rainwater noted this phenomenon. He observed that contemporary discussions of black poverty ignored the work of Davis and other black scholars of a previous generation. He wrote, "The current researches on Negro subculture represent a refining and updating of patterns which have been described, for example, by Frazier in the '30s, Cayton and Drake and Allison Davis in the '40s, Kardiner and Rohrer and Edmonson in the '50s. The fact that the larger society has been indifferent to their findings does not make the current studies 'a new and ominous phenomenon.'"[63]

St. Clair Drake observed this same process of marginalization in the thinking of Daniel Patrick Moynihan. In 1968 Moynihan published an article in *Commentary* that criticized black scholars for failing to have adequately studied black poverty.[64] Dumbfounded, Drake rebuked Moynihan for "deploring what he feels to be a scarcity of insightful research *on* Negroes *by* Negroes," all the while ignoring entire bodies of relevant scholarship.[65] His exhibit A was Allison Davis, whom Moynihan had failed to even mention.

Moynihan responded contradictorily. He claimed to know Davis's work intimately, but he bizarrely explained that Davis "seemed too much of a contemporary to locate in the misty past of the 1930's."[66] Either he did not really know Davis's extensive contributions, having credited them to Davis's white collaborators, or perhaps he did not even think of Davis as black, since Davis's work was not merely about race and the black experience—which most white commentators continued to view as black scholars' only potential area of expertise. Davis's many contributions to other topics, including social class, socialization, and intelligence testing, perhaps confused the embattled Moynihan. Regardless, Moynihan revealed the many ways in which the marginalization of black scholars could proceed.

In taking issue with other arguments made by Moynihan, Drake also revealed the mounting criticism of the culture-of-poverty idea. Like most black intellectuals and a growing number of white liberals, Drake disparaged Moynihan for his "constantly reiterated hypothesis that so much 'structural damage' has been done to Negro personalities and institutions."[67] The unfolding of history seemed to delegitimize Moynihan's ideas at every turn. The civil rights movement at home and the decolonization movement abroad testified to the power of even the most oppressed black people to be agents of social transformation. The power and spirit of the movement directly challenged Moynihan's portrait of the black poor as passive victims locked in self-perpetuating cultures of pathology.

If Moynihan had taken seriously the work of scholars such as Allison Davis, he might have saved himself some embarrassment and censure.[68] But like other white liberals of the sixties, he ignored Davis to his detriment.

As it turned out, liberals' misguided conceptions of the culture of poverty backfired politically. Conservatives seized upon that notion to undermine efforts to combat poverty altogether. They often adulterated liberals' ideas, but they also followed many liberals' lead in ignoring the structural, material aspects of poverty while emphasizing its cultural dimensions.[69] This tactic empowered neoconservatives such as Nathan Glazer to prescribe behavioral solutions to poverty, such as adopting a middle-class ethic, while avoiding issues of systemic inequity.[70]

In the process, conservatives were abetted by the general conflation of poverty as a whole with the urban, ghetto poverty of African Americans. Lost was the fact that there were many more poor whites than poor blacks. But as white Americans misinterpreted President Johnson's War on Poverty as benefiting only black people, many of them refused to support the program. To make matters worse, many fled the Democratic Party, believing that the government was no longer on "their" side but had taken the side of minorities and liberal interest groups.

Although this confluence of forces was beyond the control of liberal critics of the culture of poverty, those liberals would have helped their cause had they not so problematically conceptualized, emphasized, and stigmatized the cultural aspects of poverty. In all of this, Allison Davis would have been a useful guide.

Even as Davis's research productivity slowed in the 1950s and 1960s, he continued to play significant roles in major social developments. In both direct and indirect ways, he helped to make racial desegregation and antipoverty programs a success. *Brown* and Head Start stood out as monumental liberal achievements in these years, and the roles that Davis played within each are revealing. His scholarship generally supported both developments, even though social engineers used it selectively to further their own causes. In *Brown*, this meant drawing from the parts of Davis's work that could at least imply a level of damage to or frustration among black people, while ignoring his emphasis on resilience and adaptability. In Head Start, this meant ignoring Davis's call for more sustained educational support throughout the entire schooling process. Regarding the culture of poverty, this again meant ignoring much of Davis's work on poverty and emphasizing instead the profound damage that results from being poor.

In the middle of the twentieth century, such damage imagery proved useful in winning important court cases and mobilizing white people against social injustice. But it was also a deeply flawed way to build a movement for social change. Instead of including oppressed peoples in the fight and empowering them as foot soldiers, it excluded them as beyond the pale and presumed condescendingly that it was up to more affluent whites to effect change. This furthered the cultural gap between the races and the classes, and it made it difficult to find common ground. Furthermore, pity came at the expense of arguments for change based upon the shared goals of full citizenship rights, equal opportunity, and freedom from discrimination, which could have united people in common cause. In the ideological context of the 1950s and 1960s, however, such approaches simply did not win out. Davis's example makes clearer the historical landscape of the period, if also the many missed opportunities to achieve progressive change.

Conclusion

As a young man in the 1920s, Allison Davis carved out a place among the black intelligentsia by rebuking many of its positions. His emphasis on class divisions within the black community and on direct leadership of the black masses in the South challenged mainstream thinking. Through herculean resolve and remarkable political acumen, he later led the way among his peers by entering social science and integrating the faculties of predominantly white universities. He was an insurgent who effected change by confronting the racial divide and transforming scholarship. The success of his efforts depended upon his ability to work with the whites who controlled the system and to ultimately win the contest of ideas through the sheer vigor of his research. He mastered that role, and as difficult as it was for him personally, he had a significant impact on American social thought.

By the late 1960s, a new generation of young black radicals had come to the fore. Empowered by the civil rights movement but also chastened by the limitations of campaigns for racial integration, Black Power activists were more separatist. They sought to advance the freedom struggle by cultivating racial pride and developing independent black institutions. Notions of "Afrocentricity" and proclamations that "Black is beautiful" pervaded the movement, prompting activists to grow out their hair, to celebrate their African heritage, and to recognize their ties to other oppressed, colonized peoples of the world. For the new radicals looking to carve out their own positions as race leaders, assimilation into white society seemed to involve an unacceptable effacement of black identity, as well as an objectionable accommodation to a racist society.

Given such priorities, many young radicals criticized the older generation of black leaders for being too conservative. Allison Davis was one such figure who could suddenly appear too white, too assimilated into white institutions, too intellectual, and too distant from grassroots activism. In 1974 St. Clair Drake noted that "Davis has been criticized by some for not being deeply rooted in the black community."[1]

But as Drake knew well, Davis believed in the role that intellectuals had to play in the black freedom struggle. He had strategically entered social science to further the environmentalist revolution in American social thought. His fight underpinned the civil rights movement, and it helped to make possible the new tactics and priorities of the next generation. In the process, he risked his life to conduct research in the Deep South, exploding notions that intellectual pursuits were always safe ones confined within the ivory tower. As Drake put it, "I like to remember that [Davis] could have spent his life working on nineteenth-century English literature. But he didn't. He made his commitment in terms of choice of problem, and if he never walked a picket line, if he never signed anything for the N.A.A.C.P., I would argue that Davis made a definite commitment and that his commitment has had its value in social change. His publication list is proof."[2]

Not coincidentally, at the very time that some black radicals were writing Davis off as too conservative, elements of white society began upholding him as an important symbol of black achievement and racial inclusion. The well-earned, if sometimes token, recognition took several forms. Several universities offered him prestigious visiting professorships. He accepted temporary posts at Berkeley, Michigan, Columbia, and Illinois, and he declined an offer from Cambridge. Numerous schools also invited Davis to give named lectures in education, such as the Leo Franklin Lecture at Wayne State University in 1966, the Du Pont Lecture at the University of Delaware in 1966, and the Frederick Douglass Lecture at the University of Rochester in 1967.[3]

Other universities awarded Davis an honorary degree. If receiving degrees from institutions such as Tuskegee Institute and Northwestern left him feeling unambiguously honored, the same was not the case with his alma mater, Williams College. Williams recognized Davis in 1974, but the occasion did little to placate his lingering resentment toward the school. Even though half a century had passed, it still felt like yesterday. The humiliations remained foremost in his mind.[4] As he was about to receive his honorary degree, he whispered to his family, "What took them so long."[5] Nevertheless, when his son Gordon also received an honorary degree from Williams, in 1982, Allison seemed to have finally made peace with the school, recognizing how far it had come in

FIGURE 10.1. The Davis family in Evanston, Illinois, on June 17, 1978, after Allison received an honorary degree from Northwestern University. Back row, from left to right: Lois Mason (Allison's second wife), Allison Davis, and Karen Davis (Allison's daughter-in-law). Front row, from left to right: Cullen Davis and Jared Davis (Allison's grandchildren). Courtesy of the Davis Family.

acknowledging and addressing its history of racism. In 2012 Williams College renamed its Multicultural Center "The Davis Center" to honor him and his brother, John Aubrey Davis.[6]

The University of Chicago also honored Davis. Hoping partly to uphold him as a symbol of its own racial progressiveness, Chicago made him the first John Dewey Distinguished Service Professor in Education in 1970. The university also held a symposium in Davis's honor shortly before his death in 1983, fittingly calling it "Race, Class, Socialization and the Life Cycle."[7] Many of his closest friends and colleagues participated in honoring the depth and breadth of his career.

In addition, Davis received numerous other forms of recognition for his accomplishments. In 1972 the prestigious American Academy of Arts and Sciences elected him to membership, making him the first scholar selected from the field of education in the organization's almost two-hundred-year history. In 1971 the journal *Education* selected him as one of the "Gold Medal Educators

of the 1960s" and named him the 1971 "Leader in Education."[8] The federal
government, too, began to recognize Davis. Seeking to highlight its own progress on the race issue, the government offered Davis positions in Lyndon
Johnson's Commission on Civil Rights, the Department of Labor's Commission on Manpower Retraining, the Conference to Ensure Civil Rights, and the
White House Task Force on the Gifted.[9]

Other notable honors came after Davis died on November 21, 1983. The
most significant was his postage stamp, issued in February 1994, ushering in
Black History Month that year. Davis's inclusion there placed him among a
handful of black pioneers, including Harriet Tubman, W. E. B. Du Bois, and
Martin Luther King Jr.[10] The Postal Service's description nicely captured
Davis's significance: "He challenged the cultural bias of standardized intelligence tests and fought for the understanding of the human potential beyond
racial class and caste. His work helped end legalized racial segregation and
contributed to contemporary thought on valuing the capabilities of youth from
diverse backgrounds."[11] This stamp, in turn, brought a bit more attention to
Allison Davis.[12]

In 2005 Davis's family partnered with the University of Chicago, the Chicago Park District, and the Chicago Community Trust to build the Allison
Davis Garden near the University of Chicago in Washington Park. At a large
dedication ceremony, speakers discussed how the park "separated the heart
of the university from Woodlawn, a predominantly African-American neighborhood."[13] They emphasized how Davis had, throughout the course of his
long career at Chicago, daily crossed the physical boundaries separating the
university from the neighboring black communities. The attendees celebrated
him as someone who both physically and symbolically transgressed racial barriers and confronted America's color line. They hoped that Davis's leadership
might inspire a renewed dedication to the principles of racial inclusion in a city
still terribly divided along race and class lines.[14]

Although Allison Davis must have appreciated such honors, he understood
all too well just how much remained to be done in the battle for racial justice.
That awareness prompted him to spend the final years of his life—after finally
retiring from Chicago in 1978—completing yet another book. *Leadership, Love,
and Aggression* (1983) conveyed his own struggle with transforming the devastating effects of racial oppression into socially productive ends. With the support of grants from the Spencer Foundation and the MacArthur Foundation,
Davis analyzed the lives and careers of Frederick Douglass, W. E. B. Du Bois,
Richard Wright, and Martin Luther King Jr. These psychological biographies

explored how each figure dealt with racial discrimination and to what extent each was able to transform his righteous anger into productive action. In King he found his greatest example of someone who turned the hate targeted at him into love, which he then successfully harnessed to build a peaceful social movement that benefited the most oppressed Americans. Davis shared King's goals, for he believed that it was only through love and conscious struggle that people could transcend hate and make the most of life.[15]

Accordingly, the best way to honor a man like Davis is not to lavish awards upon him. It is to try to live up to his high ideals, which include social justice, equal opportunity, and freedom from race and class constraints. Unfortunately, those constraints have hardly lessened in the last half century. Davis's own success revealed the contradictions of a society in which overt racism and de jure segregation were increasingly challenged, but in which institutional racism thrived and continued to circumscribe the lives of African Americans. The positive attention devoted to successful black people such as Allison Davis too often served as evidence to white America that racism is no longer a problem in the United States. A passing glance at sociological research, however, highlights the absurdity of such a notion. De facto segregation, mass incarceration, and structural unemployment have combined to ensure that African Americans as a group suffer from the worst education, housing, medical care, nutrition, and violence.[16] This leads not only to a far lower quality of life for the average black person but also to a significantly shorter life.[17] To understand the nature of such a pernicious inequity, one must grasp its structural nature, which is precisely the task to which Davis dedicated his life. His work remains as relevant as ever.

Hagiography does little to help those most oppressed, but close attention to bold humanistic ideas and their role in social affairs is instructive. The case of Allison Davis shows how America's system of race and class stratification helped to produce a man ideally situated to lay bare those very systems. As a victim of racial oppression and yet a beneficiary of the finest education available at the time, he was uniquely positioned to reveal the nature of America's social structure. His example highlights how particular individuals can take advantage of liberal strains within American social thought for their own ends. He used the environmentalist methods and assumptions of social anthropology, culture-and-personality, and educational theory to expose the social forces that circumscribed the lives of racial minorities and the poor. His life's work, including his literary writings during the New Negro Renaissance, his social-science classics *Deep South* and *Children of Bondage*, his efforts within the field of education, and much more, were dedicated to eliminating arbitrary social constraints so that all people could develop into their best selves. His entire career reflected that goal, even as he calibrated his shifting approaches to evolving contexts.

The best way to understand Allison Davis's career is to view it as part of the larger black freedom struggle. Born into a despised caste, Davis had little choice but to become part of that struggle. In pursuing the modest aspirations of becoming educated, securing a job, voting, and eating lunch with colleagues, Davis found himself consistently denied and penned in. By continuing to strive for such basic goals, he invariably became part of the freedom struggle for racial equality. But Davis was of another mold altogether. He channeled his righteous indignation over racial injustice into an effective program of action. Swallowing the daily affronts to his humanity, he dedicated himself to a near-singular pursuit of scholarship that would debunk the racist, hereditarian thinking prevalent within American society and that would expose the environmental roots of group differences. Even as he grew weary and waxed pessimistic about the possibilities for change, he continued to speak and live his truth about the equal capacities of all races and peoples of the world.

Davis's story helps us to understand the nature and texture of the larger black freedom struggle. For one thing, we should see ordinary acts of living and striving as part of that struggle. The labors of innumerable slaves and sharecroppers to merely survive in rigidly oppressive environments were as much a part of the freedom struggle as any other effort. More often than not, it was the shifting winds of historical change that presented new opportunities for activists, and that activists helped to bring about in the first place. Allison Davis, for his part, used education and social science in his struggle, as both became increasingly accessible to black people in the interwar period. He seized upon the opportunity to wage the environmentalist battle of ideas. His example shows how black people were indispensable parts of the environmentalist revolution in social thought, even though the power structure marginalized their contributions. The nature of Davis's activities and the level of his successes were new, but the struggle itself was not.

By placing African Americans such as Davis at the center of the environmentalist revolution, we gain a better sense of the larger civil rights movement. Historians have recently sought to broaden traditional interpretations of the movement to include more than only the southern battle against Jim Crow at midcentury, expanding our sense of the freedom struggle chronologically, geographically, and conceptually.[18] One result has been the inclusion of efforts within interwar America, which often took more radical forms, including the focus on economic justice as well as civil rights.

Davis, through his career-long emphasis on class, makes clearer what one element of this earlier, more radical struggle looked like. In particular, he underlines the importance of ideas within movement politics. He and some of his peers recognized that campaigns for social justice depended upon winning Americans over to the idea that racial inequality was a social problem, not a biological one. His life's work showed how caste and class, not heredity, delimited African Americans' lives. In the process, he posed the radical argument that rich and powerful Americans exploited racial inequality for their own class-based ends; he thereby implied that class struggle needed to accompany racial struggle. Such ideas infused grassroots activism and supported attempts at interracial organizing in interwar America.[19]

Davis's environmentalist scholarship also shaped the "heroic" phase of the postwar civil rights movement. *Brown v. Board of Education*, for instance, made tangible the connections between environmentalist ideas and movement politics. The justices in *Brown* relied upon the work of Davis and others in their ruling, reasoning that segregation was unconstitutional because it created an environment that discriminated against black students to devastating effect. After the decision, activists took up the court's ruling to challenge Jim Crow in every institution and to make desegregation a reality on the ground. Environmentalist ideas therefore pervaded the movement and directed its energies.

Davis's story also illustrates how elements of the earlier and more radical phase of the black freedom struggle persisted into the 1950s and beyond. Davis continued to emphasize class inequalities, and class became his dominant research paradigm at Chicago. Cognizant of how race and class were linked, he attacked the class biases within intelligence tests, combated class discrimination in industry and the schools, and fought broadly for antipoverty programs. He recognized that black rights depended upon more than equal access to mainstream institutions, so he focused his attack upon ameliorating the class inequalities that disproportionately affected African Americans. He argued that poor people needed good jobs, stable wages, and suitable places to live in order to become full members of society.[20] Even as the postwar context caused him to muffle some of his radical views, he continued to quietly make the case for the redistribution of wealth and the social and economic empowerment of the poor. In this way, his work represents a more radical aspect of the civil rights movement, even as emphases on racial integration and equal access loomed large.

Davis's career also links the earlier radical phase of the civil rights movement with the later radicalism of the 1960s. Through Davis's story, we see how civil rights activists did not merely discover institutional racism after the heroic phase of the movement ended. Rather, individuals within the movement had been concerned with these issues all along, and when the movement radicalized in the mid-1960s, it had a radical tradition—and empirical data—from which to draw. Davis therefore reminds us of the notable continuities underlying the shifting contours of the larger freedom struggle. As the recent biographical turn in civil rights historiography suggests, and of which this book is a part, taking the long and close view of activists' lives is thus deeply insightful.[21]

Finally, Davis's role as a pioneer within the heroic phase of the civil rights movement is notable. His pathbreaking appointment to the University of Chicago in 1942 made clear the many changes afoot within American race relations at that time, and it highlighted the attributes required of racial pioneers. Davis had to deftly negotiate the politics of the conservative academy by building strong alliances with influential white academics. His undisputed scholarly success enabled him to secure his position and then further develop and broadcast his progressive ideas, even though his own contributions were often marginalized through his collaboration with white scholars. His appointment at Chicago therefore testified to the significance of academia as both a physical and intellectual terrain for the civil rights struggle, even as it underscored the intractability of racial inequality within universities and beyond.

Davis's story, however, is of more than only historiographical value. Many of his ideas are directly relevant, and even pressingly urgent, today. For one, his examination of the structural nature of race and class is deeply important. Race and class stratification are persistent elements of America's social structure. Later investigators' focus on "institutional" inequality was in many ways simply a reformulation of Davis's and his colleagues' structural thought. That thought is particularly significant within the context of America's current "neoliberal" moment, when an excessively individualistic and agent-based model of human behavior prevails even while inequality mounts. This heightened individualism only exacerbates a deeper strain of exceptionalism within American culture: some Americans see their country as a "classless" land of opportunity for all. Davis's emphasis on the persistence of structural inequality and the lack of opportunity can serve as a valuable counterweight to this overwrought sense of individualism.

Similarly, Davis's explanation of the interconnections between race and class remains important. In scrutinizing how those two systems functioned together in complementary ways, Davis anticipated the study of "intersectionality," in which scholars consciously explore how class, race, gender, sexuality, and other social systems interact to cement inequality. Davis's and his colleagues' caste-and-class framework was a pioneering form of this type of work. Decades later, sociologist William Julius Wilson explained how his early research was limited because he "paid little attention to the role of class in understanding issues of race." When he finally turned to studying the two systems together, such as in his influential *The Declining Significance of Race* (1978), he observed that "a preoccupation with race and racial conflict obscures fundamental problems that derive from the intersection of class with race." This was an insight Davis had come to four decades earlier, and one that governed his extensive body of research at midcentury. Wilson, like other scholars, would have benefited from engaging with it.[22]

Scholars today, of course, also cannot ignore the centrality of other systems, most notably gender, which Davis and his colleagues did largely ignore. Despite their considerable reliance upon the work of women in both their home lives and their scholarly careers, the primarily male social scientists of Davis's time often took for granted the gendered nature of their world. Adding an analysis of sex and gender to Davis's work would have greatly strengthened it. Allison Davis cannot be understood apart from his forty-year intellectual and emotional partnership with Elizabeth Davis, who, given the chance, might have become just as prolific and influential a scholar as her husband.

Yet it would be anachronistic to criticize Allison Davis and his colleagues for insights growing out of a powerful women's movement that occurred largely after Davis's career. In the context of their times, these scholars were pioneering in opening up new lines of research. Furthermore, their focus on just a few categories of inequality also had value, because studies of intersectionality sometimes obfuscate in their complexity.

Second, Davis's analyses of socialization are significant. Along with other culture-and-personality theorists, Davis helped to move structural theorists beyond the tendency to erect abstract social systems that were only tangentially linked with actual individuals. He showed that race and class are tangible realities in the lives of individuals, experienced through the family, the school, and other socializing agents. Yet Davis challenged the holistic, totalizing conceptions of culture held by many of his fellow culture-and-personality theorists. He showed that American society was differentiated along class lines and hence had many distinct class cultures, rather than a single, unified national one.

Davis's social-psychological orientation was similarly compelling. His emphasis on overt behavior rather than thought and ideology could fairly be criticized for downplaying the role of long-term values in directing people's behavior, but his focus on observable behavior and the environmental forces conditioning it was vital. Davis grasped that people are best understood less as stable creatures embodying a consistent set of behaviors and values than as resilient beings who behave very differently depending on the immediate context. This type of thinking allowed him to recognize the power of the social environment to shape behavior, and it enabled him to describe how individuals adopt new behaviors when the environment changes. For this reason, Davis was able to avoid the flaws of many "culture-of-poverty" theorists who saw poverty as a closed, deep-seated system that perpetually warps individuals and teaches them unalterable values.

Third, Davis's criticisms of intelligence testing remain relevant today. Despite the devastating critiques that he and others have issued over the years, the tests continue to be used in schools, businesses, and other sectors of society. As journalist Nicholas Lemann explains, modern intelligence testing often takes the guise of "aptitude testing," which is only a slightly modified form of intelligence testing. Both types of tests rely heavily on academic skills such as reading comprehension and vocabulary. Lemann argues that the United States—through the Educational Testing Service, which institutionalized the Scholastic Aptitude Test (SAT), the Graduate Record Examination (GRE), the Medical College Admissions Test (MCAT), the Law School Admissions Test (LSAT), and the Graduate Management Admissions Test (GMAT)—has become "the most thoroughly IQ-tested society in the world."[23] Despite abundant evidence that the tests are mainly barometers of social affluence rather than intellectual ability and that they do not even accurately predict a person's academic success in later years, these tests remain deeply embedded within American education. Davis saw the tests for what they really are: tools that reflect, legitimize, and actively perpetuate social disparities, all the while shoring up the meritocratic myth.[24]

Fourth, Davis's conception of education as a public good rather than a private investment remains vital today. Amid a struggling economy and a neoliberal assault on public institutions, Americans are increasingly viewing education in narrowly individualistic and utilitarian ways. Davis and his colleagues at the University of Chicago understood education far more broadly as a bulwark of democracy. They knew that a democratic system relies on an informed and empathic citizenry equipped to question power and to productively engage fellow citizens in reasoned debate. Davis thus attacked all things antidemocratic within the schools, especially segregation and unfair sorting practices. Rather than pit students against one another in competition, reflecting the larger stratified society, Davis argued, schools should be laboratories for diversity and engagement, as well as mechanisms for social mobility. In the twenty-first century, when social inequality approaches that of the Gilded Age, a more informed and engaged citizenry remains as important as ever.

Davis also has much to offer in terms of pedagogy. As a prerequisite for mutual engagement, Davis insisted that teachers and students should learn intimately about one another's lives. He understood that poor and minority students had much to "teach" more privileged students and their teachers about the world, so he promoted class discussion and debate as major pedagogical tools. Furthermore, he advised teachers to gain sociological and anthropological knowledge about their students and to forge alliances with the students' parents and the larger community.

Given his stress on productive engagement, Davis valued social studies and the humanities above all other fields. He understood that the liberal arts are unrivaled in fostering empathy and promoting social knowledge. Moreover, he knew that social science has as much practical value as did any physical or applied science (despite the current emphasis on science, technology, engineering, and math [STEM] education). Davis appreciated the deeper value of a humanistic education, which prepares students not merely to meet the increasing demands of employers but to actually question the nature and fairness of those demands in the first place, and to recognize how to change them.

Along with this, Davis promoted education that is rooted in the lives and interests of the specific students in the classroom. He recommended an education that was highly tailored, and hence relevant, to the lives of America's richly diverse students—not a standardized education that so many support today. He believed that only by investing in all students and in all public schools, and by training students to think critically and socially, could American democracy be made to thrive. America's twenty-first-century education "reform" movement, which is based heavily on privatizing education, attacking democratic forms of power such as teacher unions, and proliferating charter schools and STEM courses, would have been anathema to a democratically minded thinker such as Davis.

In adopting many of these positions, Davis followed in the footsteps of John Dewey. Despite the men's shared ties to the University of Chicago, there is no evidence that they had a personal relationship. Rather, it is likely that Dewey influenced Davis mainly through his profound impact on American education in general and on the University of Chicago in particular. As the chief architect of progressive education, Dewey inspired Davis and countless other educators to help create an educational system that was relevant, student-centered, equitable, and not least, transformational. It was therefore fitting that Davis rose to assume Chicago's first John Dewey Distinguished Service Professorship of Education.

Finally, Davis's general intellectual mode—a type of American existentialism—could be of value to Americans today. Davis faced squarely the final tragedy and ultimate purposelessness of life. As people around him became caught up with trivial pursuits engineered seemingly to avoid those darker realities, Davis faced them head on and used them to construct the most meaningful life possible.[25] He channeled his ennui and his righteous anger over injustice into socially productive ends. Rather than shrinking from the most profound human questions or getting caught up in the rat race, he probed the nature of human existence and ultimately devised a humanistic goal and purpose, which was to ease human suffering and to better the lives of others. As he understood it, "the alternatives remain the same as in all other ages. We can scuttle—or we can sail the seas. *Navigare necesse est; non vivere est.* 'One must chart his course and set sail; it is not enough merely to exist.'"[26]

ACKNOWLEDGMENTS

I am happy to acknowledge many of the specific people and institutions that have made this book possible. But I first want to recognize the countless other people—librarians, archivists, general library staff, scholars, and teachers—whose often thankless labors abetted all of my work. Without them, and without our society's continuing investment in the humanities, books like this would not exist.

A variety of institutions supported the research and writing of this book. Foremost among them was the University of Colorado. The Department of History provided extensive research support through annual grants, and it offered me one and a half years of writing support through a Roaring Fork Fellowship and the Jack C. and Jean L. Thompson Endowed Fellowship in American History. The Center for the Humanities and the Arts awarded me an Eaton Travel Grant, and it organized an individualized workshop with veteran editor Edward Dimendberg. Dimendberg gave me confidence in the project and walked me through how to approach publishers.

A number of archives supported my research. The University of Chicago Library awarded me a Robert L. Platzman Memorial Fellowship to allay research expenses, and it provided excellent guidance in helping me locate relevant materials. The same was true of Fisk University and the Rockefeller Archive Center, where Jessie Carney Smith and Nancy Adgent, respectively, were very helpful. I could scarcely have asked for better environments for conducting archival research.

Not least of all, the Department of History at Case Western Reserve University helped to bring this book to fruition. Its fellowship in African American

Studies proved essential to completing the book revisions in a timely manner. Many thanks to Rhonda Williams for instituting the fellowship and supporting my work, and to Kenneth Ledford and others at Case who made Cleveland a wonderful place to spend a year.

As essential as institutions were in supporting my research, it was the character of the individuals who inhabited them which has made all the difference. Mark Pittenger was an excellent mentor who provided guidance and support at every turn, while also letting me find my own way. His careful reading of an early version of my manuscript improved it immensely. So, too, did that of Paul Sutter, a first-rate historian from whom I have learned a great deal. The same is true of Virginia Anderson, who influenced me greatly.

Phoebe Young read the entire manuscript and gave me thoughtful feedback. Anthropologist Paul Shankman did the same, and he did so throughout the entire writing process. His early enthusiasm for my research inspired me to push forward. If Shankman helped me to see the value of the project beyond only the discipline of history, Peter H. Wood helped me to ground it in black history. At every stage, Peter went out of his way to strengthen the ideas and clarity of my work. Perhaps even more important, he served as a friend who modeled generosity and intellectual curiosity—the two best traits, I think, for any historian.

I am also thankful to a wide range of teachers and mentors who have supported me over the years. At Illinois Wesleyan, Shu-chin Wu demonstrated the vitality of history at a formative time in my life. Later, at Illinois State University, the Department of History was an embarrassment of riches. Almost every professor I encountered there went out of his or her way to encourage me to become a better historian. Richard Soderlund, Anthony Crubaugh, Alan Lessoff, Andrew Hartman, Ross Kennedy, Richard Hughes, and Agbenyega Adedze are only a few of them. Amy Wood has long supported me as both a mentor and a friend. I am deeply grateful to them all.

I am also grateful to the University of Chicago Press and those there who have helped turn my manuscript into a book. My manuscript editor, Ruth Goring, has made this book much nicer to read. My editor, Timothy Mennel, expertly navigated me through the entire process, and he did so with grace and steadfast support. Not least, he arranged for three excellent outside readers. Each of them provided sound suggestions for revisions while also sharing their enthusiasm for the book. I thank them for their hard work and commitment. Two of the readers remained anonymous, but one of them, Alford Young Jr., waived anonymity. I am thus happy to be able to thank him personally for his important contributions.

The two sons of W. Allison Davis—Allison S. Davis and Gordon J. Davis—proved to be invaluable resources for this project. Ever since I first reached out to them, they have been wellsprings of both inspiration and insight. They opened up their family records, made themselves available for interviews and e-mail correspondence, and shared their family photographs, many of which are in this book and have greatly enriched it. Yet their contributions extend beyond mere research support. They also helped to humanize their father, enabling me to render a fuller portrait of the man. Even more, they allowed me to see the direct relevance of my research for the present, and for that I am deeply grateful.

Finally, I want to acknowledge friends and family who have sustained me over the years and who have shaped me in countless ways. Kate Pole, Chris Morris, Natalie Mendoza, Liz Lawrence, Lindsey Cantwell, Chris Foss, Seth Ellis, and Tim McDonald are only a few of them. Above all, thanks to my parents, Dennis and Sharon Varel; my grandmother, Edith Ivie; my brother, Steve Varel; and my partner, Michelle Penn, who generously created the index for this book. I have relied heavily upon them throughout my life—for inspiration, emotional support, intellectual guidance, and financial backing. It is to them that I dedicate this book, with all my love.

ARCHIVAL ABBREVIATIONS

ADP SCRC UCL: Allison Davis Papers, Special Collections Research Center, University of Chicago Library, Chicago, Illinois

DFR: Davis Family Records, Allison S. Davis Jr., Chicago, Illinois

FUSC JARC: Fisk University, Special Collections, J. A. Rogers Collection, John Hope and Aurelia E. Franklin Library, Nashville, Tennessee

FUSC JARC ADFF: Fisk University, Special Collections, J. A. Rogers Collection, Allison Davis Fellowship File, 1932–42, John Hope and Aurelia E. Franklin Library, Nashville, Tennessee

FUSC JARC UCAD: Fisk University, Special Collections, J. A. Rogers Collection, University of Chicago, Allison Davis, 1941–1947, John Hope and Aurelia E. Franklin Library, Nashville, Tennessee

GEBA RAC: General Education Board Archives, Rockefeller Archive Center, Sleepy Hollow, New York

JADPF NPRC: John A. Davis Personnel File, National Personnel Records Center, St. Louis, Missouri

RFA RAC: Rockefeller Foundation Archives, Rockefeller Archive Center, Sleepy Hollow, New York

SCRC UCL: Special Collections Research Center, University of Chicago Library, Chicago, Illinois

SCUA UMAL: Special Collections and University Archives, University of Massachusetts Amherst Libraries, Amherst, Massachusetts

WLWP SCRC UCL:　W. Lloyd Warner Papers, Special Collections Research Center, University of Chicago Library, Chicago, Illinois

UCPR SCRC UCL:　University of Chicago Press Records, Special Collections Research Center, University of Chicago Library, Chicago, Illinois

NOTES

INTRODUCTION

1. John Aubrey Davis, "Remarks upon the Occasion of the Issuance of a Commemorative Stamp in Honor of Dr. W. Allison Davis at Williams College, Williamstown, Massachusetts, February 1, 1994," draft 3, 1/27/94, DFR.

2. Allison Davis, "Commencement Address, University of Chicago, 1975," Allison Davis Papers, Box 62, Folder 19, SCRC UCL.

3. In African-American history, see Dallas L. Browne, "Across Class and Culture: Allison Davis and His Works," in *African-American Pioneers in Anthropology*, ed. Ira E. Harrison and Faye V. Harrison (Urbana: University of Illinois Press, 1999), 168–90; Joan Oleck, "Allison Davis: 1902–1983," in *Contemporary Black Biography*, ed. Shirelle Phelps (Detroit: Gale Research, 1996), 12:38–41; and Daryl Michael Scott, *Contempt and Pity: Social Policy and the Image of the Damaged Black Psyche, 1880–1996* (Chapel Hill: University of North Carolina Press, 1997), 27–29, 35–37, 39, 52–54, 64–66, 124, 128, 167, 198, 223. In biography, see Morris Finder, "Davis, Allison," *American National Biography Online*, http://www.anb.org/articles/14/14–01164 .html (accessed October 1, 2014). In anthropology, see St. Clair Drake, "In the Mirror of Black Scholarship: W. Allison Davis and *Deep South*," in *Education and Black Struggle: Notes from the Colonized World* (Cambridge MA: Harvard Educational Review, 1974), 42–54; St. Clair Drake, "Reflections on Anthropology and the Black Experience," *New Perspectives on Black Education*, special issue of *Anthropology & Education Quarterly* 9, (Summer 1978): 85–95; St. Clair Drake, "Anthropology and the Black Experience," *Black Scholar* 11 (September/October 1980): 4, 21–24; John S. Gilkeson, *Anthropologists and the Rediscovery of America, 1886–1965* (Cambridge: Cambridge University Press, 2010), 94–96, 132; and Faye V. Harrison, "The Du Boisian Legacy in Anthropology," *Critique of Anthropology* 12 (September 1992): 246–51. In sociology, see James B. McKee, *Sociology and the Race Problem: The Failure of a Perspective* (Urbana: University of Illinois Press, 1993), 153, 171–73, 174, 182–86; Pierre Saint-Arnaud, *African American Pioneers of Sociology: A Critical History*, trans. Peter Feldstein (Toronto: University of Toronto Press, 2009), 78, 91, 134; and Vernon J. Williams Jr., *From a Caste to a Minority: Changing Attitudes of American Sociologists toward Afro-Americans, 1896–1945* (Westport, CT: Greenwood,

1989), 165. In education, see Morris Finder, *Educating America: How Ralph W. Tyler Taught America to Teach* (Westport, CT: Praeger, 2004), 43–46; Michael R. Hillis, "Allison Davis and the Study of Race, Social Class, and Schooling," *Journal of Negro Education* 64 (Winter 1995): 33–41; Ellen Condliffe Lagemann, *An Elusive Science: The Troubling History of Educational Research* (Chicago: University of Chicago Press, 2000), 152–53, 155, 179, 234; and Andrea Marie Macaluso, "Allison Davis and the Historical Development of His Sociological Concepts: 'Cultural Deprivation' and 'Compensatory Education: 1925–1983'" (PhD diss., Loyola University Chicago, 1996). In general social science, see Alice O'Connor, *Poverty Knowledge: Social Science, Social Policy, and the Poor in Twentieth-Century U.S. History* (Princeton, NJ: Princeton University Press, 2001), 63–64, 66, 75, 76, 85, 86, 87, 89, 95, 97, 107, 198, 209.

4. Books on Johnson and Frazier alone include Patrick J. Gilpin and Marybeth Gasman, *Charles S. Johnson: Leadership beyond the Veil in the Age of Jim Crow* (Albany: State University of New York Press, 2003); Richard Robbins, *Sidelines Activist: Charles S. Johnson and the Struggle for Civil Rights* (Jackson: University Press of Mississippi, 1996); Anthony M. Platt, *E. Franklin Frazier Reconsidered* (New Brunswick, NJ: Rutgers University Press, 1991); Jonathan Scott Holloway, *Confronting the Veil: Abram Harris, Jr., E. Franklin Frazier, and Ralph Bunche* (Chapel Hill: University of North Carolina Press, 2002); and James E. Teele, ed., *E. Franklin Frazier and Black Bourgeoisie* (Columbia: University of Missouri Press, 2002).

5. "Caste," as Davis defined it, will be discussed at length in chapter 4. But briefly, Davis defined caste not as a permanently subordinate group but as an entire system of racial stratification. In the American context, he saw it as pertaining specifically to white and black Americans, with blacks' subordination being enforced through economic, social, political, cultural, and legal means.

6. Joanne Meyerowitz, "'How Common Culture Shapes the Separate Lives': Sexuality, Race, and Mid-Twentieth-Century Social Thought," *Journal of American History* 96 (March 2010): 1083.

7. The case of black anthropologist Louis Eugene King is a good example. See Ira E. Harrison, "Louis Eugene King, the Anthropologist Who Never Was," in *African-American Pioneers in Anthropology*, ed. Harrison and Harrison, 70–84.

8. Margaret Mead, *And Keep Your Powder Dry: An Anthropologist Looks at America* (New York: William Morrow, 1942).

9. Davis, Allison, 1934, 1935, Letter from Allison Davis to Horace Mann Bond, May 17, 1935. Horace Mann Bond Papers (MS 411), SCUA UMAL.

10. Daniel P. Moynihan, "The Professors and the Poor," *Commentary*, August 1968, https://www.commentarymagazine.com/article/theprofessorsandthepoor/ (accessed June 15, 2015).

11. Daniel P. Moynihan, letter to the editor, *Commentary*, November 1968; St. Clair Drake, "Poverty, Sociology and Finks," *Commentary*, November 1968, https://www.commentarymagazine.com/article/povertysociologyfinks/ (accessed June 15, 2015).

12. On race and social science in interwar America, see Jerry Gershenhorn, *Melville J. Herskovits and the Racial Politics of Knowledge* (Lincoln: University of Nebraska Press, 2004); and Gilpin and Gasman, *Charles S. Johnson.* On southern intellectual life in interwar America, see Daniel Joseph Singal, *The War Within: From Victorian to Modernist Thought In the South, 1919–1945* (Chapel Hill: University of North Carolina Press, 1982). On the Harlem Renaissance, see David Levering Lewis, *When Harlem Was in Vogue* (New York: Alfred A. Knopf, 1981). On

black intellectual life, see Harold Cruse, *The Crisis of the Negro Intellectual: A Historical Analysis of the Failure of Black Leadership* (New York: William Morrow, 1967), and James O. Young, *Black Writers of the Thirties* (Baton Rouge: Louisiana University Press, 1973).

13. Kenneth Eells, Allison Davis, Robert J. Havighurst, Virgil E. Herrick, and Ralph Tyler, *Intelligence and Cultural Differences: A Study of Cultural Learning and Problem-Solving* (Chicago: University of Chicago Press, 1951).

14. For an intellectual biography that takes up the dilemma of being a black intellectual as its primary theme, see Kenneth Robert Janken, *Rayford Logan and the Dilemma of the African-American Intellectual* (Amherst: University of Massachusetts Press, 1993).

15. These efforts span the social sciences. Three landmark volumes within anthropology— Davis's primary field—are Lee D. Baker, *From Savage to Negro: Anthropology and the Construction of Race, 1896–1954* (Berkeley: University of California Press, 1998); Faye V. Harrison, ed., *Decolonizing Anthropology: Moving Further toward an Anthropology for Liberation* (Washington, DC: American Anthropological Association, 1991); and Harrison and Harrison, eds., *African-American Pioneers in Anthropology*. Within sociology, two notable works include Saint-Arnaud, *African American Pioneers of Sociology*; and Aldon Morris, *The Scholar Denied: W. E. B. Du Bois and the Birth of Modern Sociology* (Berkeley: University of California Press, 2015).

16. Attempts to identify early black pioneers in anthropology have all failed to mention her. See Drake, "Reflections on Anthropology and the Black Experience," 94–95; Harrison and Harrison, eds., *African-American Pioneers in Anthropology*; and Martin Kilson, *Transformation of the African American Intelligentsia, 1880–2012* (Cambridge, MA: Harvard University Press, 2014), 202.

CHAPTER ONE

1. Allison Davis, novelistic drafts, DFR. From here forward, I will use "novelistic drafts" to refer to the autobiographical novel that Davis worked on at various points in his life but which he never completed or published. I rely upon this source especially for the first third of Davis's life, when the novel was most complete and most clearly autobiographical. After corroborating the novel with other historical sources, and after consulting the Davis family, I agree with them that this section of the novel speaks directly to Davis's own experiences. That said, Davis did alter certain minor facts, and some of the specific stories and quotes should not be taken as definitive, literal truths. Still, the novelistic drafts do distill Davis's perceptions of his experiences as a young man, and they do add valuable specificity to his life. For that reason I have included them here and incorporated them into my narrative.

2. Allison Davis, *Leadership, Love, and Aggression* (San Diego: Harcourt Brace Jovanovich, 1983), 150–51.

3. W. E. B. Du Bois, *The Souls of Black Folk* (1903; repr., New York: Dover, 1994), 2, 3.

4. Ibid., 2.

5. War Department, "Abstract of Official Record of Civilian Employee," JADPF NPRC.

6. W. B. Allison to Frank W. Palmer, July 6, 1899, JADPF NPRC; Private Secretary to Chas. A. Stillings, January 4, 1908, JADPF NPRC.

7. John Aubrey Davis to Gordon Davis, August 27, 1997, DFR.

8. Caroline Gaskins, "Copy of the Will of Caroline Gaskins Davis Chinn," in *The Davises: Fons et Origo*, vol. I, DFR.

9. Dorothy Davis Lucas, "The Carlisle Connection: James Mandeville Carlisle and Caroline Gaskins Davis Chinn," in *The Davises: Fons et Origo*, vol. I, DFR.

10. "Messenger for War Department Dies," *Sunday Star* (Washington), April 21, 1928.

11. John Aubrey Davis, quoted in Martin Kilson, "Political Scientists and the Activist-Technocrat Dichotomy: The Case of John Aubrey Davis," in *African American Perspectives in Political Science*, ed. Wilbur C. Rich (Philadelphia: Temple University Press, 2007), 174.

12. Eric S. Yellin, *Racism in the Nation's Service: Government Workers and the Color Line in Woodrow Wilson's America* (Chapel Hill: University of North Carolina Press, 2013), 61–62.

13. Ibid., 127.

14. War Department, "Abstract of Official Record of Civilian Employee," JADPF NPRC.

15. Chief Clerk to John A. Davis, May 17, 1913, JADPF NPRC.

16. John R. Bey to the Public Printer, July 7, 1913, JADPF NPRC.

17. John A. Davis to Cornelius Ford (Public Printer), July 20, 1913, JADPF NPRC; John A. Davis to Samuel B. Donnelly (Public Printer), May 16, 1913, JADPF NPRC.

18. Ibid.

19. Allison Davis, novelistic drafts, DFR.

20. O. K. Miller to John A. Davis, March 19, 1914, in *The Davises: Fons et Origo*, vol. I, DFR.

21. "Public Sale of Valuable Personal Property," April 1, 1914, in *The Davises: Fons et Origo*, vol. I, Davis DFR.

22. Davis, novelistic drafts, DFR.

23. Dorothy Davis Lucas, in *The Davises: Fons et Origo*, vol. I, DFR.

24. Davis, novelistic drafts, DFR.

25. Dorothy Davis Lucas, "Sale of the Farm and Thereafter," in *The Davises: Fons et Origo*, vol. I, DFR.

26. Davis, novelistic drafts, DFR.

27. Kenneth Robert Janken, *Rayford Logan and the Dilemma of the African-American Intellectual* (Amherst: University of Massachusetts Press, 1993), 20.

28. Mary Gibson Hundley, *The Dunbar Story, 1870–1955* (New York: Vintage, 1965), 70.

29. Thomas Sowell, "Black Excellence: The Case of Dunbar High School," *Public Interest* 35 (Spring 1974): 8–9.

30. Hundley, *Dunbar Story*, 16.

31. Williams College Transcript, box 406, folder 5, FUSC JARC ADFF.

32. Walter A. Jackson, *Gunnar Myrdal and America's Conscience: Social Engineering and Racial Liberalism, 1938–1987* (Chapel Hill: University of North Carolina Press, 1990), 102.

33. Allison S. Davis, interview with the author, December 30, 2014.

34. Dallas L. Browne, "Across Class and Culture: Allison Davis and His Works," in *African-American Pioneers in Anthropology*, ed. Ira E. Harrison and Faye V. Harrison (Urbana: University of Illinois Press, 1999), 171.

35. Davis, novelistic drafts, DFR.

36. Ibid.

37. Booker T. Washington, quoted in Constance McLaughlin Green, *The Secret City: A History of Race Relations in the Nation's Capital* (Princeton, NJ: Princeton University Press, 1967).

38. Langston Hughes, quoted in Arnold Rampersad, *The Life of Langston Hughes*, vol. 1, *1902–1941: I, Too, Sing America* (New York: Oxford University Press, 1986), 99–100.

39. For a good account of black Washington and the black bourgeoisie, see Willard B. Gatewood, *Aristocrats of Color: The Black Elite, 1880–1920* (Bloomington: Indiana University Press, 1990).

40. Davis, novelistic drafts, DFR.

41. Peter Perl, "Race Riot of 1919 Gave Glimpse of Future Struggles," *Washington Post*, March 1, 1999.

42. David Levering Lewis, *When Harlem Was in Vogue*, new ed. (New York: Penguin, 1996), 19.

43. Ibid.

44. Perl, "Race Riot of 1919."

45. Ibid.

46. Browne, *Across Class and Culture*, 171.

47. Davis, novelistic drafts, DFR.

48. Ibid.

49. Ibid.

50. Allison Davis, "A Glorious Company," in *Ebony and Topaz: A Collecteana*, ed. Charles S. Johnson (1927; repr., Freeport, NY: Books for Libraries, 1971), 156.

51. Sterling A. Brown, "A Son's Return: 'Oh Didn't He Ramble,'" in *Perspectives: A Williams Anthology*, ed. Frederick Rudolph (Williamstown, MA: Williams College, 1983), 320–21; "The Talented Black Scholars Whom No White University Would Hire," *Journal of Blacks in Higher Education* 58 (Winter 2007/2008): 81.

52. Davis, novelistic drafts, DFR.

53. Harry A. Garfield to James E. Gregg, April 14, 1925, DFR.

54. Davis, novelistic drafts, DFR.

55. Janken, *Rayford Logan*, 27.

56. Davis, novelistic drafts, DFR.

57. Ibid.

58. Brown, "Son's Return," 323, 324.

59. Allison Davis, quoted in Barbara P. Turner, "Profile of Allison Davis; The Man and His Research," *Education at Chicago* 2 (Autumn 1972): 23.

60. Joanne V. Gabbin, *Sterling A. Brown: Building the Black Aesthetic Tradition* (Westport, CT: Greenwood, 1985), 23.

61. Harry A. Garfield to Appointment Office at Harvard University, March 20, 1925, DFR.

62. George E. Howes's Confidential Report on Candidate for Scholarship, 1931, Box 406, Folder 5, FUSC JARC ADFF.

63. Ibid.

64. Carroll Lewis Maxcy's Confidential Report on Candidate for Scholarship, 1931, box 406, folder 5, FUSC JARC ADFF.

65. Brown, "Son's Return," 328.

66. Gabbin, *Sterling A. Brown*, 24.

67. Brown, "Son's Return," 330.

68. Gabbin, *Sterling A. Brown*, 28.

69. Davis, novelistic drafts, DFR.

70. Harvard's elite did run Radcliffe College, for women, as well. Laurel Thatcher Ulrich, "Introduction: Rewriting Harvard's History," in *Yards and Gates: Gender in Harvard and Radcliffe History*, ed. Laurel Thatcher Ulrich (New York: Palgrave Macmillan, 2004), 3.

71. Wendell E. Pritchett, *Robert Clifton Weaver and the American City: The Life and Times of an Urban Reformer* (Chicago: University of Chicago Press, 2008), 20.

72. Marcia Graham Synnott, *The Half-Opened Door: Discrimination and Admissions at Harvard, Yale, and Princeton, 1900–1970* (Westport, CT: Greenwood, 1979), 47, 83–84; James Weldon Johnson, "Attacks Harvard on Negro Question" (1930), in *Varieties of the Black Experience at Harvard: An Anthology*, ed. Werner Sollors, Thomas A. Underwood, and Caldwell Titcomb (Cambridge, MA: Harvard University Press, 1986), 87; Nell Painter, "Jim Crow at Harvard: 1923," *New England Quarterly* 44 (December 1971): 629.

73. Allison Davis, curriculum vitae, ADP SCRC UCL, box 1, folder 2.

74. Werner Sollors, Thomas A. Underwood, and Caldwell Titcomb, "Sterling A. Brown," in *Varieties of the Black Experience*, 103.

75. Brown, "Son's Return," 330.

76. St. Clair Drake, "In the Mirror of Black Scholarship: W. Allison Davis and *Deep South*," in *Education and Black Struggle: Notes from the Colonized World*, ed. Institute of the Black World (Cambridge, MA: Harvard Educational Review, 1974), 44.

77. J. David Hoeveler Jr., *The New Humanism: A Critique of Modern America, 1900–1940* (Charlottesville: University Press of Virginia, 1977), 3.

78. Irving Babbit, *Literature and the American College: Essays in Defense of the Humanities* (Boston: Houghton, Mifflin, 1908), 30.

79. Hoeveler, *New Humanism*, 42.

80. Babbitt, *Literature and the American College*, 64.

81. Irving Babbitt, *Rousseau and Romanticism* (Boston: Houghton Mifflin, 1919), xxiii.

82. Hoeveler, *New Humanism*, 40.

83. See Irving Babbitt, "Matthew Arnold," in *Spanish Character and Other Essays* (Boston: Houghton Mifflin, 1940), 48–65.

84. Quoted in Hoeveler, *New Humanism*, 8–9.

85. Allison S. Davis, interview by the author, December 30, 2014.

86. St. Clair Drake, "Studies of the African Diaspora: The Work and Reflections of St. Clair Drake," in *Against All Odds: Scholars Who Challenged Racism in the Twentieth Century*, ed. Benjamin P. Bowser and Louis Kushnick (Amherst: University of Massachusetts Press, 2002), 90.

87. Davis, quoted in Turner, "Profile of Allison Davis," 23.

88. W. Allison Davis to Harry A. Garfield, April 12, 192[5], DFR.

89. Harry A. Garfield to W. Allison Davis, April 14, 1925, DFR.

90. Ibid.

91. John Aubrey Davis, *How Management Can Integrate Negroes in War Industries* (New York: New York State War Council, 1942); and John Aubrey Davis, *Regional Organization of the Social Security Administration: A Case Study* (New York: Columbia University Press, 1950). For a study of Davis's years in the Fair Employment Practices Committee, see Martin Kilson, "Political Scientists and the Activist-Technocrat Dichotomy: The Case of John Aubrey Davis,"

in *African American Perspectives in Political Science*, ed. Wilbur C. Rich (Philadelphia: Temple University Press, 2007), 169–92.

92. Dorothy Davis Lucas, "Sale of the Farm and Thereafter," in *The Davises: Fons et Origo*, vol. I, DFR; Allison Davis, "Account of Papa's Death," in ibid.

93. Lewis, *When Harlem Was in Vogue*, 18–19.

94. Raymond Wolters, *The New Negro on Campus: Black College Rebellions of the 1920s* (Princeton, NJ: Princeton University Press, 1975), 17.

95. W. E. B. Du Bois, "Returning Soldiers" (1919), in *The Portable Harlem Renaissance Reader*, ed. David Levering Lewis (New York: Viking, 1994), 5.

96. See Adriane Lentz-Smith, *Freedom Struggles: African Americans and World War I* (Cambridge, MA: Harvard University Press, 2009); and Mark Whalan, *The Great War and the Culture of the New Negro* (Gainesville: University Press of Florida, 2008).

97. On Wilsonianism and anticolonial nationalism, see Erez Manela, *The Wilsonian Moment: Self-Determination and the International Origins of Anticolonial Nationalism* (Oxford: Oxford University Press, 2007).

98. For a great overview of black education in the South, see James D. Anderson, *The Education of Blacks in the South, 1860–1935* (Chapel Hill: University of North Carolina Press, 1935).

99. Wolters, *New Negro on Campus*, 18.

100. William M. Banks, *Black Intellectuals: Race and Responsibility in American Life* (New York: W. W. Norton, 1996), 95–96.

101. Wolters, *New Negro on Campus*, 230.

102. Janken, *Rayford Logan*, 63–64.

103. Jonathan Spiro, *Defending the Master Race: Conservation, Eugenics, and the Legacy of Madison Grant* (Burlington: University of Vermont Press, 2009), 237–40.

104. On Jim Crow's international flight, see Glenda Gilmore, *Defying Dixie: The Radical Roots of Civil Rights, 1919–1950* (New York: W. W. Norton, 2008), 21–28.

105. Wolters, *New Negro on Campus*, 26.

106. "Memorandum regarding Hampton Institute," Oct. 10, 1923, box 174, folder 1626, series 1, GEBA RAC.

107. Wolters, *New Negro on Campus*, 232–34.

108. Quoted in ibid., 235.

109. Ibid.

110. Drake, "Studies of the African Diaspora," 88.

111. St. Clair Drake, quoted in George C. Bond, "A Social Portrait of John Gibbs St. Clair Drake: An American Anthropologist," *American Ethnologist* 15 (1988): 766.

112. Drake, "Studies of the African Diaspora," 88–89.

113. Wolters, *New Negro on Campus*, 249–50.

114. Wayne J. Urban, *Black Scholar: Horace Mann Bond, 1904–1972* (Athens: University of Georgia Press, 1992), 40–41.

115. Loren Miller, "The Unrest among Negro Students at a White College: The University of Kansas," *Crisis* 34 (August 1927): 187–90. See also Charles S. Johnson, "More Student Unrest," *Opportunity* 3 (June 1925): 164.

116. Drake, "In the Mirror of Black Scholarship," 44.

117. Davis remained a paragon of professionalism and a master of winning white administrators' support. For example, the white principal of Hampton in 1931, Arthur Howe, wrote a letter of recommendation for Davis, stating: "He is a bright man and writes readily and is scholarly in his pursuit of learning." Howe went on to call Davis "unusually fine," "upright," and "most deserving in all matters of character." Arthur Howe to Edwin Embree, November 12, 1931, Box 406, Folder 5, FUSC JARC ADFF.

118. St. Clair Drake, "Reflections on Anthropology and the Black Experience," *Anthropology & Education Quarterly* 9, New Perspectives on Black Education (Summer 1978): 91.

119. Wolters, *New Negro on Campus*, 270.

120. See also Andrew J. Rosa, "The Roots and Routes of 'Imperio': St. Clair Drake, the Formative Years," *American Studies* 52 (November 2012): 68–69; and Andrew J. Rosa, "New Negroes on Campus: St. Clair Drake and the Culture of Education, Reform, and Rebellion at Hampton Institute," *History of Education Quarterly* 53 (August 2013): 222–28.

121. Drake, "In the Mirror of Black Scholarship," 44.

122. Drake, "Reflections on Anthropology and the Black Experience," 91.

123. Drake, "In the Mirror of Black Scholarship," 44.

124. Drake, quoted in Bond, "Social Portrait of John Gibbs St. Clair Drake," 766.

125. Davis, Allison, 1902–1983, Letter from Allison Davis to W. E. B. Du Bois, February 17, 1930, W. E. B. Du Bois Papers (MS 312), SCUA UMAL.

126. Drake, "Studies of the African Diaspora," 90, 86.

127. Lloyd Warner to Edwin Embree, August 15, 1935, box 409, folder 1, FUSC JARC, St. Clair Drake Fellowship File.

128. Enoch P. Waters, *American Diary: A Personal History of the Black Press* (Chicago: Path, 1987), 58–59.

129. Drake, "In the Mirror of Black Scholarship," 44.

130. Davis, quoted in Turner, "Profile of Allison Davis," 22.

131. Ibid.

CHAPTER TWO

1. Allison Davis, "The Negro Deserts His People," *Plain Talk* 4 (January 1929): 53.

2. Allison Davis, "A Glorious Company," in *Ebony and Topaz: A Collecteana*, ed. Charles S. Johnson (1927; repr., Freeport, NY: Books for Libraries Press, 1971), 156.

3. Ibid., 156, 157.

4. See Johnson quoted in Joanne V. Gabbin, *Sterling A. Brown: Building the Black Aesthetic Tradition* (Westport, CT: Greenwood, 1985), 28.

5. Charles S. Johnson, for instance, took a representative position on integration, or assimilation, over separation. See Charles S. Johnson, "On Garvey and the 'Garvey Movement,'" *Opportunity* 6 (January 1928): 5–6.

6. Lewis, introduction to *Harlem Renaissance Reader*, xv.

7. Lewis, *When Harlem Was in Vogue*, xx.

8. Henry Louis Gates Jr. and Gene Andrew Jarrett, introduction to *The New Negro: Readings on Race, Representation, and African American Culture, 1892–1938*, ed. Gates and Jarrett (Princeton, NJ: Princeton University Press, 2007), 1–3.

9. For a detailed and classic treatment of this rebellion, see Henry F. May, *The End of American Innocence: A Study of the First Years of Our Own Time*, new ed. (New York: Columbia University Press, 1992). See also Christine Stansell, *American Moderns: Bohemian New York and the Creation of a New Century* (New York: Henry Holt, 2000). See also Randolph Bourne, "Trans-national America," *Atlantic Monthly* 118 (July 1916): 86–97.

10. Lewis, introduction to *Harlem Renaissance Reader*, xx–xxv.

11. Ibid., xxxi–xxxii.

12. See Langston Hughes, "Negro Artist and the Racial Mountain," in *Harlem Renaissance Reader*, 91–95; and W. E. B. Du Bois, "Criteria for Negro Art," in *Harlem Renaissance Reader*, 103.

13. Lewis, introduction to *Harlem Renaissance Reader*, xxi–xli.

14. Patrick J. Gilpin and Marybeth Gasman, *Charles S. Johnson: Leadership beyond the Veil in the Age of Jim Crow* (Albany: State University of New York, 2003), 21.

15. See, for instance, "Contest Awards," *Opportunity* 4 (May 1926): 156–57.

16. William M. Banks, *Black Intellectuals: Race and Responsibility in American Life* (New York: W. W. Norton, 1996), 77.

17. Davis's letters to Du Bois reveal that he was often annoyed by the slow pace with which Du Bois reviewed his work. See, for instance, Allison Davis to W. E. B. Du Bois, June 27, 1927, W. E. B. Du Bois Papers (MS 312), SCUA UMAL. Over time, though, Davis impressed Du Bois, and Du Bois began soliciting him for more writing.

18. Allison Davis, "Fighters," *Opportunity* 6 (June 1928): 175. Despite this prominence, Davis is absent from Henry Louis Gates Jr. and Evelyn Brooks Higginbotham, eds., *Harlem Renaissance Lives from the African American National Biography* (Oxford: Oxford University Press, 2009), which includes brief biographies of hundreds of the most significant contributors. The foremost scholar of the Renaissance, David Levering Lewis, also fails to mention Davis in his comprehensive and standard account of the Renaissance, *When Harlem Was in Vogue*. In George Hutchinson's excellent study of the movement, he mentions Davis only once, and only in the context of one of his critical essays, "Our Negro Intellectuals." See George Hutchinson, *The Harlem Renaissance in Black and White* (Cambridge, MA: Harvard University Press, 1995), 168, which refers to Davis as an anthropologist. (In general, Davis's literary output has been overshadowed by his social science career.)

Daryl Michael Scott and Alice O'Connor are two of the few scholars to recognize Davis as an important figure of the movement, comparable to the better-known E. Franklin Frazier. See Daryl Michael Scott, *Contempt and Pity: Social Policy and the Image of the Damaged Black Psyche, 1880–1996* (Chapel Hill: University of North Carolina Press, 1997), 65; and Alice O'Connor, *Poverty Knowledge: Social Science, Social Policy, and the Poor in Twentieth-Century U.S. History* (Princeton, NJ: Princeton University Press, 2001), chaps. 2–3. Note also the inclusion of Davis's "Our Negro Intellectuals" in Henry Louis Gates Jr. and Gene Andrew Jarrett, eds., *The New Negro: Readings on Race, Representation, and African American Culture, 1892–1938* (Princeton, NJ: Princeton University Press, 2007), 246–50.

19. Allison Davis, "To Those Dead and Gone," *Crisis* 34 (November 1927): 303.

20. Allison Davis, "Gospel for Those Who Must," *Crisis* 35 (July 1928): 232. This poem is divided into two parts: "The Leader" and "Fighters." Davis published "Fighters" in *Opportunity* the month before. See Allison Davis, "Fighters," *Opportunity* 6 (June 1928): 175.

21. Allison Davis, "Our Negro 'Intellectuals'" (1928), in *New Negro: Readings on Race*, 249.

22. W. E. B. Du Bois, introduction to "Savage or Serene" by Allison Davis, *Crisis* 36 (May 1929): 157.

23. Allison Davis, "On Misgivings," *Crisis* 34 (August 1927): 192.

24. For more on American as well as African American existentialism, see George Cotkin, *Existential America* (Baltimore: Johns Hopkins University Press, 2003).

25. For a concise overview of Victorianism as a culture, see Daniel Walker Howe, "American Victorianism as a Culture," *American Quarterly* 27 (December 1975): 507–32.

26. Du Bois, "Criteria for Negro Art," 103.

27. William Archibald Dunning, *Reconstruction: Political and Economic, 1965–1877* (1907; repr., New York: Harper and Brothers, 1962), 267.

28. V. P. Franklin, *Living Our Stories, Telling Our Truths: Autobiography and the Making of the African-American Intellectual Tradition* (New York: Scribner, 1995), 15–16.

29. For more on the generational divide among black intellectuals, see James O. Young, *Black Writers of the Thirties* (Baton Rouge: Louisiana University Press, 1973).

30. This is what many establishment figures, such as Jessie Fauset, did. Her novels, including *There Is Confusion* (1924) and *Plum Bum* (1929), focused on the black elite and issue of passing.

31. Davis, "In Glorious Company," 156.

32. Lewis, *Harlem Renaissance Reader*, 624.

33. Sterling A. Brown, "Our Literary Audience," (1930), in *The New Negro: Readings on Race*, 387.

34. For one of the most significant articles laying out the younger writers' mindset, see Langston Hughes, "The Negro Artist and the Racial Mountain," *Nation* 122 (June 23, 1926).

35. Lewis, *Harlem Renaissance Reader*, 156, 300–301.

36. Wallace Thurman, "*Harlem*: A Forum of Negro Life," in *Harlem Renaissance Reader*, 630.

37. Lewis, *Harlem Renaissance Reader*, 624.

38. Davis, "Our Negro 'Intellectuals,'" 248.

39. Ibid., 247.

40. Ibid., 247–48.

41. Daniel, Victor, Letter from Victor Daniel to Editor of the *Crisis*, July 24, 1928, W. E. B. Du Bois Papers (MS 312), SCUA UMAL.

42. Du Bois, W. E. B. (William Edward Burghardt), 1868–1963, Letter from W. E. B. Du Bois to Allison Davis, September 5, 1928, W. E. B. Du Bois Papers (MS 312), SCUA UMAL.

43. Davis, "Our Negro 'Intellectuals,'" 248, 250.

44. See, for example, the remarkable similarity between Davis's poem "Fighters" and Brown's poem "Strong Men." They embody the same critical realism and emphasize the fortitude, humility, and heroic nature of the ordinary toiling black person. Davis, "Fighters," *Opportunity* 6 (June 1928): 175; Brown, "Strong Men," *Opportunity* 8 (September 1930): 265.

45. Sterling A. Brown, "Our Literary Audience," (1930), in *New Negro: Readings on Race*, 387.

46. Brown, "Steady and Unaccusing," 355–56.

47. Brown, "Our Literary Audience," 386.

48. Ibid., 389.

49. Sterling Brown, *Southern Road* (New York: Harcourt, Brace, 1932). Alain Locke, "Sterling Brown: The New Negro Folk-Poet," in *Varieties of the Black Experience at Harvard: An Anthology*, ed. Werner Sollors, Thomas A. Underwood, and Caldwell Titcomb (Cambridge, MA: Harvard University Press, 1986), 70–76.

50. Tidwell and Tracy, *After Winter*, xxiii.

51. Davis, "Negro Deserts His People," 49.

52. Allison Davis, "The Second Generation," *Crisis* 35 (March 1928): 87.

53. Davis, "Negro Deserts His People," 49–54.

54. Wayne J. Urban, *Black Scholar: Horace Mann Bond, 1904–1972* (Athens: University of Georgia Press, 1992), 229.

55. Davis, "Negro Deserts His People," 50.

56. Ibid., 51.

57. Urban, *Black Scholar*, 229.

58. Banks, W. Randolph, Letter from W. Randolph Banks to Editor of the Crisis, March 1, 1928, W. E. B. Du Bois Papers (MS 312), SCUA UMAL.

59. Berry, S. Paul, Letter from S. Paul Berry to Editor of the *Crisis*, March 9, 1928, W. E. B. Du Bois Papers (MS 312), SCUA UMAL.

60. Brown, "Our Literary Audience," 389.

61. Du Bois, W. E. B. (William Edward Burghardt), 1868–1963, Letter from W. E. B. Du Bois to W. Randolph Banks, April 14, 1928, W. E. B. Du Bois Papers (MS 312), SCUA UMAL.

62. See Malcolm Cowley, *Exile's Return: A Literary Odyssey of the 1920s* (1934; repr., New York: Penguin Books, 1951).

63. Ironically, Lewis named his protagonist after Irving Babbitt, whom he and many other American critics savaged but whom Davis found insightful. Brown, "Son's Return," 328.

64. For example, see E. Franklin Frazier, "Racial Self-Expression," in *Ebony and Topaz*, 121.

65. See also Allison Davis, "Savage or Serene," *Crisis* 36 (May 1929): 157, 173. This is another philosophical piece very similar to "On Misgivings."

66. Davis, "On Misgivings," 192.

67. Langston Hughes, "Our Wonderful Society: Washington," *Opportunity* 6 (August 1927): 226.

68. St. Clair Drake, quoted in George C. Bond, "A Social Portrait of John Gibbs St. Clair Drake: An American Anthropologist," *American Ethnologist* 15 (1988): 768.

69. E. Franklin Frazier, "La Bourgeoisie Noire," in *Harlem Renaissance Reader*, 179–80.

70. Davis, "Negro Deserts His People," 49.

71. Davis, "Our Negro 'Intellectuals,' " 249–50.

72. Ibid., 249.

73. George Schuyler, "The Negro-Art Hokum," in *Harlem Renaissance Reader*, 97.

74. George S. Schuyler, "Our Greatest Gift to America," in *Ebony and Topaz*, 122–24.

75. Davis, "Our Negro 'Intellectuals,' " 249.

76. Davis, "Negro Deserts His People," 51.

77. Christopher Robert Reed, *The Rise of Chicago's Black Metropolis, 1920–1929* (Urbana: University of Illinois Press, 2011), 71–117.

78. Davis, "Negro Deserts His People," 51, 52.

79. Ibid., 52–53. For an account of early civil rights activism in Mississippi, see Charles M. Payne, *I've Got the Light of Freedom: The Organizing Tradition and the Mississippi Freedom Struggle* (Berkeley: University of California Press, 1996).

80. Davis, "Negro Deserts His People," 54, 52.

81. Abram Harris, "Economic Foundations of American Race Division," *Social Forces* 5 (1927): 470, 478.

82. Jonathan Scott Holloway, *Confronting the Veil: Abram Harris Jr., E. Franklin Frazier, and Ralph Bunche, 1919–1941* (Chapel Hill: University of North Carolina Press, 2002), 56, 3.

83. Martin Kilson, *Transformation of the African American Intelligentsia, 1880–2012* (Cambridge, MA: Harvard University Press, 2014), 102.

84. See, for instance, "A&P Hires 2 Clerks," *Washington Tribune*, September 28, 1933; John Aubrey Davis, "We Win the Right to Fight for Jobs," *Opportunity* 16 (August 1938): 230–37.

85. For more on early Black Nationalism, see Judith Stein, *The World of Marcus Garvey: Race and Class in Modern Society* (Baton Rouge: Louisiana University Press, 1986), 5–10.

86. Davis, "Negro Deserts His People," 53.

87. Young, *Black Writers of the Thirties*, 63.

88. Lewis, *When Harlem Was in Vogue*, xx; Lewis, introduction to *The Portable Harlem Renaissance Reader*, xxi–xli.

89. For some recent accounts decentering Harlem, see Davarian L. Baldwin and Minkah Makalani, eds., *Escape from New York: The New Negro Renaissance beyond Harlem* (Minneapolis: University of Minnesota Press, 2013); Davarian Baldwin, *Chicago's New Negroes* (Chapel Hill: University of North Carolina Press, 2007); and David Canton, *Raymond Pace Alexander: New Negro Lawyer in Philadelphia* (Jackson: University Press of Mississippi, 2010).

CHAPTER THREE

1. Allison Davis, "The Study of Society," pp. 1–2, ADP SCRC UCL, box 30, folder 13.

2. St. Clair Drake, "Studies of the African Diaspora: The Work and Reflections of St. Clair Drake," in *Against All Odds: Scholars Who Challenged Racism in the Twentieth Century*, ed. Benjamin P. Bowser and Louis Kushnick (Amherst: University of Massachusetts Press, 2002), 90.

3. For a classic formulation of this cultural transition, see Warren I. Susman, "The Culture of the Thirties," in *Culture as History: The Transformation of American Society in the Twentieth Century* (New York: Pantheon Books, 1984), 150–83.

4. William M. Banks, *Black Intellectuals: Race and Responsibility in American Life* (New York: W. W. Norton, 1996), 104–5.

5. St. Clair Drake, "Reflections on Anthropology and the Black Experience," *New Perspectives on Black Education*, special issue of *Anthropology & Education Quarterly* 9, (Summer 1978): 92.

6. Charles S. Johnson, *The Negro College Graduate* (Chapel Hill: University of North Carolina Press, 1938), 10.

7. Banks, *Black Intellectuals*, 93.

8. On women fighting scientific sexism, see Rosalind Rosenberg, *Beyond Separate Spheres: Intellectual Roots of Modern Feminism* (New Haven, CT: Yale University Press, 1982).

9. David A. Hollinger, "Ethnic Diversity, Cosmopolitanism, and the Emergence of the American Liberal Intelligentsia," in his *In the American Province: Studies in the History and Historiography of Ideas* (Bloomington: Indiana University Press, 1985), 56–73.

10. A quick glance at the pages of *Opportunity* or *Crisis* in the 1920s and 1930s reveals the extent to which literary expression was allied with scientific research. Anthropologists such as Ruth Benedict and Edward Sapir are two prominent social scientists who pursued literary and scientific projects. See Richard Handler, "Vigorous Male and Aspiring Female: Poetry, Personality, and Culture in Edward Sapir and Ruth Benedict," in *Malinowski, Rivers, Benedict and Others: Essays on Culture and Personality*, ed. George W. Stocking Jr. (Madison: University of Wisconsin Press, 1986), 127–55; Richard Handler, "Ruth Benedict and the Modernist Sensibility," in *Modernist Anthropology: From Fieldwork to Text*, ed. Marc Manganaro (Princeton, NJ: Princeton University Press, 1990), 163–80; and Richard Handler, "The Dainty Man and the Hungry Man: Literature and Anthropology in the Work of Edward Sapir," in *Observers Observed: Essays on Ethnographic Fieldwork*, ed. George W. Stocking Jr. (Madison: University of Wisconsin Press, 1983), 208–32.

11. Dorothy Ross, "Modernism Reconsidered," in *Modernist Impulses in the Human Sciences, 1870–1930*, ed. Dorothy Ross (Baltimore: Johns Hopkins University Press, 1994), 2.

12. Allison S. Davis, Interview with the author, December 30, 2014.

13. "Pneumonia Victim: Del. Physician Succumbs; Was Sick for Week," in *The Davises: Fons et Origo*, vol. I, Davis Family Papers.

14. Mount Holyoke. "A Detailed History," https://www.mtholyoke.edu/about/history /detailed (maintained by the Mount Holyoke Department of History), accessed March 18, 2015.

15. Allison Davis, application for Rosenwald Fellowship, December 6, 1931, box 406, folder 5, FUSC JARC ADFF.

16. St. Clair Drake, "In the Mirror of Black Scholarship: W. Allison Davis and *Deep South*," in *Education and Black Struggle: Notes from the Colonized World* (Cambridge, MA: Harvard Educational Review, 1974), 42, 43, 45.

17. See Lee D. Baker, *From Savage to Negro: Anthropology and the Construction of Race, 1896–1954* (Berkeley: University of California Press, 1998), 32–37.

18. St. Clair Drake, "Anthropology and the Black Experience," *Black Scholar* 11 (September/ October 1980): 2–31; Drake, "Reflections on Anthropology and the Black Experience," 85–109.

19. Letters of support for Davis application for Rosenwald Fellowship, December 6, 1931, Fisk box 406, folder 5, FUSC JARC ADFF.

20. *Fellows of the Social Science Research Council*, 1925–1951 (New York, 1951), 86.

21. *The Social Science Research Council: Seventh Annual Report, 1930–1931* (New York, 1931), 49. For more information regarding the nature of the Southern Fellows program, initiated in 1930, see *The Social Science Research Council: Fifth Annual Report, 1928–1929* (New York, 1929), 28.

22. *The Rockefeller Foundation Annual Report, 1931* (New York: Rockefeller Foundation, 1931), 250–51; "Report upon the Utilization of the Rockefeller Grant for Research to the Division of Anthropology of Harvard University," July 14, 1933, folder 339, box 4045, Series 200-U.S., sub-Series S-Social Sciences, Record Group 1.1-Projects, RFA RAC.

23. Earnest A. Hooton to Dr. Edmund E. Day, June 29, 1934, folder 339, box 4045, Series 200-U.S., sub-Series S-Social Sciences, Record Group 1.1-Projects, RFA RAC.

24. Mildred Warner, "Will You Come to Australia?" in "W. Lloyd Warner; Social Anthropologist," by Mildred Hall Warner, Burleigh Gardner, Robert J. Havighurst, and Associates, with corrections, n.d. WLWP SCRC UCL, box 5, folder 1, p. 1.4.

25. For more on the Rosenwald Fund, see Edwin R. Embree and Julia Waxman, *Investment in People: The Story of the Julius Rosenwald Fund* (New York: Harper and Brothers, 1949); and Alfred Perkins, *Edwin Rogers Embree: The Julius Rosenwald Fund Foundation Philanthropy and American Race Relations* (Bloomington: Indiana University Press, 2011).

26. Allison Davis's Harvard University transcript, box 406, folder 5, FUSC JARC ADFF; Davis to Embree, November 30, 1931, box 406, folder 5, FUSC JARC ADFF.

27. Allison Davis, "The Communal Composition of Songs In South and South-East Africa, with Remarks upon the Ritual Status of Songs," circa 1932, ADP SCRC UCL, box 13, folder 9.

28. Allison Davis, "Witchcraft, Rain-Making, and Divination in South Africa," circa 1932, ADP SCRC UCL, box 13, folder 14.

29. Earnest A. Hooton, *Up from the Ape* (New York: Macmillan, 1931), 396, 502, 575.

30. Elizabeth S. Davis, "Rites of Passage among the Ashanti," ADP SCRC UCL, box 1, folder 7.

31. Hubert B. Ross, Amelia Marie Adams, and Lynne Mallory Williams, "Caroline Bond Day: Pioneer Black Physical Anthropologist," in *African-American Pioneers in Anthropology*, ed. Ira E. Harrison and Faye V. Harrison (Urbana: University of Illinois Press, 1999), 37–50; Werner Sollors, Caldwell Titcomb, and Thomas A. Underwood, eds., *Blacks at Harvard: A Documentary History of African-American Experience at Harvard and Radcliffe* (New York: New York University Press, 1993), 181–87.

32. Burleigh Gardner, "Yankee City: 1930–35," in "W. Lloyd Warner; Social Anthropologist," WLWP SCRC UCL, box 5, folder 1, p. 6.7.

33. Mildred Warner, "Early Life and Berkeley Student Days," in "W. Lloyd Warner; Social Anthropologist," WLWP SCRC UCL, box 5, folder 1.

34. Drake, "Anthropology and the Black Experience," 20.

35. Emile Durkheim, *The Division of Labor in Society*, trans. W. D. Halls (1893; repr., New York: Free Press, 1984), 61, 83–86; Robert J. Havighurst, "Australia: Radcliffe-Brown and the Murgin Research: 1926–28," in "W. Lloyd Warner; Social Anthropologist," WLWP SCRC UCL, box 5, folder 1.

36. Robert Lowie, introduction to *A Black Civilization: A Social Study of an Australian Tribe* by W. Lloyd Warner (New York: Harper and Brothers, 1937), xvii.

37. W. Lloyd Warner and Paul S. Lunt, *The Social Life of a Modern Community* (New Haven, CT: Yale University Press, 1941), 3–4.

38. Burleigh Gardner, "Warner, Harvard, and the Rockefeller Foundation," in "W. Lloyd Warner; Social Anthropologist," WLWP SCRC UCL, box 5, folder 1, pp. 4.5–4.6.

39. Mary R. Gardner, Burleigh Gardner, and Allison Davis, "The Natchez Research," in "W. Lloyd Warner; Social Anthropologist," WLWP SCRC UCL, box 5, folder 1, p. 7.1.

40. *The Social Life of a Modern Community* (1941); *The Status System of a Modern Community* (1942); *The Social Systems of American Ethnic Groups* (1945), *The Social System of the Modern Factory* (1947); *The Living and the Dead* (1959).

41. St. Clair Drake wrote of Davis's involvement: "Davis had briefly worked with Warner in Newburyport, Massachusetts (Yankee City), in the small black section of town. Davis's man-

uscript, which should have been part of the Yankee City Series, was never published." The reasons for exclusion are not clear, but Drake implies racism in the decision. Apparently Newburyport only had about eighty black residents, so Warner may not have deemed that population consequential enough. St. Clair Drake, "Studies of the African Diaspora," 92.

42. Warner and Lunt, *Social Life of a Modern Community*, 35-36.

43. Drake, "Studies of the African Diaspora," 93.

44. Allison Davis, Burleigh B. Gardner, and Mary R. Gardner, *Deep South: A Social Anthropological Study of Caste and Class* (Chicago: University of Chicago Press, 1941), 59.

45. Ibid.

46. See C. Wright Mills, "The Social Life of a Modern Community, by W. Lloyd Warner; Paul S. Lunt," *American Sociological Review* 7 (April 1942): 263-71.

47. For more on Warner's methodological approach, see W. Lloyd Warner, "Social Anthropology and the Modern Community," *American Journal of Sociology* 46 (May 1941): 785-96.

48. Ibid., 788.

49. Allison Davis to George R. Arthur, 1932, box 406, folder 5, FUSC JARC ADFF.

50. Allison Davis, official essay for Rosenwald fellowship, December 6, 1931, box 406, folder 5, FUSC JARC ADFF.

51. Drake, "Studies of the African Diaspora," 88; St. Clair Drake, "Negro America and the Africa Interest" in *The American Negro Reference Book*, ed. John P. Davis (Englewood Cliffs, NJ: Prentice-Hall, 1966), 662-705.

52. Allison Davis, official essay for Rosenwald Fellowship, December 6, 1931, box 406, folder 5, FUSC JARC ADFF.

53. For Lorenzo Dow Turner's classic demonstration of the persistence of African cultural traditions among the Gullah people in coastal South Carolina, see his *Africanisms in the Gullah Dialect* (Chicago: University of Chicago Press, 1949).

54. Walter Cline, letter of support for Allison Davis's Rosenwald Fellowship application, December 6, 1931, box 406, folder 5, FUSC JARC ADFF.

55. E. A. Hooton to Edwin Embree, February 8, 1932, box 406, folder 5, FUSC JARC ADFF.

56. Alain Locke, letter of support for Allison Davis's Rosenwald fellowship application, December 7, 1931, box 406, folder 5, FUSC JARC ADFF.

57. Allison Davis to Edwin Embree, November 30, 1931, box 406, folder 5, FUSC JARC ADFF.

58. Allison Davis to George R. Arthur, October 8, 1932, box 406, folder 5, FUSC JARC ADFF.

59. Hortense Powdermaker, *Stranger and Friend: The Way of an Anthropologist* (New York: W. W. Norton, 1966), 36.

60. Jonathan Scott Holloway, *Confronting the Veil: Abram Harris Jr., E. Franklin Frazier, and Ralph Bunche, 1919-1941* (Chapel Hill: University of North Carolina Press, 2002), 180-81.

61. Drake, "In the Mirror of Black Scholarship," 45.

62. Drake, "Reflections on Anthropology and the Black Experience," 92.

63. Allison Davis to George R. Arthur, October 8, 1932, box 406, folder 5, FUSC JARC ADFF.

64. Allison Davis to George R. Arthur, November 21, 1932, box 406, folder 5, FUSC JARC ADFF.

65. David M. Kennedy, *The American People in the Great Depression: Freedom from Fear*, pt. 1 (Oxford: Oxford University Press, 1999), 383–84.

66. Allison Davis, "Commencement Address, University of Chicago, 1975," ADP SCRC UCL, box 62, folder 19.

67. Allison Davis, Allison Davis Papers, box 66, folder 4, SCRC UCL.

68. Davis's flight from Nazi Germany coincided with that of many German, Jewish intellectuals. The consequences of this intellectual "sea change" to the United States and elsewhere in Europe were profound. See H. Stuart Hughes, *The Sea Change: The Migration of Social Thought, 1930–1965* (New York: Harper and Row, 1975).

69. Powdermaker, *Stranger and Friend*, 36.

70. These included, for example, Alfred Kroeber and Robert Lowie at Berkeley, Edward Sapir at the University of Chicago and then Yale, Clark Wissler at Yale, and Margaret Mead and Ruth Benedict at Columbia.

71. Ruth Benedict's *Patterns of Culture* (1934) was the definitive statement of this generation of cultural anthropologists.

72. Jerry D. Moore, *Visions of Culture: An Introduction to Anthropological Theories and Theorists*, 3rd ed. (Lanham, MD: AltaMira, 2009), 117.

73. Ibid.

74. Sir James G. Frazer, preface to *Argonauts of the Western Pacific* by Bronislaw Malinowski (1922; repr., New York: E. P. Dutton, 1961), vii–xiv.

75. These books include *Myth in Primitive Society* (1926), *Crime and Custom in Savage Society* (1926), *Sex and Repression in Savage Society* (1927), and *The Sexual Life of Savages* (1929).

76. Bronislaw Malinowski, *Argonauts of the Western Pacific* (1922; repr., New York: E. P. Dutton, 1961), xvi.

77. Bronislaw Malinowski, *The Sexual Life of Savages* (New York: Eugenics Publishing, 1929), xxiii.

78. Powdermaker, *Stranger and Friend*, 35.

79. Ibid., 37.

80. Bronislaw Malinowski, letter of support for Allison Davis's Rosenwald Fellowship application, December 7, 1931, box 406, folder 5, FUSC JARC ADFF.

81. Powdermaker, *Stranger and Friend*, 38.

82. For a scathing critique of functionalism, see Betty Friedan, *The Feminine Mystique* (New York: W. W. Norton, 1963), 126–49. For criticisms of British social anthropology, see George W. Stocking Jr., "Radcliffe-Brown and British Social Anthropology," in *Functionalism Historicized: Essays on British Social Anthropology*, ed. George W. Stocking Jr. (Madison: University of Wisconsin Press, 1984), 131–32.

83. Powdermaker, *Stranger and Friend*, 38.

84. Harrison and Harrison, eds., *African-American Pioneers in Anthropology* (Urbana: University of Illinois Press, 1999).

85. Drake, "Reflections on Anthropology and the Black Experience," 94–95. Besides himself and Allison Davis, Drake included Zora Neale Hurston, Caroline Bond Day, Mark Hanna Watkins, and Katherine Dunham on his list of pre–World War II black anthropologists. Notably, this list included two women with only limited formal training and actual practice in the discipline. Elizabeth Davis more than met these qualifications, yet Drake still omitted her, likely be-

cause he submerged her contributions under those of her husband, effectively rendering her professionally invisible. A group of scholars has recently sought to confront these kinds of problems by laying out a bold agenda for an intellectual history of black women. See Mia Bay, Farah J. Griffin, Martha S. Jones, and Barbara D. Savage, eds., *Toward an Intellectual History of Black Women* (Chapel Hill: University of North Carolina Press, 2015).

86. Lancelot Hogben, quoted in the introduction to *Lancelot Hogben: Scientific Humanist*, ed. Adrian Hogben and Anne Hogben (Woodbridge, Suffolk, UK: Merlin, 1998), x-xi.

87. Elazar Barkan, *The Retreat of Scientific Racism: Changing Concepts of Race in Britain and the United States between the World Wars* (Cambridge: Cambridge University Press, 1992), 229.

88. Gary Werskey, *The Visible College: The Collective Biography of British Scientific Socialists of the 1930s* (New York: Holt, Rinehart and Winston, 1978), 65.

89. Hogben, *Lancelot Hogben*, 114.

90. Barkan, *Retreat of Scientific Racism*, 230.

91. Hogben, *Lancelot Hogben*, 114-15.

92. Anthony M. Platt, *E. Franklin Frazier Reconsidered* (New Brunswick, NJ: Rutgers University Press, 1991), 46.

93. Allison Davis himself engaged in this type of science in order to subvert it. At the LSE he "received the permission of sir Arthur Keith, the leading authority on fossil man and craniology, to begin a series [of measurements] on African crania, under his direction, at the Museum of the Royal College of Surgens." It is unclear how much of this research Davis ever carried out, or what exactly he concluded from it, but he was no doubt critical of it and hoped to challenge presumptions about African inferiority, which he and other black intellectuals understood as racial prejudice masquerading as objective science. Allison Davis to George R. Arthur, October 8, 1932, box 406, folder 5, FUSC JARC ADFF.

94. Barkan, *Retreat of Scientific Racism*, 231-35.

95. George W. Stocking Jr., "The Scientific Reaction against Cultural Anthropology, 1917–1920," in *Race, Culture, and Evolution: Essays in the History of Anthropology* (New York: Free Press, 1968), 300-306.

96. Otto Klineberg, *Negro Intelligence and Selective Migration* (New York: Columbia University Press, 1935); Otto Klineberg, *Race Differences* (New York: Harper and Brothers, 1935).

97. Barkan, "Mobilizing Scientists against Nazi Racism," 185.

98. Hogben, *Lancelot Hogben*, 121.

99. Barkan, *Retreat of Scientific Racism*, 231.

100. Allison Davis, "The Socialization of the American Negro Child and Adolescent," *The Present and Future Position of the Negro in the American Social Order*, special issue of *Journal of Negro Education* 8 (July 1939): 266.

101. Barkan, *Retreat of Scientific Racism*, 235; Werskey, *Visible College*, 107-9.

102. Hogben, *Lancelot Hogben*, 122.

103. Allison Davis to George R. Arthur, October 8, 1932, box 406, folder 5, FUSC JARC ADFF.

104. Lancelot Hogben, letter of support for Allison Davis's 1939 Rosenwald Fellowship application, box 406, folder 5, FUSC JARC ADFF.

105. Allison Davis, "The Distribution of Blood Groups and Its Bearing on the Concept of Race," *Sociological Review* 27 (January 1935): 19-34; part 2 in the next issue 28 (April 1935):

183–200. The article was also reprinted in Lancelot Hogben, *Political Arithmetic: A Symposium of Population Studies* (London: G. Allen and Unwin, 1938), 503–31; and it was discussed in Julian Huxley, *We Europeans: A Survey of Racial Problems* (London: J. Cape, 1935), 128, 130–33.

106. Davis, "Socialization of the American Negro Child and Adolescent," 266.

107. Davis, "Distribution of Blood Groups," 200.

CHAPTER FOUR

1. Allison Davis, quoted in St. Clair Drake, "In the Mirror of Black Scholarship: W. Allison Davis and *Deep South*," in *Education and Black Struggle: Notes from the Colonized World* (Cambridge, MA: Harvard Educational Review, 1974), 47.

2. St. Clair Drake, "Reflections on Anthropology and the Black Experience," *New Perspectives on Black Education*, special issue of *Anthropology and Education Quarterly* 9 (Summer 1978): 93.

3. Glenda Gilmore, *Defying Dixie: The Radical Roots of Civil Rights, 1919–1950* (New York: W. W. Norton, 2008), 109.

4. The story of the Scottsboro Boys is ably told by Dan T. Carter, *Scottsboro: A Tragedy of the American South* (Baton Rouge: Louisiana State University Press, 1969); and James E. Goodman, *Stories of Scottsboro* (New York: Pantheon Books, 1994).

5. St. Clair Drake, "Studies of the African Diaspora: The Work and Reflections of St. Clair Drake," in *Against All Odds: Scholars Who Challenged Racism in the Twentieth Century*, ed. Benjamin P. Bowser and Louis Kushnick (Amherst: University of Massachusetts Press, 2002), 89.

6. Ibid., 92–93.

7. These research efforts resulted in two monographs: John Dollard, *Caste and Class in a Southern Town* (1937; repr., New York: Harper and Brothers, 1949); and Hortense Powdermaker, *After Freedom: A Cultural Study in the Deep South* (New York: Viking, 1939).

8. Wayne J. Urban, *Black Scholar: Horace Mann Bond, 1904–1972* (Athens: University of Georgia Press, 1992), 64–67.

9. Lloyd Warner to Edmund Day, September 11, 1933, folder 339, box 4045, Series 200-U.S., sub-Series S-Social Sciences, Record Group 1.1-Projects, RFA, RAC.

10. Mary R. Gardner, Burleigh Gardner, and Allison Davis, "The Natchez Research," in "W. Lloyd Warner; Social Anthropologist," by Mildred Hall Warner, Burleigh Gardner, Robert J. Havighurst, and Associates, with corrections, n.d. WLWP SCRC UCL, box 5, folder 1, page 7.6.

11. Powdermaker, *Stranger and Friend*, 139.

12. Will W. Alexander to Allison Davis, October 11, 1933, ADP SCRC UCL, box 27, folder 11; Will W. Alexander to Allison Davis, October 19, 1933, ADP SCRC UCL, box 27, folder 11.

13. Gardner, Gardner, and Davis, "Natchez Research," 7.8.

14. Ibid., 7.9.

15. Allison Davis to Dorothy Beale Davis, February 17, 1982, DFR.

16. Gardner, Gardner, and Davis, "The Natchez Research," 7.9.

17. Horace Mann Bond to Allison Davis, October 5, 1934, Davis, Allison, 1934, 1935, Horace Mann Bond Papers (MS 411), SCUA UMAL.

18. Gardner, Gardner, and Davis, "Natchez Research," 7.2.

19. Joan Oleck, "Allison Davis: 1902–1983," *Contemporary Black Biography*, ed. Shirelle Phelps (Detroit: Gale Research, 1997), 12:40.

20. Allison Davis, quoting a man named Isaac in his field notebook on October 22, 1933, ADP SCRC UCL, box 27, folder 10.

21. Allison Davis, Burleigh B. Gardner, and Mary R. Gardner, *Deep South: A Social Anthropological Study of Caste and Class* (Chicago: University of Chicago Press, 1941), 26–27.

22. See Allison Davis, "The Negro Deserts His People," *Plain Talk* 4 (January 1929): 49–54.

23. Gardner, Gardner, and Davis, "Natchez Research," 7.12.

24. Ibid., 7.8, 7.9.

25. Ibid., 7.9–7.10.

26. Lloyd Warner to Edmund Day, September 11, 1933, folder 339, box 4045, Series 200-U.S., sub-Series S-Social Sciences, Record Group 1.1-Projects, RFA, RAC.

27. Ibid., viii–ix.

28. Ibid.

29. Davis, Gardner, and Gardner, *Deep South*, vii.

30. Gardner, Gardner, and Davis, "Natchez Research," 7.17.

31. Davis, Gardner, and Gardner, *Deep South*, viii.

32. Gardner, Gardner, and Davis, "Natchez Research," 7.17.

33. Drake, "Reflections on Anthropology and the Black Experience," 92.

34. Drake, "Studies of the African Diaspora," 92.

35. Charles S. Johnson, "Report on the Manuscript of *Deep South*," UCPR SCRC UCL, box 145, folder 7, p. 3.

36. Faye V. Harrison and Ira E. Harrison, "Introduction: Anthropology, African Americans, and the Emancipation of a Subjugated Knowledge," in *African-American Pioneers in Anthropology*, ed. Ira E. Harrison and Faye V. Harrison (Urbana: University of Illinois Press, 1998), 19, 20.

37. Lloyd Warner to Allison Davis, March 18, 1934, ADP SCRC UCL, box 27, folder 11.

38. W. Lloyd Warner, "American Caste and Class," *American Journal of Sociology* 42 (September 1936): 234–37. See also W. Lloyd Warner, "Formal Education and the Social Structure," *Journal of Educational Sociology* 9 (May 1936): 524–31.

39. Warner, "American Caste and Class," 234.

40. W. Lloyd Warner and Allison Davis, "A Comparative Study of American Caste," in *Race Relations and the Race Problem: A Definition and an Analysis*, ed. Edgar T. Thompson (Durham, NC: Duke University Press, 1939), 229, 231–32. See Celestin Bougle, *Essais sur le régime des castes*, 3rd ed. (Paris: Alcan, 1935); Herbert Risley, *The Tribes and Castes of Bengal: Ethnographic Glossary* (Calcutta: Bengal Secretariat Press, 1891); and Emile Senart, *Caste in India: The Facts and the System*, trans. E. Denison Ross (London: Methuen, 1930).

41. Warner and Davis, "Comparative Study of American Caste," 236.

42. G. J. Laing to W. Lloyd Warner, October 19, 1939; University of Chicago Press to Howard H. Moore, December 17, 1940; Charles S. Johnson, "Report on Manuscript of *Deep South*," 1939, UCPR SCRC UCL, box 145, folder 7.

43. Lloyd Warner to Edwin Embree, May 18, 1936, box 409, folder 1, FUSC JARC, St. Clair Drake Fellowship File.

44. Lloyd Warner to Edwin Embree, August 15, 1935, box 409, folder 1, FUSC JARC, St. Clair Drake Fellowship File.

45. Davis, Gardner, and Gardner, *Deep South*, 3-4, 15-20, 41, 49-57.

46. Ibid., 238.

47. Ibid., 237.

48. Ibid., 221-22, 228.

49. Ibid., 245.

50. Ibid., 249.

51. Allison Davis, "The Negro Church and Associations in the Lower South," June 1, 1940, ADP SCRC UCL, box 33, folder 21; Gunnar Myrdal, *An American Dilemma: The Negro Problem and Modern Democracy*, 20th anniv. ed. (orig. 1944; New York: Harper and Row, 1962).

52. For an understanding of what Myrdal asked of Davis, see "Memorandum on Questions to be Covered by Allison Davis," July 10, 1939, ADP SCRC UCL, box 33, folder 19. He asked Davis to include "a considerable amount of descriptive material."

53. Davis, Gardner, and Gardner, *Deep South*, 250.

54. Ibid., 197.

55. Davis, "Negro Church and Associations in the Lower South," 46, 49, 52.

56. Drake, "In the Mirror of Black Scholarship," 47.

57. Faye V. Harrison, "The Du Boisian Legacy in Anthropology," *Critique of Anthropology* 12 (September 1992): 247.

58. Davis, Gardner, and Gardner, *Deep South*, 352-57.

59. Drake, "In the Mirror of Black Scholarship," 51-53. Ibid., 53.

60. Burleigh Gardner, "Human Relations in Industry and Social Research: 1940-1960," in "W. Lloyd Warner; Social Anthropologist," WLWP SCRC UCL, box 5, folder 6.

61. Drake, "Studies of the African Diaspora," 93.

62. Mary Ann Dzuback, *Robert M. Hutchins: Portrait of an Educator* (Chicago: University of Chicago Press, 1991), 163.

63. Drake, "In the Mirror of Black Scholarship," 52.

64. Davis, Gardner, and Gardner, *Deep South*, 454, 465-66.

65. Drake, "Studies of the African Diaspora," 98.

66. Drake, "In the Mirror of Black Scholarship," 52.

67. Allison Davis to Edwin Embree, March 25, 1942, box 406, folder 5, FUSC JARC ADFF.

68. "Profit and Loss on Davis: DEEP SOUTH," October 21, 1964, UCPR SCRC UCL, box 145, folder 7.

69. University of Chicago Press, "Memo To: Teachers of Sociology," May 18, 1948, UCPR SCRC UCL, box 146, folder 1.

70. Joseph Haas (of *Chicago Daily News*), "Anti-Negro Structure Attacked," *Cincinnati, Ohio Enquirer*, April 9, 1966.

71. Drake, "In the Mirror of Black Scholarship," 53-54.

72. Allison Davis, quoted in Barbara P. Turner, "Profile of Allison Davis; The Man and His Research," *Education at Chicago* 2 (Autumn 1972): 22.

73. *Christian Century*, November 6, 1941, UCPR SCRC UCL, box 146, folder 1,; Elesha J. Coffman, *"The Christian Century" and the Rise of the Protestant Mainline* (Oxford: Oxford University Press, 2013), 6, 222.

74. Arthur Rex, "White Stereotypes of the Negro," *Protestant*, May 1944, 24–26.

75. "Book Review: *Deep South*," *New York Age*, November 22, 1941; review of *Deep South* by Allison Davis, Burleigh B. Gardner, and Mary R. Gardner," *Nation*, April 4, 1942, UCPR SCRC UCL, box 146, folder 1.

76. Daniel Bell, "Caste and Class," *New Leader*, May 16, 1942.

77. A. G. N., review of *Deep South*, by Allison Davis, Burleigh B. Gardner, and Mary R. Gardner, *The Republican: The National Magazine for Republicans* (December 1941), UCPR SCRC UCL, box 146, folder 1.

78. Some examples include the *Kansas City Call*, the *Durham, N.C. Times*, the *Commercial Appeal* [Memphis, TN], the *NC Herald-Sun*, the *Virginia Pilot*, and the *Observer* [Charlotte, NC]. UCPR SCRC UCL, box 146, folder 1.

79. H. C. Nixon, "South's 2-Race, 2-Caste System," *Morning Tennessean*, September 27, 1942.

80. Anonymous review of *Deep South* by Allison Davis, Burleigh B. Gardner, and Mary R. Gardner, *Virginia Teachers Bulletin* (January 1942): 39–(?), UCPR SCRC UCL, box 146, folder 1.

81. Moreau B. Chambers, "A Glance at New Books," *Clarion-Ledger* [Jackson, MS], November 2, 1941.

82. Ibid.

83. Edwin Embree to Allison Davis, March 25, 1942, box 406, folder 5, FUSC JARC ADFF.

84. *Wichita Daily Times*, November 12, 1941, UCPR SCRC UCL, box 146, folder 1.

85. See, for instance, B. A. McC., review of *Deep South* by Allison Davis, Burleigh B. Gardner, and Mary R. Gardner, *Sociology and Social Research* 220 (March 1942), UCPR SCRC UCL, box 146, folder 1.

86. John Dollard, review of *Deep South* by Allison Davis, Burleigh B. Gardner, and Mary R. Gardner, *American Anthropologist*, October–December 1942, 705.

87. W. E. B. Du Bois, review of *Deep South* by Allison Davis, Burleigh B. Gardner, and Mary R. Gardner, *Annals of the American Academy of Political and Social Science* 220 (March 1942): 275.

88. Margaret Mead, "Class and Caste Study," *New York Herald Tribune*, December 7, 1941.

89. Review of *Deep South* by Allison Davis, Burleigh B. Gardner, and Mary R. Gardner," *Nation*, April 4, 1942. See also review of *Deep South* by Allison Davis, Burleigh B. Gardner, and Mary R. Gardner," *Quarterly Review of Biology* 17 (June 1942), 171; Daniel Bell, "Caste and Class," *New Leader*, May 16, 1942; and Charles H. Wesley, review of *Deep South* by Allison Davis, Burleigh B. Gardner, and Mary R. Gardner, *The United States, 1865–1900* 1 (September 1941–August 1942): 47–48, UCPR SCRC UCL, box 146, folder 1.

90. Jefferson Davis Bragg, review of *Deep South* by Allison Davis, Burleigh B. Gardner, and Mary R. Gardner, *Mississippi Valley Historical Review* 28 (March 1942): 646.

91. Lewis C. Copeland, review of *Deep South* by Allison Davis, Burleigh B. Gardner, and Mary R. Gardner, *American Journal of Sociology* 48 (November 1942): 432–33.

92. Thomas D. Clark, review of *Deep South* by Allison Davis, Burleigh B. Gardner, and Mary R. Gardner, *Journal of Southern History* 8 (August 1942): 439.

93. The best overview of this shift is Sarah E. Igo's *The Averaged American: Surveys, Citizens, and the Making of a Mass Public* (Cambridge, MA: Harvard University Press, 2007). For

an analysis of how this shift affected political culture, see Lizabeth Cohen, *A Consumers' Republic: The Politics of Mass Consumption in Postwar America* (New York: Vintage Books, 2003), 292–344.

94. Clark, review of *Deep South*, 439.

95. Dollard, review of *Deep South*, 705.

96. Robert Schmid, review of *Deep South* by Allison Davis, Burleigh B. Gardner, and Mary R. Gardner, *American Sociological Review* 7 (April 1942): 263.

97. For a positive review syndicated widely, see Thomas A. Webster, "The Browsing Reader," *The Call* (Kansas City), November 15, 1941; Thomas A. Webster, "Books on the Negro," *Carolina Times* (Durham, NC]., January 31, 1942; Thomas A. Webster, "Book Review: *Deep South*," *Chicago Defender*, February 14, 1942.

98. Alain Locke, "Who and What Is 'Negro'?" *Opportunity* 20 (March 1942): 86.

99. Charles S. Johnson, *Growing Up in the Black Belt: Negro Youth in the Rural South* (1941; repr., New York: Schocken Books, 1967), 325–26; Charles. S. Johnson, "Race Relations and Social Change," in *Race Relations and the Race Problem*, 291–302; E. Franklin Frazier, "Sociological Theory and Race Relations," *American Sociological Review* 12 (June 1947): 270; Oliver C. Cox, *Caste, Class, and Race: A Study in Social Dynamics* (New York: Modern Readers Paperbacks, 1948); Oliver C. Cox, "Class and Caste: A Definition and a Distinction," *Journal of Negro Education* 13 (Spring 1944): 139–49; and Oliver C. Cox, "The Modern Caste School of Race Relations," *Social Forces* 21 (December 1942),"220.

100. Howard W. Odum, "Southern Caste and Class," *Saturday Review of Literature*, February 28, 1942.

101. See Donald Young, *American Minority Peoples: A Study in Racial and Cultural Conflicts in the United States* (New York: Harper and Brothers, 1932); and Vernon J. Williams Jr., *From a Caste to a Minority: Changing Attitudes of American Sociologists toward Afro-Americans, 1896–1945* (Westport, CT: Greenwood, 1989).

102. Myrdal, *American Dilemma*, 873, 876.

103. Ibid., 952–54.

104. Walter A. Jackson, *Gunnar Myrdal and America's Conscience: Social Engineering and Racial Liberalism, 1938–1987* (Chapel Hill: University of North Carolina Press, 1990), 227, 219.

105. . Wright Mills, "The Social Life of a Modern Community, by W. Lloyd Warner; Paul S. Lunt," *American Sociological Review* 7 (April 1942): 263–71.

106. Robin M. Williams, response to Allison Davis, "American Status Systems and the Socialization of a Child," *American Sociological Review* 6 (June 1941): 356.

107. Clifton R. Jones, "Social Stratification of the Negro Population in a Small Southern Town," *Journal of Negro Education* 15 (Winter 1946): 159.

108. Grace Browning, review of *Deep South* by Allison Davis, Burleigh B. Gardner, and Mary R. Gardner, *Social Science Review* (September 1942), UCPR SCRC UCL, box 146, folder 1.

109. Herbert Aptheker, "The Black Belt," *New Masses*, January 6, 1942; Arthur Brown, review of *Deep South* by Allison Davis, Burleigh B. Gardner, and Mary R. Gardner, *Science and Society* 7 (Spring 1943), UCPR SCRC UCL, box 146, folder 1.

110. Brown, review of *Deep South*.

111. Edward A. Ross to Lloyd Warner, November 27, 1941, box 406, folder 5, FUSC JARC ADFF.

112. Margaret Mead, "Class and Caste Study," *New York Herald Tribune*, December 7, 1941.

113. Wendy L. Wall, *Inventing the "American Way": The Politics of Consensus from the New Deal to the Civil Rights Movement* (New York: Oxford University Press, 2008), 8.

114. Margaret Mead, *And Keep Your Powder Dry: An Anthropologist Looks at America* (New York: William Morrow, 1942), 58.

115. Ellen Schrecker, *Many Are the Crimes: McCarthyism in America* (Boston: Little, Brown, 1998), xiii.

116. Brooks, "American Class and Caste," 210.

CHAPTER FIVE

1. John Dollard, *Criteria for a Life History: With Analyses of Six Notable Documents* (New Haven, CT: Yale University Press, 1935), 276.

2. St. Clair Drake, quoted in George C. Bond, "A Social Portrait of John Gibbs St. Clair Drake: An American Anthropologist," *American Ethnologist* 15 (1988): 780.

3. W. Allison Davis and Robert J. Havighurst, *Father of the Man: How Your Child Gets His Personality* (Boston: Houghton Mifflin, 1947), viii.

4. Edwin R. Embree and Julia Waxman, *Investment in People: The Story of the Julius Rosenwald Fund* (New York: Harper and Brothers, 1949), 85, 98–99.

5. Joe M. Richardson, "A White New Orleans Philanthropist Helps Build a Black University," *Journal of Negro History* 82 (Summer 1997): 332–33.

6. Mary R. Gardner, Burleigh Gardner, and Allison Davis, "The Natchez Research," in "W. Lloyd Warner: Social Anthropologist," by Mildred Hall Warner, Burleigh Gardner, Robert J. Havighurst, and Associates, with corrections, n.d. WLWP SCRC UCL, box 5, folder 1, page 7.9.

7. David M. Kennedy, *The American People in the Great Depression: Freedom from Fear*, pt. 1 (Oxford: Oxford University Press, 1999), 237–39.

8. Bruce Kuklick, *Black Philosopher, White Academy: The Career of William Fontaine* (Philadelphia: University of Pennsylvania Press, 2008), 41.

9. *Annual Report of the General Education Board, 1934–35* (New York: General Education Board, 1936), 47–48.

10. St. Clair Drake, "Reflections on Anthropology and the Black Experience," *New Perspectives on Black Education*, special issue of *Anthropology and Education Quarterly* 9 (Summer 1978): 95.

11. Allison Davis, "A Proposal for a Comparative Study of Negro Societies in New Orleans and the Caribbean Islands," ADP SCRC UCL, box 3, folder 9.

12. Ibid.

13. See Margaret Mead, *Coming of Age in Samoa: A Psychological Study of Primitive Youth for Western Civilization* (New York: William Morrow, 1928).

14. Lloyd Warner to Edwin Embree, August 15, 1935, box 409, folder 1, FUSC JARC, St. Clair Drake Fellowship File.

15. St. Clair Drake, *The Redemption of Africa and Black Religion* (Chicago: Third World, 1971); St. Clair Drake, *Black Folk Here and There: An Essay in History and Anthropology*, 2 vols. (Los Angeles: Center for Afro-American Studies, University of California at Los Angeles, 1987–90); and St. Clair Drake, "Value Systems, Social Structure, and Race Relations in the British Isles" (PhD diss., University of Chicago, 1954).

16. Drake, "Reflections on Anthropology and the Black Experience," 92–95.

17. Allison Davis, "The Study of Society," ADP SCRC UCL, box 30, folder 13, page 1.

18. Chas G. Gomillion, regional director of the US Works Progress Administration, to Allison Davis, February 8, 1936, ADP SCRC UCL, box 8, folder 17.

19. S. Walter Stern, chairman of the Committee to Investigate the Desirability of Forming an Urban League in New Orleans, to Davis, October 10, 1936, ADP SCRC UCL, box 30, folder 6.

20. Stuart K. Jaffary, chairman of the Tulane University School of Social Work, to Allison Davis, January 11, 1936, ADP SCRC UCL, box 30, folder 6.

21. "The black cabinet" refers to the African American officials serving Franklin Delano Roosevelt's administration during the 1930s. Robert C. Weaver was one of the most important members of this group. For an example of Weaver's correspondence with Davis, see Robert C. Weaver, Office of the Secretary of the US Department of Interior, to Allison Davis, February 13, 1936, ADP SCRC UCL, box 8, folder 17.

22. Committee on Co-ordination and Prevention, "Summary of the Findings and Tentative Report of the Committee on Co-ordination and Prevention," ADP SCRC UCL, box 30, folder 6.

23. Floyd W. Reeves, foreword to *Children of Bondage: The Personality Development of Negro Youth in the Urban South* by Allison Davis and John Dollard (Washington, DC: American Council on Education, 1940), viii.

24. Robert L. Sutherland's "A Recommendation for a Demonstration Project in the Personality Adjustment of Negro Youth," October 1939, box 558, folder 5962, Series 1, GEBA RAC.

25. "A Proposal for a Study of the Racial Factor in the Personality Development of Negro Youth," December 9, 1937, box 558, folder 5965, Series 1, GEBA RAC.

26. W. W. Brierley to Doctor Zook, December 6, 1939, box 558, folder 5962, Series 1, GEBA RAC.

27. Harry Stack Sullivan, a psychologist and important theorist within culture-and-personality, collaborated briefly with Frazier and Johnson in their projects, but the culture-and-personality orientation did not guide their research. For more on Sullivan's role in the Frazier and Johnson projects, see FUSC JARC, Charles S. Johnson Collection, 1892–1956, box 17, folders 14–18.

28. "Biographical History," Guide to the John Dollard Papers, Yale University, http://drs.library.yale.edu:8083/HLTransformer/HLTransServlet?stylename=yul.ead2002.xhtml.xsl&pid=mssa:ms.1758&clear-stylesheet-cache=yes (accessed March 28, 2015).

29. Regna Darnell, *Edward Sapir: Linguist, Anthropologist, Humanist* (Berkeley: University of California Press, 1990), 334–35.

30. For a good overview of the culture-and-personality movement and of the relationships among major figures such as Edward Sapir, Ralph Linton, Margaret Mead, Karen Horney, Harry Stack Sullivan, and Erich Fromm, see Joanne Meyerowitz, " 'How Common Culture Shapes the Separate Lives': Sexuality, Race, and Mid-Twentieth-Century Social Thought," *Journal of American History* 96 (March 2010): 1057–84. See also Nathan G. Hale Jr., *The Rise and Crisis of Psychoanalysis in the United States: Freud and the Americans, 1917–1985* (New York: Oxford University Press, 1995); and George W. Stocking Jr., ed., *Malinowski, Rivers, Benedict and Others: Essays on Culture and Personality* (Madison: University of Wisconsin Press, 1986).

31. John S. Gilkeson, *Anthropologists and the Rediscovery of America, 1886–1965* (Cambridge: Cambridge University Press, 2010), 120.

32. Paul Shankman, *The Trashing of Margaret Mead: Anatomy of an Anthropological Controversy* (Madison: University of Wisconsin Press, 2009), 114–15.

33. Edward Sapir, "Cultural Anthropology and Psychiatry," *Journal of Abnormal and Social Psychology* 27 (October–December 1932): 229–42; Edward Sapir, "The Emergence of the Concept of Personality in a Study of Culture," *Journal of Social Psychology* 5 (August 1934): 408–15.

34. Sapir, "Emergence of the Concept of Personality," 410.

35. Sapir, "Cultural Anthropology and Psychiatry," 229–33.

36. Ibid., 233–34, 236.

37. Sapir, "Emergence of the Concept of Personality," 414, 415.

38. Dollard, *Criteria for a Life History*, 14, 3, 16.

39. Ibid., 222, 4.

40. Ibid., iii.

41. Darnell, *Edward Sapir*, 337.

42. Mark A. May, quoted in Darnell, *Edward Sapir*, 390.

43. John Dollard, Neal E. Miller, Leonard W. Doob, O. H. Mowrer, and Robert R. Sears, *Frustration and Aggression* (New Haven, CT: Yale University Press, 1939), 21–22, 60–68.

44. For more on neo-Freudianism, see Hale, *Rise and Crisis of Psychoanalysis*, 135–43, 173–79; and William C. Manson, "Abram Kardiner and the Neo-Freudian Alternative in Culture and Personality" in *Malinowski, Rivers, Benedict and Others*, 72–94.

45. Dollard et al., *Frustration and Aggression*, 56, 72–76.

46. Mark A. May, foreword to *Social Learning and Imitation* by Neal E. Miller and John Dollard (New Haven, CT: Yale University Press, 1941) vii.

47. John Dollard, *Caste and Class in a Southern Town* (1937; repr., New York: Harper and Brothers, 1949).

48. Miller and Dollard, *Social Learning and Imitation*, 2.

49. Darnell, *Edward Sapir*, 396.

50. Steven Weiland, "Life History, Psychoanalysis, and Social Science: The Example of John Dollard," *South Atlantic Quarterly* 86 (Summer 1987): 269–70.

51. John Dollard, "John Dollard: Caste and Class Revisited," interview by William R. Ferris, *Southern Cultures* 10 (Summer 2004): 10–11.

52. Ibid., 11.

53. Allison Davis and John Dollard, *Children of Bondage: The Personality Development of Negro Youth in the Urban South* (Washington, DC: American Council on Education, 1940), xxiii.

54. Bonita Valien, acting-departmental secretary for the American Youth Commission, to Allison Davis, December 3, 1938, ADP SCRC UCL, box 30, folder 4.

55. John Dollard, "Staff Meeting; Dr. Dollard: Re: Wilbur Scott," September 16, 1938, ADP SCRC UCL, box 31, folder 5.

56. "Goes to Yale," *Afro American*, February 11, 1939.

57. Davis and Dollard, *Children of Bondage*, xix, xvi–xvii.

58. Allison Davis to Edwin Embree, July 10, 1940, box 406, folder 5, FUSC JARC ADFF.

59. Allison Davis to Robert Havighurst, September 20, 1939, box 558, folder 5962, series 1, GEBA RAC; Allison Davis to Fred McCuistion, November 17, 1939, box 558, folder 5962, series 1, GEBA RAC.

60. Davis and Dollard, *Children of Bondage*, xix, xxvii.

61. "A Proposal for a Study of the Racial Factor in the Personality Development of Negro Youth," December 9, 1937, box 558, folder 5965, Series 1, GEBA RAC.

62. Davis and Dollard, *Children of Bondage*, 255–56.

63. Ibid., 13, 82, 143.

64. Ibid., 265.

65. Ibid., 8, 10, 266.

66. Ibid., 265.

67. Ibid., 269, 266.

68. Ibid., 35–39.

69. Ibid., 265, 94–95.

70. For comparable views about the white ethnic poor, see E. Wight Bakke, *The Unemployed Worker: A Study of the Task of Making a Living without a Job* (New Haven, CT: Yale University Press, 1940); and E. Wight Bakke, *Citizens without Work: A Study of the Effects of Unemployment upon the Worker's Social Relations and Practice* (New Haven, CT: Yale University Press, 1940). For further background, see Mark Pittenger, *Class Unknown: Undercover Investigations of American Work and Poverty from the Progressive Era to the Present* (New York: New York University Press, 2012), 112, 123.

71. Davis and Dollard, *Children of Bondage*, 50, 96.

72. Ibid., 267, 269.

73. Ibid., 243–45, 251.

74. Ibid., 247.

75. Ibid., 251.

76. See, for example, Eugene D. Genovese, *Roll, Jordan, Roll: The World the Slaves Made* (New York: Pantheon Books, 1974); Herbert G. Gutman, *The Black Family in Slavery and Freedom, 1750–1925* (New York: Pantheon Books, 1976), and Lawrence W. Levine, *Black Culture and Black Consciousness: Afro-American Folk Thought from Slavery to Freedom* (London: Oxford University Press, 1977).

77. Davis and Dollard, *Children of Bondage*, 23–42, 27.

78. Ibid., 35–42.

79. Stanley Milgram, *Obedience to Authority: An Experimental View* (New York: Harper and Row, 1974).

80. Allison Davis, "Author Questionnaire," November 16, 1950, UCPR SCRC UCL, box 165, folder 3.

81. "A Proposal for a Study of the Racial Factor in the Personality Development of Negro Youth," December 9, 1937, box 558, 5965, series 1, GEBA RAC.

82. "Report on the Negro Youth Study," box 558, folder 5965, series 1, pp. 3–4, GEBA RAC.

83. Allison Davis to Edwin Embree, December 19, 1940, box 406, folder 5, FUSC JARC, ADFF.

84. Allison Davis to Fred McCuistion, November 17, 1939, box 558, folder 5962, series 1, GEBA RAC.

85. Fred McCuistion to Allison Davis, December 4, 1939, box 558, folder 5962, series 1, GEBA RAC.

86. Allison Davis, "The Socialization of the American Negro Child and Adolescent," *The Present and Future Position of the Negro in the American Social Order*, special issue of *Journal of Negro Education* 8, (July 1939): 264-74.

87. Allison Davis, "American Status Systems and the Socialization of a Child," *American Sociological Review* 6 (June 1941): 345-56; Allison Davis, "Racial Status and Personality Development," *Scientific Monthly* 57 (October 1943): 354-62.

88. Allison Davis, "Child Training and Social Class," in *Child Behavior and Development* by R. G. Barker, J. S. Kounin, and H. F. Wright (New York: McGraw-Hill, 1943); Allison Davis to Edwin Embree, November 17, 1941, box 406, folder 5, FUSC JARC ADFF.

89. Allison Davis to Edwin Embree, October 29, 1940, box 406, folder 5, FUSC JARC ADFF.

90. Allison Davis to Edwin Embree, November 17, 1941, box 406, folder 5, FUSC JARC ADFF.

91. Robert Havighurst to Robert Sutherland, October 7, 1940, box 558, folder 5965, series 1, General Education Board Archives, RAC.

92. Edwin Embree to Allison Davis, September 18, 1940, box 406, folder 5, FUSC JARC ADFF.

93. Edwin Embree to Will Alexander, Charles S. Johnson, Raymond Paty, and Henry Allen Moe, November 14, 1940, box 406, folder 5, FUSC JARC ADFF.

94. See anonymous review of *Children of Bondage* by Allison Davis and John Dollard," *Journal of Educational Sociology* 15 (September 1941): 62; Warren M. Banner, review of *Children of Bondage* by Allison Davis and John Dollard, *Opportunity* 18 (October 1940): 317-19; and Guy B. Johnson, review of *Children of Bondage* by Allison Davis and John Dollard, *The Negro Caravan* by Sterling A. Brown, Arthur P. Davis and Ulysses Lee, *12 Million Black Voices: A Folk History of the Negro in the United States* by Richard Wright and Edwin Rosskam, *The Negro in Tennessee, 1865-1880* by Alrutheus Ambush Tayler, and *Gullah: Negro Life in the Carolina Sea Islands* by Mason Crum, *Social Forces* 20 (May 1942): 511.

95. Max Meenes, review of *Children of Bondage* by Allison Davis and John Dollard, *Journal of Negro Education* 10 (January 1941): 88.

96. Wayne Dennis, review of *Children of Bondage* by Allison Davis and John Dollard, *American Journal of Psychology* 55 (January 1942): 149.

97. Richard Sutherland, "Comments on Criticisms of Davis-Dollard Typoscript," 1939, ADP SCRC UCL, box 32, folder 2.

98. Leonard S. Cottrell Jr., review of *Negro Youth at the Crossways: Their Personality Development in the Middle States* by E. Franklin Frazier, and *Children of Bondage: The Personality Development of Negro Youth in the Urban South* by Allison Davis and John Dollard, *American Journal of Sociology* 47 (July 1941): 114; O. W. E., review of *Children of Bondage* by Allison Davis and John Dollard, *Phylon* 2 (First Quarter 1941): 91.

99. Meenes, review of *Children of Bondage*, 88.

100. Donald C. Marsh, review of *Children of Bondage* by Allison Davis and John Dollard, *American Sociological Review* 7 (August 1942): 575.

101. Anonymous review of *Children of Bondage* by Allison Davis and John Dollard, *Journal of Educational Sociology* 15 (September 1941): 62.

102. Davis, Allison, 1934, 1935, letter from Allison Davis to Horace Mann Bond. May 17, 1935, Horace Mann Bond Papers (MS 411), SCUA UMAL.

103. O. W. E., review of *Children of Bondage*, 92.

104. Cottrell, review of *Negro Youth at the Crossways* and *Children of Bondage*, 114.

105. Clyde Kluckhohn and Henry A. Murray, eds., *Personality in Nature, Society, and Culture*, 2nd ed. (New York: Alfred A. Knopf, 1961), xviii.

106. Allison Davis and Robert J. Havighurst, "Social Class and Color Differences in Child-Rearing," in ibid., 308–20; and Allison Davis, "American Status Systems and the Socialization of the Child," in ibid., 567–76.

107. Marsh, review of *Children of Bondage*, 575.

108. Dennis, review of *Children of Bondage*, 149; anonymous review of *Children of Bondage*, *Journal of Educational Sociology*, 62.

109. Cottrell, review of *Negro Youth at the Crossways* and *Children of Bondage*, 113.

110. Ibid., 112.

111. Allison Davis to Edwin Embree, November 17, 1941, box 406, folder 5, FUSC JARC ADFF.

112. Cottrell, review of *Negro Youth at the Crossways* and *Children of Bondage*, 113.

113. Banner, review of *Children of Bondage*, 319.

114. Allison Davis to Edwin Embree, October 29, 1940, box 406, folder 5, FUSC JARC ADFF.

115. W. M. Brewer, review of *Children of Bondage* by Allison Davis and John Dollard, *Journal of Negro History* 26 (January 1941): 113, 115.

116. Ibid., 113–14.

117. Social scientists, of course, were not the only ones beginning to confront and debate ideas of racism and damage. Richard Wright's searing novels *Native Son* (1940) and *Black Boy* (1945), and Sidney Meyer' classic documentary film *The Quiet One* (1948), which included commentary by James Agee, explored these same issues in other arenas.

118. John P. Jackson Jr., *Social Scientists for Social Justice: Making the Case against Segregation* (New York: New York University Press, 2001), 36; Robert K. Merton, "What It Costs to Be Denied," *New York Times*, May 20, 1951; and Alice O'Connor, *Poverty Knowledge: Social Science, Social Policy, and the Poor in Twentieth-Century U.S. History* (Princeton, NJ: Princeton University Press, 2001), 86–87. Daryl Michael Scott, on the other hand, makes clear in his authoritative study of damage imagery in American social science that *Children of Bondage* generally eschewed such emphases on damage. See Daryl Michael Scott, *Contempt and Pity: Social Policy and the Image of the Damaged Black Psyche, 1880–1996* (Chapel Hill: University of North Carolina Press, 1997), 35–36, 53–54.

119. Allison Davis, "The Culture of the Slum," ADP SCRC UCL, box 77, folder 18.

120. Alice O'Connor has made this point about *Children of Bondage*. Her claim, though, that Davis and Dollard's book "anticipated a more general trend in the literature by assessing psychological damage as a measure of social disadvantage, and by tracing its origins to the lower-class family," misses the larger implication of the book's belief in change and adaptability. See O'Connor, *Poverty Knowledge*, 65.

121. Harold Lief, Daniel Thompson, and William Thompson, *The Eighth Generation: Cultures and Personalities of New Orleans Negroes*, ed. John H. Rohrer and Munro S. Edmundson (New York: Harper and Brothers, 1960), 1.

CHAPTER SIX

1. Edwin Embree to Edgar B. Stern, February 24, 1942, box 182, folder 6, FUSC JARC UCAD.

2. L. S. Mayo to William A. Davis, September 16, 1931, Allison Davis Records, Harvard Alumni Directory, Harvard University Archives, Cambridge, Massachusetts.

3. William M. Banks, *Black Intellectuals: Race and Responsibility in American Life* (New York: W. W. Norton, 1996), 130.

4. It is difficult to establish with certainty who was the first black person with a full-time appointment at a white university, and it depends partly upon how this particular milestone is defined and measured. James D. Anderson acknowledges that Julian H. Lewis became an assistant professor of pathology at the University of Chicago in 1922, but he argues that Lewis's was only a "nominal appointment" as his primary employment was through Provident Hospital. Anderson concludes, "All evidence points to Allison Davis's appointment in 1941 [actually 1942] as the starting date for the employment of African American scholars in regular faculty positions at northern white universities." I follow Anderson's thinking here. James D. Anderson, "Race, Meritocracy, and the American Academy during the Immediate Post-World War II Era," *History of Education Quarterly* 33 (Summer 1993): 154.

5. Harvard Sitkoff, *A New Deal for Blacks: The Emergence of Civil Rights as a National Issue* (New York: Oxford University Press, 1978), 190-99.

6. Glenda Gilmore, *Defying Dixie: The Radical Roots of Civil Rights, 1919-1950* (New York: W. W. Norton, 2008), 106-33.

7. See Michael Denning, *The Cultural Front: The Laboring of American Culture in the Twentieth Century* (London: Verson, 1997).

8. St. Clair Drake, "Studies of the African Diaspora: The Work and Reflections of St. Clair Drake," in *Against All Odds: Scholars Who Challenged Racism in the Twentieth Century*, ed. Benjamin P. Bowser and Louis Kushnick (Amherst: University of Massachusetts Press, 2002), 93.

9. Gilmore, *Defying Dixie*, 157-200.

10. Wendy L. Wall, *Inventing the "American Way": The Politics of Consensus from the New Deal to the Civil Rights Movement* (New York: Oxford University Press, 2008), 8.

11. "Seven Days in Open Lifeboat Hell, but Seaman Finds U.S. Jim Crow Worse," *Afro-American*, August 1, 1943.

12. For a good overview, see David Clay Large, *Nazi Games: The Olympics of 1936* (New York: W. W. Norton, 2007).

13. Christopher Robert Reed, *The Rise of Chicago's Black Metropolis, 1920-1929* (Urbana: University of Illinois Press, 2001), 9-33.

14. James T. Patterson, *Grand Expectations: The United States, 1945-1974* (New York: Oxford University Press, 1996), 20.

15. Anderson, "Race, Meritocracy, and the American Academy," 157.

16. Ibid.

17. Gilbert Belles, "Scope Note," 1968, FUSC JARC.

18. Alfred Perkins, *Edwin Rogers Embree: The Julius Rosenwald Fund Foundation Philanthropy and American Race Relations* (Bloomington: Indiana University Press, 2011), 106.

19. Edwin R. Embree and Julia Waxman, *Investment in People: The Story of the Julius Rosenwald Fund* (New York: Harper and Brothers, 1949), 134.

20. Alfred Perkins, "Welcome Consequences and Fulfilled Promise: Julius Rosenwald Fellows and 'Brown v. Board of Education,' " *Journal of Negro Education* 72 (Summer 2003): 344–56.

21. Davis-Embree correspondence, box 406, folder 5, FUSC JARC ADFF.

22. St. Clair Drake Fellowship File, box 409, folder 1, FUSC JARC; John Aubrey Davis Fellowship File, box 406, folder 4, FUSC JARC.

23. Allison Davis, Application for Fellowship Renewal, 1940, box 406, folder 5, FUSC JARC ADFF.

24. Victor Goldkind, "Social Stratification in the Peasant Community: Redfield's Chan Kom Reinterpreted," *American Anthropologist* 67 (August 1965): 863–84.

25. Robert Redfield, letter of support for Allison Davis's fellowship renewal, 1940, box 406, folder 5, FUSC JARC ADFF.

26. For example, in a methods course in cultural anthropology, Redfield exposed Davis to Mead's culture-and-personality emphases on socialization as well as Benedict's conception of a "culture-pattern," which used "culture" as the primary social structure. Allison Davis, "A Criticism of 'Sex and Temperament in Three Primitive Societies,' " November 30, 1939, ADP SCRC UCL, box 12, folder 8.

27. Allison Davis, "Final Examination, Anthropology 228," Spring 1940, ADP SCRC UCL, box 11, folder 14.

28. Allison Davis, *Social-Class Influences upon Learning* (Cambridge, MA: Harvard University Press, 1948), 83.

29. Lloyd Warner, letter of support for Allison Davis's fellowship renewal, 1940, box 406, folder 5, FUSC JARC ADFF.

30. Morris Finder, *Educating America: How Ralph W. Tyler Taught America to Teach* (Westport, CT: Praeger, 2004), 44.

31. Allison Davis résumé, 1941, box 406, folder 5, FUSC JARC ADFF; Michael R. Hillis, "Allison Davis and the Study of Race, Social Class, and Schooling," *Journal of Negro Education* 64 (Winter 1995): 34.

32. Edwin Embree to Edgar B. Stern, February 24, 1942, box 182, folder 6, FUSC JARC UCAD.

33. Special to the *New York Times*, "Educators Study Aids to Teachers: Meet at Chicago to Open 3 Year Collaboration Program To Improve Schools," *New York Times*, October 8, 1939.

34. Woodie Thomas White, "The Study of Education at the University of Chicago" (PhD diss., University of Chicago, 1977), 462. See also Mary Ann Dzuback, *Robert M. Hutchins: Portrait of an Educator* (Chicago: University of Chicago Press, 1991), 180, 329.

35. Edwin Embree to Edgar B. Stern, February 24, 1942, box 182, folder 6, FUSC JARC UCAD.

36. Robert M. Hutchins to Lessing Rosenwald, January 13, 1942, box 182, folder 6, FUSC JARC UCAD; Perkins, *Edwin Rogers Embree*, 209.

37. Ibid.

38. Edgar B. Stern to Edwin Embree, February 9, 1942, box 182, folder 6, FUSC JARC UCAD.

39. Joe M. Richardson, "A White New Orleans Philanthropist Helps Build a Black University," *Journal of Negro History* 82 (Summer 1997): 328–33.

40. Edgar B. Stern to Edwin Embree, February 10, 1942, box 182, folder 6, FUSC JARC UCAD.

41. Ibid.

42. Cross Reference Record, February 9, 1942, box 182, folder 6, FUSC JARC UCAD.

43. Edwin Embree to the Trustees of the Rosenwald Fund, February 9, 1942, box 182, folder 6, FUSC JARC UCAD.

44. Edwin Embree to Edgar B. Stern, February 24, 1942, box 182, folder 6, FUSC JARC UCAD.

45. Walter A. Jackson, *Gunnar Myrdal and America's Conscience: Social Engineering and Racial Liberalism, 1938–1987* (Chapel Hill: University of North Carolina Press, 1990), 97.

46. Howard Odum to Edwin Embree, March 12, 1942, box 182, folder 6, FUSC JARC UCAD.

47. Docket from the Rosenwald Fund Board Meeting, April 10, 1942, box 182, folder 6, FUSC JARC UCAD.

48. Michael R. Hillis, "Allison Davis and the Study of Race, Social Class, and Schooling," *Journal of Negro Education* 64 (Winter 1995): 34.

49. Bruce Kuklick, *Black Philosopher, White Academy: The Career of William Fontaine* (Philadelphia: University of Pennsylvania Press, 2008), 84.

50. "Biographical Note," Guide to the ADP SCRC UCL.

51. Notably, the fact that Davis had a PhD in a field other than education was also not at all strange in the context of Chicago's Department of Education at the time. Under Ralph Tyler's leadership, the department recruited various scholars from other fields, including Harold Dunkel in philosophy and Robert Havighurst in physics. See White, "Study of Education," 394.

52. Morris Finder, "Davis, Allison," in *American National Biography Online*, http://www.anb.org/articles/14/14-01164.html (accessed March 28, 2015).

53. Dzuback, *Robert M. Hutchins*, 143.

54. JBHE Foundation, "The Talented Black Scholars Whom No White University Would Hire," *Journal of Blacks in Higher Education* 58 (Winter 2007/2008): 81.

55. Gwenda Blair, "In Traditional Chicago, The Politics of Fitting In," *New York Times*, November 6, 2003.

56. Enoch P. Waters, *American Diary: A Personal History of the Black Press* (Chicago: Path, 1987), 69–73.

57. Elisabeth Bumiller, "Lincoln Center Homecoming for Jazz Lover," *New York Times*, August 21, 1998; Blair, "In Traditional Chicago."

58. Lloyd S. Tireman to Allison Davis, November 10, 1943, box 182, folder 6, FUSC JARC UCAD. To be sure, in this particular instance Tireman, who was a progressive and a professor of education at the University of New Mexico, warned Davis to stay away not because of his own racial prejudice. Rather, he understood the explosiveness of the issue in the state, which he had experienced firsthand. For more on Tireman, see David L. Bachelor, *Educational Reform in New Mexico: Tireman, San José, and Nambé* (Albuquerque: University of New Mexico Press, 1991).

59. Allison S. Davis, interview by the author, December 30, 2014.

60. Bumiller, "Lincoln Center Homecoming for Jazz Lover."

61. Allison Davis to Ralph Tyler, May 1948, Tyler, Ralph W., Papers, box 8, folder 6, SCRC UCL.

62. "Appointing of Dr. Allison Davis to the University Faculty." letter to William Allison Davis, December 5, 1941, DFR.

63. Ralph Tyler to Edwin Embree, February 19, 1945, and March 29, 1945; Allison Davis to Edwin Embree, February 13, 1945, box 182, folder 6, FUSC JARC UCAD.

64. For more details, and for the listing of Davis's publications, see Ralph Tyler to Edwin Embree, March 29, 1945, box 182, folder 6, FUSC JARC UCAD.

65. White, "Study of Education," 464.

66. Dorothy A. Elvidge to Robert Hutchins, April 27, 1945, box 182, folder 6, FUSC JARC UCAD.

67. Jackson, *Gunnar Myrdal and America's Conscience*, 274–75.

68. President's Commission on Civil Rights, *To Secure These Rights: The Report of the President's Committee on Civil Rights* (New York: Simon and Schuster, 1947), 157, 160, 162, 166, 169.

69. Allison Davis, quoted in Barbara P. Turner, "Profile of Allison Davis; The Man and His Research," *Education at Chicago* 2 (Autumn 1972): 24.

70. On Davis as a successful teacher of white southern students, see Ralph Tyler to Edwin Embree, March 29, 1945, box 182, folder 6, FUSC JARC UCAD.

71. Edwin Embree to Edgar B. Stern, February 24, 1942, box 182, folder 6, FUSC JARC UCAD.

72. Dallas L. Browne, "Across Class and Culture: Allison Davis and His Works," in *African-American Pioneers in Anthropology*, ed. Ira E. Harrison and Faye Harrison (Urbana: University of Illinois Press, 1999), 173.

73. "Davis Made Professor at U. of C.," *Chicago Defender*, June 13, 1942; "Davis Gets Teaching Post at U. of Chicago," *Afro-American*, June 20, 1942.

74. See, for instance: "Goes to Yale," *Afro American*, February 11, 1939; "Testing the I.Q. of the Test Takers," editorial, *Chicago Defender*, July 7, 1945; "U. Of C. Project to Devise IQ Test Fair to All Groups," *Chicago Defender*, July 14, 1945; "Davis to Revise Intelligence Tests," *Chicago Bee*, July 7, 1945.

75. Jesse E. Weston to Allison Davis, September 16, 1945, ADP SCRC UCL, box 46, folder 1.

76. Fred G. Wale, "Chosen for Ability," *Atlantic Monthly* 180 (July 1947): 81–85.

77. Anderson, "Race, Meritocracy, and the American Academy," 173.

78. Ibid., 174.

79. Allison Davis, quoted in Turner, "Profile of Allison Davis," 23–24; John Hope Franklin, "The Dilemma of the American Negro Scholar," in *Soon, One Morning: New Writing by American Negroes, 1940–1962*, ed. Herbert Hill (New York: Alfred A. Knopf, 1966), 71.

80. See, for example, Kevin M. Kruse, *White Flight: Atlanta and the Making of Modern Conservatism* (Princeton, NJ: Princeton University Press, 2005).

81. Fabio Rojas, *From Black Power to Black Studies: How a Radical Social Movement Became an Academic Discipline* (Baltimore: Johns Hopkins University Press, 2007).

82. JBHE Foundation, "Black Heritage Award for an African-American Educator," *Journal of Blacks in Higher Education* 3 (Spring 1994): 23.

83. On Du Bois, see Jackson, *Gunnar Myrdal and America's Conscience*, 25–27. On Cox, see Christopher A. McAuley, *The Mind of Oliver C. Cox* (Notre Dame, IN: University of Notre Dame Press, 2004).

84. For an excellent study of the dilemmas of the black scholar in this period, see Kenneth Robert Janken, *Rayford Logan and the Dilemma of the African-American Intellectual* (Amherst: University of Massachusetts Press, 1993).

85. St. Clair Drake, "Poverty, Sociology, and Finks," excerpt from *Commentary* magazine. ADP SCRC UCL, box 1, folder 12.

86. JBHE Foundation, "Black Heritage Award for an African-American Educator," 23.

87. See Jules Tygiel, *Baseball's Great Experiment: Jackie Robinson and His Legacy* (New York: Oxford University Press, 1983).

CHAPTER SEVEN

1. Allison Davis, *Social-Class Influences upon Learning* (Cambridge, MA: Harvard University Press, 1948), 10–11.

2. Margaret Mead, *And Keep Your Powder Dry: An Anthropologist Looks at America* (New York: William Morrow, 1942), viii, 16–17; Peter Mandler, *Return from the Natives: How Margaret Mead Won the Second World War and Lost the Cold War* (New Haven, CT: Yale University Press, 2013). For a critical take on anthropology's entanglements with the national security state, see David H. Price, *Cold War Anthropology: The CIA, the Pentagon, and the Growth of Dual Use Anthropology* (Durham, NC: Duke University Press, 2016).

3. Ruth Benedict quoted in Mandler, *Return from the Natives*, 17.

4. Wayne J. Urban, *Black Scholar: Horace Mann Bond, 1904–1972* (Athens: University of Georgia Press, 1992), 26.

5. Ellen Condliffe Lagemann, *An Elusive Science: The Troubling History of Education Research* (Chicago: University of Chicago Press, 2000), 150–51.

6. For background on the reconfiguration of Chicago's Department of Education, see Woodie T. White Jr., "The Decline of the Classroom and the Chicago Study of Education, 1909–1929," *American Journal of Education* 90 (February 1982): 144–74. For a discussion of the "second" Chicago School of Sociology and its interdisciplinary efforts in this period, see Gary Alan Fine, ed., *A Second Chicago School? The Development of a Postwar American Sociology* (Chicago: University of Chicago Press, 1995).

7. Lagemann, *Elusive Science*, 134–44.

8. Robert J. Havighurst, "Chicago: 1935–1960," in "W. Lloyd Warner; Social Anthropologist" by Mildred Hall Warner, Burleigh Gardner, Robert J. Havighurst, and associates, with corrections, n.d. WLWP SCRC UCL, box 5, folder 1, page 9.14.

9. Ralph W. Tyler, "What Is the Committee on Human Development?" Tyler, Ralph W., Papers, box 11, folder 12, SCRC UCL.

10. Allison Davis and Robert J. Havighurst, "Human Development and Intergroup Education," *Journal of Educational Sociology* 18 (May 1945): 536.

11. The list of books includes Kenneth Eells et al., *Intelligence and Cultural Differences: A Study of Cultural Learning and Problem-Solving* (Chicago: University of Chicago Press, 1951);

Robert J. Havighurst, *Adolescent Character and Personality* (New York: J. Wiley, 1949); Robert J. Havighurst, *Human Development and Education* (New York: Longmans, Green, 1953); Robert J. Havighurst et al., *The American Veteran Back Home* (New York: Longmans, Green, 1951); Robert J. Havighurst et al., *Growing Up in River City* (New York: J. Wiley, 1962); Robert J. Havighurst and Ruth Albrecht, *Older People* (New York: Longmans, Green, 1953); August de Belmont Hollingshead, *Elmtown's Youth: The Impact of Social Classes on Adolescents* (New York: J. Wiley, 1949); Robert F. Peck and Robert J. Havighurst, *The Psychology of Character Development* (New York: J. Wiley, 1960); W. Lloyd Warner, *Democracy in Jonesville* (New York: Harper, 1949); and W. Lloyd Warner, *Social Class in America* (Chicago: Science Research Associates, 1949).

12. Havighurst, "Chicago: 1935–1960," 9.14. See also W. Lloyd Warner, "Memorandum for the Committee on Human Development," Tyler, Ralph W., Papers, box 12, folder 5, SCRC UCL.

13. W. Lloyd Warner, Robert J. Havighurst, and Martin B. Loeb, *Who Shall Be Educated? The Challenge of Unequal Opportunities* (New York: Harper and Brothers, 1944), xi–xii.

14. Ibid., 61.

15. Ibid., 81.

16. W. Allison Davis and Robert J. Havighurst, *Father of the Man: How Your Child Gets His Personality* (Boston: Houghton Mifflin, 1947), 33, 75.

17. Ibid., 223.

18. Allison Davis and Robert J. Havighurst, "Social Class and Color Differences in Child-Rearing," *American Sociological Review* 11 (December 1946): 699.

19. Ralph Tyler to Edwin Embree, March 29, 1945, box 182, folder 6, FUSC JARC UCAD.

20. Davis and Havighurst, "Social Class and Color Differences in Child-Rearing," 709.

21. Davis and Havighurst, *Father of the Man*, 84.

22. Ibid., 28.

23. "Conant 'Dares' Scientists to Urge Social Research," *Daily Boston Globe*, December 28, 1947; "Science Finds Bullies Are the 'Softies': Middle Class Is More Spartan," *Chicago Daily Tribune*, December 30, 1947; Harry Hansen. "Magazine of Books: Robert A. Millikan Plans to Publish Autobiografy [*sic*]," *Chicago Daily Tribune*, April 25, 1948.

24. Alfred L. Baldwin, review of *Father of the Man: How Your Child Gets His Personality* by W. Allison Davis and Robert J. Havighurst, *Quarterly Review of Biology* 22 (December 1947): 369.

25. John W. M. Whiting and Irvin L. Child, *Child Training and Personality* (New Haven, CT: Yale University Press, 1953), 66–67.

26. Ellsworth Faris, review of *Father of the Man: How Your Child Gets His Personality* by W. Allison Davis and Robert J. Havighurst," *American Journal of Sociology* 53 (March 1948): 401.

27. Burleigh Gardner, "Human Relations in Industry and Social Research: 1940–1960," in "W. Lloyd Warner; Social Anthropologist," WLWP SCRC UCL, box 5, folder 6, pp. 10.2–10.4. William Foote Whyte, *Human Relations in the Restaurant Industry* (New York: McGraw-Hill, 1948).

28. "Lecture Conferences on Labor Relations to Begin June 27," *Chicago Daily Tribune*, June 11, 1945; "U. of C. Lecturer to Begin a Series on India Friday," *Chicago Daily Tribune*, July 15, 1945.

29. William Foote Whyte, ed., *Industry and Society* (New York: McGraw-Hill, 1946), 3.

30. Allison Davis, "The Motivations of the Underprivileged Worker," in *Industry and Society*, 86.

31. For an excellent critique of the framework of "deprivation" within social science, see Mical Raz, *What's Wrong with the Poor? Psychiatry, Race, and the War on Poverty* (Chapel Hill: University of North Carolina Press, 2013).

32. Davis, "Motivations of the Underprivileged Worker," 94–96, 89, 103.

33. Ibid., 91–93.

34. Ibid., 100.

35. Ibid., 104–5, 94.

36. Olivier Zunz, *Why the American Century?* (Chicago: University of Chicago Press, 1998), 102.

37. Ibid. 103.

38. Pierre Martineau, "Social Classes and Spending Behavior," *Journal of Marketing* 23 (October 1958): 125–29; Pierre Martineau, *Motivation in Advertising: Motives That Make People Buy* (New York: McGraw-Hill, 1957), 164–65.

39. Burleigh Gardner, "Human Relations in Industry and Social Research: 1940–1960," in "W. Lloyd Warner; Social Anthropologist," WLWP SCRC UCL, box 5, folder 6, p. 10.8.

40. Walter A. Jackson, *Gunnar Myrdal and America's Conscience: Social Engineering and Racial Liberalism, 1938–1987* (Chapel Hill: University of North Carolina Press, 1990), 281.

41. Ibid.

42. Hortense Powdermaker, *Probing Our Prejudices: A Unit for High School Students* (New York: Harper and Brothers, 1944), vi.

43. Woodie Thomas White, "The Study of Education at the University of Chicago" (PhD diss., University of Chicago, 1977), 473–78.

44. William Heard Kilpatrick, foreword to *Intercultural Education in American Schools: Proposed Objectives and Methods* by William E. Vickery and Stewart G. Cole (New York: Harper and Brothers, 1943), xiii, xiv.

45. Vickery and Cole, *Intercultural Education*, 67, 109–13.

46. St. Clair Drake, "In the Mirror of Black Scholarship: W. Allison Davis and *Deep South*," in *Education and Black Struggle: Notes from the Colonized World* (Cambridge, MA: Harvard Educational Review, 1974), 53.

47. Jackson, *Gunnar Myrdal and America's Conscience*, 285. See also Leah N. Gordon, *From Power to Prejudice: The Rise of Racial Individualism in Midcentury America* (Chicago: University of Chicago Press, 2015).

48. Thomas F. Pettigrew, *The Sociology of Race Relations: Reflection and Reform* (New York: Free Press, 1980), 133.

49. R. M. MacIver, ed., *Group Relations and Group Antagonisms* (New York: Harper and Brothers, 1944), vii.

50. Vickery and Cole, *Intercultural Education*, 22.

51. Allison Davis, "Socialization and Adolescent Personality," *43rd Yearbook of the National Society for the Study of Education: Adolescence*, pt. 1, ed. Nelson B. Henry (Chicago: University of Chicago Press, 1944), 198. For an example of early theorizing on acculturation that influenced Davis, see Robert Redfield, Ralph Linton, and Melville Herskovits, "Memorandum for the Study of Acculturation," *American Anthropologist* 38 (January–March 1936): 149–52.

52. From this point forward I will continue to use *underprivileged* to refer to poor and minority peoples whom Davis and his colleagues identified as lacking the social advantages of other groups. The term is now archaic, and readers today may find it condescending and misleading. Yet it was the language that Davis and his colleagues used, and so it is necessary and appropriate to use when discussing Davis's ideas.

53. Grant in Aid to University of Chicago, August 2, 1943, box 174, folder 5286, series 1, GEBA RAC.

54. Ibid.

55. Allison Davis, "The Public Schools and the Cultural Assimilation of Americans of Negro, Mexican, and Chinese Background," July 1944, ADP SCRC UCL, box 45, folder 6.

56. Allison Davis, "The School's Most Costly Weakness: The Education of National, Racial, and Underprivileged Groups in California," *Yearbook of California Elementary School Principals' Association*, 1945, 51.

57. Allison Davis, "The School's Most Costly Weakness: The Public Schools and the Cultural Assimilation of Americans of Negro, Mexican, and Chinese Background," August 1944, ADP SCRC UCL, box 45, folder 2.

58. Allison Davis, "Some Basic Concepts in the Education of Ethnic and Lower-Class Groups," ADP SCRC UCL, box 77, folder 7.

59. Ibid.

60. As with caste theory, Frazier's disciplinary training in sociology and his sensitivity to the politics of representing black people informed his dismissal of African influences on American blacks. Herskovits, on the other hand, because of his disciplinary training in cultural anthropology and his relative white privilege, was more ardent in seeing African cultural continuities. For some of their writings on the issue, see Melville J. Herskovits, *The Myth of the Negro Past* (New York: Harper and Brothers, 1941); and E. Franklin Frazier, *The Negro Family in the United States* (Chicago: University of Chicago Press, 1939). A considerable body of good historical literature exists on these debates. See Jerry Gershenhorn, *Melville J. Herskovits and the Racial Politics of Knowledge* (Lincoln: University of Nebraska Press, 2004), 93–120; Lawrence W. Levine, "African Culture and Slavery in the United States," in *Global Dimensions of the African Diaspora*, ed. Joseph E. Harris (Washington, DC: Howard University Press, 1993), 99–107; and Albert J. Raboteau, "African Religions in America: Theoretical Perspectives," in *Global Dimensions of the African Diaspora*, 65–79.

61. Frazier, *Negro Family in the United States*; E. Franklin Frazier, *The Negro in the United States* (New York: Macmillan, 1949).

62. Jackson, *Gunnar Myrdal and America's Conscience*, 268.

63. Davis, "Some Basic Concepts in the Education of Ethnic and Lower-Class Groups."

64. Davis, "School's Most Costly Weakness."

65. Allison Davis, "The Public Schools and the Acculturation of Working-Class Children," ADP SCRC UCL, box 44, folder 12.

66. Ibid.

67. Davis, "Some Basic Concepts in the Education of Ethnic and Lower-Class Groups."

68. Davis, "Public Schools and the Acculturation of Working-Class Children."

69. Davis, "School's Most Costly Weakness."

70. Robert J. Havighurst and Allison Davis, "Child Socialization and the School," *Review of Educational Research* 13 (February 1943): 29.

71. John Dewey, *Freedom and Culture* (New York: Capricorn Books, 1939).

72. Davis, "Public Schools and the Acculturation of Working-Class Children."

73. Davis, "School's Most Costly Weakness."

74. Ralph Tyler to A. R. Mann, December 28, 1944, and February 13, 1945, box 496, folder 5286, Series 1, GEBA RAC.

75. Allison Davis to Ralph Tyler, June 26, 1945, box 496, folder 5286, series 1, GEBA RAC.

76. Allison Davis to Flora M. Rhind, January 7, 1946 and March 17, 1947, box 496, folder 5286, series 1, GEBA RAC.

77. Allison Davis, "The Public Schools and America's Most Successful Racial Democracy: Hawaii," 1947, ADP SCRC UCL, box 45, folder 10.

78. "23rd Annual Institute for Social Research to Open Tomorrow," *Chicago Daily Tribune*, August 3, 1944.

79. Carey McWilliams, "The Mexican Problem in Southern California," Carey McWilliams Papers (Collection 1243), Department of Special Collections, Charles E. Young Research Library, University of California, Los Angeles.

80. "Lt. Col. Taylor to Be Speaker at South Shore: Avalon Park PTA to Hold Fathers Night," *Chicago Daily Tribune*, November 18, 1945; "Allison Davis, Negro Educator, Will Give Talk at Sheil School," *Chicago Daily Tribune*, August 3, 1943.

81. "Schools Termed People's Ladder," *New York Times*, June 29, 1951.

82. Havighurst and Davis, "Human Development and Intergroup Education," 539.

83. Ibid.

84. Allison Davis, "Changing the Culture of the Disadvantaged Student," ADP SCRC UCL, box 77, folder 12. Allison Davis, "Applied Research upon Group and Individual Therapy for Delinquents," October 11, 1948, ADP SCRC UCL, box 77, folder 5.

85. Allison Davis, "Education for the Conservation of Human Resources," *Progressive Education* 27 (May 1950): 224; Allison Davis, "Developing an Improved Primary Curriculum," *Educational Leadership* 7 (December 1949): 175–80.

86. Davis, "Changing the Culture of the Disadvantaged Student."

87. Gunnar Myrdal, *An American Dilemma: The Negro Problem and Modern Democracy*, 20th anniv. ed. (orig. 1944; New York: Harper and Row, 1962), 929.

88. Lizabeth Cohen, *A Consumers' Republic: The Politics of Mass Consumption in Postwar America* (New York: Alfred A. Knopf, 2003), 166–91; Jackson, *Gunnar Myrdal and America's Conscience*, 283; and John P. Jackson Jr., *Social Scientists for Social Justice: Making the Case against Segregation* (New York: New York University Press, 2001), 64.

89. St. Clair Drake, "Anthropology and the Black Experience," *Black Scholar* 11 (September/October 1980): 23.

90. St. Clair Drake, "Reflections on Anthropology and the Black Experience," *New Perspectives on Black Education*, special issue of *Anthropology and Education Quarterly* 9 (Summer 1978): 88.

91. Sudhir Alladi Venkatesh, *American Project: The Rise and Fall of a Modern Ghetto* (Cambridge, MA: Harvard University Press, 2000), 9.

92. For a scholar calling for further examination into the application of culture-and-personality theory, see Joanne Meyerowitz, "'How Common Culture Shapes the Separate Lives': Sexuality, Race, and Mid-Twentieth-Century Social Thought," *Journal of American History* 96 (March 2010): 1083–84.

CHAPTER EIGHT

1. Allison Davis and John Dollard, *Children of Bondage: The Personality Development of Negro Youth in the Urban South* (Washington, DC: American Council on Education, 1940), 90.
2. Paul Davis Chapman, *Schools as Sorters: Lewis M. Terman, Applied Psychology, and the Intelligence Testing Movement, 1890–1930* (New York: New York University Press, 1988), 42, 83.
3. JoAnne Brown, *The Definition of a Profession: The Authority of Metaphor in the History of Intelligence Testing, 1890–1930* (Princeton, NJ: Princeton University Press, 1992), 37.
4. Chapman, *Schools as Sorters*, 19.
5. Brown, *Definition of a Profession*, 35–38. See also Harold B. Dunkel, "Judd's Debt to Wundt," *School Review* 85 (August 1977): 535–51.
6. Allison Davis and Robert J. Havighurst, "Measurement of Mental Systems: Can Intelligence Be Measured?," *Scientific Monthly* 66 (April 1948): 302.
7. Leila Zenderland, *Measuring Minds: Henry Herbert Goddard and the Origins of American Intelligence Testing* (Cambridge: Cambridge University Press, 1998), 90–92.
8. Chapman, *Schools as Sorters*, 112–13.
9. Brown, *Definition of a Profession*, 6–7.
10. Ibid., 45–46.
11. Chapman, *Schools as Sorters*, chaps. 4–5.
12. Allison Davis, *Social-Class Influences upon Learning* (Cambridge, MA: Harvard University Press, 1948), 70–78.
13. Richard C. Maclaurin, "Educational and Industrial Efficiency," *Science* 33 (1911): 101–3; "Measuring the Mind," anonymous editorial, *Nation* 94 (1912): 486.
14. William C. Bagley, "Educational Determinism, or Democracy and the I.Q.," *School and Society* 15 (April 1922): 373–84. See also Thomas J. McCormack, "A Critique of Mental Measurements," *School and Society* 15 (1922): 686–92. For the back-and-forth between Bagley and Terman, see Lewis M. Terman, "The Psychological Determinist, or Democracy and the IQ," *Journal of Educational Research* 6 (June 1922): 57–62; and William C. Bagley, "Professor Terman's Determinism," *Journal of Educational Research* 6 (December 1922): 376–85.
15. Horace M. Bond, "Intelligence Tests and Propaganda," *Crisis* 28 (June 1924): 61–64; Horace M. Bond, "What the Army 'Intelligence' Tests Measured," *Opportunity* 2 (July 1924): 197–202.
16. Walter Lippmann, "The Mental Age of Americans," *New Republic*, October 25, 1922, 213–15; "The Mystery of the 'A' Men," *New Republic*, November 1, 1922, 246–48; "The Reliability of Intelligence Tests," *New Republic*, November 8, 1922, 275–77; "Tests of Hereditary Intelligence," *New Republic*, November 22, 1922, 328–30; "A Future for the Tests," *New Republic*, November 29, 1922, 9–11. For Terman's response, see Lewis M. Terman, "The Great Conspiracy; or the Impulse Imperious of Intelligence Testers Psychoanalyzed and Exposed by Mr. Lippmann," *New Republic*, December 27, 1922, 1–15.

17. Lewis M. Terman, "The Possibilities and Limitations of Training," *Journal of Educational Research* 10 (December 1924): 340.

18. Brown, *Definition of a Profession*, 7–9, 138; Arthur R. Jensen, *Bias in Mental Testing* (New York: Free Press, 1980), 368.

19. Wayne H. Holtzrnan and Roger W. Russell, "Otto Klineberg: A Pioneer International Psychologist," *International Journal of Psychology* 27 (October 1992): 364–65; Jackson, *Social Scientists for Social Justice*, 20–23.

20. Otto Klineberg, *Negro Intelligence and Selective Migration* (New York: Columbia University Press, 1935); Otto Klineberg, *Race Differences* (New York: Harper and Brothers, 1935).

21. Allison Davis, "The Culture of the Slum," ADP SCRC UCL, box 77, folder 18.

22. Ibid.

23. Allison Davis to George R. Arthur, October 8, 1932, box 406, folder 5, FUSC JARC ADFF; see also Allison Davis, "The Distribution of Blood Groups and Its Bearing on the Concept of Race," *Sociological Review* 27 (January 1935): 19–34; pt. 2 in the next issue: 28 (April 1935): 183–200.

24. Allison Davis, "GEB Study of the Cultural Factors in Intelligence," ADP SCRC UCL, box 52, folder 1.

25. S. Stansfeld Sargent, review of *Intelligence and Cultural Differences* by Kenneth Eells, Allison Davis, Robert J. Havighurst, Virgil E. Herrick, and Ralph Tyler, *American Journal of Sociology* 58 (September 1952): 209; Ellen Condliffe Lagemann, *An Elusive Science: The Troubling History of Education Research* (Chicago: University of Chicago Press, 2000), 136.

26. See, for instance, Kurt Lewin, "Survey of Activities at Iowa in Recent Years," ADP SCRC UCL, box 33, folder 8.

27. Bonita Valien, acting-departmental secretary for the American Youth Commission, to Allison Davis, December 3, 1938, ADP SCRC UCL, box 30, folder 4.

28. Davis and Dollard, *Children of Bondage*, 90.

29. Allison Davis, "The School's Most Costly Weakness: The Public Schools and the Cultural Assimilation of Americans of Negro, Mexican, and Chinese Background," August 1944, ADP SCRC UCL, box 45, folder 2, p. viii.

30. Ibid.

31. Robert J. Havighurst, "Chicago: 1935–1960," in "W. Lloyd Warner; Social Anthropologist," by Mildred Hall Warner, Burleigh Gardner, Robert J. Havighurst, and associates, with corrections, n.d. WLWP SCRC UCL, box 5, folder 6, p. 9.23.

32. University of Chicago, "Proposal for the Development and Standardization of a Verbal Test of General Intelligence That Will Measure and Offer a Means of Comparing Abilities of Children of All Socio-economic Levels," January 31, 1945, box 496, folder 5289, series 1, GEBA RAC.

33. A. R. Mann to Robert Hutchins, January 19, 1945, box 496, folder 5289, series 1, GEBA RAC.

34. Havighurst, "Chicago: 1935–1960," 9.23.

35. Davis, *Social-Class Influences upon Learning*, 85.

36. Ibid., 40; See also: W. Lloyd Warner, Marchia Meeker, and Kenneth Eells, *Social Class in America: A Manual of Procedure for the Measurement of Social Status* (Chicago: University of Chicago Press, 1949).

37. Kenneth Eells, Allison Davis, Robert J. Havighurst, Virgil E. Herrick, and Ralph Tyler, *Intelligence and Cultural Differences: A Study of Cultural Learning and Problem-Solving* (Chicago: University of Chicago Press, 1951).

38. Ralph Beatley to Allison Davis, November 22, 1947, Tyler, Ralph W., Papers, box 8, folder 6, SCRC UCL; "Noted Chicago Educator to Give Inglis Lecture," *Daily Boston Globe*, March 21, 1948.

39. Davis, *Social-Class Influences upon Learning*, 6.

40. Ibid., 13–22.

41. Ibid., 29.

42. Ibid., 41, 45.

43. Ibid., 50; ADP SCRC UCL, box 13, folder 2.

44. Nicholas Lemann, "The Great Sorting," *Atlantic* 276 (September 1995): 84.

45. Davis, *Social-Class Influences upon Learning*, 57.

46. Ibid., 59–60.

47. Ibid., 66–67, 69.

48. For more on the rise of cultural nationalism and consensus culture, see Philip Gleason, "World War II and the Development of American Studies," *American Quarterly* 36, no. 3 (1984): 343–58; Sarah E. Igo, *The Averaged American: Surveys, Citizens, and the Making of a Mass Public* (Cambridge, MA: Harvard University Press, 2007); and Wendy Wall, *Inventing the "American Way": The Politics of Consensus from the New Deal to the Civil Rights Movement* (Oxford: Oxford University Press, 2008).

49. Allison Davis, "Some Basic Concepts in the Education of Ethnic and Lower-Class Groups," ADP SCRC UCL, box 77, folder 7.

50. Davis, *Social-Class Influences upon Learning*, 79, 82.

51. Specifically, he cites Edward Sapir, *Language* (New York: Harcourt, Brace, 1939); and M. Swadesh, "Siglo XX," in *La nueva filología*, vol. 4 ([Mexico City]: Biblioteca Nacional de Maestros, 1941).

52. Davis, *Social-Class Influences upon Learning*, 82, 84–85.

53. Ibid., 85–88.

54. Ibid., 88, 94–96.

55. Ibid., 94–96.

56. Allison Davis, "Author Questionnaire," November 16, 1950, UCPR SCRC UCL, box 165, folder 3.

57. Allison Davis to Flora Rhind, November 10, 1948, box 496, folder 5290, series 1, GEBA RAC.

58. Allison Davis and Robert J. Havighurst, "Measurement of Mental Systems: Can Intelligence Be Measured?," *Scientific Monthly* 66 (April 1948): 301–16.

59. Henry E. Garrett, "Negro-White Differences in Mental Ability in the United States," *Scientific Monthly* 65 (October 1947): 333. To be sure, Garrett was a minority voice among social scientists in this period. Numerous scholars criticized his article, most notably anthropologist Ashley Montagu. See Ashley F. Montagu, "Racial Intelligence," *Scientific Monthly* 66 (January 1948): 81–82.

60. Arthur S. Otis, "Can Intelligence Be Measured? (A Reply to Davis and Havighurst)," *Scientific Monthly* 67 (October 1948): 312–13. For another example of a test maker who resisted

Davis's ideas, see Ernest W. Tiegs, editor-in-chief of the California Test Bureau, to Ernest A. Haggard, February 10, 1950, ADP SCRC UCL, box 46, folder 1.

61. Lemann, "Great Sorting," 87.

62. Robert J. Havighurst and W. Allison Davis, "(A Rejoinder to Mr. Otis)," *Scientific Monthly* 67 (October 1948): 313–14.

63. Ibid., 314.

64. Orval Hobart Mowrer to Allison Davis, September 25, 1948, ADP SCRC UCL, box 46, folder 1.

65. Allison Davis to Flora Rhind, November 10, 1948, box 496, folder 5290, series 1, GEBA RAC.

66. Kenneth Eels to Tyler, Bloom, Havighurst, Haggard, Hess, and Davis, August 17, 1951, ADP SCRC UCL, box 46, folder 1.

67. *Book Review Digest*, February 1953; *Elementary School Journal* 52 (1952): 365; *U.S. Quarterly Book Review* 7 (1951): 394. See UCPR SCRC UCL, box 165, folder 3.

68. Irving Lorge, "Implications of *Intelligence and Cultural Differences*" by Kenneth Eells, Allison Davis, Robert J. Havighurst, Virgil E. Herrick, and Ralph Tyler, *Teachers College Record*. January 1953, UCPR SCRC UCL, box 165, folder 3.

69. Charles F. Harding, review of *Intelligence and Cultural Differences* by Kenneth Eells, Allison Davis, Robert J. Havighurst, Virgil E. Herrick, and Ralph Tyler, *American Anthropologist* 56 (February 1954): 152.

70. Denton Coker, review of *Intelligence and Cultural Differences* by Kenneth Eells, Allison Davis, Robert J. Havighurst, Virgil E. Herrick, and Ralph Tyler, *Review and Expositor*, 1954, UCPR SCRC UCL, box 165, folder 3.

71. William H. Sewell, review of *Intelligence and Cultural Differences* by Kenneth Eells, Allison Davis, Robert J. Havighurst, Virgil E. Herrick, and Ralph Tyler, *American Sociological Review* 18 (April 1953): 221. For a test maker conveying similar ideas, see Ernest W. Tiegs, editor-in-chief of the California Test Bureau, to Ernest A. Haggard, February 10, 1950, ADP SCRC UCL, box 46, folder 1.

72. Sargent, review of *Intelligence and Cultural Differences*, 209–10.

73. Allison Davis, "Poor People Have Brains Too," *Phi Delta Kappan* 30 (April 1949): 294–95; Allison Davis, "Socio-economic Influences on Learning," *Phi Delta Kappan* 32 (January 1951): 253–56.

74. Allison Davis, "Developing an Improved Primary Curriculum," *Educational Leadership: Journal of the Association for Supervision and Curriculum Development, N.E.A.* 7 (December 1949): 175–80; Allison Davis, "Author Questionnaire," November 16, 1950, UCPR SCRC UCL, box 165, folder 3.

75. Allison Davis to Fred D. Wieck, September 28, 1949, UCPR SCRC UCL, box 165, folder 2; "Standard Intelligence Tests Held Remiss in Evaluating Children's Mental Capacities," *New York Times*, March 23, 1950.

76. Allison Davis to Anna Rosenberg, assistant secretary of defense, April 8, 1951, ADP SCRC UCL, box 46, folder 1; "Youth Conference Schedule," *Washington Post*, December 3, 1950.

77. Edward A. Richards, ed., *Proceedings of the Midcentury White House Conference on Children and Youth* (Raleigh, NC: Health Publications Institute, 1951), 13.

78. Catherine E. Kerr, "Race in the Making of American Liberalism, 1912–1965," (Ph.D. diss., Johns Hopkins University, 1995), 240.

79. Jackson, *Social Scientists for Social Justice*, 111.

80. Allison Davis, "Socio-economic Influences upon Children's Learning," in *Proceedings of the Midcentury White House Conference*, 77–83. He published much of this in Allison Davis, "Education for the Conservation of Human Resources," *Progressive Education* 27 (May 1950): 221–22. For another article that reiterated the same ideas, see Allison Davis, "Ability and Survival," *Survey* 87 (February 1951): 60–63.

81. Davis, "Education for the Conservation of Human Resources."

82. Ibid.

83. Dorothea Andrews, "U.S. Wastes Manpower, Parley Told: Class Conflict between Adults, Children Blamed by Educator," *Washington Post*, December 6, 1950; "Baby's Thumb Sucking Laid to Parental Zeal," *Chicago Daily Tribune*, December 6, 1950; Elsie Carper, "U.S. Public Education System Not Democratic, Says Dr. Davis," *Washington Post*, December 10, 1950; "China Poses Grave Risk, Truman Says," *Los Angeles Times*, December 6, 1950.

84. "China Poses Grave Risk, Truman Says," *Los Angeles Times*, December 6, 1950.

85. For an overview of American foreign policy in these years, see George C. Herring, *From Colony to Superpower: U.S. Foreign Relations since 1776* (Oxford: Oxford University Press, 2008), 595–650. For an overview of McCarthyism, see Ellen Schrecker, *Many Are the Crimes: McCarthyism in America* (Boston: Little, Brown, 1998).

86. Allison Davis to Flora Rhind, November 10, 1948, box 496, folder 5290, series 1, GEBA RAC.

87. Benjamin Fine, "Education in Review: Teacher Shortage Remains Greatest Problem, According to School Administrators," *New York Times*, February 27, 1949.

88. Fine, "Education in Review;" "5000 Educators Open Conference," *Washington Post*, March 27, 1949.

89. Lawrence E. Davis, "Educator Defends Validity of the IQ," *New York Times*, February 28, 1949.

90. Lyle M. Spencer to Allison Davis, August 1, 1950, ADP SCRC UCL, box 46, folder 1.

91. J. F. Graham to Allison Davis, February 24, 1949, box 496, folder 5290, series 1, GEBA RAC.

92. Franklin Patterson to Davis, March 10, 1949, box 496, folder 5290, series 1, GEBA RAC.

93. W. Hugh Stickler to Allison Davis, on March 2, 1949, box 496, folder 5290, series 1, GEBA RAC.

94. T. Malcolm Brown to Allison Davis, March 4, 1949, box 496, folder 5290, series 1, GEBA RAC.

95. Gail B. Willis to Allison Davis, September 5, 1945, ADP SCRC UCL, box 46, folder 1.

96. Fine, "Education in Review."

97. Benjamin Fine, "12 Billions Asked to Build Schools: Long-Range Program Proposed at Coast Conference to End a Dangerous Shortage," *New York Times*, February 21, 1949.

98. John M. Harmon to Allison Davis, March 1, 1949; E. W. McDaid to Allison Davis, March 3, 1949; Burton Rogers to Allison Davis, March 1, 1949, box 496, folder 5290, series 1, GEBA RAC.

99. R. D. Baldwin to Allison Davis, March 9, 1949, box 496, folder 5290, series 1, GEBA RAC.

100. Burton Rogers to Allison Davis, March 1, 1949, box 496, folder 5290, series 1, GEBA RAC.

101. "Testing the I.Q. of the Test Takers," editorial, *Chicago Defender*, July 7, 1945.

102. Ibid.

103. "Davis to Revise Intelligence Tests," *Chicago Bee*, July 7, 1945.

104. Jacqueline Lopez, "U. Of C. Project to Devise IQ Test Fair to All Groups," *Chicago Defender*, July 14, 1945.

105. See, for instance, Harold Seashore, director of Test Division for the Psychological Corporation, to Davis, February 2, 1950, ADP SCRC UCL, box 46, folder 1.

106. See Donald S. Napoli, *Architects of Adjustment: The History of the Psychological Profession in the United States* (Port Washington, NY: Kennikat, 1981), 30–41, 86–152.

107. Flora M. Rhind to Allison Davis, October 29, 1948, box 496, folder 5289, series 1, GEBA RAC.

108. Allison Davis to Lyle M. Spencer, August 16, 1950, ADP SCRC UCL, box 46, folder 1.

109. Allison Davis and Kenneth Eells, *Davis-Eells Test of General Intelligence or Problem-Solving Ability: Manual* (New York: World Book Company, 1953).

110. Allison Davis to Anna Rosenberg, assistant secretary of defense, April 8, 1951, ADP SCRC UCL, box 46, folder 1.

111. Jensen, *Bias in Mental Testing*, 644.

112. Davis and Eells, *Davis-Eells Test*, 4–5.

113. Ibid., 60; Robert D. Hess, "Controlling Culture Influence in Mental Testing: An Experimental Test," *Journal of Educational Research* 49 (September 1955): 58.

114. Henry Angelino and Charles L. Shedd, "An Initial Report of a Validation Study of the Davis-Eells Tests of General Intelligence or Problem Solving Ability," *Journal of Psychology* 40 (January 1955): 35–38; William Coleman and Annie W. Ward, "A Comparison of Davis-Eells and Kuhlman-Finch Scores of Children from High and Low Socio-economic Status," *Journal of Educational Psychology* 46 (December 1955): 465–69; H. Glen Ludlow, "Some Recent Research on the Davis-Eells Game," *School and Society* 84 (October 1956): 146–48; Victor H. Nolls, "Relation of Scores on Davis-Eells Test of General Intelligence to Social Status, School Achievement, and Other Intelligence Test Results," *American Psychologist* 13 (1958): 394; Merle W. Tate and Charlotte E. Voss, "A Study of the Davis-Eells Test of Intelligence," *Harvard Educational Review* 26 (Fall 1956): 374–87.

115. Sidney Rosenblum, James E. Keller, and Ned Papania, "Davis-Eells ('Culture-Fair') Test Performance of Lower-Class Retarded Children," *Journal of Consulting Psychology* 19 (June 1955): 54.

116. Lee J. Cronbach, "Five Decades of Public Controversy over Mental Testing," *American Psychologist* 30 (1975): 8.

117. Allison Davis, quoted in Barbara P. Turner, "Profile of Allison Davis; The Man and His Research," *Education at Chicago* 2 (Autumn 1972): 22.

118. "City Life Aids Negroes' I.Q., Seminar Told," *Chicago Tribune*, March 17, 1965; "Life in North Said to Boost Negroes' IQ," *Washington Post*, March 17, 1965.

119. Ralph McGill, "IQ Tests Are Unfair," *Boston Globe*, February 6, 1964.

120. Robert L. Williams, "Scientific Racism and the IQ: The Silent Mugging of the Black Community," *Psychology Today* (May 1974): 32.

121. Paul Delaney, "Black Psychologist Fighting Use of Intelligence Tests He Says Reflect White Middle-Class Values," *New York Times*, May 13, 1975.

122. Williams, "Scientific Racism and the IQ," 101.

123. Robert L. Williams, "Abuses and Misuses in Testing Black Children," *Counseling Psychologist* 2 (Fall 1971): 67.

124. David K. Cohen, "Jurists and Educators on Urban Schools: The Wright Decision and the Passow Report," *Teachers College Record* 70 (December 1968): 233–50.

125. J. Skelly Wright, quoted in Jensen, *Bias in Mental Testing*, 28.

126. Ibid., 28–29.

127. Jensen, *Bias in Mental Testing*, 32.

128. Richard J. Herrnstein, "I.Q.," *Atlantic Monthly* (September 1971): 43–64; Arthur R. Jensen, "How Much Can We Boost IQ and Scholastic Achievement?" *Harvard Educational Review* 39 (Winter 1969): 1–123. For context, see Cronbach, "Five Decades of Public Controversy," 1–6; and Mark Snyderman and Stanley Rothman, *The IQ Controversy, the Media and Public Policy* (New Brunswick, NJ: Transaction Books, 1988), 1–41.

129. Jensen, *Bias in Mental Testing*, 13.

130. Stephen J. Gould, *The Mismeasure of Man* (New York: W. W. Norton, 1981); Paul L. Houts, ed., *The Myth of Measurability* (New York: Hart, 1977); Leon J. Kamin, *The Science and Politics of IQ* (Potomac, MD: Lawrence Erlbaum, 1974); and Andrew J. Strenio, *The Testing Trap* (New York: Rawson, Wade, 1981).

131. Richard J. Herrnstein and Charles Murray, *The Bell Curve: Intelligence and Class Structure in American Life* (New York: Free Press, 1994). Stephen J. Gould had published his famous critique of intelligence tests, *The Mismeasure of Man*, in 1981, but he revised and expanded it in 1995 in order to directly refute *The Bell Curve*. A variety of intellectuals also published an important compendium in response to *The Bell Curve*. See Russell Jacoby and Naomi Glauberman, eds., *The Bell Curve Debate: History, Documents, Opinions* (New York: Times Books, 1995).

CHAPTER NINE

1. Benjamin S. Bloom, Allison Davis, and Robert Hess, *Compensatory Education for Cultural Deprivation* (New York: Holt, Rinehart and Winston, 1965), 6.

2. Allison Davis, quoted by Gordon J. Davis, e-mail message to author, July 26, 2015.

3. Allison S. Davis, interview with the author, December 30, 2014; Allison Davis to George Allen Mason, March 28, 1974, ADP SCRC UCL, box 1, folder 2.

4. Reed Ueta, e-mail message to author, June 10, 2016.

5. Allison Davis, *Psychology of the Child in the Middle Class* (Pittsburgh: University of Pittsburgh Press, 1960).

6. See Allison Davis, "Personality and Social Mobility," *School Review* 65 (Summer 1957): 135–43; and Allison Davis, "The Ego and Status Anxiety," in *The State of Sciences*, ed. Leonard D. White (Chicago: University Chicago Press, 1956), 212–28.

7. Allison Davis and Robert D. Hess, *Achievement in Adolescence and Young Adulthood* (Washington, DC: US Office of Education, 1963).

8. Allison Davis, "Caste, Economy, and Violence," *American Journal of Sociology* 51 (July 1945): 7–15; Allison Davis, "Racial Status and Personality Development," *Scientific Monthly* 57 (October 1943): 354–62; Allison Davis, "Retrospect, 1965: Power and Caste," in *Deep South:*

A Social Anthropological Study of Caste and Class, abr. ed. (Chicago: Phoenix Books, 1965), 337–46.

9. Thurgood Marshall, quoted in Walter A. Jackson, *Gunnar Myrdal and America's Conscience: Social Engineering and Racial Liberalism, 1938–1987* (Chapel Hill: University of North Carolina Press, 1990), 292.

10. John P. Jackson Jr., *Social Scientists for Social Justice: Making the Case against Segregation* (New York: New York University Press, 2001), 139.

11. Kenneth B. Clark, "The Effects of Segregation and the Consequences of Desegregation: A Social Science Statement," *Minnesota Law Review* 37 (1952–53): 429.

12. Jackson, *Social Scientists for Social Justice*, 174.

13. Daryl Michael Scott, *Contempt and Pity: Social Policy and the Image of the Damaged Black Psyche, 1880–1996* (Chapel Hill: University of North Carolina Press, 1997), 125–36.

14. Allison Davis, "Racial Status and Personality Development," *Scientific Monthly* 57 (October 1943): 359.

15. Allison Davis, "The Socialization of the American Negro Child and Adolescent," *Journal of Negro Education* 8 (July 1939): 264–74; Clark, "Effects of Segregation and the Consequences of Desegregation," 430.

16. Scott, *Contempt and Pity*, 129–30.

17. Ibid., 187–202.

18. Jackson, J*Social Scientists for Social Justice*, 168.

19. Clark and others later published that research in "Desegregation: An Appraisal of the Evidence," *Journal of Social Issues*, 1953. See also Jackson, *Social Scientists for Social Justice*, 168–72; Wayne J. Urban, *Black Scholar: Horace Mann Bond, 1904–1972* (Athens: University of Georgia Press, 1992), 168–70.

20. Alfred Perkins, "Welcome Consequences and Fulfilled Promise: Julius Rosenwald Fellows and 'Brown v. Board of Education,'" *Journal of Negro Education* 72 (Summer 2003): 351.

21. Jackson, *Social Scientists for Social Justice*, 96–97.

22. "Court Said to End 'a Sense of Guilt,'" *New York Times*, May 18, 1954.

23. Jackson, *Social Scientists for Social Justice*, 195–96.

24. Benjamin Fine, "Races Declared Equal in Brains," *New York Times*, October 16, 1956.

25. Floyd Fleming, quoted in John P. Jackson Jr., "'Racially Stuffed Shirts and Other Enemies of Mankind': Horace Mann Bond's Parody of Segregationist Psychology in the 1950s," in *Defining Difference: Race and Racism in the History of Psychology*, ed. Andrew S. Winston (Washington, DC: American Psychological Association, 2004): 267.

26. Richard Russell, quoted in ibid.

27. Eve Edstrom, "Scientists Reject Idea of Negro Inferiority," *Washington Post and Times Herald*, October 16, 1956.

28. "Experts Deny Negro Lacking in Brainpower," *Chicago Daily Tribune*, October 16, 1956.

29. Ibid.

30. Fine, "Races Declared Equal in Brains," October 16, 1956.

31. Critics tended to focus on problems stemming from affluence, such as conformity and ennui in suburban life and the corporate environment. See, for example, Vance Packard, *The Status Seekers: An Exploration of Class Behavior in America and the Hidden Barriers that Affect*

You, Your Community, Your Future (New York: D. McKay, 1959); David Riesman, Nathan Glazer, and Reuel Denney, *The Lonely Crowd: A Study of the Changing American Character* (New Haven, CT: Yale University Press, 1950); and William H. Whyte, *The Organization Man* (New York: Simon and Schuster, 1956).

32. Maris A. Vinovskis, *The Birth of Head Start: Preschool Education Policies in the Kennedy and Johnson Administrations* (Chicago: University of Chicago Press, 2005), 6.

33. James T. Patterson, *Grand Expectations: The United States, 1945–1974* (New York: Oxford University Press, 1996), 311–70.

34. Many other journalists and researchers tracked poverty in these years as well, but they had a smaller national impact. For instance, Harry Caudill's *Night Comes to the Cumberlands: A Biography of a Depressed Area* (Boston: Little, Brown, 1963) was an important expose of rural poverty in America.

35. Michael Harrington, *The Other America: Poverty in the United States* (Baltimore: Penguin Books, 1963), 21–22.

36. Vinovskis, *Birth of Head Start*, 6.

37. Scott Stossel, *Sarge: The Life and Times of Sargent Shriver* (Washington. DC: Smithsonian Books, 2004), 337–38; Dwight MacDonald, "The Invisible Poor," *New Yorker*, January 19, 1963, 82–132.

38. Lyndon Johnson, quoted in Stossel, *Sarge*, 333, 334.

39. Valora Washington and Ura Jean Oyemade Bailey, *Project Head Start: Model and Strategies for the Twenty-First Century* (New York: Garland, 1995), 21–22, 24.

40. Ibid., 22; Vinovskis, *Birth of Head Start*, 10. On Bloom's years at Chicago, see Thomas R. Guskey, "The Early Years," in *Benjamin S. Bloom: Portraits of an Educator*, ed. Thomas R. Guskey, 2nd ed. (Lanham, MD: Rowman and Littlefield Education, 2012), 16–17; Guskey, "The University of Chicago's Board of Examinations," in *Benjamin S. Bloom*, 28–29.

41. Thomas R. Guskey, "Stability and Change in Human Characteristics," in *Benjamin S. Bloom*, 59.

42. Benjamin S. Bloom, *Stability and Change in Human Characteristics* (New York: John Wiley and Sons, 1964), 77, 87–91, 127.

43. Bloom, Davis, and Hess, *Compensatory Education for Cultural Deprivation*, 6.

44. Ibid.

45. "Educator Hits ADC Program 'Shortcoming,'" *Chicago Daily Tribune*, December 8, 1962.

46. Ibid.

47. "Plan Session on Fair Youth Opportunities," *Chicago Tribune*, February 27, 1964; "City Schools Fail to Do Job, Say Speakers," *Chicago Tribune*, March 13, 1964; "City Life Aids Negroes' I.Q., Seminar Told," *Chicago Tribune*, March 17, 1965.

48. "City Schools Fail to Do Job, Say Speakers."

49. "C.C.C.O. Urges Naming of 3 to School Board," *Chicago Tribune*, April 12, 1964; "Propose 7 for School Board," *Chicago Tribune*, April 4, 1964; "I.V.I. Proposes 7 for School Board Posts," *Chicago Tribune*, April 9, 1964; "Urban League Offers 4 for School Board," *Chicago Tribune*, March 18, 1964.

50. Walter H. Waggoner, "Allison Davis, Psychologist, Dies: Wrote About Blacks in America," *New York Times*, November 22, 1983.

51. "Obituary: James Coleman, Sociology," *University of Chicago Chronicle* 14 (March 30, 1995), http://chronicle.uchicago.edu/950330/coleman.shtml (accessed March 28, 2015).

52. James S. Coleman et al., *Equality of Educational Opportunity* (Washington, DC: US Government Printing Office, 1966), 3–23; Ellen Condliffe Lagemann, *An Elusive Science: The Troubling History of Education Research* (Chicago: University of Chicago Press, 2000), 196.

53. Coleman et al., *Equality of Educational Opportunity*, 3–23.

54. Jean Yavis Jones, *Head Start—A History of Legislation, Issues and Funding* (Washington, DC: Library of Congress, 1978), 4; Washington and Bailey, *Project Head Start*, 24. Other studies, of course, showed the long-term significance and cost effectiveness of Head Start. Indeed, extensive studies of Head Start became a mainstay within social science. See Raymond C. Collins, *Head Start: A Review of Research with Implications for Practice in Early Childhood Education* (n.p.: ERIC Clearinghouse, 1984).

55. Daniel Patrick Moynihan, "The Negro Family: The Case for National Action," US Department of Labor, http://www.dol.gov/dol/aboutdol/history/moynchapter5.htm (accessed March 28, 2015). For an account of how the War on Poverty evolved into the system of mass incarceration, see Elizabeth Hinton, *The War on Poverty to the War on Crime: The Making of Mass Incarceration in America* (Cambridge, MA: Harvard University Press, 2016).

56. The Moynihan Report continues to be fiercely debated. For a recent assessment of Moynihan's arguments in relation to novel social science research, see Gregory Acs, Kenneth Braswell, Elaine Sorensen, and Margaret Austin Turner, "The Moynihan Report Revisited," Urban Institute, 2013, http://www.urban.org/UploadedPDF/412839-The-Moynihan-Report-Revisited.pdf (accessed March 28, 2015). For a sympathetic account of Moynihan, see James T. Patterson, *Freedom Is Not Enough: The Moynihan Report and America's Struggle over Black Family Life from LBJ to Obama* (New York: Basic Books, 2010).

57. See Michael B. Katz, *The Undeserving Poor: From the War on Poverty to the War on Welfare* (New York: Pantheon Books, 1989), 36–43; Hylan Lewis, "Culture of Poverty? What Does It Matter?," in *The Culture of Poverty: A Critique*, ed. Eleanor E. Leacock (New York: Simon and Schuster, 1971), 345–63; and Charles A. Valentine, *Culture and Poverty: Critique and Counterproposals* (Chicago: University of Chicago Press, 1968).

58. Allison Davis, "A Constructive Program for ADC," ADP SCRC UCL, box 77, folder 16.

59. Allison Davis, "Survival and Defense in Slum Life," ADP SCRC UCL, box 80, folder 11.

60. Ibid.

61. Davis, Constructive Program for ADC."

62. "U. of Chicago Sets Parley on Poor Class," *Chicago Daily Tribune*, April 12, 1962.

63. Lee Rainwater, "Cancer of the Cities: Two Views," letter to the editor, *Washington Post, Times Herald*, February 11, 1967.

64. Daniel P. Moynihan, "The Professors and the Poor," *Commentary*, August 1968, https://www.commentarymagazine.com/article/theprofessorsandthepoor/ (accessed June 15, 2015).

65. St. Clair Drake, "Poverty, Sociology & Finks," *Commentary*, November 1968, https://www.commentarymagazine.com/article/povertysociologyfinks/ (accessed June 15, 2015).

66. Daniel P. Moynihan, letter to the editor, *Commentary*, November 1968, https://www.commentarymagazine.com/article/povertysociologyfinks/ (accessed June 15, 2015).

67. Drake, "Poverty, Sociology & Finks."

68. Several critics at the time hit on the central weaknesses of Moynihan's arguments. In an article in *Commonweal*, white sociologist Herbert Gans refrained from stigmatizing matriarchal families and even pointed to the stability of extended kinship systems. At a White House conference in November 1965, black sociologist Hylan Lewis gave a paper that implicitly critiqued Moynihan's crisis-oriented rhetoric, explaining that class more than race was the issue at stake. Patterson, *Freedom Is Not Enough*, 78–79, 83–84.

69. To be sure, the culture-of-poverty idea could just as easily be used for conservative ends, though that was not typically the case in the 1950s and 1960s. For one example, see Edward C. Banfield, *The Moral Basis of a Backward Society* (Glencoe, IL: Free Press, 1958).

70. Nathan Glazer, "The Culture of Poverty: The View from New York City," in *The Poor: A Culture of Poverty or a Poverty of Culture?*, ed. Alan Winter (Grand Rapids: William B. Eerdmans, 1971), 39–48.

CONCLUSION

1. St. Clair Drake, "In the Mirror of Black Scholarship: W. Allison Davis and *Deep South*," in *Education and Black Struggle: Notes from the Colonized World* (Cambridge, MA: Harvard Educational Review, 1974), 54.

2. Ibid.

3. ADP SCRC UCL, box 1, folder 2.

4. Davis Center, "W. Allison Davis '24," Williams College, http://davis-center.williams.edu /daviscenter/allison-davis/ (accessed March 28, 2015).

5. Gordon Davis, e-mail message to author, January 2015.

6. "History of the Davis Center," Williams College, http://davis-center.williams.edu/about /history-of-the-mcc/ (accessed March 28, 2015). There is also now a lecture series in honor of Allison Davis at both Williams Colleage and Northwestern University.

7. Allison Davis Papers, "Biographical Note," Special Collections Research Center, University of Chicago Library.

8. "U. of C. Professor Is Honored," *Chicago Tribune*, February 13, 1972.

9. "Davis, Allison," in *Africana: The Encyclopedia of the African and African American Experience*, 2nd ed. (Oxford: Oxford African American Studies Center, 2012), http://0-www .oxfordaasc.com.libraries.colorado.edu/article/opr/t0002/e1161?hi=0&highlight=1&from=quick &pos=1#match (accessed March 28, 2015); Walter H. Waggoner, "Allison Davis, Psychologist, Dies: Wrote about Blacks in America," *New York Times*, November 22, 1983.

10. Bill McAllister, "Blacks' Stamp Presence," *Washington Post*, January 21, 1994; Bill McAllister, "Stamps & Coins," *Washington Post*, December 17, 1993; Bill McAllister, "Heritage Series, Flying High," *Washington Post*, April 7, 1995.

11. Finder, "Davis, Allison."

12. Dallas L. Browne, "Across Class and Culture: Allison Davis and His Works," in *African-American Pioneers in Anthropology*, ed. Ira E. Harrison and Faye Harrison (Urbana: University of Illinois Press, 1999), 168–90; Michael R. Hillis, "Allison Davis and the Study of Race, Social Class, and Schooling," *Journal of Negro Education* 64 (Winter 1995): 33–41; Joan Oleck,

"Allison Davis: 1902–1983," *Contemporary Black Biography*, ed. Shirelle Phelps (Detroit: Gale Research, 1996), 12:38–41; JBHE Foundation, "Black Heritage Award for an African-American Educator," *Journal of Blacks in Higher Education* 3 (Spring 1994): 23.

13. Mike Stevens, *Hyde Park Herald*, November 3, 2004.

14. Jeremy Adragna, "Ground-Breaking Prof Honored at Weekend Garden Opening," *Hyde Park Herald*, September 14, 2005; "New Allison Davis Garden in Washington Park Honors a Pioneer and a Recommitment to Inclusion," Hyde Park-Kenwood Community Conference, http://www.hydepark.org/parks/washington/DavisGard.htm (accessed March 28, 2015).

15. Allison Davis, *Leadership, Love, and Aggression* (San Diego: Harcourt Brace Jovanovich, 1983), xi.

16. Ta-Nehisi Coates, "This Is How We Lost to the White Man," *Atlantic*, May 1, 2008, http://www.theatlantic.com/magazine/archive/2008/05/-this-is-how-we-lost-to-the-white-man/306774/ (accessed March 28, 2015); Gregory Acs, Kenneth Braswell, Elaine Sorensen, and Margaret Austin Turner, "The Moynihan Report Revisited," Urban Institute, 2013, http://www.urban.org/UploadedPDF/412839-The-Moynihan-Report-Revisited.pdf (accessed March 28, 2015).

17. Robert Pear, "Gap in Life Expectancy Widens for the Nation," *New York Times*, March 23, 2008.

18. Mark Brilliant, *The Color of America Has Changed: How Racial Diversity Shaped Civil Rights Reform in California, 1941–1978* (New York: Oxford University Press, 2010); Mary Dudziak, *Cold War Civil Rights: Race and the Image of American Democracy* (Princeton, NJ: Princeton University Press, 2000); Glenda Gilmore, *Defying Dixie: The Radical Roots of Civil Rights, 1919–1950* (New York: W. W. Norton, 2008); Jacquelyn Dowd Hall, "The Long Civil Rights Movement and the Political Uses of the Past," *Journal of American History* 91 (March 2005): 1233–63; Peniel E. Joseph, "The Black Power Movement: A State of the Field," *Journal of American History* 96 (December 2009): 751–76; Danielle L. McGuire, *At the Dark End of the Street: Black Women, Rape, and Resistance—a New History of the Civil Rights Movement from Rosa Parks to the Rise of Black Power* (New York: Vintage Books, 2010); Robert Self, *American Babylon: Race and the Struggle for Postwar Oakland* (Princeton, NJ: Princeton University Press, 2003); Thomas J. Sugrue, *Sweet Land of Liberty: The Forgotten Struggle for Civil Rights in the North* (New York: Random House, 2008); Patricia Sullivan, *Days of Hope: Race and Democracy in the New Deal* (Chapel Hill: University of North Carolina Press, 1996).

19. For one attempt to link ideas to the civil rights movement, see Ted Ownby, ed., *The Role of Ideas in the Civil Rights South* (Jackson: University of Mississippi Press, 2002).

20. Allison Davis, "The Motivations of the Underprivileged Worker," in *Industry and Society* (New York: McGraw-Hill, 1946), 86.

21. The biographical turn has been particularly important in highlighting the role of women within the movement. Some notable books include Katherine Mellen Charron, *Freedom's Teacher: The Life of Septima Clark* (Chapel Hill: University of North Carolina Press, 2009); Chana Kai Lee, *For Freedom's Sake: The Life of Fannie Lou Hamer* (Urbana: University of Illinois Press, 1999); Kay Mills, *This Little Light of Mine: The Life of Fannie Lou Hamer* (New York: Dutton, 1993); Barbara Ransby, *Ella Baker and the Black Freedom Movement: A Radical Democratic Movement* (Chapel Hill: University of North Carolina Press, 2003). For the

biographical turn in history as a whole, see "AHR Roundtable: Historians and Biography," *American Historical Review* 114 (June 2009): 573–661; and Barbara Caine, *Biography and History* (New York: Palgrave Macmillan, 2010).

22. William Julius Wilson, *The Declining Significance of Race: Blacks and Changing American Institutions*, 3rd ed. (Chicago: University of Chicago Press, 2012), ix. Wilson did not cite Davis in the book.

23. Nicholas Lemann, "The Great Sorting," *TAtlantic* 276 (September 1995): 88.

24. For more on this, see David C. McClelland, "Testing for Competence Rather Than for 'Intelligence,'" *American Psychologist* 28 (January 1973): 1–14.

25. For an interesting analysis of this phenomenon, in which Americans invent ways to be busy to avoid confronting their existential angst, see Tim Kreider, "The Busy Trap," *New York Times*, June 30, 2012.

26. Allison Davis, "Commencement Address, University of Chicago, 1975," ADP SCRC UCL, box 62, folder 19.

INDEX

Cole, Fay-Cooper, 138
Cole, Stewart, 161
Coleman, James S., 209
Coleman Report, 209
Color, Class, and Personality, 126
Color and Human Nature, 113
Color Struck, 49
Columbia University: cultural anthropology, 6, 48, 75, 79, 114; Allison Davis, 127, 133, 185, 216; John Aubrey Davis, 36, 138; intelligence testing, 176, 183; racism of faculty, 48, 79, 183
Commentary magazine, 7
Commission on Civil Rights, 146, 209
Commission on Interracial Cooperation, 72, 84
Commission on Manpower Retraining, 209
Committee on Human Relations in Industry, 157
Committee on Intercultural Education, 161
Committee on Interracial Cooperation, 141
Common Club Tennis Team, 28
Commonweal, 280n68
communism: anti-communist fear, 96–97, 152, 187–88; anti-communist persecution, 9, 73, 106; black communists, 59–60; Communist Party USA, 82, 136; Marxism, 5, 71, 97; Marxist, 8, 92, 95–96, 104; Scottsboro Boys and, 82; Warner's conception of class, 70
Compensatory Education for Cultural Deprivation, 208
Conference to Insure Civil Rights, 209
Congress of Industrial Organizations, 136
Cook, Mercer, 21
Cooke, Robert E., 209
Cooper, Anna Julia, 20
Copeland, Lewis C., 101
"Cordelia the Crude," 50
Cornell University, 127
Cottrell, Leonard, 129–30
Council of Intercultural Relations, 152
Cox, Oliver C., 3, 102, 149

Crisis: campus protests, 40–41; intelligence testing, 175; the New Negro Renaissance, 45–47, 49, 51, 53
Criteria for a Life History, 115
Cullen, Countee, 46
cultural anthropology: Columbia, 6, 114; distinction from social, 75; dominance of, 5; holism, 75, 105, 114–15, 117; "patterns of culture," 110, 114–15, 129; Robert Redfield and, 138–39, 262n26
"culture-and-personality": *Brown v. Board of Education*, 200; *Children of Bondage*, 108–9, 113–18, 125, 129, 131; Davis's work, 219, 260n26; figures in, 256n27; human development, 151; intelligence testing, 171; interdisciplinary, 5–6, 144; *Social-Class Influences on Learning*, 179; socialization, 223
Czechoslovakia, 187

Darnell, Regna, 114, 116
Davis, Allison Stubbs, 134–35, 196–97
Davis, Benjamin O., 21
Davis, Cullen, 217
Davis, Dorothy, 15, 18, 36
Davis, Elizabeth Stubbs: background and education, 64–68; Chicago, 134–35; *Children of Bondage*, 118–19; John Aubrey Davis's graduation, 197; death, 196; the Deep South, 10, 81, 83–89, 93, 96, 103; Dillard, 109; Europe, 73–74, 76–77; marginalization of, 10, 77, 88, 223, 235n16, 248–49n85; partnership with Davis, 223; Washington, D.C., 186
Davis, Gabrielle Beale, 14–15, 18, 23, 25
Davis, Gordon, 134–35, 145, 196–97, 216
Davis, Jared, 217
Davis, John Abraham: character, 13–19, 25, 28; Allison Davis's graduation, 31; death of, 36; dreams for children, 23; life and demotion at GPO, 13–19, 25
Davis, John Aubrey: civil rights work, 60, 203; Columbia, 138; education and career, 36; family, 18, 197; memories of father, 15; Williams College, 217

Franco, Francisco, 136

Franklin, John Hope, 36, 148–49, 203

Frazier, E. Franklin: AYC project, 113; black academic, 36; black institutions, 104; Chicago School, 4, 102; collaboration with Henry Stack Sullivan, 256n27; correspondence with Davis, 148; culture of poverty, 210, 212; Davis compared with, 165, 241n18; dismissal of African influence, 268n60; influential, 3, 127; New Negro Renaissance, 46, 56–57; racial solidarity, 59; relevance of Africa to black Americans, 64, 72, 165

Freedom and Culture, 167

Freud, Sigmund, 116–17

Frost, Robert, 29–30, 32, 44, 46

Frustration and Aggression, 116

Gabbin, Joanne, 29

Gaines v. Missouri, 137

Galton, Francis, 173

Gambia, 21

Gardner, Burleigh: Chicago, 157, 160; *Deep South*, 92, 95–96, 100, 103, 118; *Deep South* fieldwork, 83–89; intelligence testing, 205

Gardner, Mary, 83–89, 96, 101, 103

Garfield, Harry, 35–36

Garrett, Henry E., 183, 272n59

Garvey, Marcus, 44, 60

General Education Board: AYC, 112–13; Davis, 146, 163–64; Dillard, 109; Havighurst, 153; intelligence testing, 178, 184, 191

Georgia, 49, 58, 113, 140

Germany: Berlin, 2, 73–74, 81, 136; East Germany, 187; Freudianism, 116; Hamburg, 82; Nazi Germany, 136, 190, 248n68

Ghana, 67

Gilded Age, 225

Ginsberg, Morris, 74

Glazer, Nathan, 213

Goddard, Henry Herbert, 174

"Gospel for Those Who Must," 46

Gould, Stephen Jay, 276n131

Government Printing Office, 13–16, 18

grants: General Education Board, 178; MacArthur Foundation, 218; Social Sciences Research Council, 65; Spencer Foundation, 218

Great Depression: African Americans, 60, 62, 120, 127, 136; black institutions, 104; "caste and class," 8; Davis's finances, 91; *Deep South*, 7, 96–97; Dillard, 109, 111; and environmentalism, 135; London, 73; poverty, 206; radicalism, 190; social thought, 79; youth, 112

Great Migration, 37–38, 136, 205

Greenwich Village, 45

Gregg, James E., 35, 39, 41

Grimké, Angelina, 20

Growing Up in the Black Belt, 113

Guatemala, 163, 167

Haggard, Ernest A., 178

Haldane, J. B. S., 177, 184

Hall, G. Stanley, 173–74

Hampton Institute: African history, 71; Arthur Howe, 72; Davis's appointment, 13, 35–37; New Negro Renaissance, 61; provincial, 55, 64; racial discrimination and segregation, 39–40, 53–55; St. Clair Drake, 89; students' backgrounds and class, 42; student protests, 40–41, 44, 53; Washington model, 39; white support for Davis, 240n117; writer's club, 41

Harding, Charles F., 185

Harlem, 43–44, 50, 61

Harlem, 50

Harlem Renaissance, 45. *See also* New Negro Renaissance

Harlem Shadows, 50

Harrington, Michael, 206, 210

Harris, Abram, 3, 59, 148

Harrison, Faye, 89, 95

Harrison, Ira, 89

Harvard University: anthropology at, 66–69; Sterling Brown and, 52; Burleigh Gardner, 83, 157; *Children of Bondage* at,